Design Management

Placed at the nexus between marketing and organisational studies, this book breaks a new ground on the intersection of these two disciplines with design management. With the latest marketing thinking assigning greater emphasis on organisations co-creating value with consumers and other stakeholders by placing them at the heart of the product/service development process, it has never been more important to integrate marketing and organisational perspectives into design management.

This text explores the importance of managing design strategies, design processes, and design implementation in a way that it puts the human and the society at the centre, contributing to organisational success, customer gratification, and social welfare. Drawing from a variety of scholarly research and personal commercial insights, this book integrates key concepts of marketing, innovation, and design to provide an in-depth discussion of the subject of design management.

With end-of-chapter exercises, case studies, and reflective insights, *Design Management: Organisation and Marketing Perspectives* is an essential text for students in design management, marketing, and innovation, or for anyone interested in gaining an in-depth understanding of how design can be successfully managed in order to generate the best answers to contemporary global challenges.

Sotiris T. Lalaounis is a Lecturer in Marketing and Design Management in the Department of Organisation Studies at the University of Exeter Business School. Following a postgraduate degree in Design and Digital Media from the University of Edinburgh, he worked in design consultancies, and earned his PhD in Design Management from the Centre for Creative Industries at Glasgow Caledonian University. His thesis investigated business development issues in the creative industries, and his current research interests include organisational paradoxes, ambidexterity, and creative firms.

This book presents a highly informative, contemporary and accessible text on Design Management, an essential resource for students of design, marketing, and management.

Rachel Cooper, OBE, Distinguished Professor of Design Management and Policy, Lancaster University, UK.

Design Management is a treasure trove of ideas for combining design, creativity, and marketing management. Sotiris Lalaounis has brought together an exquisite blend of examples, plans, and principles that highlight and demonstrate the key role of design in successful product and service offerings. The result will stimulate and inspire both designers and marketers.

Russell W. Belk, Professor of Marketing, Kraft Foods Canada Chair in Marketing, York University, Canada.

In this book Sotiris Lalaounis has made a very welcome contribution to the still too rare literature about the management of design. It is a well-crafted and easy to read book that draws upon relevant theory to explain what designers do, and the value that they bring to organisations. The chapters cover the main issues that non-designers will need to understand in order to use design effectively in their own work. Each chapter contains a critical reflection on the issues raised in the chapter by experts in the field. This book will be useful to business and management students and managers alike.

Alison Rieple, Professor of Strategic Management, University of Westminster, UK.

Design Management

Organisation and Marketing Perspectives

Sotiris T. Lalaounis

LONDON AND NEW YORK

First published 2018
by Routledge
2 Park Square, Milton Park, Abingdon, Oxon OX14 4RN

and by Routledge
711 Third Avenue, New York, NY 10017

Routledge is an imprint of the Taylor & Francis Group, an informa business

British Library Cataloguing-in-Publication Data
A catalogue record for this book is available from the British Library

Library of Congress Cataloging-in-Publication Data
A catalog record for this book has been requested

ISBN: 978-1-138-64806-7 (hbk)
ISBN: 978-1-138-64807-4 (pbk)
ISBN: 978-1-315-62666-6 (ebk)

Typeset in Times New Roman
by Book Now Ltd, London

To Mum, Dad, Antonia, and Spyros
To Graham, Evgenia, and Paulina

Contents

Figures

Images

Tables

Foreword

> Every human being is a designer. Many also earn their living by design - in every field that warrants pause, and careful consideration, between the conceiving of an action and a fashioning of the means to carry it out, and an estimation of its effects.
>
> (Potter, 1969, p. 10)

This phrase captured my heart in 1973. It converted me into an evangelist for the power of design; however, I soon realised as a practising designer that this was not the case in many organisations; indeed, design as a function was frequently seen as a subset of marketing. Later as an academic I realised that the 'serious money' did not see design as a credible discipline except as a professional and technical training. I set about to change this, as have others in the field.

Design is no longer a niche subject; yet it has, in the past, frequently been relegated to a group of slightly 'arty' people or 'creative' types. When it comes to saving the world, the economy, the environment, and society, most people turned to the scientists, the economists, the engineers, and maybe business. These are the valued topics governments seek to support in universities alongside the critical and high culture value of some arts and humanities. These functions in business, finance, law, marketing, engineering, and production were the premier departments. However, over the last 50 years, 'Design' as a discipline, as a practice, and a particular lens on mankind and the material world has slowly been seeking to establish itself as a critical contributor, first to organisations and business and then to society and the environment.

I was recently commissioned to conduct a study on the 'Value of Design in Innovation'. Yet another study on the value of design, obviously there is still some convincing to do. However, studies on the definitions, uses, value, and impact of design, such as *The Cox Review of Creativity in Business* (Cox, 2005), *Leading Business by Design* (Design Council, 2013) and *€Design – Measuring Design Value* (BCD Barcelona Design Centre, 2014), have all helped to build confidence in design and expand understanding of design's strategic position in industry. But these are 'ephemera of the moment'; what builds confidence is knowledgeable and skilled people who are able to draw on a comprehensive body of knowledge to deliver solutions, generate new insights, and influence decisions that mould the organisation and indeed society.

Finally, we have a body of knowledge that we can turn to. This book has drawn on the entire body of literature that has emerged since the 1960s. It is no surprise that the marketing and design perspective is the starting point; marketing has always needed to focus outside the unit and the organisation, using that insight to deliver products and services to the customer, doing so by drawing on design to 'style' the offer. However, we now know that design insight, approach, and management offers more for marketing and the whole organisation. This book illustrates so clearly how design and design management are synonymous with creativity and innovation and also demonstrates the breadth of design research methods and insight that offer value and alternative perspectives. It also sets design uniquely and thoughtfully in the context of bias in decision making and in the context of managing paradoxes in organisations.

Today the boundaries of organisations are fluid, as indeed is the notion of marketing. We are now living in multiple worlds, we travel momentarily between the physical and the digital world. We are free (or we think we are) to connect with anyone and everyone, to influence organisations, to consult our customers, to create together. Everyone is part (or potentially part) of the development process. As a result, organisations who address this product/service/system … are in fact designing the human experience. That experience includes co-design and co-creation; in developed countries, at least, we have increased access to data and information and to low-cost manufacturing; we have access to informal skill development and co-production through maker-spaces, 'hackerthons', etc.; so open data for experimentation and facilities for experimentation. Indeed, a situation where we are returning to everyone being a designer. *But we still need design management.*

We need design management because we need design and designerly approaches to thinking about the complex global challenges. For example, the 'digital world', especially via the 'Internet of Things', is increasingly supporting our daily life, our health and well-being, and our cultural experience; yet, it poses unknown threats; it affects our privacy, informs our attitudes and values, our safety and security. Already this book is illustrating how design can consider the relationship between humans and things. We must also consider how design management can manage and monitor potential emergent qualities of open design, co-design, and the Internet of Things, both positive and negative. We have yet to consider the role of design management in a world of robots and artificial intelligence, when objects design objects.

Furthermore, despite the enticements of the digital world to solving problems of consumption and connection, we still live in a physical world that has a number of stresses, including an aging and growing population and resource scarcity. Fundamentally we will need to design more efficient ways of living and using resources, new ways of caring and supporting each other, new ways of moving about, new approaches to governance, indeed new ways of living. Design leadership that can harness creativity and innovation, that can connect knowledge between science and social science, will be necessary in all organisations, public and private.

This book brings together seminal theories and the foundational material of design management alongside contemporary research and commentary to deliver a fundamental platform upon which design management knowledge and action can be built and used for the benefit of everyone.

Professor Rachel Cooper, OBE
Distinguished Professor of Design Management and Policy
Director, ImaginationLancaster
Chair, Lancaster Institute for the Contemporary Arts
Lancaster University, Lancaster, UK

References

BCD Barcelona Design Centre. (2014). *€Design – Measuring design value: Guidelines for collecting and interpreting design data.* Retrieved from www.bcd.es/site/unitFiles/6733/A_proposal_for_a_future_Barcelona_Manual_on_Design_BCD.pdf

Cox, G. (2005). *The Cox review of creativity in business: Building on the UK's strengths.* London: HM Treasury.

Design Council. (2013). *Leading business by design: Why and how business leaders invest in design.* Coventry, UK: Warwick Business School and Design Council.

Potter, N. (1969). *What is a designer.* London: Studio Vista.

Acknowledgements

Throughout the process of writing this textbook, there has been a number of people who have provided me with great support and encouragement.

First, I would like to thank my colleagues in the Department of Organisation Studies at the University of Exeter Business School, and my very bright and passionate students on the Design Management and Marketing module (academic year 2016–2017) for their feedback while teaching the material presented in this textbook.

I am extremely grateful to staff at Routledge, and in particular Amy Laurens and Laura Hussey, for their continuous guidance and support throughout the process of writing this textbook. Special thanks to Nicola Cupit (previously at Routledge) who believed in this project right from the start and offered enormous help and support in the initial stages of my writing.

I would also like to extend my warmest thanks to the following academic colleagues and friends for their contributions in the form of the reflective pieces featured at the end of every chapter of this textbook, as well as for their feedback on preliminary drafts: Professor Russell W. Belk, Dr. Alex Thompson, Professor Natalie W. Nixon, Dr. Mary Maclachlan, Professor Bruce M. Wood, Professor Constantine Andriopoulos, Tony Coffield, Dr. Katerina Karanika, and Dr. Lindsay Stringfellow.

Furthermore, I would like to thank Professor Rachel Cooper, OBE, for writing the foreword for this textbook. Your contribution and feedback on the final manuscript is truly appreciated.

Big love to Liz, Wiz, Susie, Luca, Graham G. Sr., and George – thank you for your love and encouragement.

Finally, my deepest love to my Mum and Dad, Uncle Costas, Antonia, Spyros, Graham, Evgenia, and Paulina – thank you all for your continuous love and support.

Sotiris T. Lalaounis
Exeter, UK

1 Introduction

Design management and the creative economy

Chapter aims and learning outcomes

This chapter aims to:

1 Discuss the development of marketing and commerce from ancient civilisations to the contemporary post-modern society.
2 Explore the development of design management practice and the three overarching paradigms in design management.
3 Understand the creative industries, the creative economy, and their role in the wider economy and society.
4 Discuss design sustainability and ecological intentional design.
5 Determine the overarching synergy between design management and marketing paradigms in post-modern society.

This chapter essentially aims to extend our understanding of the development of design management over the years and its role in contemporary society. Perhaps some would question the purpose and use of such a critical review of the subject. In response to such doubts, we can turn out attention to the work of Tadajewski (2009), a marketing scholar specialising in disciplinal history who argues that a very good starting point for understanding a discipline is by reviewing the history of the field, from its first inception as an academic discipline, exploring the influences that have impacted the subject areas over the years as they stand in the present day. In addition, George Santayana, the famous Spanish-born philosopher, argued that "those who do not know their history are likely to make similar mistakes to those of their intellectual predecessors" (cited in Tadajewski, 2009, p. 13). Therefore, understanding the history of design management thought and practice will allow us to avoid making the same intellectual mistakes and helps us shape a better understanding of design management from organisational and marketing perspectives, which is the fundamental aim of this book.

Development of design management: A critical review

Marketing and commerce: Ancient traditions

Before we attempt to understand the development of the design management discipline, it is important to explore the advances of commerce and marketing from ancient civilisations to our contemporary post-modern world. The reason for such endeavour is the fact that the connections between design, commerce, and marketing have been very profoundly strong across different eras of human development. Especially over the last few centuries, there has been closer integration between the development of design and marketing.

> Product design has always been of keen interest to marketers. Medieval craftsmen sought to curry favour with the quality of their ecclesiastical ornamentation, and railroads of the 1930s attracted passengers with the visual impact of their streamlined locomotives and comfort of their Pullman cars. Today companies like Apple achieve record profits during a major recession because of leadership in design.
>
> (Bloch, 2011, p. 378)

In 1984, Kotler and Alexander-Rath recognised the importance of design as part of the organisation's marketing strategy, but argued that it had been neglected by organisations despite its imperative value. Undoubtedly, there has been significant progress since then as organisations have deepened their understanding of the role of design in innovation, which consequently leads to product differentiation (Lalaounis, Wood, & Evans, 2011). Nowadays, numerous organisations recognise that "marketing interacts with research and development, industrial design, engineering, and manufacturing" (Zhang, Hu, & Kotabe, 2011, p. 360) during the new product development (NPD) process. But the connections between design and marketing go beyond product design and the NPD process. In our contemporary society, there is an ever-growing need to manage design to achieve organisational objectives and contribute to social welfare. As a result, this has elevated the importance of design in the corporate world and in the wider society. But let us take things from the beginning.

Some would be surprised to read that the start of the history of marketing, a discipline so contemporary in comparison to other social sciences, is not placed during the Industrial Revolution but traced in the ancient world. Indeed, there are various forms of trade shown in 6,000 years of recorded history. In fact, one can find evidence of commerce, in the form of branding, advertising, and packaging, in ancient sites scattered across the Mediterranean Sea, such as those attributed to ancient civilisations of Greece, Rome, and Etruria. According to Shaw (1995), ancient Greek Socratic philosophers Plato and Aristotle discussed macro-marketing issues, such as how marketing can be integrated into society. Wengrow (2008) indicates that brands in the form of labels or seals can be traced back to prehistory and the Bronze Age society. The use of these kinds of brand was very administrative – to signify ownership, place of origin, or jurisdiction. The earliest manufactured goods in 'mass' production were clay pots. These were 'marked' by their makers with their thumbprints or symbols, such as a star or a cross, rather than their initials. These symbols are the earliest form of brand logotypes. In ancient Rome, commercial law was developed to protect the origin and title of potters' marks, with evidence, even then, of imitations and counterfeit products (Blackett, 2003).

Following the fall of the Roman Empire, the mutually interdependent system of trade between the Mediterranean and the West European peoples collapsed, and the use of brands was mainly on local scale with the exception of distinguishing marks used by noble groups, royal families, and governments (e.g. the Hapsburg family's coat of arms, or Japan's imperial chrysanthemum symbol) (Blackett, 2003). The use of brands evolved to indicate content and quality of the product as trade became more specialised. Volume manufacture of fine porcelain, furniture, and tapestries by royal patronage increased, and laws for watermarking of paper and hallmarking of gold and silver objects were enforced in the seventeenth and eighteenth centuries (Blackett, 2003); such laws are still used to this day. In addition, at that stage, besides quality, brands were also used to signify authority, ownership, and status because factories manufactured not only perishable but also durable goods (Moor, 2007). This led to branding becoming a means of separating production from consumption (as explored in Chapter 8), a separation that contemporary branding still depends on to an extent. In the Middle Ages, Medieval schoolmen such as St Augustus of Hippo and St Thomas of Aquinas wrote about macro-marketing issues such as how marketing can be practiced in an ethical manner and without sin (Jones & Shaw, 2002).

ETRUSCAN VASES.

Thumbprints or symbols on clay pots as first forms of brand logotypes.

However, it was the Industrial Revolution in the eighteenth century which was the springboard for the development of the first set of principles of marketing. During the industrial boom, we saw the development of mass production, higher levels of trade among different regions, improved distribution and transportation, and enormous social changes such as the increase of urbanisation, the birth of working and middle classes, luxury consumption, and more interactions among consumer cultures. According to Bartels (1988), the term 'marketing' was first used as a noun, hence a label of a particular practice, sometime between 1906 and 1911 in the UK. However, Tadajewski (2009) points out that the first use of the term is a subject of intellectual contestation with some scholars placing its first use as far back as 1561 (Shaw, 1995). The 1900s' meaning of the term 'marketing' was strongly associated with the work of sales departments which were becoming extremely common. The first meaning of the term was related to the combination of factors that had to be taken into consideration prior to the undertaking of selling activities. The combination of these efforts was the essence of marketing at that stage. Marketing was a characteristic of the period in the development of the 'market economy', the system where the market regulates and runs society, and has evolved to a refined system of thought and practice.

Blackett (2003) argues that the Industrial Revolution phenomenon led to the brand revolution of the nineteenth and early twentieth centuries. Manufacturing and communications advances opened up the western world and led to the mass-marketing of consumer goods. Many of today's best known brands, such as *Coca-Cola*, *Heinz Baked Beans*, and *Quaker Oats*, date from this era. "Hand in hand with the introduction of these brands came early trade mark legislation. This allowed the owners of these brands to protect them in law" (Blackett, 2003, p. 15). In the same period, we also saw the founding of many well-known advertising agencies, some of which still dominate the sector, e.g., *J Walter Thompson*, which provided further push to the development of brands. The first ever registered trademark in the UK was *Bass Beer's Red Triangle*, first registered in 1876, and still used by the organisation today. Innovation in packaging and printing meant that manufacturers had the ability to place their mark on their products; thus, instead of selling in bulk to retailers who then placed the product into their own unmarked packaging, they had a way to differentiate their own product from others and communicate a message through the images used in promotional materials. This highlighted the significant role of branding in fiercely competitive environments (Moor, 2007). The development of the marketing profession is also strongly associated with the history of professional associations such as the American Marketing Association – established as the American Marketing Society in 1931 – and the UK's Chartered Institute of Marketing established in 1911 as the Sales Managers' Association and incorporated by Royal Charter in 1989.

Bass beer triangle – first registered trademark in the UK.

The period since World War II is described by Blackett (2003) as the 'brand explosion' period. Brands are now symbols of worldwide economies on a demand-led rather than a command-led system. This was a result of developments such as the collapse of communism, the birth of mass communication systems and the Internet, and improved transportation. However, brands, along with the capitalist market system, have been criticised over the years. We can see such criticism mounting; attacks by anti-globalisation activists on *Starbucks* or *McDonald's* stores are simple manifestations of such anger. This also demonstrates the fact that brands have also become political symbols beyond their economic jurisdiction. On a positive note, this has made organisations realise that they have to understand the political, social, and economic impact of their activities – brands are central to these activities (Hales, 2011).

Design management practice

The first person to be attributed the ability to marry the activities of designing and managing is Josiah Wedgewood, an English master of pottery who established a very successful, world-renowned ceramic pottery business by combining the beauty and art of designing with a set of management skills (Cooper & Junginger, 2011a). Letters written by Wedgwood to his friend, Thomas Bentley, provide us with "a unique picture of the mind of an entrepreneur during the early stages of industrialisation, revealing the problems he faced and the solutions he developed. In particular, they show the unprecedented importance that design was to have in the production of his wares" (Forty, 1986, pp. 17–18). The industrial society, and its early manifestations such as the opening of the National Gallery in 1832 and the Great Exhibition in 1851, created the context in which the subject would be born (Best, 2006, 2015). World's Fairs like the Great Exhibition at Crystal Palace provided the platform for discussions about the influence of machines on the role of design in society. Many, like Henry Cole, the principal organiser of the exhibition, believed that the effect of machines involved the separation of the responsibility for the appearance of a product from the tasks of fabricating it, leading to, in their opinion, the quality of design deteriorating (Forty, 1986). On the other hand, such exhibitions were supported by the UK government with the aim of improving public taste and educating artisans. The underlying reason for such endeavour was the fact that the development of machine production had made design more valuable to manufacturers. In retrospect, the use of machine at that stage was still limited, and any arguments against machines were fuelled by Victorian writers' misunderstanding and prejudices. Generally speaking, the Great Exhibition ignited the debate on the effect of machines on the quality of design, a discussion which is still contemporary (Forty, 1986). Nowadays, we agree on the interdependence of design and machines, and most of us welcome machines as a way of improving design process and design artefacts.

The Great Exhibition at Crystal Palace in 1851.

Peter Behrens, the designer appointed by the German electronics manufacturer AEG, is the archetypical design manager of the early twentieth century, whose role was to shape the corporate identity, buildings, posters, and actual products of the organisation, enjoying senior-level influence within AEG. In 1915, the Design and Industries Association was established in the UK to facilitate the collaboration of manufacturers, designers, distributors, economists, and critics, as well as to seek the involvement of the UK government in the promotion of good design. Two more professional institutions were also formed: the Society of Industrial Arts (later the Chartered Society of Designers) in 1930, and the Council of Industrial Design (CID) (later the Design Council) in 1944 (Best, 2006, 2015), which furthered the consolidation of designers to promote their occupation.

By 1950, there was a renewed interest in design management in the UK, the US, and Germany, due to the industriousness after World War II which enhanced production and the urge to develop new markets. The reasons behind such attitude were a shortage of many traditional manufacturing materials such as metals and steel used in war production in the US and the need to rebuild large devastated areas and propose new ways of living to populations that have simply lost everything in the UK and Germany (Cooper & Junginger, 2011a). In the decade that followed (1950s), we saw the foundation of design consultancies by prominent names such as Terence Conran, Wally Ollins, Michael Wolf, and Michael Peters; all these firms are still big players in the design consultancy sector.

The term 'design management' was introduced in 1965 by the Royal Society of the Arts when the 1964 Presidential Medals for Design Management were bestowed on the recommendation of the CID, making design management more salient to academics and practitioners. It is noteworthy that although design management is applied to all design disciplines, there is a subtle separation in today's education curriculum. Design management is applied to architecture in the form of project management for construction, compared with manufacturing-related design disciplines which have embraced wider concerns of design management as an academic discipline and professional practice, because they have evolved to appreciate the business dimensions in which they operate (Cooper & Junginger, 2011a).

However, during that period, only few management scholars explored design management; most seemed to focus their attention on marketing, strategy, and NPD as emergent subjects. Other professional associations have also played an important role in the development of the design management practice. The Design Management Institute (DMI) was established at the Massachusetts College of Art in Boston in 1975, and ten years later, it became an independent entity with its own membership programme. In the UK, the Design Business Association was established in 1986, bringing together businesses in the design sector.

The evolution of design management thought

Design management was taught for the first time as part of a business school curriculum at the London Business School in 1976, and its Design Management Unit was established in 1982. The first programme on design management at a UK design school was launched at the same time by the Royal College of Art, and many other programmes followed in other academic institutions. Unfortunately, many of these programmes proved unsustainable. As Cooper and Junginger note, it is worth trying to identify the reasons preventing "design management building a sustainable legacy that could thrive in either management or design schools – and survive long after funding money has dried up" (2011a, p. 19).

Design magazines such as *Industrial Design* (USA) and *Design* (UK), peer-reviewed journals such as *Design Studies* (established in 1979), the *Design Management Journal* (established in 1989), the *Design Journal* and *Design Issues*, or publications such as the *Design Management Review* (with a more practitioner focus), and specific conferences such as those run by the DMI became the main arenas for exploring the management of design and its challenges and have been central to the practice and academic thought of design management. However, the term design management is not always applied to scholarly work published in these journals because to some it is too narrow and to others it is a muddled term as it has many interpretations. Indeed, the latter has been one of the main problems of the subject area. Perhaps similar to marketing, in its attempt to attract a broader audience and advocate for its application in different contexts, it has lost its focus and disciplinal boundaries, which are required for a subject to be clear and distinct from others (Shaw & Jones, 2005).

Before we begin our discussion of the current status of the academic discourse on the subject, it is important to provide some definitions of design management in order to avoid misinterpretations of the term. Indeed, there is no single universally agreed definition, just like there is not a single definition of 'design' and 'business' (Best, 2006, 2015). The first formal definition was provided by Farr (1965) in his *Design* magazine article.

> Design management is the function of defining a design problem, finding the most suitable designer, and making it possible for him to solve it on time and within a budget. This is a consciously managed exercise which can apply to all the areas where designers work.
>
> (Farr, 1965, p. 48)

This definition manifests the fact that design management was at that point of time in its embryonic stage and was viewed from a more practical perspective. Many years after, Gorb (1990) offered his own definition which demonstrated the fact that design management discourse had evolved to be something more 'managerial'. He defined the discipline as follows:

> The effective deployment by line managers of the design resources available to an organisation in the pursuance of its corporate objectives. It is therefore directly concerned with the organisational place of design, with the identification of specific design disciplines which are relevant to the resolution of key management issues, and with the training of managers to use design effectively.
>
> (Gorb, 1990, p. 2)

In simple terms, Best (2006, 2015) suggests that design management is involved in *the management of the design strategy, the design process, and the design implementation.* Perhaps a lack of a formal definition is a simple manifestation of the confusion which Cooper and Junginger (2011a) noticed with regard to the boundaries of the discipline and what purpose it fulfils within the field of design itself. Some scholars discuss the value of design; some explore its role and location in the organisation; while some others seek to define design management and set the boundaries of its practice by identifying methods and assigning tasks (Cooper & Junginger, 2011a). However, the confusion can be justified according to Pilditch (1976), who argues that designing as an activity is closely linked with the activities of organising and managing. In fact, organising and managing can be part of designing since design is undertaken by an individual or a group in the context of a certain entity, be it an organisation (private or public), a community, or a voluntary group. Initially Pilditch (1976) did not feel the need to address design management as a subcategory for design and its role in the organisation (he later addressed design management specifically). Similarly, fifteen years earlier, Falk (1961) identified design as part of the 'art of management', "a subject, which, at the very heart of its nature, strikes at the heart of social behaviour" (p. 12). Based on this *interconnectedness among the activities of designing, managing, and organising*, we can identify another side of design management which is gradually picking up in management and business schools. This relates to the "transferability of design concepts, practices, and methods to managerial and organisational problems as well as to the possibilities design practice holds for strategy and policy formulation and implementation" (Cooper & Junginger, 2011a). This means that designing and managing are less the polar opposites we often think of them to be.

Paradigms of design management

According to Cooper and Junginger (2011a), if we were to organise design management discourse, we would determine three overarching paradigms. The first is about the concepts and ideas of *design practice*, in terms of how it is to be done and what it should be concerned with. The second paradigm is about the surrounding *methods of design management*, the *characteristics of a manager*, and *what can be managed*. The third paradigm involves what we discussed above: the principles and practices, concepts, matters, and methods of *design as a general human capability* (Figure 1.1). Most of the scholarly work on design management from the 1960s to the start of the twenty-first century has concentrated on the first two paradigms.

The first paradigm in design management has articulated many arguments related to the value of professional design to a firm which makes a case for employing in-house designers or working with external designers (based in a design consultancy). These arguments were based on the fact that there is a need for attractive products and services, a corporate requirement for innovation, and a market desire for differentiation. The second paradigm has developed

> methods and practices to structure the design process, introduce predictability and cost control. This emphasised skills in writing a design brief and managing the design and delivery process. It focuses on the role of design in solving market-related design problems.
>
> (Cooper & Junginger, 2011a, pp. 23–24)

Within this paradigm, these problems included the design of products, brands, and services in a commercial context. Therefore, the focus here is about how to deliver the design contribution effectively and efficiently, through more design-aware managers, design consultants who influence boardroom decision making, or through a new profession of design management.

The third paradigm, however, goes beyond the foci of the first two and provides a challenge and an opportunity for all organisations regardless of their nature, i.e., commercial or non-profit. Many scholars (e.g. Bolland & Collopy, 2004; Brown, 2009; Chick & Micklethwaite, 2011; Hands, 2009) have explored how design management can influence services, public policy, management, and the society at large through concepts such as 'design for society', 'design thinking', 'sustainable design', and 'managing as designing', which are discussed in this book. This has helped to set design management free from its somehow limiting realms of specific design specialties and has elevated its value as a general organisational capability (Cooper & Junginger, 2011a). For instance, when it comes to design

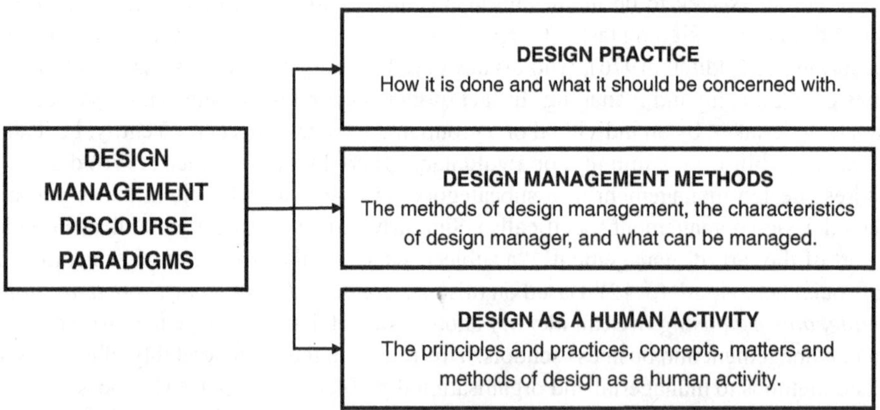

Figure 1.1 Design management discourse methods.

thinking, *IDEO*, the iconic global design consultancy, has been extremely successful in demonstrating the potential of design thinking for organisations and the role of the design manager in igniting and facilitating design thinking in the corporate environment. Bolland and Collopy (2004) take a step further and argue that managers should act not only as decision-makers but also as designers. It becomes evident that this third paradigm broadens the scope of design management by articulating the value of design to people, societies, environments, and organisations and by recognising it as a fundamental human capability. On this basis, Cooper and Junginger (2011a) determined the key characteristics of the third paradigm as follows: (1) a focus on human problems, (2) a more advanced concept of the nature of the 'product' and how 'things' come into being (although, besides things, we can also design processes and activities), (3) a comprehensive and systematic design approach that facilitates for emergence, (4) a plethora of design methods which are inclusive, participatory, and/or collaborative, and (5) design is situated in the context of changing, organising, and managing.

The effect of the third paradigm in design management debate is manifested by a reorganisation into two overlapping strands of empirical research and practice. The first group involves work carried out in relation to creating products, places, communications, involving the management of process and people, and the promotion of the role of design in creating physical contribution to the strategic goals of the organisation. The second group is concerned with developing the organisational capacity to adopt the design approach in order to respond to change and external challenges. These two strands can and do operate separately, yet they interact and overlap with each other. As Cooper and Junginger comment,

> the existence of these two strands is one of the strongest indicators that design requires careful management, the design manager of the future will need to know how, when and where these two strands link up. Hands-on experience, theoretical knowledge, a grasp of the past and of the technology of today, will allow the design manager to address the challenges of tomorrow.
>
> (Cooper and Junginger, 2011a, p. 27)

Problems and critique

The above quote highlights the need for the design manager to have a good grasp of the past. This is perhaps more challenging to achieve in the case of design management than other disciplines because unlike marketing, for instance, there is not a generic history of design management. Best (2006, 2015) and Cooper and Junginger (2011a) have been two of the very few, if not the only, attempts to explore genealogies of design management – the former in the form of a timeline offered in the first pages of her popular textbook on design management (Best, 2006, 2015, pp. 20–25), and the latter in the introductory chapter of the *Handbook of Design Management* edited by Cooper and Junginger themselves, from which the above section has drawn a lot. This indicates a significant problem. If we refer back to Santayana's thinking, a lack of knowledge of the history of the discipline means that it is likely that scholars and practitioners will make the same mistakes as their intellectual predecessors. Such risk is acknowledged by Cooper and Junginger who provide the following observation.

> Design management remains a field that prefers to concern itself with the here and now and with the future, in particular the future of products and services. The links to the origins and traditions of design management are rather weak … We increasingly found this lack of connection and reflection problematic; questions and answers tend to be repetitive and often reinvented. We see a need for a full researched history of design management that looks both into the origins of design and of management and how they interconnect.
>
> (Cooper and Junginger, 2011b, p. 542)

Failing to understand the historical development of design management can be extremely problematic and dangerous for the subject matter. While addressing this empirical gap in the historical analysis of the discipline is beyond the scope of this chapter, the above section aimed to provide a brief overview of the discipline's history drawing from the scarce sources available, hoping that such brief overview, albeit limited, can provide us with a solid background foundation upon which we can base our subsequent discussion of various intellectual concepts.

Creative economy and the society

Defining the creative industries and the creative economy

In the late 1990s, the UK's Department for Culture, Media, and Sport (DCMS) established its Creative Industries Unit and Task Force which published the *Creative Industries Mapping Document* in 1998 providing a definition of the '*creative industries*'. They defined the creative industries as:

> Those industries which have their origin in individual creativity, skill and talent and which have a potential for wealth and job creation through the generation and exploitation of intellectual property. This includes advertising, architecture, the art and the antiques market, crafts, design, designer fashion, film and video, interactive leisure software, music, the performing arts, publishing, software and computer games, television and radio.
>
> (DCMS, 1998, 2001)

This definition has proven, paradoxically, both a useful and a confusing concept. It is useful for three reasons: (1) it demonstrates the economic value of culture, media, and design by recognising creativity as a significant input into contemporary economies which are characterised by elements of 'culturalisation' (see Du Gay & Pryke, 2002; Lash & Urry, 1994), digitisation, and highly designed goods and services; (2) it generates a provisional convergence of a range of sectors which have not been traditionally linked with each other; and (3) the sectors included under this term move from the non-commercial to the high-tech and commercial arena (Hartley, Potts, Flew, Cunningham, Keane, & Banks, 2013).

However, at the same time, there are many problems with DCMS's definition. First, as mentioned above, the definition converges previously unrelated sectors; such convergence has generated high levels of criticism. It has been suggested that such classification of disparate sectors under one umbrella was orchestrated by the UK government in order to make Britain look a world leader in a field that the country had defined by and for itself (Hartley et al., 2013). In addition, if we were to accept this definition, then one could claim that science is not creative and that advertising is creative but marketing is not. There has been a mixed reaction from different industries, some welcoming and some ignoring the term, depending on their objectives. More specifically, the definition suggests that the creative industries are based on 'individual creativity, skill and talent' and lead to the 'generation of intellectual property'; these statements are challenged by Bilton (2007) who argues that these are questionable assumptions made by politicians about the meaning and the purpose of creativity. He contends that as a result the definition is meaningless since most industries, businesses, and workers are associated with this definition, and no self-respecting organisation could admit to lacking creativity, skill, and talent. Similarly, according to Troilo (2015), all industries are essentially creative, so it is difficult to differentiate one from another based on creativity. However, he suggests that if we understand the relevance that consumers associate with the creative content that products and services offer in an industry, then we resolve the questions around the uniqueness of the creative industries. He proposes that:

> Instead of considering creativity as the input of production processes, we need to think of creativity as the output. (All sectors make products and services that spring from a creative idea, but only in certain sectors do customers associate value of a product or service primarily with its creative content).
>
> (Troilo, 2015, p. 4)

To avoid the aforementioned problems, Howkins suggests that

> it is best to restrict the term 'creative industry' to an industry where brain work is preponderant and where the outcome is intellectual property. This definition does not pretend to include all industries where creativity takes place. Creativity takes place anywhere. But it does include industries where brain work is the determining motif. It seems more reasonable than including, say, copyright but not patents; or advertising but not marketing.
>
> (Howkins, 2005, p. 119)

The above statement resonates with Jones, Lorenzen, and Sapsed, who emphasise that "even if there are elements of creativity in most human endeavour, not all industries are organised principally to take advantage of and capture the market value of human activity" (2015, p. 3). This means that we should not include under the term every human activity merely because it has an element of creative effort. Therefore, many have questioned the coherence of what constitutes the creative industries. The definition seems to have been driven by the need for government policy intervention, rather than being a rigorous empirically researched academic category. Nevertheless, despite its controversy, the definition has survived over the years and has been used quite extensively. Many governments around the world have adopted variations of this definition leading to viewing the status of arts and culture not as a matter for cultural policy but from the prism of economic development and wealth creation (Bilton, 2007).

Recent publications from DCMS have gone beyond the initial definition of the creative industries and have introduced the concept of the '*creative economy*', which is a more encompassing term. In this economy, products and services carry, beyond their utilitarian character and commercial value, cultural meaning. McCracken (1986) argues that such meaning is disengaged from the cultural world and transferred to goods through advertising and product design as practiced in the fashion system, which act as instruments of meaning transfer. Developed through the lens of the creative workforce, the creative economy has been defined as

> the total of creative occupations within the core creative industries (specialists), plus the creative occupations employed in other industries, for example designers or media producers working for mining companies or government departments (embedded), plus the business and administrative occupations employed in creative industries that are often responsible for managing, accounting for, and technically supporting creative activity (support).
>
> (Hartley et al., 2013, p. 57)

Therefore, the creative industries and creative occupations are now considered as subsets of the creative economy. The former includes "just those working in the creative industries irrespective of their occupation (they may either be in creative occupations or in other roles, e.g. finance)" (DCMS, 2015,

Creative economy workforce.

p. 4), whereas the latter "includes all those working in creative occupations irrespective of the industry that they work in" (DCMS, 2015, p. 5) (some are employed in the creative industries and some are not, such as in-house designers working in other industries, e.g., financial services or insurance).

The role of creative economy in the society

Statistics consistently show that there is more creative employment outside the creative industries than inside (DCMS, 2015) which raises the question of the role of creative employment in the labour market and its effects (Cunningham & Potts, 2015). This is however not the only reason we should understand how the creative economy contributes to economic growth in general. People seldom consider the creative economy as a standard source of economic growth in terms of developing new technology, capital deepening, achieving operational efficiency, generating business model innovation, and enhancing institutional evolution (Hartley et al., 2013). However, the creative economy does offer exactly these aspects; it experiments with new technologies, develops new content and applications, and creates new business models. The creative industries and the creative economy are

> broadly engaged in the coordination of new technologies to new lifestyles, new meanings and new ways of being, which in turn is the basis of new business opportunities. The creative industries [and the creative economy] are not seminal forces of material economic growth, but they are germinal in their role in coordinating the individual and social structure of novelty and in resetting the definition of the normal.
>
> (Hartley et al., 2013, p. 61)

The creative economy contributes to many developed and developing countries' GDP much more than traditional manufacturing industries. Troilo (2015) suggests that a number of changes that have occurred in contemporary society have made the creative economy well suited for satisfying the needs of organisations and individuals. First, a move *from tangibles to intangibles* as the primary source of value means that value lies in the intellectual and relational capital organisations can leverage (know-how and reputation). The creative industries provide the best evidence of the value generated by organisations. Second, consumers purchase products not only for their functional utility but also for their *symbolic value*. This means that products and brands are often used by consumers to build self-image and communicate image to others. Brands are not only physical objects but also mental objects; they are mental constructs imbued with meaning (Danesi, 2006). As Pavitt suggests, some brands are "selected to make a statement to others about ourselves as a form of communication, and branded goods are specifically designed to speak to us on an emotional and associational level. In turn, we use them to speak for us" (2000, p. 156) . Brands act as a sort of virtual real estate (Schiller, 1999) and occupy a valuable place in consumers' minds. "That position is valuable insofar as it enables a brand to subsume and appropriate what consumers do with the brand in mind as source of surplus value and profits" (Arvidsson, 2006, p. 7). This leads us to 'informational capitalism', a new form of capitalism centred on informational rather than industrial production (Arvidsson, 2006). Lury (2004) suggests that brands are objects of information and they objectify information. Brands are seen by many as symbols of capitalism of any form; they have become symbols of political ideologies and social phenomena (Klein, 2015). Consider, for instance, how *Starbucks* and *McDonald's* have come to represent globalisation and capitalism, hence making them usual targets for anti-globalisation activists. We mentioned earlier that meaning is transferred from the cultural world to products and services (McCracken, 1986). We can argue that this transfer is rather reciprocal, since the omnipresence of brands has in return transformed the cultural landscape into a commercial brandscape. Such transformation means that

> constructing and expressing emotional, aesthetic, and symbolic values assume centre stage. Blurring the borders between economy and culture, brand culture and our designed existence signals something created and consumed in the interface between art and industry, production and consumption, creativity and commerce.
>
> (Schroeder & Salzer-Mörling, 2006, p. 10)

Products delivered by the creative industries (e.g. clothes, accessories, music, magazines) communicate clearer messages about oneself than products in other industries (e.g. washing detergent, milk, and toilet tissue). This is even true in the case of purchasing virtual goods within video games and online worlds, where branded virtual goods command substantially higher prices. For instance, reading the *Economist* every week tells more about yourself than does using *Ariel* washing liquid for your clothes. In addition, many opinion formers in the creative industries (e.g. art critics) "play a central role in the process of assigning collective meaning to product categories, brands, and organisations" (Troilo, 2015, p. 12).

The third change in our contemporary society involves the '*aestheticisation of daily life*', where borders between art and daily life are fading, daily life itself becomes an aesthetic project, and images and signs play a greater role in building meaning in daily life (Featherstone, 1991). As Holt (2004) suggests, the most successful long-lasting brands are those that become cultural icons and contribute to sense-making for individuals, social groups, communities, and lifestyles on a global level. Products of the creative industries take a central role because of their high levels of aesthetic value.

The *digital revolution* is the fourth change which has brought the creative industries to the fore. Digital technologies, e.g., *Skype* or *Instagram*, have modified the way we communicate and interact, giving new forms to the way we relate to each other. This influence is articulated by the creative economy. Digital technologies have revolutionised the entire value chain in the creative industries, from production of content, to its delivery. In fact, it is now possible to separate the content from the format (or platform) of delivery. Different formats provide different ways of using the same content; this increases our creative freedom. Finally, there has been a general *blurring of boundaries between industries* that were once thought as separate; this diversification leads to indistinct industry boundaries which is a particular phenomenon in the creative industries, as previously discussed. Essentially, the creative economy has the capacity to provide organisations with better growth opportunities and individuals with symbolic resources, particularly important in our post-modern society.

The creative economy helps the wider economy and society by facilitating change and by allowing people to adapt to new ideas, systems, and processes. The role of the creative economy in the society can also be understood through the concept of '*spillovers*' (Figure 1.2). This term signifies the ways the creative economy influences the wider economy and society. According to a research report by Chapain, Cooke, De Propris, MacNeill, and Mateos-Garcia (2010) for the National Endowment for Science, Technology, and the Arts, there are three types of spillovers: (1) knowledge, (2) product, and (3) network spillovers.

Knowledge spillovers happen when new ideas and technologies developed by firms in the creative industries are applied elsewhere in the market. For example, social networking features such as *Facebook* or *LinkedIn*, originally developed by digital media firms, are employed by other organisations to manage their communications. In other design firm–client contexts, designers might channel knowledge across the client firm, beyond the original brief specified by the client, developing unexpected novelty for the client organisation (Chapain et al., 2010). In addition, open and collaborative models, with which creative businesses organise their productive and innovative activities, suitable to dynamic competitive environments, can spread to businesses that engage with the creative industries, a phenomenon described by Potts and Morrison (2008) as a creative 'nudging innovation'.

Another form of knowledge spillovers includes labour flows where creative professionals such as designers, advertisers, or software developers are employed outside the creative industries (as explained above, these are the creative occupations out with the creative industries yet part of the wider creative economy) who bring to these organisations new techniques, ideas, ways of working, and skill sets that can induce innovation in their corporate environment (Chapain et al., 2010). Creative professionals might also start spin-off companies in a different sector (Steve Jobs & Steve Wozniak

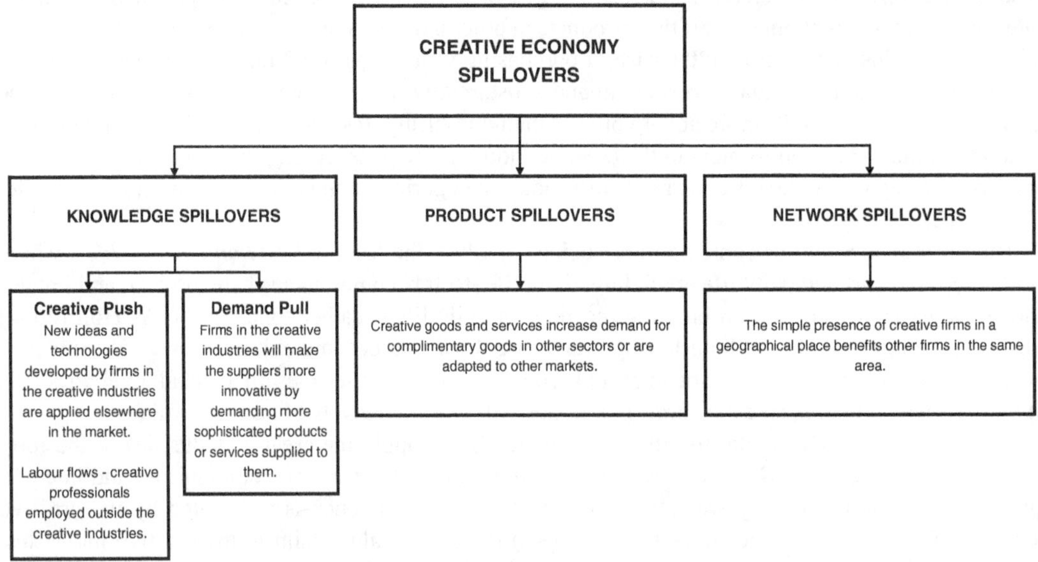

Figure 1.2 Creative economy spillovers.

were initially employed by *Atari*, a video games developer). These two forms are considered the 'creative push' knowledge spillovers; however, there can also be 'demand pull' knowledge spillovers where the firms in the creative industries will make the suppliers more innovative by demanding more sophisticated products or services supplied to them. For example, game developers will demand new and updated hardware and software from computer chip and server technology suppliers in order to design more advanced computer games.

Creative goods and services increase demand for complimentary goods in other sectors or are adapted to other markets – this phenomenon is termed as '*product spillovers*'. Consider, for instance, the ubiquity of online music which consequently increases the attractiveness of mp3 players such as *iPods* (Chapain et al., 2010). Finally, '*network spillovers*' occur where the simple presence of creative firms in a particular geographical place benefits other firms in the same area (Hartley et al., 2013). In his seminal book, *The Rise of the Creative Class*, Florida (2004) determined that 'creative cities' with a prosperous cultural scene can attract knowledge workers who can then be employed by other local businesses or may attract foreign investment from companies drawn in by the strong local pool of talent. However, this has proven to be a contentious thesis and does not always appear to hold up. Despite many attempts to recreate creative cultures like that of Silicon Valley, these do not seem to be easily recreated in other areas. Yet, Storper and Venables (2004) suggest that, generally speaking, the creative industries can create an 'urban buzz' or atmosphere which encourages local collaboration and innovation.

Beyond the wider recognition and organisational adoption of design as a means for successful product and service development, a significant contribution of creative firms to the wider economy relates to, as discussed above, their adoption of collaborative organisational models which can be adapted to other businesses in other sectors. Their systems, process, and ways of thinking can offer invaluable lessons to firms in any sector wishing to innovate. Design thinking, a paradigm extensively explored in Chapter 3, advocates for the adoption of the way designers think and work by any organisation regardless of its offering and the sector it belongs to, allowing for innovation to flourish. Many organisations around the world have been mentored by design firms such as *IDEO* in terms of adapting its innovative organisational models (Brown, 2009). Kilian, Sarrazin, and Yeon (2015), in their article for *McKinsay & Company*, urge organisations to instil design in their corporate ethos by means of design thinking. They claim that organisations ought to embed "empathy to put customers, clients and end users at the centre of the problem-solving equation" (Kilian et al., 2015, p. 1) within their business and quote Herbert Simon, the Nobel laureate, who stated that the act of design "devises courses of action aimed at changing existing situations into preferred ones" (1988, p. 67).

Design sustainability

Beyond influencing the way firms are organised and managed and how products and services are developed and marketed, design management plays a fundamental role in society through the concept of design sustainability. Chick and Micklethwaite (2011) argue that sustainable design should not be viewed as different from mainstream design. Instead, it should be an essential element of 'good' design. They contend that design thinking is an approach and attitude whose nature is to consider issues of sustainability.

> Design is increasingly recognised as a key element of the contemporary focus on the need for greater ecological and societal sustainability … Design thinking … [suggests] a wider role for design in addressing our biggest societal challenges.
>
> (Chick & Micklethwaite, 2011, p. 13)

Design has become a central point for sustainability because poorly designed industrial systems, products, and buildings contribute to environmental and social degradation. However, Stegall (2006) argues that popular views on 'design for the environment' are not enough to solve the environmental and social problems in the world because such views merely focus on a product's physical attributes such as material construction, energy use, manufacture, transportation, and disposal, without considering the fact that in order to be truly sustainable there is a need to ensure that every person uses the product in a responsible manner and returns it for recycling at the end of the product's life. In order for sustainability to become a reality, there is a need for persuading the general public to adopt a sustainable behaviour.

The role of the designer goes beyond simply creating sustainable products, to envisioning products, processes, and services that encourage such sustainable behaviour. Buchanan argues that through their products and technologies, "designers have directly influenced the actions of individuals and communities, changed attitudes and values, and shaped society in surprisingly fundamental ways" (1989, p. 93). However, this has not always been a positive influence. For instance, designers have responded to our constant drive to achieve efficiency, one of the four fundamental dimensions in what Ritzer (2011) describes as the 'McDonaldised society', by creating disposable products (e.g. cameras, cups, and cutlery) which reduce the time and energy spent on cleaning or storing products but have at the same time led to increased material consumption, uncontrollable pollution, and enormous amount of waste. McDonaldisation, as a social phenomenon, has also led to the creation of 'McJobs' which exploit low-wage workers and treat them in a mechanistic way. This, of course, was not something intentional, yet it highlights that the social and cultural impact of such products and processes was not taken into account to the required level. Products and services have to be functional, aesthetically pleasing, ergonomic, safe, environmental benign, easy to manufacture, as well as they have to have other characteristics specific to their use – all these can be achieved by design. Besides all these characteristics, design is "an art of thought and communication that can induce in others a wide range of beliefs about practical life for the individual and for groups" (Buchanan, 1989, p. 94). If we fail to recognise this, the products might create unconscious and unintentional arguments about how people should live.

Instead, understanding design's role in society can lead to providing appropriate products and services for a more sustainable consumption and, dare we say, more 'sustainable materialism', a term which, from the outset, sounds like an oxymoron. Belk (2017) explored the role of design in the so-called *sharing economy*, where people opt to pay for access to environments and products than following the usual ownership patterns, with sharing ventures such as *Airbnb* (accommodation), *Uber* (taxi rides), and *Steal* (access to designer bags). If we were to go back to our previous example, instead of disposable objects, sustainable design alternatively encourages the production of reusable objects that can be shared. Belk (2017) argues that, while many (e.g. Schor, 2014) question the sustainable nature of such sharing ventures, the net effect of sharing on the environment can be positive. Ronald Inglehart's (1981, 2008) post-materialism hypothesis suggests that by satisfying lower order material needs in Maslow's typology, we move on to higher, less material needs like love and self-actualisation. This forms a more post-material society, more likely found in developed rather than developing countries. *Post-materialism* might allow or demand more sustainability, and design ought to play its significant role in achieving this. Belk (2017) argues that, in this post-materialistic society,

> as we learn to share more and own less, we may realise that materialistic acquisitiveness imposes a great burden of ownership. To the extent that we can be happy with ready access to things rather than personally archiving, maintaining, and safeguarding them, sharing may truly offer a substantial step toward sustainability.
>
> (Belk, 2017, p. 168)

Design that has brought more problems to society and the environment can be termed as 'unconscious design', and the alternative to this is termed by Stegall as '*intentional design*', which recognises "that any artefact makes an argument for how people should live and what values they should hold" (Stegall, 2006, p. 58). Therefore, drawing from Buchanan (1989), Stegall (2006) argues that designers should encourage a constructive way of life, influence social behaviour, and play an important role in the transition to a sustainable society (Stegall, 2006). Therefore, the purpose of intentional design is to make sure that new products combine materials and resources which are environmentally conscious and at the same time they communicate values and lifestyles which promote a sustainable society. Stegall (2006) argues that such a philosophy can be understood as a sum of four interconnected, hierarchical components: (1) a *philosophy of spirit*, which suggests that design should aim to create an environment where humans can live a meaningful, peaceful, and fulfilling life in harmony with the natural world; (2) the *philosophy of purpose* (the most important part) which guides the designers to the set of values, attitudes, and characteristics they should promote, and leads to what Orr (1992) calls 'ecological literacy', i.e., the awareness of environmental issues, caring for the environment, and practicing a sustainable behaviour; (3) "the *philosophy of form and function* which addresses how a product interacts with the physical world, its ecosystems, and its people before, during, and after its useful life" (Stegall, 2006, p. 61); and (4) *philosophy of resources*, which brings our discussion to McDonough and Braungart's (2010) 'cradle-to-cradle' model. This model is based on the basic principle in the natural environment which determines that the waste of a living organism is the food of another. In summary, design can help humans achieve these four philosophical components in order to establish a society that exists in harmony with the natural world, achieving true environmental and social sustainability.

A fantastic example of such harmony is the Vancouver Convention Centre designed by LMN architects, which is the world's first LEED (Leadership in Energy and Environmental Design) Platinum convention centre that "fully integrates the urban ecosystem at the intersection of a vibrant downtown

(Continued)

(Continued)

Vancouver Convention Centre designed by LMN Architects. (Photos courtesy of LMN Architects.)

core and one of the most spectacular natural ecosystems in North America" (LMN Architects, 2016). Besides this recognition, the building received numerous other accolades, such as the Committee on the Environment Award and three National AIA Design awards – one for architecture, one for interior design, and one in the regional and urban design category.

The above discussion provides evidence for the fact that design needs to be managed in a way that it is accountable not only to commercial standards but also to ethical and environmental standards. "A designer [and design manager] must be professionally, culturally and socially responsible for the impact his or her design [and design strategy have] on the citizenry" (Joziasse, 2011, p. 409), i.e., the community. Bhamra, Hernandez, and Mawle (2013) identified four approaches which organisations can follow in their efforts to design for sustainability. First, '*improvement*', which, as an incremental approach, allows the design manager to direct

> small modifications to the outputs of design by considering, as far as possible, both environmental and social aspects that result in products, services and systems that have better performance in the three dimensions: people, planet, and profit. Usually these dimensions are related to current legislation and to continual benchmarking within the industry sector, influenced by regulations and policies, both of which are drivers for change.
>
> (Bhamra et al., 2013, pp. 107–108)

Second, '*redesign*', although an incremental approach too, is more proactive than the improvement approach, as it considers the design's impact over an entire life cycle. In this case, the overall design concept does not change; however, the way design details are executed is modified which can result in resource use reductions, in terms of the materials used and how much energy the product consumes in its entire life (Bhamra et al., 2013). A third approach involves '*developing new concepts*', which is a more radical approach requiring the designer "to think about the underlying needs and how they can be fulfilled, rather than focusing on methods of improving the current design" (Bhamra et al., 2013, p. 113). This endeavour requires a more holistic approach and multidisciplinary teams collaborating to generate a new design concept.

Van Hemel (1998) provides us with some guiding principles to achieve the rethinking of existing solutions, including (1) dematerialisation, which is not simply reducing material usage (as in the case of redesign) but replacing a physical object entirely with an alternative way of achieving the same task, e.g., replacing digital cameras with mobile phone cameras, or answering machines with mobile phone voicemail capabilities; (2) shared use of the organisational offering, which relates to the aforementioned 'sharing economy'; (3) integration of functions, for instance, smartphones integrate online access and phone call functions; and (4) functional optimisation, where the designer scrutinises the function(s) delivered by the product to identify unnecessary aspects of the design, or aspects that can be supplied in a more sustainable way, e.g., the use of less and more sustainable packaging (Van Hemel, 1998).

Finally, a fourth approach to design for sustainability is '*system innovation*', which achieves the highest level of innovation by adopting a more strategic view and includes the collaboration of different stakeholders, such as organisations, users, communities, and governments. With this approach,

> designers are part of the development of new complete sustainable systems implying new lifestyles and ways to understand production and consumption of goods and services. This holistic approach not only responds to an evolution process but also aims to avoid the rebound effects often found as a result of partial improvements in products and services from less radical approaches.
>
> (Bhamra et al., 2013, p. 115)

Human focus as disciplinal synergy

It becomes apparent from our discussion in this chapter that the two disciplines – design management and marketing – share the same focus: the individual and the wider society. Both subjects strive for human empathy and an understanding of their role in society, achieved through consumer-centred marketing and human-centred design. This constitutes a disciplinal synergy – an imperative synergy between the two disciplines. Indeed, Bruce (2011) argues that despite some tensions,

> both disciplines are focused on the consumer and on satisfying consumer needs. This common focus fuels the relationship and also means that marketing and design [management] are symbiotic. [They] work together and produce effective outcomes for the consumer and for business. Marketing provides an ongoing customer interface and ensures that design innovation delivers value customers find appealing.
>
> (Bruce, 2011, p. 340)

Marketing professionals need to use design effectively by considering "how design fits into their business, which design specialisms to use, the contribution design can make to their business, as well as developing skills in sourcing, briefing, liaising and evaluating design" (Bruce & Cooper, 1997, p. 31).

Design management achieves the aforementioned human emphasis through design sustainability and design thinking as discussed above. Marketing responds to this focus, through the macro-marketing concept, its attention to consumer behaviour, and its understanding of social exchanges. The macro-marketing school explores how marketing affects society and how society affects marketing systems; consumer behaviour investigates the role of purchasing and consumption in society; and the concept of exchange discusses the role of social exchanges (Shaw & Jones, 2005). Even if we wanted to concentrate on commercial exchanges only (in order to avoid broadening the concept of exchange so much that we blur the boundaries of the discipline), such exchanges are ubiquitous and a fundamental part of our social structure. Commercial exchanges do not only take the form of a quid-pro-quo transaction where a financial value is exchanged for a product or service; they also include the consumer 'spending', committing time, and effort to purchase and, most importantly, use and experience the product or service created by the designer. As users, we incorporate brands in every aspect of our personal, social, and professional lives, and we exchange with brands the most important asset we have: time. Consider, for instance, your use of social media brands such as *Facebook* and *Instagram* in your personal life and your use of technology software, such as the *Microsoft Office* suite, in your professional life; we spend an enormous time with these platforms on a daily basis. As a result, we are drawn towards brands which understand us the most and those which achieve the required empathy, i.e., brands that are human-centric in what they offer.

Hence, all three concepts of macro-marketing, consumer behaviour, and exchange require a societal perspective. Such societal emphasis is also recognised in marketing management through the concept of societal marketing. The societal marketing paradigm indicates that successful marketing in the twenty-first century should achieve three important objectives – consumer satisfaction, organisational profit, and social welfare – and strives to strike a balance among these. This again recognises the pivotal role an organisation plays in the social structure. Kotler (2011), in his short paper in the *Journal of Marketing*, urged scholars and practitioners towards reinventing marketing to respond to the environmental imperative previously discussed. He argued that sustainable practice holds the following principles: (1) wants are influenced by culture and morphed by marketing practices, (2) our planet's resources are finite and fragile, (3) the earth has a limited capacity for waste and pollution, and (4) quality of life and personal happiness do not always increase with more consumption and want satisfaction. However, in the words of Paul Polan, *Uniliver*'s CEO, "the road to well-being doesn't go via reduced consumption. It has to be done via more responsible consumption" (cited in Stern, 2010). Fundamentally, we can see a connection between marketing and design through the concept of societal marketing whereby the organisation should not only ensure that it satisfies the needs and wants of every party which has a stake in the marketing exchange, but it should also enhance or at least maintain the welfare of everyone involved and the society in general. Managing design successfully will enable the organisation to achieve its societal marketing objectives: organisational profit, consumer satisfaction, and, most importantly, social welfare.

Book structure

The fundamental aim of this book is to explore design management from an organisation and a marketing perspective. This will highlight synergies between design management and marketing and improve our understanding of design management as a discipline, exploring its scope and boundaries, in response to previous calls for more clarity of the disciplinal territory and its connections with other fields. This book is structured on the basis of Best's (2006, 2015) three stages of design management: the management of design strategy, the management of design process, and the management of design implementation. Hence we will start by exploring the management of the design strategy and vision, with Chapter 2 discussing the design research process and methods, Chapter 3 debating the concept of design thinking and how it can be incorporated in the organisational DNA, and Chapter 4 exploring the necessary components of the design strategy, developed on the basis of the previous two chapters. Then we will explore how we can manage the creative process, with Chapter 5 discussing human creativity, its antecedents and outcomes, and Chapter 6 providing an understanding of how firms can organise themselves to achieve higher levels of creativity and design innovation, drawing from the field of organisation studies and in particular from literature on organisational paradoxes of innovation and the concept of ambidexterity. In addition, Chapter 7 will discuss the relationships between humans and things, the concept of experiences, and will demonstrate how design management can contribute to the creation of holistic human experiences. Chapter 8 will explore the role of design management and technology (e.g. social media) in facilitating the value co-creation process which not only puts the customer at the centre of the product and service development process but empowers him/her to co-create adverts, products, and brands that he/she will ultimately consume. The marketing potential of anthropomorphic design, which relates to concept co-creation, is also explored. In Chapter 9, we will explore how to implement design projects, through our discussion of design consultancies as professional service firms and the successful management of consultancy–client relations. In addition, Chapter 10 will explore the concept of design leadership and bring the main concepts discussed in the previous chapters together, in order to offer general concluding remarks.

Chapter review questions

You can use the following questions to reflect on the material covered in Chapter 1:

1 Discuss the three overarching paradigms in design management.
2 Explain the challenges associated with the definition of the creative industries and their relation to the concept of the creative economy.
3 Discuss the role of the creative economy in the wider economy and society.
4 Define design sustainability and discuss the four hierarchical philosophical components of ecologically intentional design.
5 Discuss the main synergy between the design management and marketing paradigms in contemporary society.

Recommended reading

1 Cooper, R., & Junginger, S. (2011a). General introduction: Design management – a reflection. In R. Cooper, S. Junginger, & T. Lockwood (Eds.), *The handbook of design management.* Oxford, UK: Berg.
2 Stegall, N. (2006). Designing for sustainability: A philosophy for ecologically intentional design. *Design Issues, 22*(2), 56–63.

Reflective thoughts

Design and marketing practice: On tempests and tea cups

Russell W. Belk
Professor of Marketing
Kraft Foods Canada Chair in Marketing
Schulich School of Business, York University, Toronto, Canada

Perhaps early farmers seeking to sell or trade their excess produce did not worry much about design. But no doubt those who cleaned up their fruits and vegetables, those who arranged them in attractive

(Continued)

(Continued)

displays, those who built stands to shield their produce from the elements, and those who created appealing signs announcing the nature of their business noticed that they attracted more consumers and could get more in return for their offerings. They were marrying design and marketing to enhance the value of their products. Later on, those who brought their produce to cities and regional fairs, developed a line of verbal pitching, and who were themselves clean and attractive representatives of their agricultural output no doubt enjoyed greater sales. They too were engaging in a combination of design and marketing. Later still, farmers from particular regions that produced higher quality fruits, vegetables, wines, olive oils, and other produce and who packaged them in attractive and informative containers likely began to benefit from regional branding. And eventually larger scale producers and intermediaries began to more formally brand their foods and beverages, advertise them, and offer them in more convenient and attractive forms including refrigerated, frozen, freeze-dried, dehydrated, microwaveable, recyclable, enriched, and condensed. Together with form and packaging innovations, designing more effective supply chains and faster transportation, genetic improvements, and more efficient farming practices led to low-cost availability of locally out-of-season items that we have come to take for granted in economically developed economies.

What is true with the role of design and marketing for food products is certainly true in the realms of clothing, furniture, homes, cars, films, videogames, phones, and many other products and services that we use daily. We have only to consider the role of design in the success of *Apple* products in the late twentieth and early twenty-first centuries. It is not that *Apple* invented the first tablet computer, MP3 player, smartphone, or computerised wristwatch. Rather they were more successful in designing the workings and appearance of these products and at enhancing the consumer–product interface and experience. And once they had established their reputation for well-designed, reliable, easy-to-use products, consumer expectations and enthusiasm helped to make the success of their later offerings more than halfway assured. Likewise, *Disney*'s and *Pixar*'s success in designing films, theme parks, stylishly retold tales, and anthropomorphised cartoon characters has helped make their new offerings increasingly successful, entertaining, and profitable. And *McDonald's* has succeeded not only by designing addictively good-tasting foods but also through appealing local decors and menus, efficient supply chains and restaurant operations, and more sustainable packaging.

Processes, products, ideas, and even personal appearances can all benefit from the potent combination of good design and good marketing. Good design is multi-modal and often includes sight, sound, feel, smell, and taste. It involves a combination of form, function, and symbolic elements that result in a better consumer experience. In marketing it is easiest to think of product design, which is one of the basic "4 Ps" of marketing. But there are many types of design, including "architectural and interior design, industrial design, engineering design, graphic design, urban design, information systems design, software design, interaction design, fashion design … organizational design, social systems design, educational systems design, workplace design, [and] healthcare design" (Nelson & Stolterman, 2012). As the systemic element of the latter design contexts suggests, design should not be conceived in isolation. The lightbulb, the bicycle, mobile phones, automobiles, and dinner plates all have had wide-ranging impacts on such far-flung areas as education, clothing, urban sprawl, laws, socialising patterns, work patterns, friendships, funerals, human and animal migration patterns, longevity, farm prices, holiday travel, nightlife, mealtimes, and much more (e.g. Bijker, 1995; Norman, 2013; Shove, Watson, Hand, & Ingram, 2007). Virtually everything about design influences more than just the sale and use of a single product. We also use the design of products to make statements about our age, gender, taste, social class, sophistication, and lifestyle (Forty, 1986). And if product and package design are not enough, marketing helps to codify and exemplify who would use a particular product and brand, in what settings, and for what purposes.

Think about something as simple as a cup – a vessel that is meant to hold beverages. Through design and marketing we can now tell at a glance if it is meant for serving tea or coffee, whether it is masculine or feminine, refined or robust, old-fashioned or contemporary, for children or adults, a family heirloom or a souvenir from a trip to New York City. Also at a glance we can tell not only who is likely to use the cup but also in what settings, in which parts of the world, and with what accompanying utensils, foods, and condiments. So powerful are these semiotic readings and associations that in a *BBC* special series, Neil MacGregor (2012) succeeded in telling *A History of the World in 100 Objects* from the British Museum. They included three cups and one Victorian tea set. These objects tell us about the origins and spread of tea from China to Europe, the impact on English tea rituals, the use of tea with sugar to fuel workers in the Industrial Revolution, the frenzied fashion to have Chinese porcelain, imitation "Chinaware" from Delft and elsewhere, women's appearance in downtown settings, restaurants and hotels, collecting behaviour, conspicuous consumption, globalisation, and a host of other rippling impacts on both European and Asian societies (e.g. Finlay 2010; Jenkins 2013; Porter 2010). And all of this from a single tea cup.

References

Bijker, W. E. (1995). *Of bicycles, bakelites, and bulbs: Toward a theory of sociotechnical change.* Cambridge, MA: MIT Press.

Finlay, R. (2010). *The pilgrim art: Cultures of porcelain in world history.* Berkeley: University of California Press.

Forty, A. (1986). *Objects of desire: Design and society from Wedgwood to IBM.* New York: Pantheon.

Jenkins, E. (2013). *A taste for China: English subjectivity and the prehistory of orientalism.* Oxford, UK: Oxford University Press.

MacGregor, N. (2012). *A history of the world in 100 objects.* London: Penguin.

Nelson, H., & Stolterman, E. (2012). *The design way: Intentional change in an unpredictable world* (2nd ed.). Cambridge, MA: MIT Press.

Norman, D. (2013). *The design of everyday things* (Rev. ed.). New York: Basic Books.

Porter, D. (2010). *The Chinese taste in eighteenth century England.* Cambridge, UK: Cambridge University Press.

Shove, E., Watson, M., Hand, M., & Ingram, J. (2007). *The design of everyday life.* Oxford, UK: Berg.

References

Arvidsson, A. (2006). *Brands: Meaning and value in media culture.* New York: Psychology Press.

Bagozzi, R. P. (1975). Marketing as exchange. *The Journal of Marketing, 39*(4), 32–39.

Bartels, R. (1988). *The history of marketing thought* (3rd ed.). Columbus, OH: Publishing Horizons.

Belk, R. W. (2017). Sharing, materialism, and design for sustainability. In J. Chapman (Ed.), *Routledge handbook of sustainable product design.* London: Routledge.

Best, K. (2006). *Design management: Managing design strategy, process and implementation.* Lausanne, Switzerland: AVA Publishing.

Best, K. (2015). *Design management: Managing design strategy, process and implementation.* London: Fairchild Books, Bloomsbury Publishing.

Bhamra, T., Hernandez, R., & Mawle, R. (2013). Sustainability: Methods and practices. In S. Walker, & J. Giard (Eds.), *The handbook of design for sustainability*. London: Bloomsbury.

Bilton, C. (2007). *Management and creativity: From creative industries to creative management*. Oxford, UK: Blackwell.

Blackett, T. (2003). What is a brand? In P. Barwise (Ed.), *Brands and branding* (pp. 13–25). London: The Economist.

Bloch, P. H. (2011). Product design and marketing: Reflections after fifteen years. *Journal of Product Innovation Management, 28*(3), 378–380.

Bolland, R., & Collopy, F. (Eds.). (2004). *Managing as designing*. Palo Alto, CA: Stanford University Press.

Brown, T. (2009). *Change by design: How design thinking transforms organisations and inspires innovation*. New York: HarperCollins.

Bruce, M. (2011). Connecting marketing and design. In R. Cooper, S. Junginger, & T. Lockwood (Eds.), *The handbook of design management*. Oxford, UK: Berg.

Bruce, M., & Cooper, R. (1997). *Marketing and design management*. London: Intl Thomson Business Press.

Buchanan, R. (1989). Declaration by design: Rhetoric, argument, and demonstration in design practice. In V. Margolin (Ed.), *Design discourse*. Chicago: University of Chicago Press.

Chapain, C., Cooke, P., De Propris, L., MacNeill, S., & Mateos-Garcia, J. (2010). *Creative clusters and innovation: Putting creativity on the map*. London: NESTA.

Chick, A., & Micklethwaite, P. (2011). *Design for sustainable change: How design and designers can drive the sustainability agenda*. Lausanne, Switzerland: AVA Publishing.

Cooper, R., & Junginger, S. (2011a). General introduction: Design management – a reflection. In R. Cooper, S. Junginger, & T. Lockwood (Eds.), *The handbook of design management*. Oxford, UK: Berg.

Cooper, R., & Junginger, S. (2011b). Conclusions: Design management and beyond. In R. Cooper, S. Junginger, & T. Lockwood (Eds.), *The handbook of design management*. Oxford, UK: Berg.

Cunningham, S., & Potts, J. (2015). Creative industries and the wider economy. In C. Jones, M. Lorenzen, & J. Sapsed (Eds.), *The Oxford handbook of the creative industries*. Oxford, UK: Oxford University Press.

Danesi, M. (2006). *Brands*. London: Routledge.

Department for Media, Culture and Sport. (1998). *Creative industries mapping document 2001*. Retrieved from www.gov.uk/government/publications/creative-industries-mapping-documents-1998

Department for Media, Culture and Sport. (2001). *Creative industries mapping document 2001*. Retrieved from www.gov.uk/government/publications/creative-industries-mapping-documents-2001

Department for Media, Culture and Sport. (2015). *Creative industries: Focus on employment 2015*. Retrieved from www.gov.uk/government/uploads/system/uploads/attachment_data/file/439714/Annex_C_-_Creative_Industries_Focus_on_Employment_2015.pdf

Du Gay, P., & Pryke, M. (Eds.). (2002). *Cultural economy: Cultural analysis and commercial life*. London: Sage.

Falk, R. (1961). *The business of management: Art or craft?* London: Penguin Books.

Farr, M. (1965). Design management: Why is it needed now? *Design, 200*, 38–39.

Featherstone, M. (1991). *Consumer culture and postmodernism*. London: Sage.

Florida, R. L. (2004). *The rise of the creative class: And how it's transforming work, leisure, community and everyday life*. New York: Basic Books.

Forty, A. (1986). *Objects of desire: Design and society from Wedgewood to IBM*. London: Thames & Hudson.

Gorb, P. (Ed.). (1990). *Design management: Papers from the London Business School*. New York: Van Nostrand Reinhold.

Hales, G. (2011). Branding. In J. J. Kourdi (Ed.), *The marketing century: How marketing drives business and shapes society*. Chichester, UK: John Wiley & Sons.

Hands, D. (2009). *Vision and values in design management*. Lausanne, Switzerland: AVA Publishing.

Hartley, J., Potts, J., Flew, T., Cunningham, S., Keane, M., & Banks, J. (Eds.). (2013). *Key concepts in creative industries*. London: Sage.

Holt, D. B. (2004). *How brands become icons: The principles of cultural branding*. Cambridge, MA: Harvard Business Press.

Howkins, J. (2005). The mayor's commission on the creative industries. In J. Hartley (Ed.), *Creative industries* (pp. 117–125). London: Blackwell.

Inglehart, R. (1981, December). Post-materialism in an environment of insecurity. *American Political Science Review, 75*(4), 880–900.

Inglehart, R. (2008). Changing values among western publics from 1970 to 2006. *West European Politics, 31*(1–2), 130–146.
Jones, C., Lorenzen, M., & Sapsed, J. (2015). Creativity: A typology of change. In C. Jones, M. Lorenzen, & J. Sapsed (Eds.), *The Oxford handbook of the creative industries*. Oxford, UK: Oxford University Press.
Jones, D. B., & Shaw, E. H. (2002). A history of marketing thought. In B. A. Weitz, & R. Wensley (Eds.), *Handbook of marketing* (pp. 39–65). London: Sage.
Joziasse, F. (2011). Design leadership: Current limits and future opportunities. In R. Cooper, S. Junginger, & T. Lockwood (Eds.), *The handbook of design management*. Oxford, UK: Berg.
Kilian, J., Sarrazin, H., & Yeon, H. (2015). *Building a design-driven culture*. London: McKinsey & Company.
Klein, N. (2015). *No logo*. Paris: Éditions Actes Sud.
Kotler, P. (2011). Reinventing marketing to manage the environmental imperative. *Journal of Marketing, 75*(4), 132–135.
Kotler, P., & Alexander Rath, G. (1984). Design: A powerful but neglected strategic tool. *Journal of Business Strategy, 5*(2), 16–21.
Lalaounis, S. T., Wood, B. M., & Evans, D. (2011). Design management: A comparative analysis of the professional status of the occupation in the UK. *Design Principles & Practice: An International Journal, 5*(6), 639–665.
Lash, S., & Urry, J. (1994). *Economies of signs and space* (Vol. 26). London: Sage.
LMN Architects. (2016). Retrieved August 20, 2016 from https://lmnarchitects.com/project/vancouver-convention-centre-west
Lury, C. (2004). *Brands: The logos of the global economy*. London: Routledge.
McCracken, G. (1986). Culture and consumption: A theoretical account of the structure and movement of the cultural meaning of consumer goods. *Journal of Consumer Research, 13*(1), 71–84.
McDonough, W., & Braungart, M. (2010). *Cradle to cradle: Remaking the way we make things*. London: MacMillan.
Moor, L. (2007). *The rise of brands*. Oxford, UK: Berg.
Orr, D. W. (1992). *Ecological literacy: Education and the transition to a postmodern world*. Albany, NY: SUNY Press.
Pavitt, J. (2000). Branding the individual. In J. Pavitt (Ed.), *Brand new*. London: Victoria & Albert Publications.
Pilditch, J. (1976). *Talk about design*. New York: Random House Business.
Potts, J., & Morrison, K. (2008). *Nudging innovation*. London: NESTA.
Ritzer, G. (2011). *The McDonaldization of society 6*. Thousand Oaks, CA: Pine Forge Press.
Schiller, D. (1999). *Digital capitalism*. Cambridge, MA: MIT Press.
Schor, J. (1998). *The overspent American: Upscaling, downshifting, and the new consumer*. New York: Harper Perennial.
Schroeder, J. E., & Salzer-Mörling, M. (2006). Introduction. The cultural codes of branding. In J. E. Schroeder, M. Salzer-Mörling, & S. Askegaard (Eds.), *Brand culture*. London: Taylor & Francis.
Shaw, E. H. (1995). The first dialogue on macromarketing. *Journal of Macromarketing, 15*(1), 7–20.
Shaw, E. H., & Jones, D. B. (2005). A history of schools of marketing thought. *Marketing Theory, 5*(3), 239–281.
Simon, H. A. (1988). The science of design: Creating the artificial. *Design Issues, 4*(1/2), 67–82.
Stegall, N. (2006). Designing for sustainability: A philosophy for ecologically intentional design. *Design Issues, 22*(2), 56–63.
Stern, S. (2010, April 5). The outsider in a hurry to shake up his company. *Financial Times*. Retrieved from www.ft.com/cms/s/0/942c64a6-404a-11df-8d23-00144feabdc0.html?ft_site=falcon&desktop=true#axzz4gCOxzVuj
Storper, M., & Venables, A. J. (2004). Buzz: Face-to-face contact and the urban economy. *Journal of Economic Geography, 4*(4), 351–370.
Tadajewski, M. (2009). A history of marketing thought. In E. Parsons, & P. MacLaran (Eds.), *Contemporary issues in marketing and consumer behaviour* (pp. 13–36). London: Butterworth-Heinemann.
Troilo, G. (2015). *Marketing in the creative industries: Value, experience and creativity*. Basingstoke, UK: Palgrave.
Van Hemel, C. G. (1998). *EcoDesign empirically explored: Design for environment in Dutch small and medium-sized enterprises* (doctoral thesis). TU Delft, Delft University of Technology, Delft, The Netherlands.
Wengrow, D. (2008). Prehistories of commodity branding. *Current Anthropology, 49*(1), 7–34.
Zhang, D., Hu, P., & Kotabe, M. (2011). Marketing – industrial design integration in new product development: The case of China. *Journal of Product Innovation Management, 28*(3), 360–373.

2 Design research

Framing the design problem and identifying design opportunities

Chapter aims and learning outcomes

This chapter aims to:

1 Discuss the origins of design research and the value of research in the design process.
2 Explore the design research processes while reflecting on the collaboration among marketers, designers, and researchers.
3 Critically examine the design research methods pursued in order to frame the design problem and/or identify design opportunities.
4 Understand how design firms (and firms in general) can establish and maintain a culture of design research.

The origins and value of design research

In the previous chapter, we indicated that the main disciplinal synergy between design management and marketing is the fact that both share the same focus: the human being. Consequently, both disciplines seek to study and understand *human behaviour* in order to provide better solutions to human problems. After all, "design, stripped to its essence, can be defined as the human capacity to shape and make our environment in ways without precedent in nature, to serve our needs and give meaning to our lives" (Heskett, 2005, p. 5). Humans have not only functional needs, satisfied through the mechanical efficiency of products and service processes, but also emotional needs. As Pilditch explains,

> the more man-made our world becomes, the more stress we face, the less contact we have with nature, the more weed emotional satisfactions that cannot be provided in traditional ways. We choose products to surround us that will fulfil our emotional requirements.
>
> (Pilditch, 1976, p. 179)

In marketing, scholars and practitioners emphasise the need for thorough consumer research to satisfy consumer needs, generate profit, and contribute to social welfare (societal marketing paradigm). Similarly, designers aim to understand the behaviour of end users, brainstorm, conceive, and test their ideas with them. This indicates that both marketing and design look to the consumer and the user, the human being, for inspiration and direction. *Apple* is an organisation where understanding the needs of the user and the market right from the start of the design process is a priority. Its new product process (ANPP) acts like a giant checklist and details exactly what every part of the organisation has to do at every stage of the product development process. "The ANPP involves every department from the outset, including functions like marketing, whose work will only be seen after the product is launched"

(Kahney, 2013). Such endeavours require conducting research on human behaviour and the continuous collaboration of marketers and designers with researchers.

Design research as a discipline was born out of necessity; designers needed to understand the users of their artefacts (Wilcox, 2016). The first real design researcher was Alvin Tilley working for *Henry Dreyfuss Associates*, a product design firm responsible for many iconic products like *Bell* telephones, *Hoover* vacuum cleaners, and *Polaroid* cameras. Tilley, a mechanical engineer by profession, began collecting information from many different sources to support his design endeavours. This led to, among other things, the publication of his book entitled *The Measure of Man and Woman: Human Factors in Design* in 1959, which is still considered an invaluable collection of anthropometric information and acts, in its revised form, as a useful tool for designers today (Wilcox, 2016). *Anthropometry* is the study of the shape and size of the human body and provides significant direction for the pursuit of human-centred design (Tilley, Anning, & Welles, 2002). During the 1960s, the design research field began to develop in the UK, including the foundation of the Design Research Society in 1966. The work of Charles Mauro and Dan Formosa in the 1970s and 1980s, respectively, contributed to the development of *ergonomics* – the application of human body knowledge to design.

Ergonomics: The application of human body knowledge to design.

Wasson (2000) explains that before the use of ethnography in design research, the dominant type of social science that designers pursued to understand the product/service user was cognitive psychology, particularly human factors research investigating what kind of product designs are the most 'natural' for consumers and are the easiest to use based on the strengths and weaknesses of human information processing abilities. This means that following this approach, usability research is limited to a consideration of what goes in the head of the consumer, without examining larger institutional and cultural contexts. Marketing research in the form of customer surveys, demographics, and historical patterns had also been used to provide statistical insights but failed to provide an understanding of how consumers fit products and services into their everyday life and to explore the cultural ideologies that influence consumers' perception of these products and services. Similarly, although focus groups can provide a more open-ended approach with regard to this, they are based on users' own accounts of their attitudes and practices which can be unreliable (Wasson, 2000).

The limitations of human factors and traditional marketing research led the design profession towards ethnographic methods which can reveal a new dimension of the user. Throughout the 1980s, the employment of social scientists including psychologists, anthropologists, and behavioural scientists in design firms increased, embracing ethnography as a dominant design research methodology. *Cheskin, The Dolbin Group, E-Lab, Fitch,* and *IDEO* are design firms considered to be the early initiators of design ethnography (Ireland, 2003). In addition, the visual nature of video-tapping as a means of recording naturally occurring consumer practices made ethnography particularly appealing to designers given the visual nature of the very own profession.

The importance of research in design is also highlighted by Schön's (1983) concept of the 'reflective practitioner' which leads to the generation of knowledge in action – knowing *how* rather than knowing *what* (Gray & Malins, 2004) – and Robson's concept of the 'practitioner-researcher' who is "someone who holds down a job in some particular areas and at the same time carries out … enquiry which is of relevance to the job" (1993, p. 446). Adopting such an approach provides the 'insider's advantage' explained by Douglas as the ability "to look at one's own creative practice [which] means taking on both a creative and a reflective role, in a sense creating a new research model which may use other models but will inevitably have its own distinct identity" (1994, p. 45). However, the insider's advantage can also prove to be a problem because practitioner-researchers might find it difficult to adopt an open-minded approach and avoid preconceptions which might cloud any issues. The way to address this problem is by exposing ideas and practices to other professionals for advice and feedback (Gray & Malins, 2004).

What we can distil from the aforementioned concepts is that designers beyond their primary role of designing shall also take a role of researchers, in the form of pursuing academic enquiry to understand design from a theoretical perspective, or in the form of conducting practical research to provide better design solutions for users. In the case of practical research carried out as part of a consumer project, there shall be close collaboration among designers, marketers, and researchers. Brown (2009) recognises that although we shall never lose respect for the designer as the 'inspired form giver', as design has moved upstream in the innovation process to tackle a wider range of problems, it requires an interdisciplinary team of behaviour scientists, psychologists, ethnographers, marketing and business experts, engineers and scientists, and even writers and filmmakers working together, following the same processes (Brown, 2009). Such interdisciplinary design project teams which can include different professionals from a plethora of different disciplines will be referred to hereafter as 'the team'.

In the foreword of the seminal book *Creating Breakthrough Ideas, The Collaboration of Anthropologists and Designers in the Product Development Industry*, John F. Sherry Jr emphasised that consumption drives culture, and anthropologists can meticulously study this drive and can advise marketers and designers appropriately. There are many different research methodologies adopted in design, but given the power of ethnography to unravel human behaviour, it provides even more invaluable implications for improving current product/service offerings, or developing new ones. At *IDEO*, joint teams of designers and human scientists get 'out there' to observe existing and potential users of the product or service (Myerson, 2004). Sherry (2002) explains very articulately the value of ethnography in the design process with the following.

> An ethically engaged ethnographer can penetrate the heart of consumer experience and render it accessible to intervention in a way that not only minimises potential harm, but also optimises the potential benefit consumers are likely to derive. This is a prosocial use of proprietary

> enquiry … When an ethnographer helps the marketers and the engineers to see the 'familiar' as 'strange', new product development leaps to an entirely different plane … The contribution of ethnography does not end with an interpretation of the ecology of consumer behaviour, although frequently this is the case. Nor does it end when the product produced has all the functional and ergonomic properties to compete favourably in the category. We live in a world of functional parity, where optimal features and benefits are the ante to get into the game. If ethnography contributes merely to the addition of bells and whistles, it falls far short of its promise. A well-designed product is increasingly evaluated on its aesthetic dimension, for the experience it helps the consumer enjoy. Ethnography lays bare the cultural erotics that consumers employ to animate the world of goods, and renders those principles accessible to creatives (designers, advertisers, and other visionaries) whose job it is to translate them into artefacts and relationships.
>
> (Sherry, 2002, pp. ix–x)

The design research process

It is important at this stage to understand the design research process. As already said, the collaboration between marketers, designers, and researchers (such as ethnographers) should be encouraged and maintained throughout the lifetime of the design project. Indeed, there are different parts where each will take a more prominent role; however, this does not mean that the other disciplines need not be involved on a permanent fashion. Quite the contrary, there is a need for continuous convergence of disciplines which goes beyond the mere provision of feedback and takes the form of collaborative co-creation. Researchers should be provided the right environment (and often time) for their expertise to be fully utilised. Designers should be given research results that point to practical implications and not only mere observational data (Wasson, 2002). "Applied ethnographic analyses cannot end with descriptions or explanations. They must draw out the implications of the cultural insights and offer practicable guidelines for future ideas" (Squires & Byrne, 2002, p. xiv). The trajectory of the design research project starts with an emphasis on marketing in the first phase, moves to an emphasis on research in the second phase, and then finishes with an emphasis on design in the third phase. However, as Figure 2.1 illustrates, this does not mean that the other two disciplines are not involved in every stage; as we have already emphasised, the collaboration should be continuous without any moments of 'handoffs' between them (Wasson, 2002).

The early stages of the design process which involve design research are often described by corporate managers as the '*fuzzy front end*'. The use of such term demonstrates the fact that design research is often perceived by the corporate world as ill-defined, random, and mysterious (Rhea, 2003). However, design research can guide the client organisation to discover what offering it needs to make, determine whom to make it for, explain the reasons for making it, and highlight the important attributes for it to be successful in the market.

In fact, Cooper and Kleinschmidt (1987) in their study of the success and failure of 203 new products determined that besides the products' advantage (including their unique features, high quality, and reduced customer costs), the 'proficiency of pre-development activities' and the 'protocol' were the most critical steps in the new product development (NPD) process. The proficiency of pre-development activities includes "undertaking proficiently a set of 'up-front' activities, namely initial screening; preliminary market assessment; preliminary technical assessment; detailed market study or marketing research; and business/financial analysis" (Cooper and Kleinschmidt, 1987, p. 180). The protocol involves a clear definition of the new product's target audience, including their needs, desires, and preferences, and the product concept, including

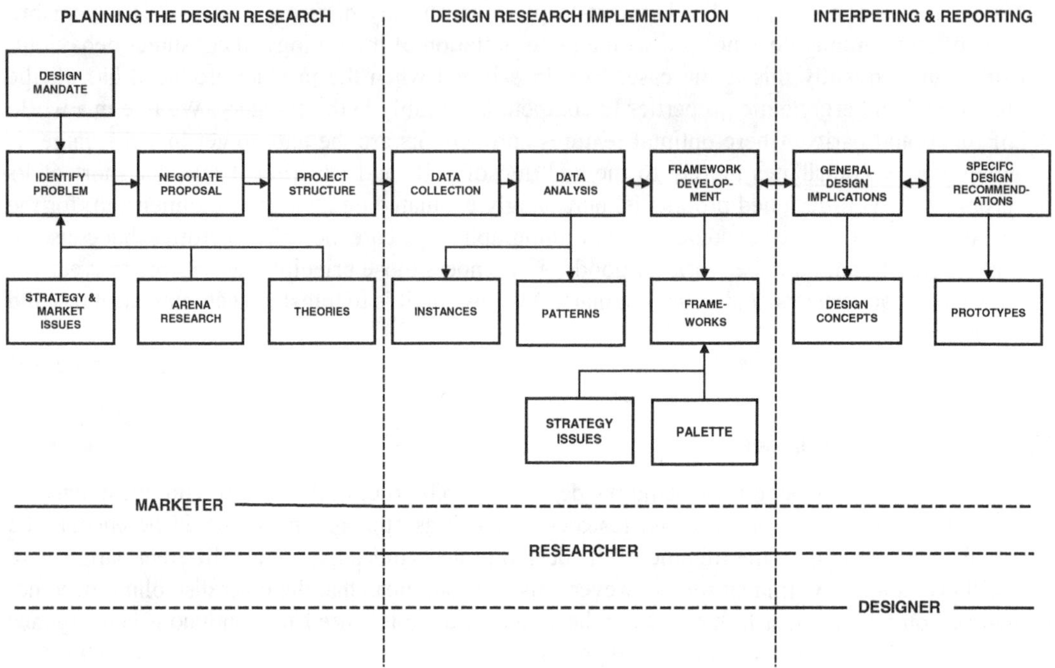

Figure 2.1 Design research process.

specifications and requirements (Cooper & Kleinschmidt, 1987). A well-executed design research process can ensure the proficiency of the pre-development activities and result to this protocol (in the form of the design brief). However, Rhea (2003) argues that design researchers often do not do a good job in presenting a coherent framework to explain how design research can lead an organisation to all these. Hence, understanding and enunciating the design research process will assist the team to make sure everyone appreciates the value of design research in the early stages of product/service development process. This is because it helps "articulate how research can turn the 'fuzzy front end' into a predictable process for inventing the future of the organisation, and advocate its value to senior management" (Rhea, 2003, p. 145).

The process outlined below draws primarily from Wasson's (2002) account of the collaborative design research process of *E-Lab*, a Chicago-based design firm founded in 1994 on the principle of equal partnership between design and research (the company was acquired by *Sapient Corporation* in 1999 and does not use its original name any more). In the first phase of the process, the team defines the problem and plans the design research project; this involves four stages, i.e., getting the mandate from the client, identifying the problem, negotiating the proposal, and defining the project structure. In the second phase, the team will carry out the design research; this phase includes three stages – data collection, data analysis, and framework development. Finally, in the third phase, the team interprets the data and indicates general design implications and specific design recommendations. It is important to remember that although this process appears linear, there are parts of the process where there is a need for multiple iterations, going back and forward between data and implications. The following part will explore these phases and stages in greater depth.

Planning the design research

The design mandate

There is a plethora of reasons that client organisations decide to pursue a design project. It could include cases such an entrepreneur deciding to start up a new company, or an existing company seeking to add a new product or service in its portfolio or aiming to make improvements to existing offerings. The ultimate drive behind such endeavours might be to defend, regain, or increase market share, and/or the firm's desire to diversify into a completely new market (Borja de Mozotta, 2003; Leblanc, 2012). This will provide an organisation the basis for a *design mandate*. Leblanc (2012) defines the mandate as the authorisation to begin the design process. This is usually provided in a written format (with or as part of a design brief) and indicates the client's project expectations. These can be very precise or vague depending on the nature of the project; incremental innovation projects tend to be more well-defined from the outset, whereas radical innovation might merely include the client intentions without specific details on the project expectations since these are not known at the start of the process. It is important that designers have an understanding of both the motivation behind a design project and the context in which a problem occurs (Leblanc, 2012).

Identifying the design problem, negotiating the proposal, and agreeing project structure

At this stage it is important for the project team to define the design problem. After all, "before a problem is resolved, it needs to be identified and articulated" (Leblanc, 2012, p. 35). However, what we consider to be the problem that needs to be fixed in the first instance with a deeper analysis might prove to be only the symptom. The onus is on the team to recognise this and address the real root of the problem – the cause (Leblanc, 2012). Thus, an important question we have to understand is what makes a problem a problem. In design, the term 'problem' can refer to both a negative and a positive situation. The former will be cases where there is something we do not approve of or disagree with, because it does not meet our expectations, needs, or wants. The latter can be simply a goal which design can pursue creatively. All disciplines will have to work together to define the problem clearly. Ultimately, the solutions proposed will have to have a direct relationship with the problem stated at this stage of the process (Leblanc, 2012).

Framing the problem in an appropriate way will influence the creative approach to be taken. Leblanc (2012) uses a vivid example to explain what we mean by *appropriate problem formation*. If, for example, we frame a design task using the phrase "design a new chair", this will lead the team to an '*object-focused design approach*' where all efforts will seek to understand how the chair is made, how it can be improved, producing sketches of new shapes, improved details, features, and perhaps an environmentally responsible solution. Nevertheless, if we phrase the design task as "how can we accommodate people's need for sitting?", then the team is likely to follow a more '*human-centred design approach*' where the team can question many assumptions such as what we understand by sitting, when it is required, how long, and how comfortable does it need to be. New and often unconventional ideas about sitting are to be expected. Such an approach will lead to creative idea generation, understanding how people can often use an object for a different purpose than what it was intended. As Leblanc states, "the initial phrasing of the problem can be a catalyst to such creative reinterpretations or it can suppress creativity" (2012, p. 36).

Following this, the team will have to *negotiate the design research project proposal* and agree this with the client. This proposal or final design brief will have to be shaped in a written form and disseminated internally and externally. This will act as the contract between the design firm and the client. It also provides a clear indication of the *structure* the project should follow. The research project proposal and the structure will indicate the methods the project will follow in order to collect the data required to resolve the problem specified.

Wasson (2002) states that factors like the client's *strategy and market issues*, the pre-existing *arena research* on the client's industry and consumers, and the *theories* which inform the researchers' understandings of social phenomena can shape this initial phase of the design research process. With regard to strategy and market issues, marketers can bring in marketing environment information generated through the use of conventional analytical models such as the PESTEL and Michael Porter's (1979, 1980) Five Forces models. On a macro-level, the PESTEL framework explores the political, economic, socio-cultural, technological, environmental (related to environmental protection), and legal factors, affecting the wider economy and society. Such analysis allows the firm to identify opportunities and threats that might affect the design project. On a micro-level, Porter's Five Forces model suggests that the nature and intensity of competition in a given sector is determined by the interaction of (1) the bargaining power of suppliers, (2) the bargaining power of buyers, (3) the threats of new entrants, (4) the threat of substitutes, and (5) the overall competitive rivalry. Mapping the results of the aforementioned levels of analyses against an understanding of the internal capabilities of the client organisation, which determine its internal strengths and weaknesses, enables the client firm to respond appropriately to external opportunities and threats (SWOT analysis). In essence, the team can identify the current market status quo and determine whether there are any market issues that need attention.

In the process of identifying the design problem, the team needs to ask the right questions related to people's behaviour. The team needs to develop the right skills to be able to explore unfamiliar things and look at familiar things in new ways (Koberg & Bagnall, 2003). Generally speaking, the team should pursue questions related to the user of the product or service, the context and experience of the user, and the characteristics of the object, the service, or the environment (Leblanc, 2012). Understanding the product or service user is fundamental in adopting a human-centred design approach. The team should refrain from making the common mistake of taking their own personal experience as the main reference and assuming other people feel the same. In deductive research, our personal experience can give us an interesting starting point and can help us to formulate a hypothesis to test. On the other hand, in inductive research, it is important we do not allow our personal experiences to bias our research process; qualitative researchers' minds should be a blank canvas in order to explore phenomena in a free-of-prejudice manner.

Analysing the *context of use* empowers the project team to establish design criteria and product/service specifications because such knowledge can influence decisions on the shape, form, weight, and materials of the product, or the elements of the service process. Understanding the *product and service experience* requires from the team an understanding of how users interact with, and experience, a product or service, the steps of the usage process, and how these can be improved. Such an understanding can be achieved through the use of scenarios. "The use of scenarios in design provides a mechanism for outlining an often-complex situation in which numerous interconnections are evident" (Cooper & Evans, 2006, p. 71). The use of scenarios as a data collection technique will be explored later on in the chapter. Finally, it is important that the team understands not only *the purpose* that users expect an object to serve but also the *values that the object reflects* (Leblanc, 2012). Users choose branded objects not only for their functional value but also for their symbolic value. Consumers incorporate in their lives brands whose personality and values correspond to their own personality and values. Previous research has determined that the greater the congruity between the characteristics of an individual's actual or ideal self and the characteristics of the brand, the greater the preference for the brand (Malhotra, 1981; Sirgy, 1982). Aaker (1997) determined that the dimensions of brand personality include sincerity, competence, fun, sophistication, and ruggedness. Similar to how an individual's personality influences our decision to like and acquaint a person, brand personalities can influence our decision to purchase and use certain brands. Brands and objects eventually become manifestations of consumers' life principles and standards; they become part of a person's extended self (Belk, 1988). Understanding the personality and values reflected in an object is, therefore, of great importance. Leblanc (2012) suggests that the team should, therefore, understand the physical, technical, and communicative characteristics of an object. The latter involves the object's semantic quality as expressed through the utility and the symbolism of the object. Being au fait with all these will allow the team to (re)discover important notions forgotten over time or reveal the origins of other that have persisted over time (Leblanc, 2012).

Design research implementation

In the second phase of the process, the team will implement the agreed design research proposal and structure, by achieving three stages: data collection (following the methods specified in the proposal and structure), data analysis, and, in the case of ethnographic studies, framework development.

Data collection

Design research can adopt a plethora of deductive or inductive data collection techniques. Deductive approaches are of quantitative nature and can include administering a survey questionnaire that will allow the team to test pre-determined hypotheses. Such techniques allow marketers, designers, and researchers to determine correlations between certain elements and answer questions primarily concerned with quantifying and measuring certain dimensions or variables. On the other hand, inductive approaches include the team conducting in-depth one-to-one interviews, focus groups, and/or ethnographic research.

This chapter aims to go beyond a discussion of the conventional data collection methods employed in marketing research. This is because despite the value of market research to NPD (and to design in general), there are limitations to traditional marketing research techniques. As Cooper and Evans (2006) point, although consumers are the most qualified to discuss their current needs and desires, they are seldom capable of anticipating what they are likely to want or consume in the future. "Designers may create new product ideas that satisfy needs consumers did not know they had" (Wasson, 2000). For instance, consider the case of the *Post-It* notes. Certainly consumers had not envisioned such a product. Even with existing products, "customers may lack the vocabulary or the palate to explain what's wrong, and especially what's *missing*" (Kelley & Littman, 2001, p. 27). Furthermore, consumers cannot instantly imagine how they will use a new product or service; hence some of their responses might be unreliable. In many cases, consumers do not really know what they want on abstract level. Therefore, the team needs to go beyond traditional marketing research techniques to gauge users' behaviour in a profound way. Samuel Craig and Douglas emphasised the need for international marketing research itself to develop and use new qualitative tools, including "projective and elicitation techniques such as collages, picture completion, analogies and metaphors, psycho-drawing and personalisation [which] can be used to encourage respondents to project their private and unconscious beliefs and personal and subjective associations" (2001, p. 87).

The need for incorporating online research techniques as a means for reducing the time, and expanding the geographical span, of international marketing research was also highlighted at the start of the new millennium (Malhotra & Peterson, 2001; Samuel Craig & Douglas, 2001). Undoubtedly, the latent needs of consumers can be unearthed using different ethnographic methods, such as field and digital ethnography (Ireland, 2003), scenarios (Manzini & Jegou, 2003), and ethno-futurism, to name a few. The numerous conventional and progressive data collection methods employed in design research will be discussed in more depth in the next section of this chapter.

Data analysis

In this stage, it is important the client understands that data does not speak on its own (Wasson, 2002). In fact, we shall not forget that raw data on its own, unanalysed, is useless. It is what we do with the data that renders it useful. Only when we analyse and interpret the data gathered, we transform this data to valuable information. Data analysis is primarily carried out by researchers, but marketers and designers need to be involved in the process too. When analysing data, we need to be careful we do not get carried away. For instance, during the analysis of ethnographic data, identifying a single dramatic episode of consumer behaviour, albeit sometimes leading to useful insight, should not be considered a crucial behaviour. What we need to look for is repeated patterns of behaviour because these expose the cultural beliefs and practices that influence a wide consumer base. A deeper analysis is required "to reveal the cultural meanings that lie beneath the surface of particular activities, tying together different kinds of user behaviours that may seem unrelated at first glance" (Wasson, 2002, p. 79). Hence the team will start first with *instances* of consumer behaviour that might be relevant. Then these instances are clustered based on their similarity into groups which produce the *patterns*. These patterns also need to be contextualised because this will lead to better design recommendations and greater client opportunities for design.

Framework development

According to Wasson (2002), the ultimate goal of the analysis of ethnographic data is the development of *frameworks* that provide both an interpretation of what has been collected and an envisioning of the design solutions for the client. The frameworks take the form of a story which illustrates the interactions between the user and the product or service, how it was integrated in people's daily routines, and the symbolic meanings attached to it. Such story provides clear implications for product or service development and the marketing efforts involved. At this stage of the process, it is important the team follows an iterative approach – going back and forward between the data and the framework. This is also the stage where designers and researchers play an equal role. The framework developed at this stage can take the form of both a verbal narrative and a graphic representation (Wasson, 2002).

Interpreting and reporting

General design implications

After the development of a satisfactory framework, the team shall turn to developing design recommendations for the client. At this stage, the role of designers increases, although the collaboration between the disciplines continues as the whole team needs to brainstorm solutions together. At this stage, the design solutions developed begin "with *general implications*, broad formulations for new product [or service] and marketing directions based on the discoveries encapsulated in the framework" (Wasson, 2002, p. 81). Ultimately the team will be able to generate some initial design concepts for the client.

Specific design recommendations

At the final stage of the process, the team – especially the designers – will come up with specific suggestions for how these concepts could be given shape in specific designs. The team can present their ideas through hand-drawn sketches, computer simulations, and three-dimensional prototypes. Since this stage requires training in technical drawing, computer graphics programmes, and the ability to work with materials for prototypes, the involvement of marketers and researchers at this stage includes primarily evaluating how the product and marketing ideas fit with research findings.

Design research methods and techniques

This section of the chapter will explore in greater depth the plethora of different data collection methods that can be employed in design research. We will start first with quantitative research methods, and then we will concentrate on qualitative, inductive approaches which provide greater data richness. However, before we pursue our discussion of different methods, it is essential to define two terms which we ought to understand in advance – 'everyday knowledge' and 'scientific knowledge'. According to Calder (1977), the philosophy of science has provided a separation between the two, albeit not an impenetrable boundary. *Everyday knowledge* refers to 'first-degree constructs' which are explanatory concepts of the everyday kind and are based on the social construction of reality by a group of people, imparted to a person through the process of socialisation within a given culture. On the other hand, *scientific knowledge* is about 'second-degree constructs', which belong to the realm of science; they are highly abstract and subject to scientific methods but should not be seen as less a construction of reality. In addition, comparing the everyday with the scientific should not be considered 'unscientific' (Calder, 1977) (Figure 2.2).

Quantitative research methods: Deduction

Calder (1977) suggests that there are two approaches to quantitative research – the descriptive approach and the scientific approach. The *descriptive approach* provides numerical information relevant to everyday (first-degree) constructs such as demographic analyses, including the breakdown of consumption figures by age. Such research is based upon everyday than scientific explanation. The *scientific approach*, on the other hand, goes beyond merely working with numerical amounts or

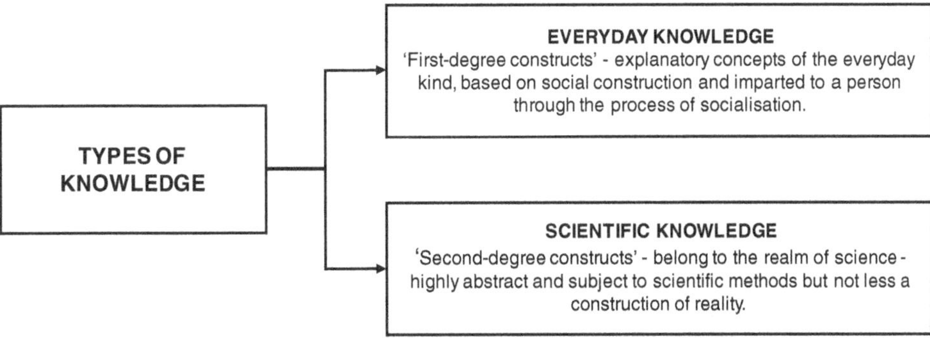

Figure 2.2 Types of knowledge.

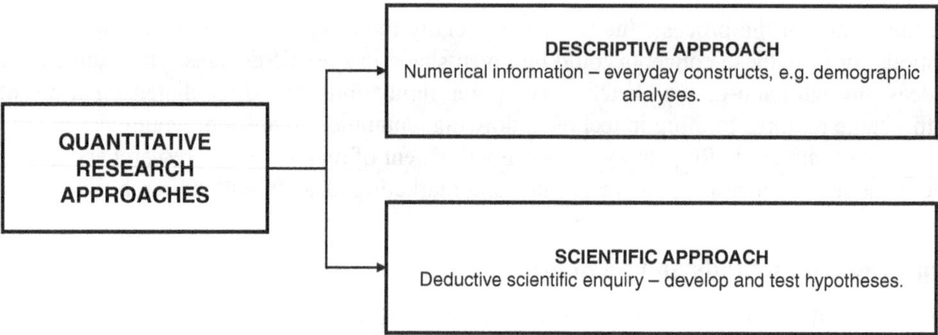

Figure 2.3 Quantitative research approaches.

rating scales. Such approach is associated with a deductive scientific enquiry. *Deduction* means that the researcher draws from existing theory (through a review of the literature) to develop a proposition (hypothesis), and then through a research framework test this proposition (Collins, 2010). The scientific approach "implies the use of second-degree constructs and causal hypotheses which are subjected to scientific methods" (Calder, 1977, p. 355). Methods used to pursue such an approach include experiments, some types of cross-sectional and panel surveys, and time series analysis. In design research, both approaches can be followed, although the second approach is more common in academic rather than commercial research (Figure 2.3).

Using statistics in design research sounds quite paradoxical because, from the outset, statistics seem to contradict design's inherent freedom and creativity (Purpura, 2003). Notwithstanding such a misconception, design research can use quantitative approaches in different ways, from practical considerations related to, for instance, time of completing tasks (descriptive approach), to validating exploratory research findings to refine theories about users' interactions with products and services (scientific approach). Quantitative research can be used at certain phases at the beginning, middle, and end of the iterative design process to provide incremental gains and benchmarks for the team. With regard to the beginning of the design process, the concept stage, the team can use quantitative research to speak to the target audience. Purpura (2003) argues that this target audience will not involve the general population but the innovators, early adopters (Robertson, 1967), and people on the fringe because they are the ones "to find new uses for old products and adopt emerging products at the earliest stage or generate new ideas" (Purpura, 2003, p. 65). *Concept testing* can be achieved through quantitative research involving the eclectic group of innovators and early adopters, which can indicate a clear winner from a few concepts. Moving from the beginning to the middle stage of the design process, the team can test features through a discrete choice analysis. *Features testing* should not be carried out separately for each feature; the goal is to understand how people will react to the entire package with all the features included and usually accompanied with a price tag. Respondents shall be exposed to each hypothetical package one at a time and using computer simulations to make the development process less costly. Such testing will allow the team to identify those features which are the most positively perceived by the respondents (Purpura, 2003).

Usability testing is appropriate midway the design process where the team will use quantitative research to determine, for instance, whether a product is usable in a timely manner that is deemed appropriate by the audience ('time to task' testing). The focus here is not aesthetics but the functionality of the product. Usability testing is best performed in laboratories to ensure the participants are not interrupted when using the product. This will allow the team to understand the users' interaction with the product and ensure incremental gains in time to complete the task, especially important when designing products used in situations where time is of essence like the case of hospitals' emergency rooms and medical equipment. At the end of the design process, the team might want to validate the findings with the relative audience. *Validation studies* will confirm what you heard from a smaller group of people with a larger and hopefully representative group of people.

Survey questionnaires

Questionnaires can be used in design where a larger sample is necessary to achieve generalisable results. In addition, the team might consider using questionnaires when the research subject is of sensitive nature because they allow the anonymity often desired when answering personal questions. Survey questionnaires can be administered on paper, online, through phone texting or phone calls. The way the questions are phrased should convey neutrality, i.e., they should not lead the respondent to an answer. Moreover, a questionnaire could leave some room for respondents to express some thoughts in their own words.

Preparing appropriate questions is crucial in order to elicit valuable responses. The team should bear in mind that some respondents might overanalyse questions, some might try to hide things, or some might try to give what they think are the right answers – how a situation should be, not how it actually is. Therefore, this might skew the results. It is important respondents are given many options to express nuances, questions are not perceived as judgemental, and (especially delicate) topics are introduced gradually (Leblanc, 2002). Questionnaires can be useful in gathering customers' feedback, for instance, after the release of a new or updated product. Such data can act as the springboard for further development. In addition, due to their deductive nature, questionnaires allow the testing of pre-determined hypotheses through high-level statistical analysis such as regression analysis. Such hypotheses could involve design problems and explore causal relationships. Nevertheless, the problem with quantitative data is that it can be too sterile to be of much use to designers in terms of translating it into sensory dimensions (Cooper & Evans, 2006).

Qualitative research methods: Induction

Qualitative research is not merely doing research without numbers and "unlike the case of quantitative research, the relationship of qualitative research to scientific and everyday knowledge dichotomy is very ambiguous" (Calder, 1977). There are three approaches to qualitative research: the exploratory, the clinical, and the phenomenological approach. The first two approaches pursue knowledge which lies on the boundary between scientific and everyday knowledge; in contrast, the third explicitly seeks everyday knowledge. The *exploratory approach* has a pre-scientific nature and aims to generate scientific constructs and validate them against everyday experience. Such an approach can take two forms: (1) pilot testing operational aspects of quantitative research such as checking the wording of questions to be used in subsequent quantitative research, or (2) the more ambiguous aim of using such research in order to generate or select theoretical ideas and hypotheses which will be tested and verified (or not) with future quantitative research. However, this does not mean that exploratory qualitative research (especially of the second type) which is not followed by a quantitative stage is useless. Quite the contrary, researchers can conduct independent exploratory qualitative research. The exploratory approach does not seek knowledge of scientific status, it is a precursor to scientific knowledge, where "its status is ultimately rooted in the creativity of the individual … [It] could be adopted to compare scientific with everyday explanations" (Calder, 1977, pp. 356–357).

A second approach, the *clinical approach*, aims to pursue qualitative research as a scientific endeavour; thus, qualitative methods are seen as an alternative to scientific quantitative approaches. There are two premises which underlie the clinical approach: (1) the constructs of everyday thought are often deceptive as explanations of behaviour, which means that what people say they do might cover the real causes of behaviour; and (2) building from the first premise, the real causes of behaviour must be uncovered through the sensitivity and clinical judgement of a specially trained analyst. Therefore, quantitative tools are not adequate for this purpose. Calder explains why:

> Clinical judgement is an analytical skill of somewhat nebulous dimensions, though much faith is placed in it. It is an ability developed largely from practical experience for diagnosing the major causes of behaviour from the complex over-determination of both unconscious and conscious causes. Although it is basically an art, as is the medical model in general, it is widely held to be scientific because clinical judgement is supposed to take scientifically valid theory as a starting point and as a problem-solving framework. The clinical approach thus attempts to make use of scientific knowledge without being bound by quantitative methods of analysis.
>
> (Calder, 1977, p. 357)

In marketing, this has been followed by borrowing methods from clinical psychology, including projective tests, free association exercises, and depth focus groups. The term 'depth' in the latter "implies seeking information that is more profound than is usually accessible at the level of interpersonal relationships" (Goldman, 1962, p. 63). Drawing from the above, the clinical approach seeks quasi-scientific knowledge, which means that although this knowledge is meant to have scientific status, "it is not fully scientific ... because it has not itself been subject to scientific methods, only to clinical judgment ... Therefore at its best the clinical approach yields quasi-scientific knowledge; at its worst, it yields phony scientific knowledge" (Calder, 1977, p. 358).

The third approach to qualitative research is the *phenomenological approach* which provides to the team "a chance to 'experience' a 'flesh and blood' consumer. It is the opportunity for the client to put himself in the position of the consumer and to be able to look at his product and his category from her vantage point" (Axelrod, 1975, p. 6).

The above is a description of a focus group, and at first glance, it might not seem different to the exploratory and clinical approaches, but the differences are actually quite profound. The experiential value of focus groups is accepted even by researchers who pursue the exploratory and clinical approaches. The phenomenological approach in marketing research (and the use of focus groups to engage in it) differs for the other two approaches because it draws from the core canon of sociological phenomenology and the work of Alfred Schutz. According to Schutz, "in philosophy, the study of phenomenology is concerned with the representation of knowledge as conscious experience" (Calder, 1977, p. 358). Schutz (1967) defined this experience as 'inter-subjectivity' where social actors share common-sense conceptions and ordinary explanations (Calder, 1977). Sociologists historically have been more concerned in deviant groups, such as gangs, whereas marketing researchers are interested in the inter-subjectivity of different groups of consumers. Calder articulately summarises the contribution of the phenomenological approach thus:

> The phenomenological approach provides a systematic description in terms of first-degree constructs of the consumption-relevant inter-subjectivity of a target segment. The description is of how consumers interpret reality in their own terms. In contrast, the clinical approach gives what is hoped to be a scientific interpretation of reality. This interpretation employs second-degree constructs representing the *intra*-subjectivity of individual consumers. The logic of the phenomenological

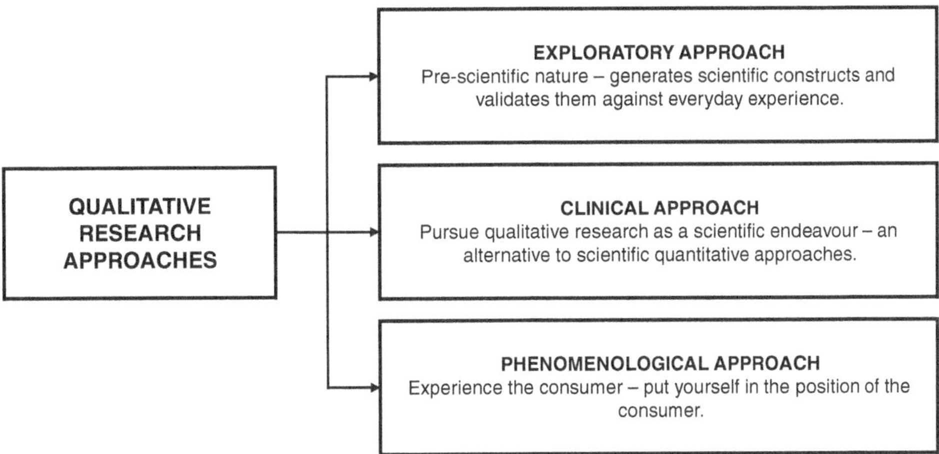

Figure 2.4 Qualitative research approaches.

> approach dictates that the researchers have close personal involvement with consumers. He or she must share, participatively or vicariously, the experience of consumers … The phenomenological approach to qualitative research seeks everyday knowledge. This knowledge is not meant to have scientific status. It is the everyday knowledge, the experience, of the consumer.
>
> (Calder, 1977, p. 360)

Design research can follow all the aforementioned approaches; especially phenomenology can be great for commercial design research, because it can provide in-depth understanding of consumer everyday knowledge and experience (Figure 2.4). It is now important to discuss the different data collection technique that can be employed by the team who wishes to pursue qualitative research.

One-to-one in-depth interviews

One-to-one in-depth interviews between a researcher and a respondent can take different forms; they can be formal and structured as well as semi-structured and conversational (Leblanc, 2002). The former strictly follows a predetermined protocol of questions, while the latter allows more flexibility which renders the discussion with more spontaneity making it more informal and establishing better rapport with the interviewee. This, however, does not mean semi-structured interviews lack a protocol of questions. Such checklist of questions still exists, but the interviewer allows the participant to elaborate more, talk about additional issues, and swiftly move from one topic to another without strict guidance. This makes the discussion seem very logical to the respondent because it has followed his/her train of thought. The onus is on the researcher to find the balance between allowing flexibility and ensuring that all topics in the protocol are sufficiently covered.

In general terms, in-depth interviews have advantages over questionnaires since they facilitate follow-up questions, additional probing, and further explanation of one's thoughts. This means that the data gathered is richer and more in-depth. Similar to questionnaires, the questions and the way they are articulated should not be suggestive or leading; instead, they must ensure neutrality. In-depth interviews are voice- or video-recorded to enable the researcher to pay full attention to what is being discussed. Quick notes during the respondent's answering allow the interviewer to highlight important points that need revisiting. This also demonstrates to the participant that he or she is being listened to which further enhances the rapport between the two people. Ireland deems that individual interviews are "ideal for learning exactly how each person feels and thinks about a topic or design, without concern for the influence of others [often a problem with focus groups – explored below] (except the moderator's influence, which really can't be avoided)" (2003, p. 25).

Focus groups

Considering the development of the design research discipline, we notice that focus group discussions directed by a moderator who follows a predetermined protocol of topics received the most attention first, due to their pervasive nature (Ireland, 2003). Focus groups and extended creativity groups can be used to explore inherent motivations, feelings, and opinions. Such technique can be used to test new product ideas and concepts with a sample of the target users and/or develop new ideas and identify future trends (Samuel Craig & Douglas, 2001). The extensive use of this data collection method led to the development of different formats. Ireland (2003) identified different types of focus groups on the basis of the group's size, including in his typology one-on-one interviews too, which we have explored separately. These types include, firstly, *traditional focus groups* where 10–12 people gather to discuss a number of topics led by a trained moderator for about 2 hours. Secondly, *mini-focus groups* include a smaller gathering of 6–8 people led by a moderator for 1–2 hours. *Dyads* are another type where a moderator interviews two friends as a pair for at least 1 hour. Dyads, or 'friendship pairs', are "a powerful forum for exploring issues that are difficult for people to articulate or for interviewing people who may be uncomfortable participating in research. For that reason, dyad interviews are frequently used with children and teens" (Ireland, 2003, p. 25). In addition, *triads* include a group of three people interviewed by a moderator following a lightly scripted guide for about an hour.

Party groups include a gathering of people who all know each other. Such gathering takes place in one person's home and lasts 2–3 hours discussing a topic under the direction of a trained moderator. Such gatherings work best for consumers and not for business people and for singular topics because this allows for deep, thoughtful, and honest conversations. *Super groups* include a gathering of 50–100 people in large auditoriums to view product design ideas or other exhibits presented on a large screen. Such gatherings are controlled by two moderators and require a very structured approach to gain rapid feedback from a larger number of people. Usually such gatherings are followed by breakout sessions where a small selection of people is chosen to discuss the topics further. Finally, *online discussion groups* allow the team to conduct the aforementioned techniques in a virtual environment. Videoconferencing platforms can help the team go beyond mere text interfaces and incorporate the study of body language which is an inherent part of face-to-face conversations and allow for better interpretation of what is being said (Ireland, 2003).

Observations

Leblanc (2012) indicates that observations are a complementary investigative technique used in the case where questions cannot be answered through surveys, interviews, or focus groups. They are also ideal when there are inconsistencies between what people say and what they actually do. Such observations involve the team writing notes in a logbook, sketching, photographing, recording, or filming product or service users. Despite the complimentary nature, Leblanc (2012) recognises observations' incredible power to direct the team to new and inspiring ideas. Collins (2010) provides a typology of different types of observations. *Structured observations* require a specific plan of what it is to be observed and how measurements are to be recorded. On the other hand, *unstructured observations* allow the team to monitor all aspects of the phenomenon which seem important. The latter might involve an element of bias so the data gathered may be combined with data gathered using other techniques. In *disguised observations*, participants are unware they are being observed; therefore, they tend to behave more naturally, whereas in *undisguised observations*, participants are aware they are being observed which might influence their behaviour. *Natural observations* take place in a natural environment, for instance, in users' homes or in business offices; in contrast, *contrived observations* take place in controlled environments purpose-built for the project in hand. In *personal observations*, the team will observe actual behaviour as it occurs, whereas in *mechanical observations*, digital tools record the behaviour and the team will then analyse the recorded data. Finally, with *participant observations*, the researcher becomes part of the group that is being observed, in contrast with *non-participant observations* where the researcher will stay in the background and does not question or communicate with the users who are being observed (Collins, 2010).

Observations could be considered a mild version of ethnographic techniques; the latter go beyond mere observations and gain a deeper "description and explanation of the culture of a group of people" (Squires & Byrne, 2002, p. xiv). In fact, Wasson (2002) claims that the act of observing naturally occurring consumer behaviours is a 'pale shadow' of ethnography because

> the need to analyse those behaviours and situate them in their cultural context is poorly understood, even though these activities are essential parts of developing a model of user experience that leads to targeted and far-reaching design solutions. One might speculate that the visual orientation of design culture makes the value of observation more immediately obvious than that of analysis.
>
> (Wasson, 2002, p. 87)

Ethnographic methods

As already mentioned, there are limitations to traditional marketing techniques because consumers can rarely predict what they will want or consume in the future, may find themselves unable to explain the product's problems or missing elements, or cannot imagine how they will use a product or service in the future (Cooper & Evans, 2006). All these points can render their responses misleading. However, this does not mean that we should not engage with users to unravel their needs and behaviours. In fact, they are a source of invaluable data. Design research borrows a number of methods from the social sciences (Cooper & Evans, 2006). Ethnographic methods are a cluster of such methods that elevate design research to a higher place. As mentioned already, ethnography enables us to describe and explain the culture of a group of people (Squires & Byrne, 2002). The word derives from the Greek *ethnos* (έθνος), which means nation, people, or folk, and *grapho* (γράφω), which means 'I write'. It is, therefore, the study of people. Cooper and Evans define ethnography as the "means of illustrating the context of everyday life, providing a holistic view of people and culture that allows understanding of attitudes and behaviour in a wider social context" (2006, p. 69). Ireland defines ethnography as "the research approach that produces a detailed, in-depth observation of people's behaviour, beliefs, and preferences by observing and interacting with them in a natural environment" (2003, p. 26). Rosenthal and Capper (2006) suggest that although ethnography is performed using special field-based observational methods managed by specialists, it is very common to combine ethnographic enquiry with traditional marketing research techniques like standard focus groups as well as market research surveys, which can test the validity and potential impact of initial qualitative insights (exploratory approach of qualitative research).

Whatever definition we want to adopt, in essence, ethnographic enquiry explores the behaviour of people in their culture. Such approach requires time and usually involves the researcher living among the people under study (natives) for long periods of time. This approach is simply described among ethnographers by the term 'going native' where the researcher is "accepted as a 'natural' part of the culture or context under study [which] minimises the impact of the researcher's presence and increases the likelihood that the observations are of more or less naturally occurring phenomenon" (Plowman, 2003, pp. 32–33). Such an approach leads to what was described by one of anthropology's founding figures, Bronislaw Malinowski (1922), as 'the imponderabilia of actual life', because it can lead to revealing behaviours that even the natives cannot explain or articulate themselves (Plowman, 2003). Such an in-depth approach is more appropriate for academic research. As Wasson explains,

> Ethnography has a narrower and somewhat different meaning in the field of design than it does for more anthropologists. In common with other kinds of applied anthropology, research is usually done more quickly and given less theoretical contextualisation, than on academic projects. In addition, however, the data collection methods and ways ethnographic materials are analysed are shaped by the particular needs of industrial designers.
>
> (Wasson, 2000, p. 382)

This means that although the team needs to learn about the context and the target audience, in similar fashion as their academic counterparts, they might not have the luxury of time due to the commercial nature of their endeavour; thus, there might be a need for ethnographic studies to last half a day or even less. This requires very well-trained and experienced researchers who can use the knowledge they have developed through previous projects to their advantage; such knowledge includes understanding segments of population who are usually of interest to businesses. Then, such researchers have the ability to quickly gather relevant data, minimise the impact of their presence, synthesise and interpret the data, and provide useful implications for design.

From an anthropological perspective, culture can be described as the "consideration of the interrelated ways that people behave, think, communicate, organise, and interact with their surroundings, objects, and each other" (Squires & Byrne, 2002, p. xiv). Individuals do not realise how and to what extent they are participating in and, therefore, are shaping culture. Culture is so natural to individuals that it is difficult for them to step back from their daily experiences and analyse these practices objectively. Culture is important because humans are engaged by products or services through their utility but also their cultural location – the 'situatedness' – through which designed products or services derive their meaning and are interpreted (Plowman, 2003). Both product/service use and interpretation are deeply cultural activities. The need to engage deeply into people's culture was also highlighted by Suchman (1995), a prominent science and technology anthropology scholar, in the context of organisational settings. When we attempt to study people in their work environment in order to understand their working practices, she believes that we ought to pursue

> [a deeper conceptualisation of] the intimate relations between work, representations, and the politics of organisations … This argument implies a reflexive engagement in our work as designers both with the images and accounts of working practices that are provided to us by organisation members and is a design practice in which representations of work are taken not as proxies for some independently existent organisational processes but as part of the fabric of meanings within and out of which all working practices – our own and others' – are made.
>
> (Suchman, 1995, p. 58)

Designers can use their own empathetic imagination in order to translate the data provided by ethnography to the products and services of the future (Cooper & Evans, 2006). Wasson (2002) argues that in order to utilise the power of ethnography in the most optimum way, there are three pre-conditions: (1) we have to recognise ethnography as a creative process and not just a mere data collection technique, (2) we must give ethnographers an equal voice in project development and execution, and (3) the work activities of designers and researchers must be integrated.

According to Ireland (2003), there are six types of ethnography. *Field ethnography* includes a person or a group of people being observed by a researcher while they go about in their normal lives. Such approach is appropriate during the first stages of the product/service development process when the team needs to understand more about the people who are the target users. Such ethnographies can last from 1 hour to several days or weeks. However, some would question the quality of data that can be gathered in an hour. Traditionally, ethnography requires time, so it might not be appropriate for rapid-paced development projects. This is where the team might consider *digital ethnography*, which has been a contemporary addition to ethnographic techniques, where we can utilise digital technology to speed up the process without jeopardising the quality of the data gathered. Similar to field ethnography, the team will observe people's daily life, but use digital cameras, laptops, virtual collaboration sites to record, transmit, edit, and present the data. With *photo ethnography*, however, the technology is not used by the team but by the people who are the subjects of the research study. Such approach involves a person who is given a camera (still or video) and is asked to capture images of his/her life and explain them with accompanied notes. The images and notes are then reviewed by the team who will interpret the data to generate conclusions. Interpreting images or videos is a very demanding task; therefore, this approach requires that the team has considerable skills and experience. As Suchman explains,

> even the most seemingly unmediated, veridical representational forms like video recordings, do not wear their meanings on their sleeves to be read definitively once and for all. Rather, the significance of recordings is contingent upon their reading in the context of particular moments of interpretation, informed by particular interests.
>
> (Suchman, 1995, p. 58)

Following this approach is suitable to cases where the presence of a researcher would bias the behaviour of people or when it is not appropriate or cost-effective for the researcher to be there, for instance, when the person is getting dressed or is travelling, respectively (Ireland, 2003).

'Real world' ethnographic enactments were first introduced in the *Real World Series* by the *MTV*, where the TV channel built an environment for a person or a group of people and then monitored their behaviour within it. This is ideal for cases where the team needs to understand how people's behaviour changes when their homes include new digital appliances and distributed computing. This approach can be a fascinating arena for studying people's lives, but it requires substantial investment from the client organisation. On the other hand, *personas* are "scenarios or profiles created to inspire and guide design. They are typically visual and textual descriptions, but ideally, they are the results of studying real people" (Ireland, 2003). Personas require a homogenous audience because by definition personas are narrow descriptions so they cannot work well when the audience is diverse. *Ethno-futurism* is often discussed as a separate technique to ethnography, so it will be explored in a section of its own, further below.

Coughlan and Prokopoff (2004) offer a precise typology of customised user-centre ethnographic techniques. These include: (1) *mock journeys* where the team simulates the user experience; (2) *shadowing,* where designers follow consumers to observe and understand their daily routines and interactions; (3) *expert walk-throughs,* which involves an 'expert' user talking through how a product is used so that the team understands complex behaviours; (4) *spatial observations,* which allow the team to experience the atmosphere of a certain space, observe behavioural patterns, and look for indications of everyday workarounds or innovations that could determine unmet needs. As Cooper and Evans explain,

> Consumers often develop workarounds when things don't work properly, and these workarounds quickly become invisible as they become habit. Thus observing people using products in daily life can lead to a clearer understanding than simply asking them how they use those products and this often leads to a breakthrough in product design.
>
> (Cooper and Evans, 2006, p. 69)

(5) *behavioural mapping,* where the team will track positions and movements within space over time using different frameworks and timelines; (6) *consumer journeys,* usually done with camera journals, where consumers record their experience throughout the 'product journey'; (7) *day-in-the-life surveys,* which encourage users to take note of their own surroundings and behaviours; (8) *extreme user interviews,* where the team will identify users who are extremely familiar with the product or service and will ask them to evaluate their experience of using it; such users are usually capable of identifying the key design problems; (9) *storytelling,* where users are encouraged to explain their experiences as a narrative or as an analogy which generates for the team rich stories and powerful characters involved in the use of the product or service; and (10) *unfocus groups* which involve a diverse group in a workshop environment. Participants in such groups are selected on the basis of their lack of product preconceptions and are asked to use different materials to make things which are relevant to the project in hand (Coughlan & Prokopoff, 2004).

Rosenthal and Capper (2006) provided us with a very detailed *process for planning* for ethnographic enquiry in product development which includes five stages. In the first stage, the team has to "*identify the objectives* to be considered during the fieldwork and subsequent analysis and reporting" (Rosenthal & Capper, 2006, p. 223). As part of formulating the objectives, it is vital to decide whether the underlying motivation for the project is to seek new opportunities and markets or to concentrate on a specific well-defined target audience. In addition, the team should *define the boundary* of the enquiry, which means understanding whether the project aims to explore a specific issue (e.g., customer interactions with a piece of software) or to understand the behaviour and motivations of a specific segment (Rosenthal & Capper, 2006, p. 223).

In the second stage, the team has to select the most *appropriate methodological approach* to follow. For instance, in cases where interaction with the participant might influence behaviour, the team might choose indirect observation techniques. In situations where it might be difficult to predict when an event of interest might occur, the team might opt to trace behaviour using technology such as recording cameras. Where the team might want to supplement observation with in-depth questioning, direct observation techniques should be selected. In general, the team should consider the project budget, timeline, resources, and the context of the research when deciding which specific methods to follow (Rosenthal & Capper, 2006, p. 223).

In the third stage, the team must define, in concert with the objectives specified, the "parameters of *the desired sample* of respondents in terms of specific qualifiers that define inclusion and assure diversity" (Rosenthal & Capper, 2006, p. 224). For instance, although the sample may be limited to a younger audience when exploring the purchase of a video game, there might be a scope to explore how other characteristics such as family background, location of household, and income affect attitudes and behaviours within the sample. For this reason, the sample might include youngsters from a range of family backgrounds, locations, and income levels to ensure diversity. It is also important that the team considers in this stage the size of the sample and where the research will take place, i.e., in one location or in multiple locations (Rosenthal & Capper, 2006).

In the fourth stage, the team should prepare the *guide of topics* that connect with the specified objectives (Rosenthal & Capper, 2006). This is more like an outline of topics instead of a formal list of pre-specified questions that is normally used in marketing research interview guides or surveys. In the fifth and final stage of the planning process, the team must make decisions about *how the data will be recorded, analysed, and presented.* This means that the team should plan the technology that might be used for recording consumer behaviour such as video or photographic cameras and voice-recording equipment, as well as the technology used for analysing data (such as the *NVivo* software for analysing textual data) and for presenting the research results, where design implications need to be discussed (Rosenthal & Capper, 2006, p. 223).

Future perspectives, scenarios, and ethno-futurism

Cooper and Evans (2006) briefly note that ethnography offers in-depth understanding of people and culture at the micro-level. They suggest that in order to move onto the macro-level, we need to combine ethnographic insight with a *futures perspective* to generate an understanding of science, politics, technology, economics, and culture, identifying global trends regarding topics such as biotechnology, life expectancy, and mobile communications. Such an approach is ideal for developing *scenarios*. The latter are defined as an "overall vision of a context as it might appear under certain conditions … [providing] a mechanism for outlining often complex situations in which numerous interconnections are evident" (Cooper & Evans, 2006, p. 71). Such endeavours allow the team not only to visualise but also describe a version of the future and transform abstract theories into tangible entities. The marriage of a futures perspective with digital ethnography is often called *ethno-futurism*. Here the team combines digital tools capturing day-to-day activities and small details of cultural significance with future perspectives, which, as explained above, explore major trends that can influence and change culture as a whole. Such approach is ideal for technology products that require understanding an individual's perspective and the broader picture, as well as for products whose success relies on trends, at least to a certain extent.

Encouraging a culture of design research

In order for a design project to be successful, it is absolutely imperative there is a close partnership between the design firm and the client organisation throughout every stage of the process, making sure that the client buys into research findings and design directions as the team develops them. This means that the client needs to get regular exposure to the project to ensure they experience the 'story' as it unfolds. Regular meetings where the client is engaged into interactive work sessions with the team should be the canon to ensure such collaboration (Wasson, 2002). Internal collaboration is also unequivocally crucial as it has already been emphasised. Marketers, designers, and researchers need to work together throughout every stage of the project. Such collaboration can be achieved by instilling a research culture within the design firm. As Zimmerman puts it, design research "represents a particular attitude about design, a willingness to look beyond the immediate concerns of crafting a specific project, an openness to integrating ideas and insights from the outside world into the design process itself" (2003, p. 185).

He suggests that in order to foster a research culture in the design firm, the management of the organisation must work hard to ensure there is a connection between the work every staff member pursues with larger cultural spheres – a link between daily design practice and the wider social context outside the company walls. He proposes six important ways that can facilitate an environment where design research can thrive. Let us explore these in detail.

First, it is important to *create a space that can encourage design research*. This can include a physical space where the team can gather together in order to facilitate brainstorming and exchange of ideas, and a virtual space, such as a section of the design firm's intranet, which allows staff to post links and thoughts about design projects and trends. *IDEO* allocates special 'project rooms' that are reserved to a team for the duration of their work, regardless of how long it takes (Brown, 2009). In addition, staff at *IDEO* start their working week with a 'show-and-tell' Monday morning meeting which is not a "stuffy, minuted affair at a boardroom table but a large, often noisy gathering at which models and concepts are shown, ideas are floated and information exchanged" (Myerson, 2004, p. 31). The need for such physical space is also discussed by Wasson who argues that "such areas [make] it possible for a team to distribute its emergent insights across various participants and objects. Individuals and groups [can] leave insights and artefacts for other team members to find and play with" (2002, p. 80).

An IDEO 'show-and-tell' meeting. (Photo courtesy of IDEO.)

A second way to encourage a research culture in the design firm is *building a design research library*. This, of course, requires some physical space, but it could also take the form of a digital space, as part of the firm's intranet. Such physical or online library can include books, novels, DVDs, magazines, and artefacts from previous design projects. The library can reflect the tastes and interests of staff, allowing them self-expression and the opportunity to shape the 'mind-space' of the organisation through cultural objects from the outside world brought into the firm (Zimmerman, 2003).

Third, staff in the design firm should also be on the *lookout for cultural events* relevant (and perhaps not only relevant) to the design projects undertaken by the design firm. These can include exhibitions, conferences, film shows, and other events related to the creative industries and beyond. Such group activities have a dual objective: they are research opportunities and an occasion for team building (Zimmerman, 2003). In addition, the design firm should organise and host events that can bring the local creative community and client organisations together in an informal 'get-together' setting that generates a discussion.

Fourth, a design firm should also *encourage and allow its staff to teach*. This can take the form of visiting lectureships at local universities or colleges as well as attending critiques, participating on panels, and giving talks and workshops. Teaching can be considered a challenging and effective form of research, and it can build bridges between the design firm and the local academic community, providing access to new talent through graduates, freelancers, and student internships (Zimmerman, 2003). Academic relationships can also foster 'blue sky projects' that can lead to radical innovation.

Fifth, another way of fostering a research culture in the design firm is to encourage staff to *pursue their own personal side projects* which can be of different types, ranging from magazine articles to essays and books, to experimental design and radical projects. Such 'blue sky' projects are encouraged at *Lunar Design*, a Silicon Valley product development consultancy, which allow team members "the complete freedom to develop solutions that are quite different from client projects, which are typically constrained by criteria such as manufacturing costs and regulatory or brand requirements" (Andriopoulos & Gotsi, 2005, p. 319). The onus is on the organisation to balance the freedom of allowing staff some time to pursue such endeavours during their work time, while not jeopardising the client work that needs to get done. Zimmerman (2003) suggests that by engaging with culture productively in their own terms outside client work, staff can bring insight into the projects they complete for the clients.

Such activities connect with the final way of encouraging a design research culture which involves *creating the context for experimentation*. Zimmerman (2003) suggests that staff can be encouraged to undertake experimental, non-commercial projects as form of design research. This can also demonstrate to clients that the design firm is at the forefront of innovative thinking. Experimentation is also praised by Brown (2009) who believes that a team should be given the time, space, and the budget to make mistakes. His principle can be summarised with the following: make mistakes and then ask for forgiveness. He quotes Alexander Pope who has famously said: *errare humanum est, perdonare divinum*, which means "to err is human, to forgive is divine" (quoted in Brown, 2009, p. 75). Brown (2009) urges firms (not only design firms) that want to facilitate design thinking in their culture, to understand that the "pre-requisite is an environment – social but also spatial – in which people know they can experiment, take risks, and explore the full range of their facilities" (Brown, 2009, p. 30). Such 'no-fear' climate is also encouraged at *Lunar Design*, which recognises that

> creativity requires constant experimentation, which implicitly involves the fear of failure. Not all creative endeavours are successful; mistakes are part of the process, and a no-fear attitude is an essential component of innovation ... [Staff] should work in an environment that tolerates mistakes and considers failure a part of the path toward achieving innovation.
>
> (Andriopoulos & Gotsi, 2002, p. 58)

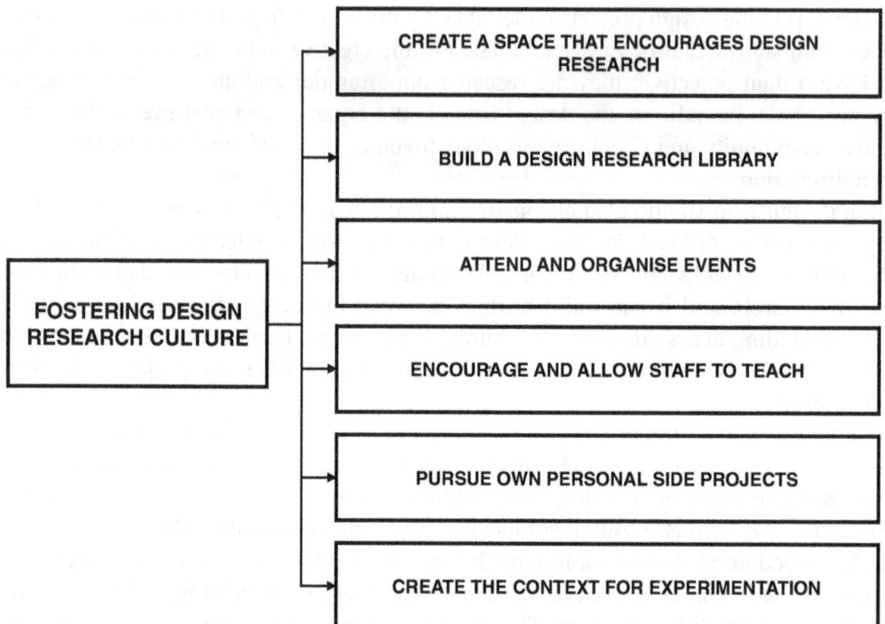

Figure 2.5 Fostering design research culture.

The above describe the plethora of ways a design firm can encourage the development of a research culture (Figure 2.5). Many of the points discussed relate closely with the process of instilling design thinking into any organisation's DNA, which is the topic explored in the next chapter.

Chapter review questions

You can use the following questions to reflect on the material covered in Chapter 2:

1 Discuss the importance of design research and ethnography in the design process.
2 Outline the different stages of the design research process.
3 Examine the different quantitative and qualitative approaches and techniques pursued in design research.
4 Explore the different ways a design firm can encourage a culture of design research.

Recommended reading

1 Wasson, C. (2000). Ethnography in the field of design. *Human Organization, 59*(4), 377–388.
2 Wasson, C. (2002). Collaborative work: Integrating the role of ethnographers and designers. In S. Squires, & B. Byrne (Eds.), *Creating breakthrough ideas: The collaboration of anthropologists and designers in the product development industry*. Westport, CT: Bergin & Garvey.
3 Rosenthal, S. R., & Capper, M. (2006). Ethnographies in the front end: Designing for enhanced customer experiences. *Journal of Product Innovation Management, 23*(3), 215–237.

Reflective thoughts

Design research and ethnography: Uncovering the consumer psyche

Dr. Alex Thompson
Senior Lecturer in Marketing
University of Exeter Business School, Exeter, UK

This chapter makes an important contribution to how we understand the design research process. It starts with the historical evolution of user-led design by tracing important challenges early designers faced when bringing the voice of the customer inside an organisation. A significant development within this chapter is the detailed considerations designers must account for in the planning process and their ability to conduct rigorous research through protocols. Design-led researchers must consider both inductive and deductive approaches to understanding user-led problems. This will help us to better understand that user-led insights are not generated through 'happenstance', but through careful consideration of data collection and analysis.

A key point readers should consider surrounds the transition of designers away from an 'inspired form giver', mentioned earlier within this chapter, to that of an 'informed researcher' who is charged with disseminating consumer information across an organisation. The job function of a designer is not only to generate new consumer insights that lead to new products and services that are relevant to users but to also ensure that information is acted upon in different cross-functional departments such as marketing, engineering, accounting, human resources, and any other area of the business that are charged with delivering customer value. Designers play a crucial role within a broader organisational architecture to ensure users are at the forefront of organisational innovation. As the chapter rightly points out, design is as much about collaboration as it is about generating user-led insights.

While this chapter advocates methodological plurality when considering framing the design research problem, which includes both quantitative and qualitative approaches, a common thread throughout this chapter is the importance of placing users at the forefront of the design process. This requires spending periods of time observing people within their homes and workplaces, trying to better understand their lives, routines, behaviours, and beliefs. This research process, which has become to be known as 'design ethnography', represents an innovative way to bring the voice of users directly into the design process.

This chapter highlights how design ethnography is a research process that is historically rooted in anthropological traditions of first-hand observation and participation in the lives of people within native cultures in order to better understand their worldviews. Through the process of first-hand observation and participation in people's lives, a process known as cultural immersion, we are able to gain a deeper understanding of individuals and their cultural belief systems. Ethnography represents more than mere observation. It involves direct participation into the lives and the culture of people. Its strength is its attempt to get at the underlying meanings of actions and beliefs within the context of a cultural group/setting.

For designers, ethnography represents a movement away from the study of native cultures, associated with traditional anthropological treatments of people, towards the study of consumer

(Continued)

(Continued)

cultures. The principles remain the same, a quest to understand people within the context of their natural environment. Instead of travelling to far-away lands, designers study people within their homes and workplaces. Due to commercial pressures, designers spend shorter periods of time with people, but their aim is still to directly participate in people's lives in order to gain access to social situations that help them to better understand their world.

Today, designers have adapted ethnographic methods in order to gain a deeper understanding of users in an attempt to understand how users interact within their environment. The strength of the method is that it places primacy on users and ensures that their needs and beliefs are at the forefront of any design-led inspiration. A critical point of discussion that this chapter raises is that users are often unable to articulate their usage of everyday products, such as beauty care, electronics, food/cooking consumption, travel, websites, etc., which are key considerations for businesses. Design-led ethnography enables researchers to capture the minutiae of everyday life, which becomes a platform for new innovations. Designers then take this understanding into the realm of business and are able to design products and services that best satisfy the needs of their constituents. This chapter highlights how these insights can become the basis for creating competitive advantage in the marketplace.

This chapter emphasises how design ethnography provides a catalyst that enables designers to see old problems in new ways. New ideas, new innovations come to light, that designers are then tasked with bringing to the fore. For some designers it takes them and their organisations into new realms of business and opportunities that could not come out of their more traditional research and development departments. For other designers it represents an organisation's first opportunity to put the voices of 'real people' behind quantitative market segmentation and more traditional inductive/deductive research approaches. The chapter rightly concludes with the importance of encouraging a 'culture of research' where designers are core facilitators in bringing and diffusing the voice of the customer throughout an organisation. Designers are not harbourers of knowledge, but active disseminators of knowledge-led design.

In the end, through credible research practice, this chapter highlights how all partners are transformed.

Questions for discussion

1. How would you go about incorporating design ethnography into your own design work? What considerations would you need to incorporate into your research to make it more ethnographic?
2. Choose an electronic device that you own. How has that product changed over time? What insights/innovations do you think drove these changes? How do you see this technology changing in the future? What research information would you need to collect to help you better understand what might be needed in the future?

References

Aaker, J. L. (1997). Dimensions of brand personality. *Journal of Marketing Research, 34*(3), 347–356.

Andriopoulos, C., & Gotsi, M. (2002). Lessons from a creative culture. *Design Management Journal (Former Series), 13*(2), 57–63.

Andriopoulos, C., & Gotsi, M. (2005). The virtues of 'blue sky' projects: How lunar design taps into the power of imagination. *Creativity and Innovation Management, 14*(3), 316–324.

Axelrod, M. D. (1975, February 28). Marketers get an eyeful when focus groups expose products, ideas, images, ad copy, etc. to consumers. *Marketing News, 8*, 6–7.

Belk, R. W. (1988). Possessions and the extended self. *Journal of Consumer Research, 15*(2), 139–168.

Borja de Mozotta, B. (2003). *Design management: Using design to build brand value and corporate innovation.* New York: Skyhorse.

Brown, T. (2009). *Change by design: How design thinking transforms organisations and inspires innovation.* New York: HarperCollins.

Calder, B. J. (1977). Focus groups and the nature of qualitative marketing research. *Journal of Marketing Research, 14*(3), 353–364.

Collins, H. (2010). *Creative research: The theory and practice of research for the creative industries.* London: Bloomsbury.

Cooper, R., & Evans, M. (2006). Breaking from tradition: Market research, consumer needs, and design futures. *Design Management Review, 17*(1), 68–74.

Cooper, R. G., & Kleinschmidt, E. J. (1987). New products: What separates winners from losers? *Journal of Product Innovation Management, 4*(3), 169–184.

Coughlan, P., & Prokopoff, I. (2004). Managing change by design. In R. J. Boland, & F. Collopy (Eds.), *Managing as designing.* Palo Alto, CA: Stanford University Press.

Douglas, A. (1994). *The creative process as material for research degrees, matrix 2: A conference on postgraduate research degrees in design and the visual arts.* Central Saint Martin's College of Art, The London Institute, London.

Goldman, A. E. (1962). The group depth interview. *The Journal of Marketing, 26*, 61–68.

Gray, C., & Malins, J. (2004). *Visualizing research: A guide to the research process in art and design.* Burlington, VT: Ashgate.

Heskett, J. (2005). *Design: A very short introduction* (Vol. 136). Oxford, UK: Oxford University Press.

Ireland, C. (2003). Qualitative methods: From boring to brilliant. In B. Laurel (Ed.), *Design research: Methods and perspectives.* Cambridge, MA: MIT Press.

Kahney, L. (2013). *Jony Ive: The genius behind Apple's greatest products.* London: Penguin.

Kelley, T., & Littman, J. (2001). *The art of innovation.* New York: Broadway Business.

Koberg, D., & Bagnall, J. (2003). *The universal traveller: A soft-systems guide to creativity, problem-solving, and the process of reaching goals.* Menlo Park, CA: Crisp Publications.

Leblanc, T. (2012). Problem finding and problem solving. In S. Garner, & C. Evans (Eds.), *Design and designing: A critical introduction.* London: Bloomsbury.

Malhotra, N. K. (1981). A scale to measure self-concepts, person concepts, and product concepts. *Journal of Marketing Research, 18*(4), 456–464.

Malhotra, N. K., & Peterson, M. (2001). Marketing research in the new millennium: Emerging issues and trends. *Marketing Intelligence & Planning, 19*(4), 216–232.

Malinowski, B. (1922). *Argonauts of the Western Pacific.* New York: E.P. Dutton.

Manzini, E., & Jegou, F. (2003). *Sustainable every day: Scenarios of urban life.* Milan, Italy: Edizioni Ambiente.

Myerson, J. (2004). *IDEO: Masters of innovation.* London: Laurence King.

Pilditch, J. (1976). *Talk about design.* London: Barrie and Jenkins.

Plowman, T. (2003). Ethnography and critical design practice. In B. Laurel (Ed.), *Design research: Methods and perspectives.* Cambridge, MA: MIT Press.

Porter, M. E. (1979). How competitive forces shape strategy. *Harvard Business Review, 57*(2), 137–145.

Porter, M. E. (1980). *Competitive strategy.* New York: Free Press.

Purpura, S. (2003). Overview of quantitative methods in design research. In B. Laurel (Ed.), *Design research: Methods and perspectives.* Cambridge, MA: MIT Press.

Rhea, D. (2003). Bringing clarity to the 'fuzzy front end': A predictable process for innovation. In B. Laurel (Ed.), *Design research: Methods and perspectives.* Cambridge, MA: MIT Press.

Robertson, T. S. (1967). The process of innovation and the diffusion of innovation. *The Journal of Marketing, 31*(1), 14–19.

Robson, C. (1993). *Real world research: A resource for social sciences and practitioner-researcher*. Oxford, UK: Blackwell.

Rosenthal, S. R., & Capper, M. (2006). Ethnographies in the front end: Designing for enhanced customer experiences. *Journal of Product Innovation Management, 23*(3), 215–237.

Samuel Craig, C., & Douglas, S. P. (2001). Conducting international marketing research in the twenty-first century. *International Marketing Review, 18*(1), 80–90.

Schön, D. A. (1983). *The reflective practitioner: How professionals think in action* (Vol. 5126). New York: Basic Books.

Schutz, A. (1967). *The phenomenology of the social world.* Evanston, IL: Northwestern University Press.

Sherry, J. F., Jr. (2002). Foreword: Ethnography, design, and customer experience: An anthropologist's sense of it all. In S. Squires, & B. Byrne (Eds.), *Creating breakthrough ideas: The collaboration of anthropologists and designers in the product development industry*. Westport, CT: Bergin & Garvey.

Sirgy, M. J. (1982). Self-concept in consumer behaviour: A critical review. *Journal of Consumer Research, 9*(3), 287–300.

Squires, S., & Byrne, B. (2002). An introduction to the growing partnership between research and design. In S. Squires, & B. Byrne (Eds.), *Creating breakthrough ideas: The collaboration of anthropologists and designers in the product development industry*. Westport, CT: Bergin & Garvey.

Suchman, L. (1995). Making work visible. *Communications of the ACM, 38*(9), 56–64.

Tilley, A. R., Anning, J., & Welles, R. (2002). *The measure of man and woman: Human factors in design* (Rev. ed.). Chichester, UK: John Wiley & Sons.

Wasson, C. (2000). Ethnography in the field of design. *Human Organization, 59*(4), 377–388.

Wasson, C. (2002). Collaborative work: Integrating the role of ethnographers and designers. In S. Squires, & B. Byrne (Eds.), *Creating breakthrough ideas: The collaboration of anthropologists and designers in the product development industry*. Westport, CT: Bergin & Garvey.

Wilcox, S. B. (2016). Framing the problem: Design research. In N. W. Nixon (Ed.), *Strategic design thinking: Innovation in products, services, experiences, and beyond.* New York: Bloomsbury.

Zimmerman, E. (2003). Creating a culture of design research. In B. Laurel (Ed.), *Design research: Methods and perspectives*. Cambridge, MA: MIT Press.

3 Incorporating design thinking into the organisational DNA

Chapter aims and learning outcomes

This chapter aims to:

1 Define design thinking and discuss its origins and characteristics.
2 Critically explore the importance of the 'wicked problems' approach in design thinking.
3 Discuss the stages of the design thinking process: inspiration (need finding), ideation (idea generation), implementation (testing).
4 Explore cognitive biases in decision making and the ways design thinking can mitigate these biases.

In the last section of Chapter 2, we discussed the ways that a design firm can encourage a prosperous culture of design research. The importance of human-centred design research is equally highlighted in the design thinking paradigm which is the focus of this chapter. Design thinking is not limited to design firms; quite the contrary, any organisation can incorporate the principles of design thinking in its corporate DNA. Exploring how this can be achieved is the overall aim of this chapter. In the first stage of the design management process, where the organisation needs to manage its design strategy, design management needs to engage design thinking in the corporate strategy (Best, 2006, 2015), interpreting the needs of customers and users, as well as achieving the potential design has in influencing the organisation from bottom up. The concept of design thinking connects with the third paradigm of design management (discussed in Chapter 1) which explores how design management can influence services, public policy, and the society at large, recognising design as a human activity (Cooper & Junginger, 2011). As already mentioned, academic and practitioner work within this paradigm proves the potential of design thinking for organisations, and the role of the design manager in igniting and facilitating design thinking in the corporate environment.

Definitions and origins of design thinking

Brown and Katz (2011) argue that there has been an underlying growing corporate interest in design in recent years. They explain this phenomenon through the shift of economic activity in the developed world from industrial manufacturing to knowledge creation, service delivery, and experience creation (Pine & Gilmore, 1998, 1999, 2011), which renders innovation as an important survival strategy for organisations. In addition, they argue that design is no longer limited to the development of new physical artefacts, but it is also concerned with the introduction of new processes, services, interactions, entertainment forms, as well as contemporary ways of communication and collaboration.

What we currently observe is the natural evolution from design to design thinking which demonstrates that business leaders and the wider society have recognised that design has become too important to be left to designers (Brown & Katz, 2011).

Before we seek to understand the origins of design thinking, it is essential to attempt to define the term. As a fairly recent concept, there is no definite consensus as to what exactly it is (Rieple, 2016). Perhaps this is where its beauty lies. Yet, there have been numerous definitions of the concept. This should not be surprising given the fact that even the well-established field of "product design with a longer history in the innovation and marketing literature still suffers from confusion introduced by the use of various definitions" (Liedtka, 2015). Herbert Simon started a revolution with the 1969 classic *The Sciences of the Artificial* book, which described design not so much as a physical process but as a way of thinking. The actual term 'design thinking' was coined in 1987 by Peter Rowe, a Professor of Architecture at the Harvard School of Design. Although his focus was on architectural design, his definition was not entirely limiting; he defined design thinking as an "account of the underlying structure and focus of inquiry directly associated with those rather private moments of 'seeking out', on the part of designers" (Rowe, 1987, p. 1).

Nevertheless, since this first reference, our understanding of design thinking has moved to more mainstream arenas, to capture its current meaning in the way that is practiced in the business environment. It has caught the attention of many leading organisations, as well as many business publications. Design has moved out of the studio and into the boardroom. It is indeed not unusual to find designers having an equal place at the decision-making table. Design thinking has moved design upstream and has achieved a higher, and its rightful, place in the corporate world. One particular design firm that has been instrumental in achieving a higher status for design thinking is *IDEO*. Founded by David Kelley, a Stanford University professor, and currently under the leadership of Tim Brown, *IDEO* has been approached by many client organisations not only to design new products, services, or experiences but to also design these client organisations per se. This does not mean that *IDEO* has progressively become a management consultancy firm, yet its approaches have informed management and organisation decisions, as well as corporate structure and culture, of many corporations.

Tim Brown, CEO and President of IDEO. (Photo courtesy of IDEO.)

Professor David Kelley, Professor of Mechanical Engineering at Stanford University and Founder of IDEO. (Photo courtesy of IDEO.)

Brown (2009) argues that

> design thinking begins with skills designers have learned over many decades in their quest to match human needs with available technical resources within the practical constraints of business. By integrating what is desirable from a human point of view with what is technologically feasible and economically viable, designers have been able to create the products we enjoy today. Design thinking takes the next step, which is to put these tools into the hands of people, who may have never thought of themselves as designers and apply them to a vastly greater range of problems.
>
> (Brown, 2009, p. 4)

Three words stand out from the above quote: '*desirable*', '*feasible*', and '*viable*'. These are the three overlapping criteria for successful ideas. *Feasibility* relates to what is functionally possible within the foreseeable future; *viability* is about what is likely to become part of a sustainable business model; and *desirability* is what makes sense to people and for people. People often view these criteria as constraints, which are 'resolved' by designers. A design thinker does not exactly resolve them, but rather achieves a harmonious balance of the three constructs (Brown, 2009) (Figure 3.1).

Brown (2008) argues that there are three spaces of innovation which need to be diffused within the organisation: (1) inspiration, which includes the problem or opportunity that motivates the search for solutions, (2) ideation, which involves the process of generating, developing, and testing ideas, and (3) implementation, which is all about the path that leads the organisation from the 'project room' to the market. These will be explored in the third section of this chapter.

Lockwood provides a more descriptive definition of design thinking, arguing that it is "a human-centred innovation process that emphasises observation, collaboration, fast learning, visualisation of ideas, rapid concept prototyping, and concurrent business analysis, which ultimately influences innovation and business strategy" (2010, p. xi). Understanding the way designers work and adopting their practices can broaden the repertoire of strategies for addressing the complex and open-ended challenges many contemporary organisations face (Dorst, 2011).

The three eras of development of design theories and methods

The history of academic understanding of the design process, advanced in the discipline often referred to as *design theories and methods*, highlights the need to make design thinking more explicit while embracing the many other disciplines which are engaged in design in a plethora of ways (Beckman & Barry, 2007).

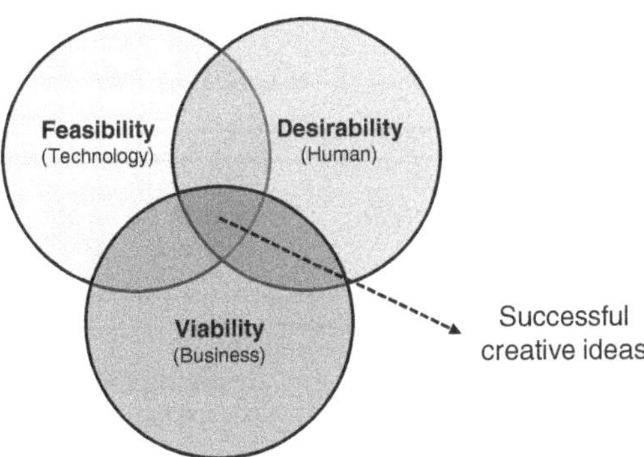

Figure 3.1 Three criteria for successful creative ideas.

The *first generation* of design theories and methods gained from the fields of operation research and cybernetics by utilising their optimisation techniques and systems thinking approaches, respectively. Such approaches favoured a process of decomposing "a complex problem into a set of smaller, well defined problems and to seek experts in the sub-disciplines to solve these problems" (Beckman & Barry, 2007, p. 26). However, such a design process was rather 'tayloristic' because the aim was to split the work in small tasks and perform them in the most optimum way individually (Taylor, 1911). This led to a mechanisation of the design process frustrating those attempting to follow this process, due to the inability to reconcile such 'first generation' methods with the complexities of real design problems, especially the values of social security and pluralism (Beckman & Barry, 2007). This led to the birth of the *second generation* of design theories and methods which focus on design as a social process. Such paradigm facilitates a more bottom-up view of the design process and relied less on experts to provide the solutions; instead, it engages a broader range of players. Practical and theoretical wisdom then shifted from the strict problem-solving process to a problem-formulating process where the core effort is to get to a collectively acceptable starting point to ensure that appropriate resources are committed to solving the problem (Beckman & Barry, 2007).

Recently, design theories and methods discourse has attempted to integrate the previous two paradigms by considering design as problem-solving process that involves players from multiple disciplines. In relation to this *third generation* of design theories and methods, Owen (1993) argues that the design process includes recognisable stages, and these, while not always in the same sequence, often begin with the analytical stages of searching and understanding and end with the synthetic stages of experimentation and invention. During the past 30 years, we have seen the codification and formalisation of the innovation process, in particular new product development, with the development of the 'stage-gate' processes executed by cross-disciplinary teams. Nevertheless, the innovation challenges faced by organisations in our contemporary post-modern world are increasingly broad and complex. Organisations are asked to provide not mere products or discrete features but complete solutions for the society in a rapidly changing technological environment (Beckman & Barry, 2007). These challenges can be described as 'wicked problems' for which design thinking can provide appropriate solutions; this constitutes the main reason many organisations have turned to designers. Designers, with their unique methods and techniques, have always been able to deal with design problems which are inherently wicked (Buchanan, 1992). Contemporary organisations' problems share the same characteristics. We will discuss the 'wicked problems' approach in design thinking further on in the chapter.

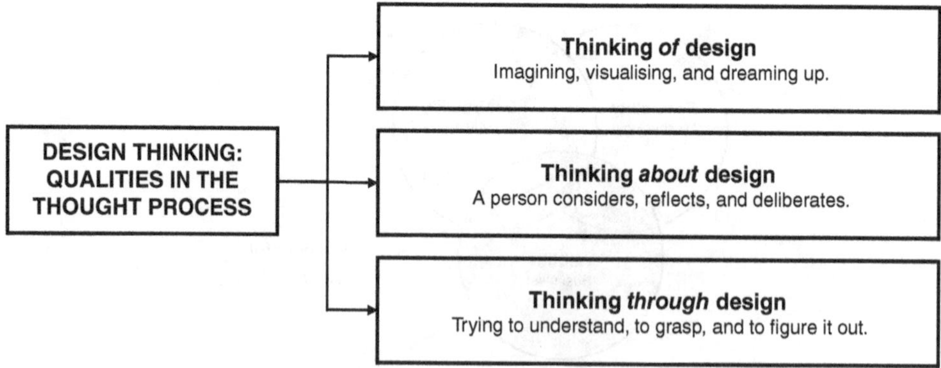

Figure 3.2 Design thinking: Three qualities in the thought process.

Design thinking and design management

A reflection on what the recent focus on design thinking has contributed to our understanding of design, and how it has informed design management, will enable us to understand design thinking better. Design thinking is not a completely new concept or practice; however, current interpretations offer new nuances which influence how we practice and theorise about design (Cooper, Junginger, & Lockwood, 2010). Design thinking encompasses all three qualities associated with the thought process: 'thinking *of*', 'thinking *about*', and 'thinking *through*'. Any dictionary will describe the activity of *thinking of* as imagining, visualising, and dreaming up. *Thinking about* something equates to an activity during which a person considers, reflects, and deliberates. Lastly, when we are *thinking through* something means we are trying to understand, to grasp, and to figure it out (Cooper et al., 2010) (Figure 3.2).

Although these qualities are distinctive to some extent, it is not always very clear whether we are thinking *about* design, thinking *of* design, or thinking *through* design; therefore, they can be concurrently pursued. Most organisations are familiar with the first two qualities. They think *about* design by answering questions of who can design and what. They also think *of* design by imagining, visualising, and dreaming up new understandings, new roles for design, as well as new practices and new applications. Therefore, organisations think *about* design as a tool for marketing and think *of* design when they design specific products and services. However, Cooper et al. explain that

> while thinking *about* and thinking *of* design are core elements of design thinking that offer reflections on the past and, in some ways, the future of design, it is the idea of thinking *through* design that currently shapes the design discourse … a new way to employ design thinking – thinking *through* design – is emerging and it promises to have a much more profound impact on the way business itself is being conducted.
>
> (Cooper et al., 2010, p. 58)

This means that thinking *through* design encourages corporate managers to 'think like designers', establishing design thinking as a core capability that elevates design in organisations beyond traditional boundaries. Design thinking has created excitement and interest among many people who had been previously unaffected by design, generating opportunities for designers to engage with various levels and functions of organisations and their management. Design thinking has liberated design activities from being 'pigeon-holed' within the product development realm, to be applied to a plethora of organisational and strategic problems (Cooper et al., 2010).

In her interview, published in the *Harvard Business Review*, Indra Nooyi, the CEO of *PepsiCo*, explains why this global organisation has incorporated design thinking into its corporate culture. Nooyi decided to make the firm more design-driven because she sought to rethink its innovation process and design new holistic experiences for its consumers. In few words, she wanted to think *through* design. In order to lead this endeavour, she brought in Mauro Porcini, *PepsiCo*'s first ever Chief Design Officer, and gave him exactly what he asked: resources, a design studio, and a seat at the top executive table. "Now our teams are pushing design through the entire system, from product creation, to packaging and labelling, to how a product looks on the shelf, to how consumers interact with it" (Nooyi, cited in Ignatius, 2015, p. 82).

Porcini explains the approach of embedding design thinking into the company's culture. He believes that any organisation firstly needs a leader who has a holistic vision for design to bring all the different types of design together (be it brand, industrial, interior, user experience, or innovation design) and manage all aspects of design in a clever way. Secondly, in order to be able to introduce change within the organisation, the design function needs to have the support at the top executive level, because any firm is apt to resist change (Porcini cited in Ignatius, 2015). Thirdly, the organisation should seek external endorsements by business leaders or designers outside the firm, from design and business publications, or in the form of awards and accolades that the firm can win. Such endorsements can act as an internal marketing activity, validating the vision to internal stakeholders, i.e., staff, managers, and shareholders, and demonstrating that the organisation is moving in the right direction and increasing their confidence in the changes taking place. Finally, it is important to have some 'quick wins', projects that will quickly prove the value of design inside the firm. Such early success can provide the basis upon which you can build a design-driven organisation and create processes that establish and maintain the new culture throughout the entire organisation (Porcini cited in Ignatius, 2015).

Therefore, as far as the implications of design thinking for design management are concerned, we can certainly say that design thinking has represented a radical paradigm shift. While design management had concentrated on individual design projects as well as on incremental improvements and developments, design thinking challenges organisations' overall way of doing business, their assumptions, values, norms, and beliefs. Thus, we are moving from the managing of the design of tangible products to the management of the design of innovation and services, from the lower level product-centred design strategies to designing entire business processes and customer experiences across many touchpoints, on the organisational level. Cooper et al. (2010) argue that design thinking has raised awareness of design management at different organisational levels and has contributed to a clearer picture of design management.

Nevertheless, it is noteworthy that design thinking has also faced some criticism over the years from a number of scholars, with some commenting on the lack of a theoretical basis (Johansson-Skoldberg, Woodilla, & Çetinkaya, 2013; Kimbell, 2011). "Design thinking has also been accused of producing incremental rather than disruptive innovation, 'losing its meaning' and becoming a 'failed experiment'" (Davis, Docherty, & Dowling, 2016). Cross (2010) and Nussbaum (2011) have claimed that the iterative, creative process has become lost in corporate efficiency, while Carlgren, Elmquist, and Rauth (2014) have accused design thinking of extending project timescales and costs, affecting motivation and adding a burden on staff. To counter such criticism, Walters (2011) has suggested addressing the tensions between design and corporate communities as well as clearly defining their roles, allowing design thinking to be a valuable process towards innovation. Konno (2014) has also argued that it is the superficial application of design thinking which undermines its value. If such superficiality is avoided, then design thinking can still be a human-centred and purposeful innovation process.

Areas of design thinking

The broad application of design thinking, and how design affects contemporary life, can be appreciated by considering the four broad areas in which design is explored. Buchanan (1992) indicated these four areas as follows: (1) the design of symbolic and visual communications, (2) the design of material objects, (3) the design of activities and organised services, and (4) the design of complex systems or environments for living, working, playing, and learning (Figure 3.3). As we explore below, these traditional design areas have been expanded through design thinking, elevating the role of design in business and society. Let us explore all four areas in more detail.

The *design of symbolic and visual communication* includes the traditional work of graphic design, including activities like typography, advertising, book and magazine production, and scientific illustration. Yet this area has expanded to include communication through photography, film, TV, and computer display. Buchanan argued that communications design was evolving into a "broader exploration of the problems of communicating ideas, and arguments through a new synthesis of words and images" which has transformed the 'bookish culture' of the past (1992, p. 9). We have certainly witnessed such development in communications design over the last 30 years.

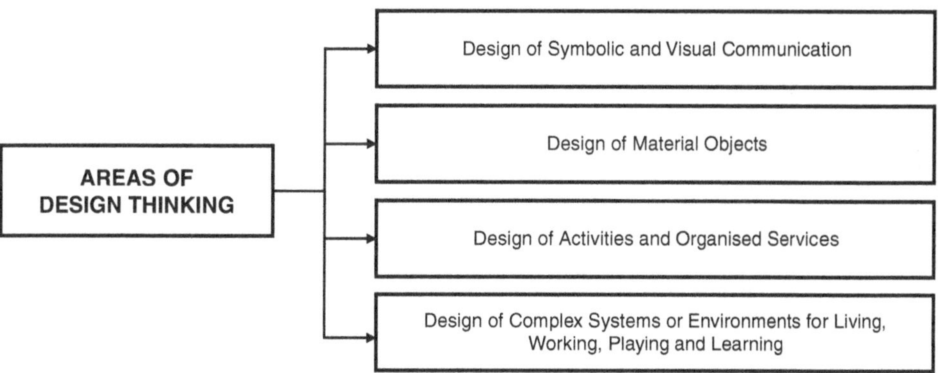

Figure 3.3 Areas of design thinking.

The *design of material objects* is traditionally associated with product design which is responsible for the form, function, and visual appearance of many everyday objects such as domestic appliances, machinery, automobiles, and clothing. This area has also expanded into a more in-depth and diverse understanding of the physical, psychological, social, and cultural relationships between objects and human beings, as well as into exploring "the problems of construction in which form and visual appearance must carry a deeper, more integrative argument that unites aspects of art, engineering and natural science, and the human sciences" (Buchanan, 1992, p. 9).

The design of activities and organised services is concerned with the management activity of logistics, where physical resources, instrumentalities, and human beings need to be co-ordinated in efficient schedules and sequences to achieve specific objectives. Design thinking has expanded this area by exploring how "decision making and strategic planning can achieve organic flow of experiences which are more intelligent, meaningful and satisfying" (Buchanan, 1992, pp. 9–10).

Finally, *the design of complex systems or environments for living, working, playing, and learning* is traditionally the responsibility of systems engineers, architects, and urban planners. In the past, such endeavour involved the functional analysis of the different parts of complex wholes and how they can be integrated in hierarchies. This area has also evolved over the years, thanks to design thinking. Nowadays, we have become more conscious of the central idea, thought, or value which expresses a balanced and functional whole, exploring the role of design in developing, sustaining, and integrating people into broader ecological and cultural environments, shaping them when desirable and adapting to them when necessary (Buchanan, 1992).

The 'wicked problems' approach in design thinking

Design thinking proposes the notion that managers should think like designers in order to solve the complex contemporary organisational and strategic problems, because the problems faced by organisations are similar to design problems, which have been described as 'wicked'. "For that reason, understanding what designers do and applying it as a methodology to complex organisational problems that require creativity and inspiration" (Rieple, 2016, p. 5) is an approach embraced by many organisations on a global basis. It is important, at this stage, to understand what we mean by 'wicked problems' in design because this will enable us to reflect on organisational problems too.

Linear model of design thinking

Bazjanac (1974) suggested that serious attention to the design process began in the middle of the twentieth century concurrently with developments in the fields of mathematics and systems science. He argues that the design process was considered then as a series of well-defined activities where scientific method principles and ideas can be applied (Bazjanac, 1974). There are many variations of the linear model, but all of its supporters argue that the design process is divided into two distinct phases: problem definition and problem solution (Buchanan, 1992). The former is the *analytical* sequence in which the designer establishes all the elements of the problem and stipulates the requirements that a successful solution must have. The latter is the *synthetic* sequence where the designer combines the various requirements and balances them against each other, producing a final plan to be carried into production (Buchanan, 1992). Despite the fact that there are some obvious points of weakness, many scientists, business professionals, and even designers continue to find this linear model attractive because of its 'logical' nature. Nevertheless, there are indeed two very important problems with this approach as explained by Buchanan: "one, the actual sequence of design thinking and decision making is not a simple linear process; and two, the problems addressed by designers do not, in actual practice, yield to any linear analysis and synthesis yet proposed" (1992, p. 15).

The properties of wicked problems

In contrast to such approaches, Horst Rittel, a mathematician, designer, and teacher, attempted to find an alternative to such a linear, step-by-step model of the design process and formulated the wicked problems approach in the 1960s (Buchanan, 1992). He was the first to highlight the 'wicked' nature of many design problems. He defined such problems as:

> a class of social system problems which are ill-formulated, where the information is confusing, where there are many clients and decision makers with conflicting values, and where the ramifications in the whole system are thoroughly confusing.
>
> (Rittel cited in West Churchman, 1967, pp. 141–142)

Rittel identified ten properties of wicked problems, which include the fact that: (1) they do not have definitive formulation – every formulation of a wicked problem corresponds to the formulation of a solution; (2) they do not have stopping rules; (3) their solutions cannot be true or false, only good or bad; (4) there is no exhaustive list of admissible operations in solving them; (5) every wicked problem has more than one possible explanation; these explanations depend on the 'weltanschauung' (the intellectual perspective) of the designer; (6) every wicked problem is a symptom of another, 'higher level', problem; (7) "no formulation and solution of a wicked problem has a definitive test" (Buchanan, 1992, p. 16); (8) solving wicked problems is a one-shot operation where there is no room for trial and error; (9) every wicked problem is unique; and (10) people who solve the wicked problems do not have the right to be wrong – they are fully responsible for their actions.

Rittel's definition of wicked problems highlights a fundamental issue which is the relationship between 'determinacy' and 'indeterminacy' in design thinking. Buchanan (1992) argues that the linear model of design thinking is based on 'determinate' problems, which have definite conditions. Thus, the designer has to precisely identify these conditions and then calculate a solution. Contrastingly, there is an inherent indeterminacy with the wicked problems approach. In order to understand what we mean by indeterminacy, it is important to note that it is quite different from 'undetermined' because it "implies that there are no definitive conditions or limits to design problems" (Buchanan, 1992, p. 16).

Reasons for the wickedness of design problems

A significant question that requires an answer at this stage is the reasons that design problems are wicked. Buchanan (1992) provides an explanation by arguing that this wickedness lies in the peculiar nature of the subject matter of design, which does not have a special subject matter of its own, except from what a designer conceives it to be. He further explains:

> The subject matter of design is potentially universal in scope, because design thinking may be applied to any area of human experience. But in the process of application, the designer must discover or invent a particular subject out of the problems and issues of specific circumstances. This sharply contrasts with the disciplines of science, which are concerned with understanding the principles, laws, rules, or structures that are necessary, embodied in existing subject matters. Such subject matters are undetermined or under-determined, requiring further investigation to make them more fully determinate. But they are not radically indeterminate in a way directly comparable to that of design.
>
> (Buchanan, 1992, pp. 16–17)

Buchanan (1992) believes that designers conceive their subject matter on two levels: the general and the particular. On the general level, they form ideas or working hypotheses about the nature of products in the world, for instance, the 'artificial' in relation to the 'natural', which indicate their wider view of the nature of design and its scope. These act as proto-philosophies ('proto' from the Greek *πρώτο*, meaning first) of design which exist within a plurality of alternative views providing essential frameworks for them to understand materials, methods, and principles of design thinking. However, we cannot claim that such philosophies are sciences of design like any natural, social, or humanistic science because design is concerned with the particular, and there is no science of the particular (Buchanan, 1992).

In fact, designers start with a quasi-subject matter, which exists within the issues and problems of specific circumstances. This means that the designer, on the particular level, must come up with a design that will lead to a particular product out of the specific possibilities of a concrete situation. "A quasi-subject matter is not an undetermined subject waiting to be made determinate. It is an indeterminate subject waiting to be made specific and concrete" (Buchanan, 1992, p. 17). Design briefs, which clients provide to design firms, do not and should not present a definition of the subject matter of a particular design application. They should provide a set of issues to be considered when attempting to resolve the problem. In those cases, where clients detail the particular features of the product to be planned, they attempt to take out the 'wickedness' of the design problems. Even in such cases though, these particular features are only a possibility that may (and should) be subject to change through discussion and arguments (Buchanan, 1992). The onus is on designers to put forward the right solution to the problem at hand.

The design thinking process

If we were to try to distil Buchanan's (1992) arguments discussed in the previous section, we could argue that "he situated design as a dialectic that took place at the intersection of constraint, contingency, and possibility" (Liedtka, 2015, p. 927). In fact, in the past 60 years, design theorists have noted the paradoxical nature of design because it seeks to find high-order solutions that accommodate seemingly opposite forces. Lewis (2000) has indicated that a paradox denotes contradictory yet interrelated elements. These elements seem logical in isolation yet irrational when appearing simultaneously. Design attempts to embrace and reconcile such paradoxes.

Unlike Rittel's work on the wicked problems in design, theorists like Schon (1982) explored the role of scientific method in the design process and viewed the design process as learning-focused, hypothesis-driven approach. Other theorists explored the areas where design and science diverge, arguing that designers are concerned with what does not yet exist, and scientists deal with explaining what does exist (Liedtka, 2015). "Scientists *discover* the laws that govern today's reality, while designers *invent* a different future" (Liedtka, 2000). Therefore, while design and science are both hypothesis-driven, the design hypothesis differs from the scientific hypothesis on the basis of abduction. According to March (1976), the mode of reasoning involved in design is abductive which means that speculative design cannot be determined logically. In short, design initiates novel forms, in contrast with science which investigates extant forms. In practical terms, "the mission of design thinking is to translate observations into insights, and insights into products and services that will improve lives" (Brown, 2009, p. 49).

Nevertheless, the above does not mean that science and design cannot converge. Quite the contrary, despite these aforementioned differences, over the last few years, according to Rieko Yajima, a biochemist working for the American Association for the Advancement of Science, there have been a plethora of initiatives to bridge art and design with science, technology, and engineering, in order to meet contemporary global challenges such as climate change and environmental sustainability. For instance, the Rhode Island School of Design has partnered with scientists to explore the role of designers and artists to tackle regional climate change and the impacts on Rhode Island's Narragansett Bay (Yajima, 2015). Yajima believes that

> at its core, the motivation that drives designers and scientists is nearly identical. Both designers and scientists possess an intense desire to understand the world around them, a passion to discover something new, the ability to test ideas through experiments or prototypes, and most important an innate desire to challenge assumptions and ask *why*. Designers enjoy challenging the status quo and ask *why* and *how* in an attempt to push forward the frontiers of knowledge.
>
> (Yajima, 2015, p. 20)

Liedtka (2015) provides a theoretical foundation for describing the design thinking process as articulated in the business world today. She argues that design thinking

> is a hypothesis-driven process that is problem, as well as solution, focused. It relies on abduction and experimentation involving multiple alternative solutions that actively mediate a variety of tensions between possibilities and constraints, and is best suited to decision contexts in which uncertainty and ambiguity are high. Iteration, based on learning through experimentation, is seen as a central task.
>
> (Liedtka, 2015, p. 927)

The above definition highlights many elements which will be explored through our discussion of the stages of the design thinking process. However, before we present these stages, it is important to take note of three important changes and additions which are regarded as critical elements of business design thinking, that were not emphasised in earlier work of design theorists: (1) the question of *who* designs, (2) the role of empathy in design thinking, and (3) the emphasis on visualisation and prototyping (Liedtka, 2015). Firstly, *the question of who designs* was raised by Moreau (2011). Buchanan (1992) noted a move from design being a sole responsibility of experts to come up with socially acceptable results, to being an opportunity for active participation of many different parties, including users, in order to reach appropriate conclusions. Garud, Jain, and Tuertscher (2008) discussed the notion of co-creation in design which was absent in earlier theories of design thinking and argued that "the distinctions between designers and users are blurred, resulting in the formation of a community of co-designers" (p. 364). Brown (2009) also highlights the importance of collaboration between creators and consumers and the fact that the boundaries at the level of both companies and individuals are blurred.

Secondly, *empathy* in design thinking has been emphasised by contemporary scholars (Leonard & Rayport, 1997; Patnaik & Mortensen, 2009) and was determined, by Brown (2008), as one of the characteristics of the profile of the design thinker. With empathy, we go beyond mere recognition of the subjectivity of the design domain, to constitute design thinking as human-centred and user-driven. In fact, as Brown argues, design thinking "is not only human-centred; it is deeply human in and of itself" (2009, p. 4). Thirdly, *visualisation and prototyping* play a vital role in design thinking. Such activities have long been important features in the fields of architecture and product development. Liedtka (2015) argues that design thinking's view of prototyping is different as its main function is to drive real-world experimentation in service to learning rather than to display, persuade, or test. The prototypes in design thinking act as 'playgrounds' (Schrage, 2013) for conversation rather than 'dress rehearsals' for new products (Liedtka, 2015).

Liedtka (2015) compared the website descriptions of design thinking process as featured on the official online space of leading design consulting organisations like *IDEO* and the Boston-headquartered *Continuum*, as well as educational institutions like Stanford University Design School and the Darden School at the University of Virginia, and noticed that despite the use of different terminology, they all share the same overarching view on the stages of the design thinking process. These stages are: (1) data gathering about user needs, (2) idea generation, and (3) testing. These stages correspond to the *three 'spaces of innovation'*: inspiration, ideation, and implementation (Brown, 2009), which we have already discussed. As Liedtka explains,

> all descriptions of the process emphasize iterative cycles of exploration using deep user research to develop insights and design criteria, followed by the generation of multiple ideas and concepts and the prototyping and experimentation to select the best ones – usually performed by functionally diverse groups working closely with users.
>
> (Liedtka, 2015, p. 927)

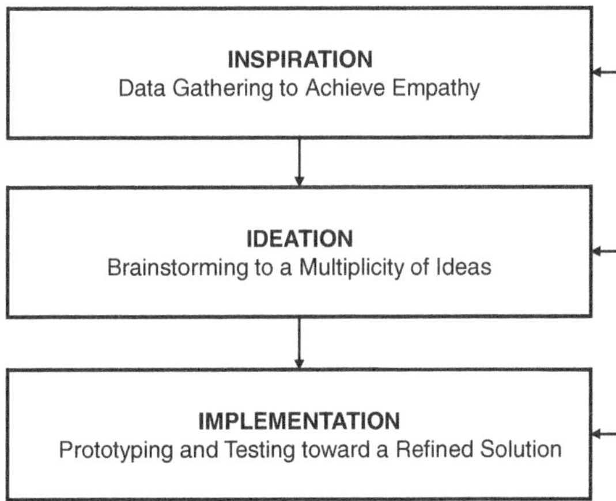

Figure 3.4 The design thinking process.

The above points towards some very important tools used during the design thinking process. In the first stage, *inspiration*, ethnographic research techniques are of outmost importance. The significance and use of ethnography in design was extensively discussed in Chapter 2. Such research techniques allow the organisation the necessary empathy, which is one of the most important values of design thinking. The second stage of *ideation* involves the use of sense-making tools, for instance, mind-mapping, to facilitate brainstorming and concept development. Thirdly, in the last stage of *implementation*, the organisation uses prototyping and testing approaches to support experimentation (Figure 3.4). In addition, visualisation and co-creation are tools which are used in every stage of the process. The remainder of this section will explore these stages and their tools in more detail.

Inspiration: Data gathering to achieve empathy

Inspiration is the starting point of the design thinking process. In this first stage, the design project team must go out in the world and observe the actual experience of the target audience, i.e., the product/service user, or community. *Ethnographic research* provides the tools to achieve this stage. What is important to concentrate on here is *empathy*, which is the guiding force for the team in this stage. The design thinker, according to Brown (2008), can view the world from multiple perspectives and takes a 'people-first' approach to come up with solutions which are desirable and meet explicit or latent needs. Tripp (2013) stresses the importance of empathy research in product and service marketing. She discusses how firms such as *Universal Studios* (in particular, *Harry Potter and the Forbidden Journey*), *NikeiD*, *Discovery Cove at SeaWorld*, *Apple*, and *Coca-Cola* have created encapsulating consumer experiences which "meet their users where they are and in a way that is contextually relevant for their lives. What they don't do is offer services [and products] only from the company's perspective" (Tripp, 2013, p. 61). She argues that empathy research is a form of design research which is very different than classic marketing research. She refers to Kolko (2010), who, by contrasting design research with marketing research, argued that although both borrow from social and behavioural sciences, marketing research attempts to predict behaviour, while design research attempts to understand culture by looking at people's styles, words, tools, and workarounds, to inspire design.

Tripp (2013) outlines seven steps that organisations can take to achieve high levels of empathy. First, the organisation needs to reframe its view of its target consumer to that of a person. The firm needs to stop calling the consumers the 'target market', but consider them as people, as stakeholders. After all, consumers as stakeholders confer social legitimacy upon the organisation. Second, it is important to focus on specific people who are willing to share their life experiences with the team and maintain an open mind by listening to the extremes of the potential user base. This is also emphasised by Brown (2009) who explains that:

> it makes sense for a company to familiarise itself with the buying habits of people who inhabit the centre of its current market, for they are the ones who will verify that an idea is valid on large scale – a fall outfit for *Barbie*, for instance, or next year's feature on last year's car. By concentrating solely on the bulge at the centre for the bell curve, however, we are more likely to confirm what we already know than learn something new and surprising. For insights at that level we need to head for the edges, the places where we expect to find 'extreme' users who live differently, think differently, and consume differently – a collector who owns 1,400 *Barbies*, for instance, or a professional car thief.
>
> (Brown, 2009, p. 44)

Third, the organisation should understand the consumer's hopes and dreams in the broader context of life. The firm needs to immerse itself into the consumer's world to view his/her life in a broader context, rather than watch from behind a two-way mirror. This will enable the team to develop 'personas' based on these people as the team navigates through its work (Tripp, 2013). Fourth, the organisation needs to understand the consumer's story and envision how it can help him/her. Fifth, the organisation will then have to consider its strategy and what might be able to offer to the consumer. This requires using the process of prototyping which is explored further below to make sure the solution is affordable and profitable. Sixth, the organisation must also ensure this solution is truly appealing to the consumer. This requires an iterative process, going back and forward, as the ideas are refined. Finally, seventh, the firm should keep the personas it has created available and refer to them when making decisions or is in need for inspiration (Figure 3.5).

Brown (2009) argues that empathy is the mental activity that moves organisations beyond thinking of people as laboratory rats or standard deviations. For this we have to "see the world through the eyes of others, understand the world through their experiences, and feel the world through their emotions" (Brown, 2009, p. 50). This quote indicates that empathy requires three levels of understanding: (1) the physical, (2) the cognitive, and (3) the emotional. The first requires the team to *physically* live through the user experience first-hand. For instance, *IDEO* designers went through the emergency

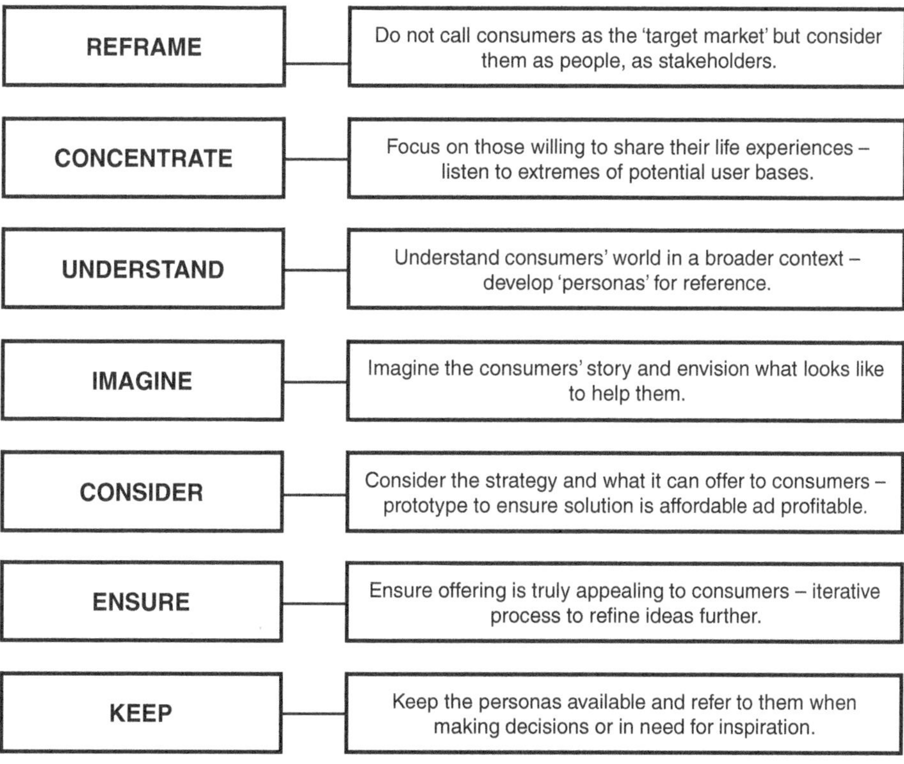

Figure 3.5 Seven steps to achieve empathy.

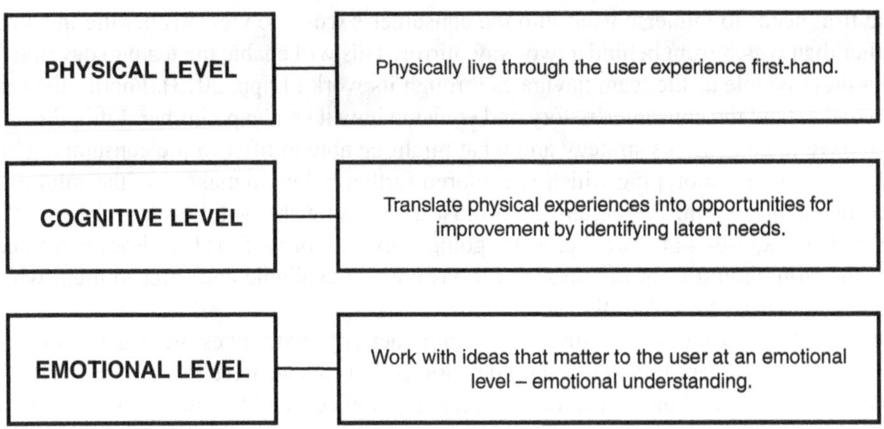

Figure 3.6 Empathy: Three levels of understanding.

room experience, from admission to examination, when trying to design a new wing for a hospital in St. Louis, Missouri, USA (Brown, 2009). The *cognitive* layer requires the firm to translate these first-hand physical experiences into opportunity by asking questions that help the team identify latent needs, which can be difficult to articulate albeit severe. This allows the team to imagine how the experience might be improved. These insights can emphasise both the new and the ordinary and familiar. The third, *emotional* layer is entered by the team when it starts working with ideas that matter to the user at an emotional level. This requires from the team emotional understanding, which can be generated by asking questions such as 'what does the user feel?', 'what touches them?', or 'what motivates them?' This, of course, is not something new; advertising agencies, even political parties, have been utilising emotional understanding for years; however, the aim here is for the organisations to turn the consumers into advocates and not adversaries (Brown, 2009) (Figure 3.6). It is clear from the above that achieving empathy requires that the organisation moves to the second and third stages of the design thinking process.

Ideation: Brainstorming to a multiplicity of ideas

In the stage of ideation, the team goes through the process of synthesis where it orders the gathered data and looks for patterns. This process can be frustrating in the beginning, because as the team is trying to make sense of the data, important decisions seem insubstantial guess-work to them. At some point, however, ideation becomes more tangible, and new concepts start to take shape leading to the next stage, that of implementation, where the team can experiment with prototypes (Brown, 2009). Design thinking at the second stage requires the team to go through four mental stages: (1) convergent thinking and (2) analysis, and (3) divergent thinking and (4) synthesis. Convergent thinking requires the team to narrow the mental focus (Amabile, 1982, 1983), *analyse* the series of inputs, in order to *converge upon* a single answer. Brown (2009) argues that such thinking allows the team to decide among existing alternatives, but it does not allow the team to probe into the future and create new possibilities. The latter can be achieved through divergent thinking, which multiply options to create choices (Brown, 2009), and requires the team to expand the mental focus, *synthesise* different insights, to come up with ideas (Amabile, 1982, 1983). The above demonstrates that convergent thinking involves analysis, whereas divergent thinking requires synthesis.

According to Amabile (1982, 1983), the creative process includes both convergent and divergent thinking. The creative process, which is explored in greater depth in Chapter 5, includes four stages: (1) the *preparation* stage, where we search for information and seek to understand the problem in hand, (2) the *incubation* stage, where we try to come up with ideas, (3) the *illumination* stage, often described as the 'a-ha!' moment, where we identify a possible solution to the problem, and (4) the *verification* stage, where we confirm that this particular idea is the best solution to the problem (Wallas, 1926) (Figure 3.7).

The first and fourth stages require convergent thinking to concentrate our mental focus on understanding the problem, and confirm that the idea suits the problem in hand, respectively. The second and third stages require divergent thinking where we need to expand our mental horizon to come up with ideas. Divergent thinking leads to outcomes which are bolder, more creatively disruptive, and more captivating. However, we need to bear in mind that disruptive thinking can increase complexity. This should not deter the organisation from pursuing divergent thinking; we should not restrict ourselves by relying only on convergent thinking. This way we would only achieve incremental innovation as opposed to radical innovation. In fact, we need both incremental and radical innovation; hence we need both types of thinking. As Brown explains,

> the process of the design thinker … looks like a rhythmic exchange between the divergent and convergent phases, with each subsequent iteration less broad and more detailed than the previous ones. In the divergent phase, new options emerge. In the convergent phase it is just the reverse: now it's time to *eliminate options* and *make choices*.
>
> (Brown, 2009, p. 68)

In the ideation stage, the organisation must encourage an attitude of experimentation among its staff. As already mentioned in Chapter 2, the team must be given the time, space, and budget to make mistakes (Brown, 2009). Such 'no-fear' climate is also supported by Andriopoulos and Gotsi (2005) in their study of *Lunar Design*'s creative culture. Staff should be allowed to make mistakes and ask for forgiveness (Brown, 2009). Experimentalism is another significant personality characteristic of the design thinker (Brown, 2008). Kolko suggests that "leaders need to create a culture that allows

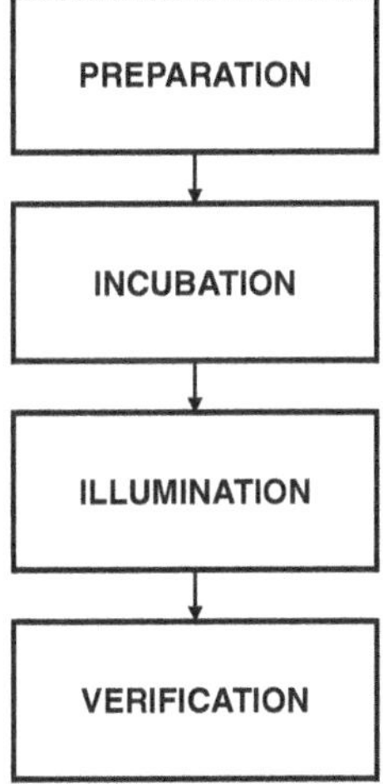

Figure 3.7 The creative process (Wallas, 1926).

people to take chances and move forward without a complete, logical understanding of a problem" (2015, p. 7). Mistakes should not be viewed as wasteful or redundant; by doing so, we transform the organisational culture to one which focuses on efficiency over innovation and this leads to incrementalism (Brown, 2009). Brown (2009) provides a set of rules for establishing such an environment for experimentation. An organisation should understand that: (1) the best ideas emerge when the entire corporate environment, including managers, designers, engineers, researchers, marketers, etc., has room to experiment, (2) those staff exposed to changing externalities (for instance, new technology, strategic threats or opportunities, a dynamic customer base) are those who will be best placed to respond and will be motivated to do so, (3) any ideas expressed should not be favoured on the basis of who comes up with them, (4) ideas which create a buzz should gain a vocal following, irrespective of their size, before they are given organisational support, (5) senior leaders should plant seeds and harvest ideas, and (6) an overarching organisational vision should be articulated and shared within the corporate environment to create a sense of direction.

The aforementioned rules lead our discussion to the importance of the brainstorming technique. While it is not the ultimate technique for idea generation, it is very useful when the organisation aims to open up a wide spectrum of ideas. Although other approaches might be important for making choices, a brainstorming session is the best for creating these choices in the first place (Brown, 2009). Tom Kelley, the General Manager of *IDEO*, and author of *The Art of Innovation*, describes the art of brainstorming in his firm:

> First, a brainstorm is not a regular meeting. It's not something you take notes at. You don't take turns speaking in any orderly way. It shouldn't consume a morning or afternoon. Sixty minutes seems to be the optimum length, in our experience, though occasionally a brainstorm can productively stretch to an hour and a half. The level of physical and mental energy required for a brainstorm is hard to sustain much longer than that. Brainstorming sessions aren't presentations or opportunities for the boss to poll the troops for hot ideas. Nor should they feel like work. And brainstorming is most definitely *not* about spending thousands of dollars at some glamorous off-site location.
>
> (Kelley & Littman, 2001, p. 56)

Kelley and Littman (2001) shared with us seven secrets for better brainstorming. First, the organisation needs to *sharpen the focus* by starting with a well-polished and articulated statement of the problem, at the right level of specificity. Second, it needs to *establish playful rules*, such as avoiding critiquing ideas without turning off critique completely, going for quantity of ideas, encouraging wild ideas, and being visual. Third, the firm *should number the ideas*; this way it will motivate the participants and set targets of the number of ideas the team wants to generate. In addition, "it's a great way to jump back and forth from idea to idea without losing track of where you are" (Kelley & Littman, 2001, p. 58). Fourth, the organisation needs to '*build and jump*'. Brainstorming involves a series of steep 'power' curves, in which momentum is built slowly, then intensely, then it starts to plateau. Kelley and Littman advise us to

> try to build on an idea. Encourage another push or introduce small variation. Or take a jump, either *back* to an earlier path you skipped by too quickly or *forward* to a completely new approach. Whatever you do, try to get into the new power curve and keep the energy up.
>
> (Kelley & Littman, 2001, p. 59)

Fifth, the organisation needs to understand the power of *spatial memory*; hence it needs ensure that brainstorming members write the flow of ideas in ways that it is visible to everyone involved.

Media used can include post-it notes and rolls of old-fashioned 'butcher-shop paper' on the tables. Sixth, the team should do some *warm-up* similar to warm-up/stretching before you start physical exercise. This is particularly essential when: (1) the group has not worked together before, (2) when many of the team members do not brainstorm frequently, and/or (3) when the team members seem distracted by pressing yet unrelated issues. Finally, seventh, the team members should get *physical*. Sketching is of outmost importance in the process. This does not mean that team members need to be visual artists. It is about getting your point across by drawing things down or using physical artefacts and materials to illustrate the verbal points articulated by team members.

The use of post-it notes to track ideas during brainstorming.

Implementation: Prototyping and testing towards a refined solution

The third stage of the design thinking process, implementation, includes *prototyping and testing* the multiple ideas generated, to select the best one. Aspelund defines prototyping as "the creation of a model or mock-up of a design to test various aspects of the idea" (2010, p. 175). One of *IDEO*'s well-known proverbs highlights the importance of prototyping in design thinking: "If a picture is worth a thousand words, a prototype is worth a thousand pictures". Brown (2009) argues that if openness to experimentation is the lifeblood of any creative organisation, then prototyping is the best evidence of this drive for experimentation. Prototyping demonstrates a willingness to go ahead and try something by building it. Prototyping is like thinking with your hands (Kelley & Littman, 2001), and despite the impression that people sometimes have that generating numerous sketches, models, and simulations slows down the process, it actually speeds up the process. Prototypes have "a very interesting paradoxical feature: They slow us down to speed us up. By taking the time to prototype our ideas, we avoid costly mistakes such as becoming too complex too early and sticking with a weak idea for too long" (Brown, 2009, p. 105). A three-dimensional prototype will demonstrate characteristics of the design that not even the most realistic computer rendering can do. "Human perception is very much geared toward objects, and we are much more able to accept an actual three-dimensional representation as 'real', even when its level of accuracy is far less than that of the printed or digital image" (Aspelund, 2010, p. 175).

Prototypes need not be working models, but need to provide the right form to an idea, in order to indicate its strengths and weaknesses and point out new directions for the next bunch of more refined and detailed prototypes. The most successful prototypes are not those that work flawlessly but those that teach the team something, be it something about the objectives of the product, service, or process designed, or even something about the designing organisation itself. Early prototypes need to be fast, rough, and cheap, because if you invest too much in an idea, you end up becoming more committed to it. Overinvesting in a refined prototype leads to two problems. "First, a mediocre idea may go too far toward realisation – or even, in the worst case, all the way. Second, prototyping process itself creates the opportunity to discover new and better ideas at minimal cost" (Brown, 2009, p. 90). Cost-efficient and easy-to-manipulate materials such as cardboard, surfboard foam, or wood can be used by the team to create a physical approximation of an idea.

Aspelund (2010) distinguishes between three types of rough prototypes: (1) *concept prototyping*, which is a rough representation of the idea, thrown together in order to communicate the basic concept; (2) *throwaway prototyping*, which is a model created in order to test a particular aspect of the design, mostly related to the functionality of the object, and may result in damaging it for the sake of testing its durability; and (3) *evolutionary prototyping*, which is a 'work-in-progress' prototype with changes being made to it as the team progresses through the development of the product (Aspelund, 2010).

So far we have talked about product prototyping. However, as already mentioned, design is also applied to services or processes. The question then is how would the team model or prototype a service or process. Prototyping things we cannot pick up involves creating *storyboards* similar to those used in film production to map out the story ahead of shooting the film, to ensure that all scenes are adequately thought through and potential problems are rooted out right from the start (Brown, 2009). Borrowing techniques from film and other creative industries, we can generate scenarios, as a form of storytelling, to describe a potential future situation or state, using words and pictures. Such scenarios could depict, for instance, the user's daily routine in order to 'observe' how he/she will use the service or go through the process. Such service could be shopping at the local supermarket or using the same supermarket's online ordering system. This leads us to what we would call *mapping out the customer journey* in the realm of customer experiences and services marketing (Richardson, 2010). Scenarios help the team to keep the focus on people. The value of mapping out the customer journey is that the team will be able to identify the various 'touchpoints', i.e., the points where the customer and the organisation interact (Brown, 2009). The more touchpoints there are, the more complicated such a map of the customer journey becomes. It is essential, therefore, to go beyond a mere timeline, to identify the exact actions of the customer at each stage, the motivations for the customer to move to the next stage, and any issues or barriers that prevent the customer from moving to the next stage (Richardson, 2010).

Prototyping is one of the techniques which allow the team to occupy all three spaces of innovation. Prototypes are inspirational because their imperfections inspire new ideas. Prototyping relates to the ideation stage because they help us to develop our ideas so that they include the necessary functional and emotional elements to meet the users' needs and desires. Prototyping is also the epitome of the implementation space of innovation because, as we have explored above, it allows the team to communicate the idea, test it, and show that it will work with the intended user (Brown, 2009).

There are also two more tools that are used throughout all the stages of the design thinking process: visualisation and co-creation. As already mentioned, being visual and sketching out ideas is a vital part of the brainstorming process. Yajima (2015) highlights the profound impact that *visualisation*, as has been contributed by artists and designers, has had on the way we understand problems and ask questions about things and, in consequence, on scientific development. She reflects on her own experience during her biochemistry studies and the colour-pencil representation of cytochrome C designed by Irving Geis, found on the cover of her undergraduate biochemistry textbook, which she identifies as her first introduction to the impact that design can have on science. In her own words,

> many scientists may be unaware that Geis, an architect, was instrumental in helping the scientific community visualise and accurately represent the early protein structures that were being solved by X-ray crystallography. He was particularly adept with using light to clarify these protein structures, making it possible to see topology, contours, and pockets that could provide insight into where chemistry and binding would be taking place. This type of visualisation redefined how scientists could ask questions about way proteins function in chemistry terms.
>
> (Yajima, 2015, p. 20)

With regard to co-creation, the emphasis is on collaboration among different disciplines and with the client (as explored in Chapter 2), to bring together diverse functions, perspectives, and experience bases (Liedtka, 2015). Seidel and Fixson (2013) identify collaboration as the centre of design thinking, where multidisciplinary and interdisciplinary teams apply design methods to a wide range of innovation challenges. According to Brown and Wyatt (2010), to establish an 'interdisciplinary' environment, the staff employed need to be 'T-shaped' and hence have strengths in two dimensions:

> On the vertical axis, every member of the team needs to possess a depth of skill that allows him or her to make tangible contributions to the outcome. The top of the 'T' is where the design thinker is made. It's about empathy for people and for disciplines beyond one's own. It tends to be expressed as openness, curiosity, optimism, a tendency toward learning through doing, and experimentation.
>
> (Brown & Wyatt, 2010, p. 34)

As already pointed out, collaboration between designers and clients is very important too. This was discussed by Garud et al. (2008), who argued about the formation of a community of co-designers in which the distinction between designers and users is blurred. The paradigm of co-creation in design is explored in more depth in Chapter 8, where we will explore the concept of prosumerism. Conveniently for us, through their empirical work, Carlgren, Rauth, and Elmquist (2016) summarise the five themes that characterise the concept of design thinking in practice: (1) an inherent user focus including empathy building, deep user understanding, and user involvement; (2) problem framing, in terms of trying to widen, challenge, and reframe the problem, instead of trying to solve it; (3) visualisation, i.e., making ideas tangible by means of representations or mock-ups; (4) experimentation and iteration – a drive "towards testing and trying things out in an iterative way, … moving between divergent and convergent ways of thinking, [and working with] … multiple solutions" (Carlgren et al., 2016, p. 47); and (5) diversity, including collaboration in diverse teams while integrating diverse external perspectives throughout the process (Carlgren et al., 2016).

Design thinking and mitigation of cognitive biases

Cognitive biases in decision making

Liedtka (2015) recognised that despite the popularity of design thinking in business press, it has not received significant attention from business and management scholars, especially in relation to how the use of design, as a thought process, can improve innovation outcomes. She sought to address this by attempting to link utility with individual cognition and decision making and by exploring design thinking "as a practice potentially valuable for improving innovation outcomes by helping decision-makers reduce their individual level cognitive biases" (Liedtka, 2015, p. 925). Extant literature on cognitive biases provides a great platform for connecting design thinking with clearly identified problems in an academic area with deep empirical base. Exploring the scholarly work on cognitive biases through the lens of design thinking, Liedtka (2015) identified nine significant and well-recorded cognitive biases, which we need to examine in detail before discussing how design thinking can help the team mitigate these biases.

The projection bias

Loewenstein and Angner (2003) discuss the 'projection' bias where individuals have the tendency to project the present into the future, leading to predictions that are too grounded to and biased towards the present and bring regressive results that stifle innovation. Gilbert, Gill, and Wilson (2002) term this kind of behaviour as 'presentism', where individuals have "the tendency to over-estimate the extent to which their future experience of an event will resemble their current experience of an event" (Gilbert et al., 2002, p. 441). Such behaviour acts as an obstacle to the development of novel ideas as well as to the evaluation of their potential success (Liedtka, 2015).

The egocentric empathy gap bias

The 'egocentric empathy gap' bias makes individuals overestimate the similarity between what they find valuable and what others find valuable (Van Boven, Dunning, & Loewenstein, 2000). People tend to project their own thoughts, preferences, and behaviours onto others (Van Bonen & Lowenstein, 2003). Nickerson (1998) terms this as the 'confirmation bias' and argues that we, as humans, tend to selectively perceive, encode, and retain information that is in line with our own desires. This leads to problems in the idea generation and implementation stages, because the ideas generated are those that their creators, and not the target users, value, and hence the assessment of the success of these ideas is also problematic (Liedtka, 2015).

The hot/cold gap bias

The 'hot/cold gap' bias indicates that the individuals' state, i.e., whether they are emotionally loaded (hot) or not (cold), influences their assessment of the value of an idea, resulting in them either over- or under-valuing the ideas (Loewenstein & Angner, 2003). For instance, people might get overexcited about an idea to a point where they are 'blinded' by their enthusiasm and they fail to predict how others, and indeed even themselves, will react in the future when their state is less emotional-laden (Liedtka, 2015).

The focusing illusion bias

It is not only emotions that can distract from an accurate assessment of an idea; individuals also have the tendency to overestimate the effect of one factor at the expense of other factors. This is described by Loewenstein and Angner (2003) as the 'focusing illusion' bias, which leads to individuals over-reacting to specific stimuli while ignoring others. Such bias can have a significant negative effect on hypothesis generation and/or testing, generating a narrow set of, and possibly less attractive, ideas (Liedtka, 2015). This goes against the value of multiplicity of ideas in design thinking, which we discussed in the previous section.

The say/do gap bias

Moving our focus onto the consumers' side, organisational decision-makers try to compensate for the aforementioned biases by *asking* consumers what they want. This results in another bias, often described as the 'say/do gap'. As already mentioned in Chapter 2, consumers are unable to accurately describe their own behaviour, or even less able to predict their future behaviour (Cooper & Evans, 2006; Fellmann, 1999). This is, of course, where ethnographic studies come into the forefront, as a means of compensating for this bias.

The planning fallacy bias

Kahneman and Tversky (1979) have indicated that even when organisational decision-makers are successful in generating new ideas, they can be overly optimistic about how well-received their ideas will be, which they call the 'planning fallacy' bias. Interestingly, humans tend to have a rosy view of the future; they seem to predict their future as including overwhelmingly positive events, while they describe their past as a balance of both positive and negative events (Armor & Taylor, 1998). Larwood and Whittaker (1997) have determined that similar overconfidence and unfounded optimism can be witnessed in organisational planning processes.

The hypothesis confirmation bias

The 'hypothesis confirmation' bias is perhaps the most recognised bias in decision making. This is where decision-makers look for explanations which are congruent with their preferred alternative (Snyder & Swan, 1978). Individuals search for facts that let them build faith in favoured solutions and avoid data which points to less favoured ones. Liedtka (2015) refers to the work of Ditto and Lopez (1992) and explains this hypothesis confirmation bias with the following:

> Decision-makers use different levels of intensity in processing information consistent with their preferences versus that which contradicts their preconceived perceptions. Information challenging any perception is more likely to be heavily scrutinized than information agreeing with the preferred solution, and alternative explanations that allow decision-makers to ignore this disconfirming data are often pursued.
>
> (Liedtka, 2015, p. 931)

In other words, as Ditto and Lopez (1992) explain, we tend to be less critical consumers of preference-consistent, than preference-inconsistent, data. Even when this bias is revealed to us, there are times where we fail to correct it. It happens to all of us. Consider, for instance, how many times you come up with a couple of ideas, out of which you prefer, say, the first one. Then you look for data that justifies why the first idea is the right idea, you ignore data that indicates it is not the best idea, as well as other data that screams the second idea is better! We all subscribe to the social realities we construct, even when we are aware that we have constructed these realities (Gilbert & Jones, 1986).

The endowment effect bias

In a similar fashion, the 'endowment effect' bias is where individuals tend to attach to what they already have, which makes giving something up (a solution in hand) more painful than the pleasure you would get from, in our case, a new and improved solution (Kahneman, 2011; Kahneman, Knetsch, & Thaler, 1991).

The availability bias

Finally, Kahneman and Tversky (1979) have also pointed out the 'availability' bias, in which individuals undervalue options or ideas that they find harder to imagine. "Because the familiarity of an idea is likely to be inversely related to its novelty, this leads to a preference for more incremental solutions" (Liedtka, 2015, p. 931).

Mitigating cognitive biases through design thinking

The above outlines the nine most prominent cognitive biases that 'would-be' innovators face, when seeking to come up and evaluate novel and value-creating ideas. However, Liedtka (2015) argues that scholars have documented a plethora of strategies that can be followed in order to mitigate these biases, and more interestingly, many of these strategies resonate with the processes and tools of design thinking. In order to demonstrate how design thinking processes and tools can mitigate the nine cognitive biases in decision making, Liedtka (2015) sorted these biases in three categories. The first category includes the projection, hot/cold gap, egocentric empathy gap, and focusing illusion biases, where decision-makers are unable to see beyond themselves and escape their own pasts, current state, personal preferences, and tendency to be excessively influenced by specific factors, respectively (Liedtka, 2015). The second category relates to the inability of consumers or users to articulately describe their own behaviour, express future needs, and provide appropriate feedback on new ideas. Therefore, this category includes the say/do gap bias. In this category, decision-makers find it difficult to develop value-creating ideas for the target users because of the lack of accurate and in-depth information about their past, present, and future behaviour (Liedtka, 2015). The third category of biases includes the availability, planning fallacy, endowment effect, and hypothesis confirmation biases, because it relates to the flaws in decision-makers' ability to test the hypotheses they have generated, and they are unimaginative, overly optimistic, and linked to initial and preferred solutions, respectively. It becomes apparent that the first category relates to biases in idea generation; the second category is about biases introduced by customers and users; and the third category relates to biases in testing the ideas (Liedtka, 2015) (Table 3.1).

Mitigating idea generation biases through design thinking

Design thinking processes and tools can mitigate the biases in the first category which relate to the decision-makers' inability to see beyond themselves, break away from their own past, and stay unaffected by their current state, personal preferences, as well as other specific influencing factors. Firstly, such mitigating strategies include the team (decision-makers) insisting on collecting, through

Table 3.1 Mitigating cognitive biases through design thinking.

Category	*Cognitive biases*	*Mitigation techniques*
Idea generation biases	Projection bias Hot/cold gap bias Egocentric empathy gap bias Focusing illusion bias	Collect deep data through ethnographic research Imagine the experience of others Collaborative work practices
Consumer bias	Say/do gap bias	Use of qualitative methodologies and prototyping tools Participant observation
Implementation biases	Availability bias Planning fallacy bias Endowment effect bias Hypothesis confirmation bias	Teaching the team to be better in hypothesis testing Work with multiple options Conduct and reflect on marketplace experiments

ethnographic research studies, deep data on users' concerns, needs, desires, and perspectives, particularly important in the inspiration (need-finding) stage, which is the first stage of the design thinking process. Through such research studies, the team can mitigate the projection bias because it will be able to immerse themselves into the user's experience and avoid looking exclusively to their own past experiences as a source of new ideas. As a result, the team will be able to generate more novel ideas (Liedtka, 2015). Ethnographic studies will also allow the team to mitigate the egocentric empathy gap bias because the data gathered will make them recognise the fact that users' preferences might be different from their own. Consequently, this will facilitate the creation of more valuable ideas. The focusing illusion bias can be mitigated through ethnographic studies because they encourage the team to maintain a broader perspective. This lessens the narrowed attention focus; hence it enables the team to introduce broader mix of alternatives (Liedtka, 2015). Finally, a deep ethnographic study will enable the team to concentrate on the users' experiences and feelings, thus maintain an objective frame of mind, unfettered by their current emotional state. As a result, pursuing such study can mitigate the hot/cold gap bias.

Secondly, mitigating strategies in this category can also involve the team by enabling them to *imagine* the experience of others in the inspiration (need-finding) stage of the design thinking process. Such enhanced ability mitigates the effects of the projection, egocentric empathy, focusing illusion, and hot/cold gap biases. The important word here is: *imagine*. Even in the case where the team lacks first-hand data, the design thinking tools of storytelling and metaphors can enhance the team's imaginative abilities. The use of stories can mitigate cognitive biases because it incites the decision-maker to pay attention to, and make sense of, data that would be otherwise missed (Liedtka, 2015). Liedtka explains the power of storytelling to mitigate these cognitive biases:

> In design thinking, visualisation methods like storytelling boost decision-makers' ability to envision experiences outside of their own. Storytelling, often partnered with ethnography, improves the novelty and value of the ideas generated by helping decision-makers take in and hold onto the rich details of the lives of those for whom they seek to create value.
>
> (Liedtka, 2015, p. 933)

Metaphor, as another visualisation technique, can help mitigate cognitive biases too. Lakoff and Johnson (1985) argue that, on the basis of linguistic evidence, most of human's ordinary conceptual system is metaphorical in nature. Individuals make sense of their experiences by creating metaphors. Understanding past experiences in this way can act as a guide to future experiences. Metaphors then become acts of 'imaginative rationality' (Lakoff & Johnson, 1985) and can stimulate the team's imaginations, and in doing so, it reduces their reliance on the past (mitigating the projection bias), broadens their vision (mitigating the focusing illusion bias), and makes them recognise different preferences (mitigating the egocentric empathy gap bias). This in turn leads to more novel and valuable ideas (Liedtka, 2015).

Thirdly, mitigating strategies in the first category can include collaborative work practices. Design thinking emphasises, and even insists, on making sure that innovation activities are carried out by diverse, multi-disciplinary teams. Consequently, design thinking can mitigate the effects of the projection, egocentric empathy gap, focusing illusion, and hot/cold gap biases (Liedtka, 2015). Collaborative working practices expose organisational members to their colleagues' perspectives and preferences and enable them to contrast them with their own, improving the novelty and value of the ideas generated. Collaboration is embedded in visualisation techniques since sketching ideas on whiteboards or writing these ideas up on post-it notes enable sharing and joint development. Co-creation, which is an important value in design thinking, by definition, requires collaboration. Liedtka, finally, suggests that

> structured sense-making and brainstorming tools facilitate team-based processes for drawing insights from ethnographic data. In addition, design values like: withholding judgement, avoiding debates, and paying particular attention to disconfirming data and the tensions difference creates, encourage more innovative team solutions.
>
> (Liedtka, 2015, p. 934)

Mitigating consumer biases through design thinking

Design thinking processes and tools can also mitigate the biases in the second category which relate to the consumers' inability to accurately articulate their experiences and predict their future actions. As a result, they are unable to adequately evaluate whether the ideas proposed will satisfy their needs and desires. This category includes the say/do gap bias, which can be mitigated by design thinking, firstly, through the use of qualitative methodologies and prototyping tools, which allow the consumer to identify and assess his/her own needs. However, these methodologies go beyond merely questioning consumers about their needs and ask them about, as well as observe, their behaviour (Liedtka, 2015). Their actions speak louder than words since consumers know more than they can articulate (Van Someren, Barnard, & Sandberg, 1994).

In the inspiration (need-finding) stage, the first stage of the design thinking process, techniques like journey mapping, job-to-be-done analyses, as well as projective tools such as collages ask users to recount an actual experience, explaining their thoughts, reactions, and levels of satisfaction at every stage. This highlights what the users tried to achieve in a relevant situation. This enables organisational members to identify needs that users cannot express themselves. Another approach to achieve similar results is "to activate more vivid mental images of the new future that help customers 'pre-experience' something novel" (Liedtka, 2015, p. 934). Gilbert et al. suggest that "just as mental images are proxies for actual events, so our reactions to these mental images may serve as proxies for our actual reactions to the events themselves" (2002, p. 432). Prototyping allows this 'pre-experience' to be achieved by providing the team with a tangible artefact which enables them to create more powerful manifestations of the future. This facilitates a better user evaluation process and the feedback gathered is more accurate.

Secondly, the say/do gap bias in this category can also be mitigated by design thinking by using methods which are not based on the user being able to diagnose their own preferences and needs or to imagine the suitability of a solution to meet them. Participant observation allows organisational members to not rely on what users say; instead, they can observe the users' behaviour, mitigating the say/do gap bias and generating ideas that are more valuable to users.

Mitigating testing biases through design thinking

Finally, design thinking processes and tools can also mitigate the biases in the third category which are concerned with decision-makers' flaws with hypothesis testing, and in particular their over-optimism (the planning fallacy bias), inability to see disconfirming data (hypothesis confirmation bias), attachment to early solutions (endowment effect bias), and preference for the easily imagined (availability bias) (Liedtka, 2015). These biases are mitigated, firstly, by teaching organisational members how they can be better in hypothesis testing through prototyping, surfacing unarticulated assumptions, and actively seeking disconfirming data. Decision-makers' hypothesis testing abilities can improve by creating the aforementioned 'pre-experience', which, as discussed above, improves the ability of users to provide feedback. This can help reduce the availability bias by helping the team imagine novel ideas more easily (Liedtka, 2015). Hypothesis testing methodologies used in design thinking allow organisational members to take part in 'cognitive rehearsals', such as thinking about the possibility of failure, which are capable of changing behaviour. Johnson and Sherman (1990) explain that the possibility of failure can motivate individuals to put more effort into the task in order to avoid such outcome.

Uncovering explicit assumptions can make hypothesis-testers describe with detail their expectancies and then describe what the data that supports and nullifies these would look like. This reduces the planning fallacy bias, i.e., over-optimism, and supports the look-out for disconfirming data (mitigating the hypothesis confirmation bias).

Secondly, testing biases can also be mitigated through design thinking by instructing decision-makers to work with multiple options and, therefore, consider and explain an array of possible outcomes, which improves the accuracy of their predictions. Such activities mitigate the planning fallacy, the hypothesis confirmation, and the endowment effect biases, in particular. The importance of 'optionality' is highlighted in design thinking processes and enables decision-makers to mitigate these biases.

Finally, testing biases can be mitigated by ensuring that decision-makers conduct, and reflect on the results of, marketplace experiments. Running experimental research and reflecting on the results can trigger an 'after-event review', which, as Ellis and Davidi (2005) argue, provides the opportunity to review both successes and failures, to understand why events happen as they do, which is, naturally, the underlying logic behind assumption testing. According to Liedtka (2015), design thinking involves field experiments to test assumptions and present prototypes to users, which achieve the purpose of after-event reviews. Ideally, such experiments are run with actual customers in real market contexts, rather than in artificial environments like conventional focus groups, and as a result, they provide accurate feedback that enables the decision-makers to evaluate the different options rigorously. Liedtka and Ogilvie (2011) argue that such field experiments provide the opportunity to assess specific assumptions with regard to value creation, execution, defensibility, and scalability. Finally, the techniques discussed earlier, used to address the different biases in idea generation, can also help mitigate biases related to testing. In particular, Nickerson (1998) suggests that perspective taking and its related ethnographic methods can mitigate the hypothesis confirmation bias too.

Chapter review questions

The following questions can help you reflect on the material covered in Chapter 3:

1 Identify the three eras of development of design theories and methods and explore their characteristics.
2 Discuss the differences between the thinking *of*, the thinking *about*, and the thinking *through* approaches, and how these approaches relate to design thinking.
3 Critically explore how traditional areas of design have developed over the last few decades through the paradigm of design thinking.
4 Outline the differences between the linear model of design thinking and the 'wicked problems' approach.
5 Discuss the properties of wicked problems and the reasons design problems can be described as wicked.
6 Explore the three important changes and additions to earlier work of design theorists, which are considered critical elements of business design thinking nowadays.
7 Discuss the three stages of the design thinking process and their associated design thinking tools and activities.
8 Explain the nine cognitive biases associated with individual decision making and explain the ways design thinking can mitigate theses biases.

Recommended reading

1 Brown, T. (2009). *Change by design: How design thinking transforms organisations and inspires innovation*. New York, NY: HarperCollins.
2 Buchanan, R. (1992). Wicked problems in design thinking. *Design Issues, 8*(2), 5–21.
3 Liedtka, J. (2015). Perspective: Linking design thinking with innovation outcomes through cognitive bias reduction. *Journal of Product Innovation Management, 32*(6), 925–938.

Reflective thoughts

Design thinking as reimagining assumptions

Professor Natalie W. Nixon
Director, MBA Strategic Design
Philadelphia University, Philadelphia, USA

Albert Einstein was credited for having said that "logic will get you from A to B. Imagination will take you everywhere". We need methods today that help us to navigate the ambiguity that is the reality in our complex world – one consisting less of linear, straight routes from A to B, but rather full of multiple scenarios which we must be able to critically assess. That reality, friends, requires imagination.

Designers are change agents. They get to shape the ways we navigate this world, whether through signage, through the comfort, protection, and semiotics coded into our garments and buildings, or through the utility and meaning garnered through objects and products. Design is also a method of inquiry: a hyper, human-centred methodology that puts people and their needs front and centre for any strategic challenge. If we just start right there, with those two principles that (1) designers are change agents and (2) design is a method of inquiry, then how more potent is Herb Simon's declaration of design *thinking* which permitted us all to conceive of ourselves as designers? We can embrace the democratic value of design thinking as outlined in this chapter. For as much as design thinking expands the provenance of design, it is also important to note that not all designers are automatically design thinkers. Design thinking is a learned skill which must be practiced in order to determine how to scale the frameworks and processes described in this chapter, in diverse environments.

Fundamentally, design thinking leads us to embrace transformation design. Transformation design is about having a systems perspective applied to the design of wicked problems and social challenges. If we were to map design as a taxonomy against something such as Maslow's Hierarchy of Needs, then design thinking takes us on a path to transformation design, which one could argue is the apex of any design function or effort.

This chapter's references to experience design, initially highlighted by Pine and Gilmore, are spot on. In our evolution from the agrarian economy to an industrial economy, and then to the service and creative economies, we find ourselves employing tools from design thinking to deliver more meaningful products, services, and experiences. Design thinking's value is that it helps us to examine the wicked problems that abound in our increasingly complex world.

Markets are made up of people. This may seem like an obvious statement, but for most businesses, this is a radical place to start. Most businesses begin with operational efficiencies, productivity, and profitability. Using design thinking means that we are more aware of the reality that markets are inconsistent, not predictive and fallible. Thus, by starting first with people and *their* needs – this is the empathy component – then we will consequently design systems, processes, and experiences that are more efficient, productive, and profitable. Enter the value of qualitative research methods in design thinking's method of inquiry. Design thinking borrowed deeply from cultural anthropology, in accessing ethnography and ethnographic research methods – observation, interviews, contextual inquiry – in order to garner the deep insight from the user's perspectives. We sometimes call it 'rapid ethnography', since in design thinking research we do not always take the extended amounts of time as anthropologists to deeply embed in a community or organisation. However, the results of ethnographic methods are invaluable when coupled with quantitative research methods in a design thinking context. The qualitative research method infused in design thinking helps to counter the nine cognitive biases this chapter outlines. And what in fact are biases? Biases are actually assumptions. Design thinking helps us to counter our assumptions by reframing our problem statements and requiring us to use our imaginations to expand beyond what the current state is and what we see. This is invaluable because we can always chisel away and edit down to practical concerns through the constraints of budgets, deadlines, and available skill sets.

Today, there are excellent resources that highlight design thinking and many open source tool kits for education and training. While we tend to map the design thinking process into 'stages' and 'phases', we know in reality that the process is rarely that neat or linear. In fact, when applying design thinking in action, the phases and stages are revisited in iterative rounds, and if anything, they become shorter and more concise as we refine our research insights.

In the complex and ambiguous environments in which we work, we are called to imagine and reimagine constantly. This chapter has aptly pointed out the paradoxical nature of design – for example, using meta-level assessment for grounded, applied work. Exploring grand scale and lofty possibilities while factoring in practical constraints is the paradox that makes design's method of inquiry dynamic and realistic. Design thinking gets us to a new way of seeing. Mark Twain once wrote that "you can't depend on your eyes when your imagination is out of focus". Practitioners of design thinking are certainly witness to this need for the imagination to challenge assumptions, reframe questions, and pursue critical methods of inquiry for problem solving.

References

Amabile, T. M. (1982). The social psychology of creativity: A consensual assessment technique. *Journal of Personality and Social Psychology, 43*, 997–1013.

Amabile, T. M. (1983). *The social psychology of creativity*. New York: Springer-Verlag.

Andriopoulos, C., & Gotsi, M. (2005). The virtues of 'blue sky' projects: How Lunar Design taps into the power of imagination. *Creativity and Innovation Management, 14*(3), 316–324.

Armor, D. A., & Taylor, S. E. (1998). Situated optimism: Specific outcome expectancies and self-regulation. In M. P. Zanna (Ed.), *Advances in experimental social psychology* (Vol. 30, pp. 309–379). New York: Academic Press.

Aspelund, K. (2010). *The design process* (2nd ed.). New York: Fairchild Books.

Bazjanac, V. (1974). Architectural design theory: Models of the design process. In W. Spillers (Ed.), *Basic questions of design theory* (pp. 3–20). Amsterdam: North-Holland.

Beckman, S. L., & Barry, M. (2007). Innovation as a learning process: Embedding design thinking. *California Management Review, 50*(1), 25–56.

Best, K. (2006). *Design management: Managing design strategy, process and implementation*. Lausanne, Switzerland: AVA Publishing.

Best, K. (2015). *Design management: Managing design strategy, process and implementation*. New York: Bloomsbury.

Brown, T. (2008). Design thinking. *Harvard Business Review, 86*(6), 84.

Brown, T. (2009). *Change by design: How design thinking transforms organisations and inspires innovation*. New York: HarperCollins.

Brown, T., & Katz, B. (2011). Change by design. *Journal of Product Innovation Management, 28*(3), 381–383.
Brown, T., & Martin, R. (2015). Design for action: How to use design thinking to make great things actually happen. *Harvard Business Review, 93*(9), 66–71.
Brown, T., & Wyatt, J. (2010). Design thinking for social innovation. *Stanford Social Innovation Review,* Winter, 30–35.
Buchanan, R. (1992). Wicked problems in design thinking. *Design Issues, 8*(2), 5–21.
Carlgren, L., Elmquist, M., & Rauth, I. (2014). Design thinking: Exploring values and effects from an innovation capability perspective. *The Design Journal, 17*(3), 403–423.
Carlgren, L., Rauth, I., & Elmquist, M. (2016). Framing design thinking: The concept in idea and enactment. *Creativity and Innovation Management, 25*(1), 38–57.
Cooper, R., & Evans, M. (2006). Breaking from tradition: Market research, consumer needs, and design futures. *Design Management Review, 17*(1), 68–74.
Cooper, R., & Junginger, S. (2011). General introduction: Design management – A reflection. In R. Cooper, S. Junginger, & T. Lockwood (Eds.), *The handbook of design management*. London: A&C Black.
Cooper, R., Junginger, S., & Lockwood, T. (2010). Design thinking and design management: A research and practice perspective. In T. Lockwood (Ed.), *Design thinking: Integrating innovation, customer experience, and brand value*. New York: Skyhorse.
Cross, N. (2010). Design thinking as a form of intelligence. In *Proceedings of the 8th Design Thinking Research Symposium (DTRS8)*, Sydney, Australia, 19–20 October, pp. 99–105.
Davis, J., Docherty, C. A., & Dowling, K. (2016). Design thinking and innovation: Synthesising concepts of knowledge co-creation in spaces of professional development. *The Design Journal, 19*(1), 117–139.
Ditto, P. H., & Lopez, D. F. (1992). Motivated scepticism: Use of differential decision criteria for preferred and nonpreferred conclusions. *Journal of Personality and Social Psychology, 63*(4), 568–584.
Dorst, K. (2011). The core of 'design thinking' and its application. *Design Studies, 32*(6), 521–532.
Ellis, S., & Davidi, I. (2005). After-event reviews: Drawing lessons from successful and failed experience. *Journal of Applied Psychology, 90*(5), 857–871.
Fellman, M. (1999). Breaking tradition. *Marketing Research, 11*(3), 20–25.
Garud, R., Jain, S., & Tuertscher, P. (2008). Incomplete by design and designing for incompleteness. *Organization Studies, 29*(3), 351–371.
Gilbert, D. T., & Jones, E. E. (1986). Perceiver-induced constraint: Interpretations of self-generated reality. *Journal of Personality and Social Psychology, 50*(2), 269–280.
Gilbert, D. T., Gill, M. J., & Wilson, T. D. (2002). The future is now: Temporal correction in affective forecasting. *Organizational Behaviour and Human Decision Processes, 88*(1), 430–444.
Ignatius, A. (2015). How Indra Nooyi turned design thinking into strategy: An interview with PepsiCo's CEO. *Harvard Business Review*. Retrieved from https://hbr.org/2015/09/how-indra-nooyi-turned-design-thinking-into-strategy
Johansson-Sköldberg, U., Woodilla, J., & Çetinkaya, M. (2013). Design thinking: Past, present and possible futures. *Creativity and Innovation Management, 22*(2), 121–146.
Johnson, M. K., & Sherman, S. J. (1990). Constructing and reconstructing the past and the future in the present. In E. T. Higgins, & R. M. Sorrention (Eds.), *Handbook of motivation and cognition: Foundations of social behaviour* (Vol. 2, pp. 482–526). New York: The Guilford Press.
Kahneman, D. (2011). *Thinking, fast and slow*. New York: Farrar, Straus and Giroux.
Kahneman, D., & Tversky, A. (1979). Intuitive prediction: Biases and corrective procedures. *Management Science, 12*, 313–327.
Kahneman, D., Knetsch, J. L., & Thaler, R. H. (1991). Anomalies: The endowment effect, loss aversion, and status quo bias. *The Journal of Economic Perspectives, 5*(1), 193–206.
Kelley, T., & Littman, J. (2001). *The art of innovation*. New York: Broadway Business.
Kimbell, L. (2011). Rethinking design thinking: Part I. *Design and Culture, 3*(3), 285–306.
Kolko, J. (2010). *Exposing the magic of design: A practitioner's guide to the methods and theory of synthesis*. Oxford, UK: Oxford University Press.
Kolko, J. (2015). Design thinking comes of age. *Harvard Business Review, 93*(9), 66–71.
Konno, N. (2014). An introduction to 'purpose engineering': An essay on 'practical wisdom' and innovation. *Kindai Management Review, 2*, 52–66.

Lakoff, G., & Johnson, M. (1985). *Metaphors we live by*. Chicago: University of Chicago Press.

Larwood, L., & Whittaker, W. (1977). Managerial myopia: Self-serving biases in organizational planning. *Journal of Applied Psychology, 62*(2), 194–198.

Leonard, D., & Rayport, J. F. (1997). Spark innovation through empathic design. *Harvard Business Review, 75*, 102–115.

Lewis, M. W. (2000). Exploring paradox: Toward a more comprehensive guide. *Academy of Management Review, 25*(4), 760–776.

Liedtka, J. (2000). In defence of strategy as design. *California Management Review, 42*(3), 8–30.

Liedtka, J. (2015). Perspective: Linking design thinking with innovation outcomes through cognitive bias reduction. *Journal of Product Innovation Management, 32*(6), 925–938.

Liedtka, J., & Ogilvie, T. (2011). *Designing for growth*. New York: Columbia Business Press.

Lockwood, T. (2010). Foreword: The importance of integrated thinking. In T. Lockwood (Ed.), *Design thinking: Integrating innovation, customer experience, and brand value*. New York: Skyhorse.

Loewenstein, G., & Angner, E. (2003). Predicting and indulging changing preferences. In G. Loewenstein, D. Read, & R. Baumeister (Eds.), *Time and decision: Economic and psychological perspectives on intertemporal choice* (pp. 351–391). New York: Russell Sage Foundation.

March, L. (1976). *The architecture of form*. Cambridge, UK: Cambridge University Press.

Moreau, C. P. (2011). Inviting the amateurs into the studio: Understanding how consumer engagement in product design creates value. *Journal of Product Innovation Management, 28*(3), 409–410.

Nickerson, R. S. (1998). Confirmation bias: A ubiquitous phenomenon in many guises. *Review of General Psychology, 2*(2), 175.

Nussbaum, B. (2011). Design thinking is a failed experiment. So what's next? *Fast Company, 6*.

Owen, C. (1993). Considering design fundamentally. *Design Processes Newsletter, 5*(3), 2.

Patnaik, D., & Mortensen, P. (2009). *Wired to care: How companies prosper when they create widespread empathy*. Upper Saddle River, NJ: FT Press.

Pine, B. J., & Gilmore, J. H. (1998). Welcome to the experience economy. *Harvard Business Review, 76*, 97–105.

Pine, B. J., & Gilmore, J. H. (1999). *The experience economy: Work is theatre and every business a stage*. Cambridge, MA: Harvard Business School Press.

Pine, B. J., & Gilmore, J. H. (2011). *The experience economy*. Cambridge, MA: Harvard Business Press.

Richardson, A. (2010). Using customer journey maps to improve customer experience. *Harvard Business Review, 15*.

Rieple, A. (2016). Theoretical context for strategic design: An introduction to design thinking. In N. W. Nixon (Ed.), *Strategic design thinking: Innovation in products, experiences, and beyond*. New York: Bloomsbury.

Rowe, P. (1987). *Design thinking*. Cambridge, MA: The MIT Press.

Schon, D. A. (1982). *The reflective practitioner: How professionals think in action*. New York: Basic Books.

Schrage, M. (2013). *Serious play: How the world's best companies simulate to innovate*. Cambridge, MA: Harvard Business School Press.

Seidel, V. P., & Fixson, S. K. (2013). Adopting design thinking in novice multidisciplinary teams: The application and limits of design methods and reflexive practices. *Journal of Product Innovation Management, 30*(S1), 19–33.

Snyder, M., & Swann, W. B. (1978). Hypothesis-testing processes in social interaction. *Journal of Personality and Social Psychology, 36*(11), 1202.

Someren, M. V., Barnard, Y. F., & Sandberg, J. A. (1994). *The think aloud method: A practical approach to modelling cognitive processes*. London: Academic Press.

Taylor, F. W. (1911). *The principles of scientific management*. London: Harper.

Tripp, C. (2013). No empathy–No service. *Design Management Review, 24*(3), 58–64.

Van Boven, L., Dunning, D., & Loewenstein, G. (2000). Egocentric empathy gaps between owners and buyers: Misperceptions of the endowment effect. *Journal of Personality and Social Psychology, 79*(1), 66.

Wallas, G. (1926). *The art of thought*. New York: Harcourt, Brace & World.

Walters, H. (2011). Design thinking isn't a miracle cure, but here's how it helps. *Fast Company, Co. Design*. Retrieved from www.fastcodesign.com/1663480/design-thinking-isnt-a-miracle-cure-but-heres-how-it-helps

West Churchman, C. (1967). Wicked problems. *Management Science, 4*(14), B-141–B-142.

Yajima, R. (2015). Catalyzing scientific innovation with design thinking. *Design Management Review, 26*(1), 18–23.

4 Strategic design management

Developing the design strategy

Chapter aims and learning outcomes

This chapter aims to:

1 Define the concepts of design strategy and strategic design.
2 Explore the strategic contributions of design, making connections with strategic management and marketing strategy concepts.
3 Discuss the different stages of the design strategy development process.
4 Understand design audit and its value to design strategy formulation.
5 Explore the different design strategies appropriate at different stages of innovation diffusion.

Building on the concepts discussed in the previous chapters, it is important to explore the ways organisations can develop a flexible design strategy successfully. Many design strategy frameworks draw from well-established concepts in strategic management and marketing strategy literature. Therefore, such an endeavour will add to the discussion of the synergies between the design management and marketing. Before we explore how the organisation can develop successful design strategies, it is important to define and understand the differences between the concepts of 'design strategy' and 'strategic design'.

Design strategy vs. strategic design

Cooper and Press (1995) in their seminal book *Design Agenda: A Guide to Successful Design Management*, a preliminary title in design management literature, argued that there are three distinct sets of design activities: (1) the development of corporate identity, (2) the design of saleable products, and (3) the design of operating environments. Their suggestion provided the basis for Olson, Cooper, and Slater's (1998) rather pragmatic definition of design strategy. They defined design strategy as "the effective allocation and coordination of design resources and activities to accomplish a firm's objectives of creating its appropriate public and internal identities, its product offerings, and its environments" (Olson et al., 1998, p. 56). However, nowadays, some will certainly argue that Cooper and Press' (1995) sets of design activities are narrow and limiting given the wider application of design in business and society, as discussed in previous chapters. More recently, Jun has provided another, more articulate definition of design strategy.

> Design strategy aims to strengthen the relationship between the company's design development and the marketing environment, helping to determine the direction of R&D and design policy. It ensures that organisational culture can be delivered through design and creates the management systems responsible for the delivery of organisational objectives.
>
> (Jun, 2008, p. 25)

An additional definition by Canada, Mortensen, and Patnaik explains that design strategy is "the interplay between design and business strategy, wherein design methods are used to inform business strategy, and strategic planning provides a context for design" (2008, p. 57). Stevens and Moultrie (2011) make a distinction between the terms 'design strategy' and 'strategic design'. They argue that 'design strategy' is a term often used to indicate a long-term plan for design implementation at product rather than corporate level. They believe that while design strategy is the sole responsibility and practice of skilled designers and design managers, "strategic design involves complex interplay of influencers and stakeholders and might not be explicitly recognised in an organisation" (Stevens & Moultrie, 2011, p. 476). Despite their distinction of the two terms, other scholars use the terms in an inter-exchangeable manner, and this is how we will use the terms here too.

Strategic contributions of design

Strategic design and corporate strategy

Given the important role of design in society and business, there is a need to understand its strategic contributions to organisations. Stevens and Moultrie (2011) published a framework demonstrating how design contributes to the formulation and implementation of corporate strategy. Based on their research with two (anonymous) organisations – a large global design and engineering firm headquartered in London, and a UK-based telecommunications technology and service delivery firm – they described such contributions in four broad foci, making references to strategic management literature: (1) competitive forces, (2) strategic fit and value creation, (3) resources and capabilities, and (4) strategic vision.

Design contributions to competitive forces

The first focus described by Stevens and Moultrie (2011) is concerned with competitive forces, since design can build market differentiation, customer intimacy and perceived value, as well as it can influence supply chain dependencies. Design can create "market positioning and differentiation by which loyalty and perceived value confer strategic advantage, reducing the threat of substitution and buyer bargaining power" (Stevens & Moultrie, 2011, p. 479) (referring to Porter, 1979, 1980, 1985; Treacy & Wiersema, 1993). Consequently design takes an external role to give form to customer perceptions and experiences directly through the product and service offerings and indirectly through corporate identity activities. Design can become a core competence, contributing to perceived customer benefits and allowing the organisation to access a plurality of markets. More specifically, in relation to Porter's (1979, 1980) 'Five Forces' model, design makes decisions on the choice of materials or components of the product or service offering ('physical evidence' in the services marketing mix) and therefore influences the bargaining power of suppliers, for instance, by minimising switching costs to avoid over-reliance on particular suppliers or technologies. Design can also impact the bargaining power of buyers by creating an emotional connection between the brand and the user to influence loyalty and preference (Stevens & Moultrie, 2011).

Design contributions to strategic fit and value creation

The second focus of design's contributions to strategy formulation and implementation relates to strategic fit and value creation. Here the contributions are achieved by "integrating and mediating between professional domains, and [by] … supporting primary and secondary value activities within the organisation and value network" (Stevens & Moultrie, 2011, p. 479). As already discussed, design activities require the collaboration of designers with other professions such as marketing, manufacturing, and research and the amalgamation of disparate expertise and viewpoints from inside and outside the organisation. Stevens and Moultrie (2011) argue that design can help improve the linkages between internal value activities, referring to Porter's (1985) 'Value Chain Analysis' model, where inbound logistics, operations, outbound logistics, marketing and sales, and (aftersales) service are the primary activities, supported by the firm's infrastructure, human resources management, technological development, and procurement which are deemed as the secondary activities. All these activities add value in the process of the product or service offering reaching the user, and design can improve the links between these activities. It can also contribute to the external role of the organisation in its sector, identifying opportunities for partnerships and generating a new industry vision (Borja de Mozota, 2003; Stabell & Fjeldstad, 1998). Design's contributions also relate to Porter's (1985) concept of strategic fit "as part of a holistic design strategy in which design is permitted to contribute across communications and identity, products and services, and environments" (Stevens & Moultrie, 2011, p. 480).

Design contributions to resources and capabilities

Design's contributions to strategy formulation and implementation has a third focus, with respect to resources and capabilities. Here, design's contributions take the form of shaping and communicating corporate culture and improving knowledge management (Stevens & Moultrie, 2011). Analytically, in relation to shaping and communicating a corporate culture, design contributes to the creation and communication of a shared vision, which is a significant discipline of the learning organisation according to Senge (1990). It is important that the organisation understands the complete picture, and this is where design can help. It can contribute to this 'systems thinking', described by Senge (1990) as the design approach where the organisation can see the 'whole'. Products, interiors, and buildings as designed material artefacts, as well as metaphors, stories, and humour as culturally mediated language (Hatch & Schultz, 1997) can also communicate and interpret the corporate vision. A corporate culture that is influenced by design enables the organisation to nurture its members with knowledge. Design is also a very important strategic (tacit) knowledge capability in its own right; hence design not only improves knowledge management systems and processes, but it is also an intellectual capability itself. The significance of this dual role is of course supported through the 'knowledge-based view' in strategy as discussed by many scholars (Barney, 1991; Grant, 1996; Manville & Foote, 1996; Wernerfelt, 1984).

Design contributions to strategic vision

The final focus of design's contributions to strategy formulation and implementation relates to strategic vision. In this case, according to Stevens and Moultrie (2011), at leadership level, design activities can view complex systems holistically, leading to the creation of a shared strategic vision. Design can help senior management explore uncertainty and assess trade-offs. Design thinking can provide the tools for exploring different perspectives and understanding what is valued by customers, employees, suppliers, and other stakeholders (Stevens & Moultrie, 2011).

Design can provide fresh perspectives and includes both formality and freedom. The latter is required in order to tackle the 'fallacy of formalisation', defined by Mintzberg (1994) as the misconception that strategy can be formulated in a formal structure and process imposed within the organisation, without allowing organisational members freedom for creativity. Design can also contribute to addressing Mintzberg's (1994) 'fallacy of predetermination', i.e., the misconception that business conditions can be predicted to any meaningful level, as well as the 'fallacy of detachment' which relates to the misapprehension that strategy should or could be grounded only to hard facts in objective isolation (Mintzberg, 1994). As already explored in Chapter 3, design thinking methods can help the organisation safely explore the future, regardless of its unknown nature, mitigating cognitive biases such as the projection bias (Liedtka, 2015) where individuals tend to project the present into the future leading to predictions that are too based on, and biased toward, the present (Loewenstein & Angner, 2003). While design relates to concepts such as strategic intent and trade-off, which are very useful to management in order to set the strategic course, predictive tools would only be valuable provided the future is an extension of the present (de Bono, 1992). As already explored, the future is seldom merely a copy of the present.

The following sections delve deeper into the contributions of design to corporate strategy in relation to the concept of strategic renewal, the development of visual recognition for the brand, as well as the use of design styling as a strategic tool.

Design management and strategic renewal

In 1994, the Dutch electronics manufacturer *Philips* partnered with *Alessi*, the Italian kitchenware producer, to develop a line of small appliances. The new products developed were pioneers in the market because their featured natural shapes managed to respond to an emerging consumer need for affection in the relationship between user and machines (Ravasi & Lojacono, 2005). Stefano Marzano, Chief Design Manager at *Philips*, explained that the *Philips-Alessi* range of products did not simply indicate a new style direction for the firm, but also

> reflected an innovative approach to the exploration of consumers' latent needs and to the use of technology in consumer products, and triggered a change in the way the company's managers looked at design. During the 1980s … design was considered primarily a competitive tool to increase the commercial appeal of new products. Later, Marzano's work emphasized the potential of design in driving brand repositioning and inspiring strategy formulation.
>
> (Ravasi & Lojacono, 2005, pp. 51–52)

Philips-Alessi home appliances.

Nowadays the above case is not a unique example. Over the last two decades, besides *Philips*, there is a plethora of other organisations which have perfected this human-centred design approach as a way to formulate strategy. *Apple* products have been embraced by a large number of consumers for their intuitive and user-friendly design which forges a triadic partnership between humans, hardware artefacts, and software applications. Other examples include audio-visual systems producer *Bang & Olufsen*, electronics giant *Sony*, and furniture maker *Kartel*. Such change of the way design is viewed by organisations is partly supported by the increasing role of culture in consumption (McCracken, 1986). Products and services have become ways of expressing lifestyle, personality, and identity; they have become extensions of people's selves (Belk, 1988). Ravasi and Lojacono (2005) developed a conceptual framework for understanding how organisations can harness the contribution of design to the process of strategic renewal.

Strategic renewal has been viewed by some scholars (Baden-Fuller & Stopford, 1994; Stopford & Baden-Fuller, 1994) as a set of activities undertaken by an organisation wishing to change its resource pattern and strategic course, in order to improve its overall economic performance. Such change might be triggered by increasing competition and a deterioration of the organisation's competitive positioning. Ravasi and Lojacono (2005) call this perspective '*renewal as corporate transformation*'. Alternatively, other scholars (Burgelman, 1991; Brown & Eisenhardt, 1997; Dougherty, 1992) have focused on product innovation and business development, viewing renewal as the search for new combinations of available technologies, supported by the creation and utilisation of product and market knowledge. Ravasi and Lojacono (2005) call this perspective '*renewal as continuous innovation*' and argue that it entails two essential characteristics: (1) it is driven by technology and product innovation instead of corporate-wide change efforts, and (2) is carried out on a permanent basis. Some might argue that these two perspectives describe different phenomena in different contexts; however, Ravasi and Lojacono's (2005) research has shown that both perspectives are necessary in order to comprehend the potential of design and designers to strategic renewal.

The design-driven strategic renewal framework developed by Ravasi and Lojacono (2005) consists of four stages: (1) the generation of ideas, (2) the evaluation and selection of ideas, (3) the revision of the design philosophy, and (4) the diffusion of new ideas. These four stages occur during two phases: the product development phase (stages 1 and 2) and the organisational development phase (stages 3 and 4) (Figure 4.1).

The two phases are essentially two processes that

> feed upon each other, as successful product innovation may inspire an overall organisational development centred on the revision of design principles and strategic intent, which in turn will affect how product innovation is carried out in design centres.
>
> (Ravasi & Lojacono, 2005, p. 54)

In the first stage of the strategic renewal framework, in-house and external designers' experimentation leads to the *generation of ideas*. This fosters a continuous process of product development which can result in regular renewal and extension of product lines and features. It is necessary that the designers' proposed ideas reflect the organisation's 'design philosophy' which directs new concept development. However, the two scholars argue that designers might sometimes diverge from the design philosophy to explore or test new approaches. They define design philosophy as the

> sort of 'genetic blueprint' of product development: a set of shared beliefs influencing designers' decisions about how a product will look and function … [and it] is made of two related components: a set of core design principles and a stylistic identity.
>
> (Ravasi & Lojacono, 2005, p. 73)

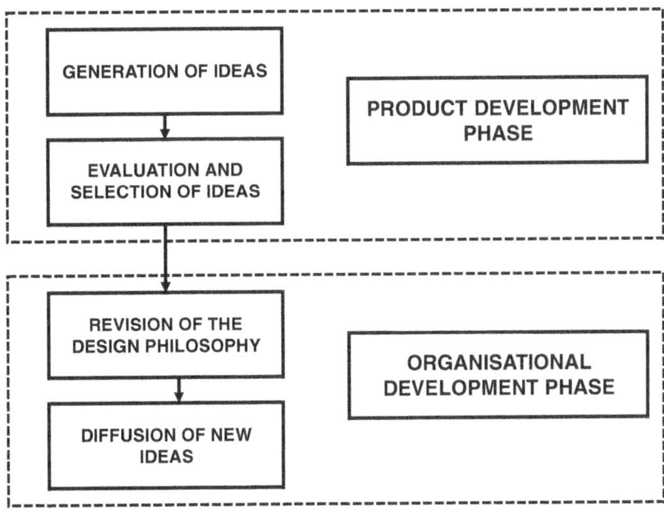

Figure 4.1 The design-driven strategic renewal framework.

The ideas generated in the first stage need to be evaluated in order for the organisation to select the most appropriate ones. Despite the fact that managers may not be responsible for the generation of ideas (although, as argued in Chapter 2, their involvement and collaboration in such endeavours is vital), the onus is on them to approve or reject the designers' ideas. This *evaluation and selection of ideas* constitutes the second stage of the process and follows criteria which include, in general terms, expected costs and revenues, fit with existing product lines, organisational features (such as technological competencies, current suppliers, and distribution channels), and organisational policies (e.g. positioning and pricing). Some ideas might be discarded because of lack of fit or because they are too bold or risky; others will be given the go-ahead for further development, and few of them will make it to final production (Ravasi & Lojacono, 2005).

During these two stages, which form the product development phase of the framework, strategic renewal tends to occur gradually and within the boundaries of current strategy and design philosophy. At times, the renewal extends from the product level to the organisational level, triggered by feedback from the market, which makes managers and designers start questioning their current conceptions, related to, for instance, market segmentation, user needs, and cultural values. This might also be induced by the unexpected success or failure of a company's new product, leading the organisation to carry out a *revision of the design philosophy*. In this stage, the organisation might choose to revise the goals and principles which drive its product innovation and consequently allow a redefinition of its strategic intent or a reconfiguration of its competitive scope (Ravasi & Lojacono, 2005).

The final stage of the design-led strategic renewal framework includes the *diffusion of the new design principles*, promoting awareness of the new design philosophy across all parts of the organisation, beyond the design centres and the corporate headquarters. This will allow all external or peripheral parties such as advertising agencies, distributors, or freelance designers to align with the new strategic intent and design philosophy of the firm. Therefore, the process demonstrates that what might start as a modest variation in product design can eventually lead to an organisation-wide renewal in values and strategic positioning (Ravasi & Lojacono, 2005).

Design and visual recognition of the brand

Concentrating on product design in particular, Karjalainen and Snelders (2010) set to explore how organisations strategically employ design to create visual recognition of their brands' core values. Drawing from their research with two firms, *Nokia* and *Volvo*, they found that these two companies fostered design philosophies that directed which design approach to follow and which design features express the core brand values. Their research led to the following thesis:

> The communication of value through design [is] modelled as a process of semantic transformation. This process specifies how meaning is created by design in a three-way relation among design features, brand values, and the interpretation by a potential customer ... Control over the process of semantic transformation [enables] managers ... to make strategic decisions over the type, strength, and generality of the relation between design features and brand values. The embodiment of brand values in a design can be strategically organised around lead products. Such products serve as reference points for what the brand stands for, and can be used as such during subsequent new product development (NPD) projects for other products in the brand portfolio.
>
> (Karjalainen & Snelders, 2010, p. 6)

Acts of semantic transformation involve transforming qualitative brand descriptions into value-based design features, which generate intended meaning of products (Karjalainen, 2004). Comparing the two cases of *Nokia* and *Volvo*, the authors identified different design philosophies as a result of the differences on their product portfolio and the market segments served. *Nokia* had a bigger product portfolio than *Volvo*, and it served more market segments; as a result, it had to apply its design features over its product portfolio in a more flexible manner. Many of *Nokia*'s designs entailed a more implicit relation between design features and brand values, whereas at *Volvo* the design philosophy was translated to design features more consistently and explicitly.

(Continued)

(Continued)

Volvo's design philosophy: Use of consistent design features across product portfolio. (Photos courtesy of Volvo.)

Karjalainen and Snelders (2010) identified six key drivers for the differences between the two organisations' design philosophies. First, the management of a visual identity of a brand is influenced by the product category the brand operates in. More specifically, the *phase of the industry life cycle* can lead to specific requirements in terms of the overall approach to design and the construction of product portfolio. The design philosophy of the organisation can also be affected by *the life cycle of a single product* (Karjalainen & Snelders, 2010). Organisations that have products with shorter life cycles, e.g., mobile phone manufacturer *Samsung* (to use a more contemporary example), are likely to consider having a dynamic design strategy as a feasible strategic choice. Design innovation is a core competence for such organisations operating in dynamic markets. In contrast, a more static design strategy is expected from *Hovis* (the UK-based bakery products manufacturer), which has a smaller portfolio with longer product cycles.

The design philosophy of the organisation is also affected by the (corporate) *brand's position*, the position the company enjoys in the sector. As a market leader in the consumer electronics industry, *Apple* (like *Nokia* in its heydays) is able to set new standards in the market, and it is more likely to try new directions for products (such as electronic watches) and their design features. *The width and structure of the organisation's portfolio* can also drive the design philosophy. The number of the organisation's product models in the market at a given time will naturally influence the required levels of consistency. If the organisation has many product models, as a result of serving many market segments, e.g., *Philips*, then a more flexible application of a design philosophy is the requirement. In comparison, if the portfolio only contains a few models, then the significance of a single product becomes greater; in fact, every product might be considered a lead product, which could have a great impact on brand recognition, and design decisions will have greater implications for brand identity. In such a case, there is usually a need for a stricter application of the design philosophy.

The *brand's heritage* is also a very important driver of design philosophy. Brand heritage is often a characteristic of organisations in mature industries, for example, *Coca-Cola* in the soft drinks industry. As Karjalainen and Snelders explain, "the prevailing image and reputation of the brand on the market affects the formation of recognition ... A strong heritage and early-established identity form

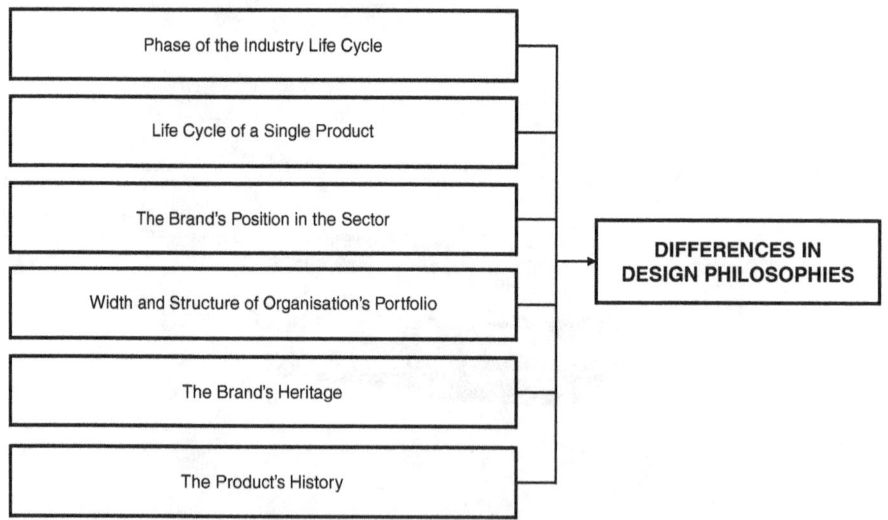

Figure 4.2 Drivers for differentiation in design philosophies.

an effective basis for brand recognition" (2010, p. 17). Finally, the *product's history* can influence its design features, having an impact on the product's overall design for a long period of time. Every designer is challenged to strike a balance between familiarity and novelty. Making design references to the past can influence future recognition of the brand. However, we have to be cautious because too much familiarity can also lead to boredom and reduced attention to the brand values expressed through the design. Managing the equation of renewal and consistency is, therefore, crucial for maintaining the visual recognition of the brand (Karjalainen & Snelders, 2010) (Figure 4.2).

It is clear that the first two drivers are external to organisations because they relate to the product category, and the last four drivers are internal to organisations deriving from the organisations' past and present brand management strategies. The requirements for designing visual recognition for the brand are industry-, organisation-, and product-dependent. In relation to semantic transformation, following a decision on the strategic approach, i.e., what design features are going to be used in the portfolio, the organisation must decide how these features should represent the core brand values.

As discussed above, an important decision the organisation must make is concerned with visual consistency of the product portfolio. Karjalainen and Snelders (2010) offer a number of guidelines on the issue of visual consistency of the product portfolio. They argue that greater consistency should be pursued if (1) the brand operates in a mature product category where there are established solutions for the interface of user and technology and a stable brand image, (2) the renewal cycle of product lines is long, (3) the brand is considered a niche or a new offering which focuses on a limited number of market segments, and (4) the brand enjoys a strong heritage and, in particular, a recognisable design identity throughout earlier product generations. Consider, for instance, how over the years *Apple* has developed recognisable iconic characteristics for its products – sleek white and silver textures and materials. Greater consistency, in such cases, can be created by referring to iconic designs from the brand's past (Karjalainen & Snelders, 2010).

Two strategies can be identified in relation to the maintenance of visual recognition of a product in the organisation's product portfolio. Organisations can aim to build coherent product portfolios where each product shares a number of explicit design features (Karjalainen & Snelders, 2010). This resonates with the idea of building 'branded houses' where organisations use one brand name for all its products (even when these are in different product categories) (Keller, Apéria, & Georgson, 2012). Alternatively, the firm might choose to create different identities for different products in its portfolio, similar to the case of 'house of brands', where the organisation will choose to have different names for different products (Keller et al., 2012).

Using design styling as a strategic tool

The role of the visual side of design in marketing and strategy was also discussed by Person, Snelders, Karjalainen, and Schoormans (2007) who explored how organisations can use design styling as a strategic tool. They argue that a product's styling can be examined with respect to not only how factors such as balance, rhythm, expression, etc., can comprehend the visual qualities of the product, but also, from a commercial perspective, in terms of "how styling can add value to new products and contribute to the bottom-line profit and long-term success of companies" (Person et al., 2007, p. 903). There can certainly be an overlap between these two perspectives because if an individual perceives a product as beautiful, appropriate, or attractive, he/she will be willing to spend more money to purchase the product (Bloch, 1995; Page & Herr, 2002). After reviewing the literature on styling in design and marketing, and through their own research, Person et al. (2007) identified that the three intermediary goals of styling in a commercial setting are *the creation of symbolic meaning, attention drawing* and *establishing recognition.* The latter connects well with Karjalainen and Snelders' (2010) work on the visual recognition of the brand, discussed above. In addition, attention drawing and establishing recognition connect well with the first layer of Keller et al.'s (2012) 'brand equity pyramid' model, where the organisation creates an identity for the brand to increase brand recall and recognition. These three intermediary goals are referred to by Person et al. (2007) as 'processes of attraction' and they are acutely interconnected because the aptitude of styling to draw attention can be considered as a precondition of using styling to create recognition, which in turn is a precondition for having consumers derive symbolic meanings from products (Person et al., 2007).

Person et al. (2007) proposed a model on strategic styling decisions over these three goals. They argue that strategic decisions are concerned with the degree of differentiation of any new product launched by the organisation, in relation to three dimensions: (1) the extant product portfolio of the organisation, (2) the succession of product generations, and (3) the products of the organisation's competitors. The organisation can achieve a different process of attraction by choosing to launch the new product in a very similar or in a very different styling to its present portfolio, its succession of product generations, and/or its competitors' products.

With respect to the organisation's *present product portfolio*, the firm might choose to launch the new product in a very similar styling in order to establish recognition by association and transfer symbolic meanings from its existing products to the new product (Karjalainen, 2004; Warell, 2001). A similar styling can assist the pairing of the new product with the current portfolio and, over time, transfer affect from the current products to the new product through Pavlov's (1927) classical conditioning process. In addition, using similar styling across the product portfolio can create the 'poster' or 'billboard' effect when the products are displayed together in a store (Keller et al., 2012; Quelch & Kenny, 1994). On the other hand, the firm might choose to launch the new product with a very different styling in order to draw attention through it being visually presented in an unusual to the organisation way. Furthermore, organisations which wish to target different market segments will opt to launch the new product in a very different way, in order to achieve distinctions among the products in their portfolio. Karjalainen (2004) identified hybrid strategies positioned between styling a product in a very similar and in a very different way to the current portfolio, such as in the case of *Nokia*, which has had "a seemingly versatile line-up in terms of visual appearance, but nurtures more consistent designs within various stylistic and functional categories" (Person et al., 2007, p. 908).

As far as the organisation's *succession of product generations* is concerned, the firm has a similar decision to make between launching the product in similar styling to the one used over time or in a very different styling. Person et al. (2007) point to *Bang & Olufsen* audio-visual systems and *Volkswagen's Golf* as exemplars of how companies use similarity over product generations. Maintaining a certain styling over the succession of product generations allows firms to (1) establish recognition for the new product since customers will be able to instantly guess the organisation behind the new product, (2) transfer symbolic meanings across the products of a brand (similar to the above case), as well as create symbolic meaning (highlighting the important stylistic characteristics that have been maintained throughout generations), and (3) develop brand icons (rendering these stylistic characteristics with a degree of iconicity) (Person et al., 2007). Alternatively, the organisation might opt to launch the new product in a very different styling to what its predecessors had. Following this approach will allow the firm to draw attention (similar to above), reposition the product in the minds of the consumers (potentially targeting a different consumer segment), and ensure that it adapts to fashion trends and customer preferences (Person et al., 2007).

Finally, the organisation must decide its stylistic strategy in comparison to the *products of the competitors*. Naturally, brand authenticity is marketing's mantra and any designer would decry imitation; however, there are cases where the organisation might choose to launch a product with similar styling to the competitors. Besides the ephemeral goals of getting the customer confused to the extent that he/she might buy an imitator by mistake, and/or persuading the customer to believe that the imitator originates from the original brand or has similarities with the original (in both instances, the firm will not develop a successful brand in the long term), such approach can actually achieve long-term strategic goals. It can establish recognition of the functionality of the product (Monö, 1997; Southgate, 1994) because similar styling can create 'points-of-parity' (POP) associations. These are attributes that are shared with competing products in the market, which are necessary for the product to be considered a legitimate member of the product category (known as category POPs) or are developed to negate the competitors' 'points-of-difference' (POD) associations (known as competitive POPs) (Keller et al., 2012). In addition, similar styling can transfer symbolic meaning as in the previous cases. Contrastingly, the organisation might choose to have a different styling to draw the consumers' attention, establish PODs by emphasising distinctiveness (consider, for instance, *Dyson* vacuum cleaners), and by improving recognition of origin (Person et al., 2007).

The design strategy development process

In order to understand how to develop a design strategy, it is important to view design and design thinking as an organisational resource, in the same way that management has always regarded money, physical property, and human resources as important resources to organisational success. On that basis, we can explore how design can be managed in a way that contributes to the organisation achieving its strategic objectives. Studying extant literature on design strategy frameworks, we can see a strong connection of these frameworks with conventional and widely accepted marketing strategy frameworks, as well as with more contemporary and cutting-edge thinking on strategic innovation management.

Drawing from the growing pedagogy of design strategy and from contemporary research on the topic, Holland and Lam (2014) developed the 4Ds of strategic design management framework. The stages of this framework correlate with the stages of the strategic marketing management process as outlined by Wilson and Gilligan (2004), as well as with a model of strategic innovation management developed by *IDEO*'s Jacoby and Rodriguez (2008). All models emulate the management practice

Figure 4.3 Design strategy development process.

of an 'internal audit–strategic vision–strategic plan–evaluation' process (see Figure 4.3) as we will discuss below. The stages of the different models are going to be explored in parallel in order to illustrate, even more clearly, the correlations between them.

Internal audit: Where are we?

In the first stage of the process, the organisation needs to conduct an internal audit to answer the question of 'where are we?' Particularly, in relation to design, Holland and Lam (2014) call this the stage of '*determining*'(the first D), where the organisation assesses its perception and confidence in the design use. An organisation needs to regularly assess its design activities and the role design and innovation have in its strategy and corporate culture. Drawing from research of its internal and external environments, the organisation needs to regularly carry out a design audit. This will allow the firm to formulate an appropriate and successful design strategy.

Design audits

Inspired by financial, management, legal, and environmental audits, Cooper and Press (1995) discussed the concept of the *design audit* and argued that, similar to any other type of audit, the design audit suffers from the same problems with respect to the question of defining its boundaries, determining the criteria for assessment, deciding on its implementation, and recognising whose responsibility it is. In preparation for the design audit, the organisation has to answer a number of *preliminary questions*. Firstly, it has to decide the levels of design audit and hence what it is going to audit. It is also imperative to determine the aim and objectives of the audit, who will be responsible for commissioning it, as well as who will undertake it. Details of the audit have to be determined in terms of the questions that it is going to address, how the data will be collected, when the audit will be carried out, and how much it will cost. It is also very important to determine from the outset what criteria will be used to determine level of achievement and what these criteria mean. The organisation should also envision what outcome is expected from the process, plan how the findings will be used or implemented, and indicate who will be responsible for acting on the recommendations. Finally, it is important to determine how the organisation will evaluate the audit process itself after its completion. This will ensure that any problems are recognised and dealt with, so that the process is improved for the next audit (Cooper & Press, 1995).

According to Cooper and Press (1995), there are four levels of the design audit. First, *the physical manifestation of design level*, where the organisation needs to analyse its visual identity, corporate design standards, product and work environments, on pre- and post-project bases. Second, the *design management level*, which includes an analysis of the design resources, the design skills and training, the design processes, procedures, guidelines, and the funding for design, including investment and return on investment. It also includes the location, services, aims and objectives of the design department, and the general project management processes followed by the organisation. Third, the *corporate culture level* which involves analysing the corporate design strategy, design awareness and understanding that exists within the organisation, who the design champions are within the organisation, the integration of design and other functions, and the organisation's current design activities. Fourth, the *environmental factors level* is concerned with an analysis of the legislation, market trends, competitor trends, and design trends which can have an impact on the corporate and design strategy (Figure 4.4).

In relation to the possible aims and objectives of the design audit, these might be, firstly, to *advise and direct strategic change* within the organisation; for instance, changes in the competitors' activity,

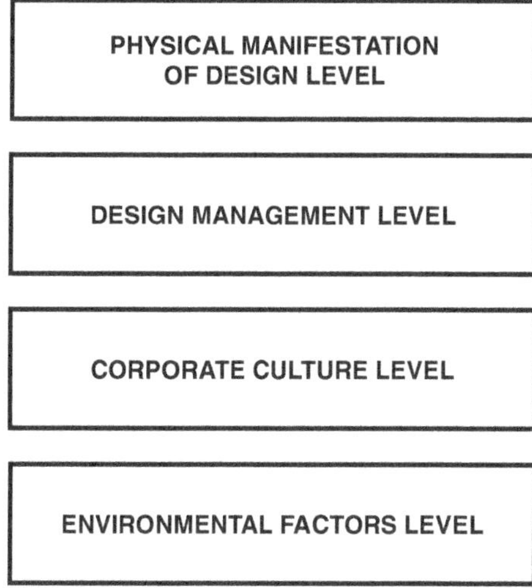

Figure 4.4 Four levels of the design audit.

as well as the dynamic market forces, might suggest the need for repositioning the organisation through a refreshed corporate identity programme. A second aim might be to *improve the overall standards of the products' design*, drawing from the results of a benchmarking process where the organisations' products are compared with those of the competitors. Thirdly, the organisation might seek to *develop a (new) design policy manual* and *monitor the implementation of this policy* on a regular basis. Finally, the firm might want to *improve design standards*; having set targets for design standards or policy, it is important that the organisation monitors its current position and identifies methods for improvement (Cooper & Press, 1995). Audits which seek to advise and direct strategic change can be carried out on an ad hoc basis or can occur in accordance with periodic strategic planning. If the aim of the audit relates to the design of a new product/service offering, then pre-project audits should occur before the onset of the product/service development or when a weakness in the current offering is identified, and post-project audits may be used to evaluate the level of success achieved by the new product/service offering. Those audits which are concerned with policy implementation tend to be performed on an annual basis. Finally, audits concerned with design management should occur at any time according to management needs (Cooper & Press, 1995).

As far as *the person who will conduct the audit* is concerned, he/she could be someone who has no vested interest in the process' outcome, has the right knowledge of how to carry out the audit and what questions to ask, and has an understanding of the design process. Thus, design managers are well placed to carry out such an audit. The decision about the person responsible for carrying out the design audit should be made based on the audit subject, the aims and objectives, and how the audit is to be undertaken. When the audit aims to assess current overall position of the organisation against competitors, external auditors are appropriate to ensure objectivity. Internal auditors are appropriate when an internal team will incorporate all key organisational functions including design, guaranteeing a broad perspective. An internal team is suitable to all levels of design audit, in particular to the 'physical' design audits. There can also be cases where an internal audit team takes over from an external auditor after his/her work has been carried out.

With one of the earliest publications on the strategic role of design in the marketing process, Kotler and Rath (1984) provided us with two sets of questions that can be asked during a design audit. One that can assist the organisation to evaluate its sensitivity to design, and one to assess its design management effectiveness. Their design sensitivity audit questions include understanding the role the company assigns to design in the marketing decision process, as well as determining to what extent design thinking is utilised in product development, environmental design, information design, and in corporate identity design work. Their proposed design management effectiveness audit questions are about identifying the orientation design staff follow, along with assessing whether or not they have an adequate budget to carry out design analysis, planning, and implementation. Another important question relates to whether or not the organisation's senior management encourage creative experimentation and design within the firm. How close is the working relationship of designers with people in marketing, sales, engineering, and research also needs to be determined. Finally, Kotler and Rath (1984) suggest that the organisation needs to assess whether or not designers are held accountable for their work through post-evaluation measurement and feedback. Irrespective of which design audit tool the organisation chooses to adopt, it is vital to ensure that the design audit covers all aspects of design from top to bottom of the organisational structure.

Determining the innovation bias

The stage of the internal audit can also include the organisation assessing its innovation bias in relation to human, technology, and business issues (Jacoby & Rodriguez, 2008). First, there might be bias as a result of the organisation narrowly defining its existing target audiences (*human bias*). The question the team might ask is how the firm can become more relevant to people outside its existing markets. Second, there might be bias in relation to how the organisation leverages new technology in the marketplace (*technology bias*). Third, *business bias* stems from a narrow view on how innovation might allow the organisation to win share from the competitors in the growing market (Figure 4.5). These three types of bias relate to the three overlapping criteria for judging the success of an idea: human desirability, technology feasibility, and business viability, respectively (Brown, 2009) (discussed in Chapter 3). Jacoby and Rodriguez (2008) argue that the most successful organisations are those that deal with the human desirability issues early in the process. As they explain:

> You must uncover human needs to design compelling user value propositions. Otherwise, why would anyone want to buy what you sell? Technology and business … are critical elements of any innovation effort, but we view them as lenses with which to enhance and refine the user value proposition as we proceed with an innovation journey. The trick is to lead with human needs and balance all three perspectives.
>
> (Jacoby and Rodriguez, 2008, p. 44)

The organisation wishing to assess the potential innovation bias within its teams and culture should ask a number of questions related to origin and outlook, decisions, and teams. It is essential to understand *where the innovation and growth projects originate in the organisation*, i.e., what function, which job role, and who exactly instigates such projects. The firm should avoid the trap of becoming too technology-driven that they value less the user-driven insights identified by its marketing team, or becoming too marketing-led where they ignore business model or technology opportunities because they deem them too risky for the brand. Therefore, identifying what is the dominant view within the organisation can help the firm understand whether it is missing opportunities (marketing myopia). Secondly, the organisation should understand *how decisions on innovation projects are made*. It is important to

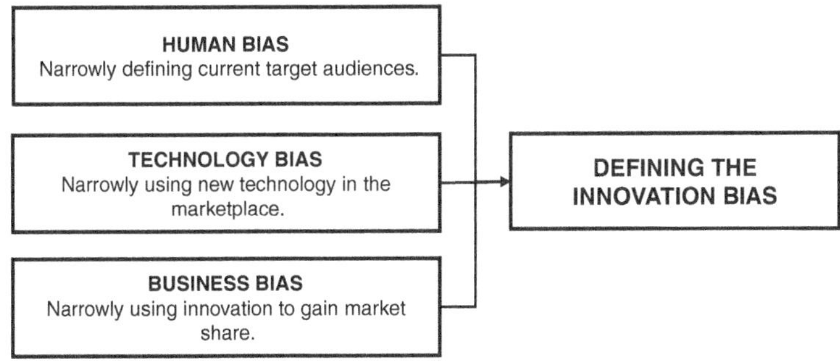

Figure 4.5 Defining the innovation bias.

ensure that powerful staff with veto rights do not shut down promising user value propositions right from the start. Thirdly, the organisation must evaluate *whether and how the people* who address the three aforementioned criteria of human desirability, technical feasibility, and business viability *work together* on the same team. There needs to be a high level of collaboration, and any handoffs need to be properly managed. Finally, the organisation must question *whether the necessary iterations between the three criteria are performed*, before making decisions to prototype, proceed, or abandon an innovation project. As Jacoby and Rodriguez explain, "once an organisation or a team realise that innovation effectiveness requires a balance of human, technical, and business factors, it is more likely to consider and frame innovation opportunities in a way that leads to success in the market" (2008, p. 45).

Strategic vision: Where do we want to go?

In the second stage of the process, the organisation needs to make a decision on its strategic vision and the general direction it wants to take; this will, therefore, answer the question of 'where do we want to go?' This is the stage in the conventional strategic marketing management process where the organisation sets its strategic direction. According to Holland and Lam (2014), this is the '*defining*' stage (the second D) where the firm needs to establish visions, strategic directions, and opportunities for design. This relates to our discussion on design research in Chapter 2, whereby organisations identify opportunities for design activities. In this stage, it is imperative to determine where the organisation wants to be in the marketplace and in the customers' mind (related to the concept of positioning in marketing terms) and how design can help the organisation to achieve that. As Holland and Lam suggest, the "effective use of design strategy will lead to the identification of alternative strategies to achieve the defined goals and support the use of creative artistic talents to differentiate the offer" (2014, p. 51).

Innovation and growth

This stage can also be associated with the second stage of the strategic innovation management process developed by Jacoby and Rodriguez (2008) where the organisation should seek to establish why it is trying to innovate. Fundamentally (and ideally) an organisation wants to innovate because it is driven by the goal of delivering experiences that make people's life better. Notwithstanding such 'altruistic' motives, realistically, an organisation aims to innovate for the additional (yet crucial) economic benefits. Profit delivered as a result of the innovation is needed to justify the expenditure of time, effort, and financial capital. In short, the main organisational goal is growth. Understanding the standard and extraordinary reasons that the organisation wants to innovate for is a very fundamental stage that needs to be completed successfully.

Strategic plan: How might we get there?

The third stage of the process involves the organisation devising the necessary plans to achieve the strategic vision determined in the previous stage. In strategic marketing management terms, this involves the organisation evaluating the routes available and making a strategic choice about how to get to its desired 'place'. Thus, this stage answers the question of 'how might we get there?' Particularly, in relation to design, this is where the organisation looks into using design thinking to develop strategies and solutions (explored in Chapter 3). Holland and Lam (2014) describe this stage as '*designing*' (the third D in their framework). They argue that this stage needs to combine what they call the 'big-D' and the 'small-d' design, which brings together systems design such as product planning and brand communication, with the actual practice of design, such as product design, packaging design, and interior design. The close relationship between the two is significant, and good communication among practitioners is pivotal for the success of the design strategy. Keinonen (2008) argues that design strategy is needed both at the 'nucleus' of the organisation, i.e., the strategic level, as well as at the tactical and operational levels. On the strategic level, the organisation turns its vision into tangible plans in relation to the organisation's brand promises and competitive advantages, and on the tactical level, in relation to unique selling propositions and the product portfolio. At the operational level, the organisation develops the design attributes in relation to every brand touchpoint. The goal here is to create differentiation and make the user experience special and memorable (Holland & Lam, 2014).

'Ways-to-grow' matrix

Jacoby and Rodriguez's (2008) strategic innovation management process includes at this stage the need for the organisation to determine how it intends to grow and innovate. In order to achieve this, they provide us with the 'Ways-to-Grow' matrix. This matrix consists of two axes, where in one axis we find 'existing users–new users', and in the other axis, 'existing offers–new offers' (see Figure 4.6).

As they explain, organic growth can be brought from differentiating within an existing market (e.g., mobile phones), creating a completely new market (e.g., introduction of the *iPad* in

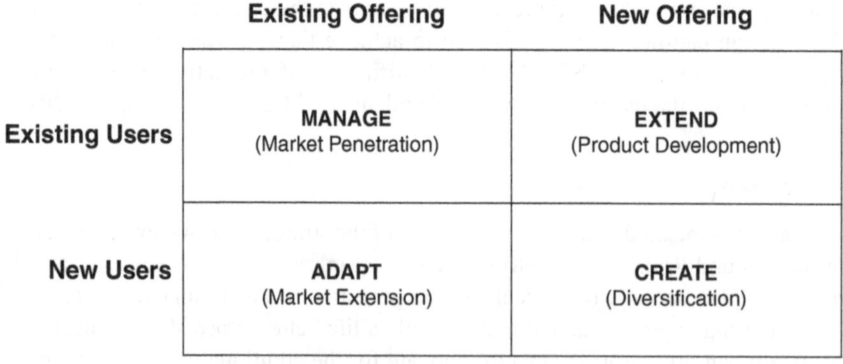

Figure 4.6 Ways-to-grow matrix.

2010), or by jump-starting a declining industry (e.g., vinyl records industry). It is certain that any business student or executive would notice the resemblance of this matrix with Ansoff's (1957) 'Growth Vector' matrix in strategic marketing management, where instead of 'offerings' we have 'products', and instead of 'users' we have 'markets'. Based on this matrix, there are four options/combinations: market penetration (targeting current markets with current products), market extension (targeting new markets with current products), product development (using new products to target current markets), and diversification (creating new products to target new markets) (Ansoff, 1957).

The four options deriving from Jacoby and Rodriguez's (2008) matrix are: (1) manage, (2) extend, (3) adapt, and (4) create. When the organisation decides that the way to grow is by targeting existing users with an existing offering, it will have to *manage* this offering through a number of choices such as raising its price, raising its usage, or attempting to win even more share from the market (similar to market penetration). The firm might choose to target existing users with new offerings, hence it will have to *extend* its brand portfolio and hence its share of the users' wallet by further leveraging existing users (similar to product development). It might decide to *adapt* by targeting new users with existing offerings in order to expand its footprint and win more share of a new market segment (similar to market extension). Finally, the organisation might select to *create* a completely new offering in order to create a new market (similar to diversification) or disrupt existing ones.

At this point, Jacoby and Rodriguez (2008) argue that it is important that the organisation articulates how it intends to grow and then match this intention to an innovation outcome. This requires an honest discussion within the organisation, which can be instigated by asking a number of questions. Firstly, the firm must identify how new is the user, hence it has to determine whether the user will experience the offering in a new context, whether this context is new for the offering, whether the offering is going to be used in a different occasion (time), what the user is trying to accomplish with the offering, and whether the users' emotions, hopes, and aspirations are new to organisation's endeavours to date. Another set of questions relate to how new the organisation should make the offering. In particular, the firm must define its value proposition in terms of the new visceral (related to beauty), reflective (conveying a sense of identity), and behavioural (functional) benefits and attributes that can be provided to the user. Preferably, the offering will include all three types of benefits and attributes (Jacoby & Rodriguez, 2008).

The organisation must also understand whether the user will have to shift his personal frame of reference in order to compare price or make decisions. This means whether there are new demand side aspects of the business model, in terms of pricing, frequency of payment, or modes of ownership, that need to be determined. The user journey needs also outlining in relation to where, when, how, and why might the user experience the offering; this means the firm needs to determine which components of messaging, sample, trial, usage, disposal, reuse, and maintenance are critical in shaping the user's experience. Finally, technology is an important issue; the organisation must determine whether it could use technologies that are new to its portfolio or new to the people who will use them (Jacoby & Rodriguez, 2008).

Following this, Jacoby and Rodriguez (2008) argue that it is important to recognise the outcome associated with the organisation's growth intention. Doing so allows the firm to design the process and evaluate its efforts with outcomes in mind. Through their experience at *IDEO*, they have distinguished three archetypes of innovation outcomes: (1) *incremental innovation* which relates to the organisation targeting existing users with existing offerings ('manage', similar to market penetration); (2) *evolutionary innovation* where the organisation targets existing users with a new offering ('extend', similar to product development) and hence extending current offerings to satisfy unmet needs of existing customers (Brown, 2009), or new users with existing offerings ('adapt', similar to market extension) and hence adapting current offerings to meet the needs of new customers (Brown, 2009); and (3) *revolutionary innovation*, where new users with new offerings forms the organisation's strategy ('create', similar to diversification). Brown (2009) argues that incremental innovation is important and the majority of the organisation's efforts will be directed towards such type of innovation, leading to the next iteration of a current product. The other two types of innovation are equally important because evolutionary innovation stretches the organisation's product base in new directions, and revolutionary innovation creates entirely new markets albeit being the riskiest type of the three. Brown (2009) argues that all types of innovation are required, because

> although the imagination may be drawn to the once-in-a-lifetime smash hits, they are few and far between. And though it may be tempting to focus on incremental projects in which business forecasts are easy to make, this short-sighted approach leaves companies vulnerable to … unforeseeable events.
>
> (Brown, 2009, p. 165)

Once the organisation has decided on the appropriate innovation process, it must assign the right people to the team and select the right outcome measures to evaluate success. This leads us to the next, and final, stage of the process.

Evaluation: How do we know when we have got there?

In the fourth and final stage of the process, the organisation needs to evaluate the outcomes, to establish whether its strategic vision has been delivered. This relates to the stage of strategic implementation and control in the strategic marketing management process (Wilson & Gilligan, 2004) and helps the firm answer the question of "how do we know when we have got there?" ('how can we ensure arrival?'). Here the organisation must evaluate its strategic activities on a regular basis to determine whether its objectives have been or are being achieved. Holland and Lam (2014) describe this as the '*deciding*' stage (the last D in their framework), and they highlight the importance of setting unambiguous performance targets. They argue that the intangibility of the qualitative benefits often included in design strategy should not be used as an excuse for a lack of rigorous measurement criteria. Even the most intangible of benefits can be determined, and as design management scholarship and practice evolves, we become more proficient at proving the links between good design and strategic success (Holland & Lam, 2014). At the strategic level, the organisation can question whether it is becoming more creative and how well design is used to generate vision and self-belief. At the tactical level, the firm may want to measure the profit generated, percentage of market share, and growth rates as a result of the design strategy. At the operational level, the firm can assess efficiency in relation to output and budget compliance and effectiveness of the strategy by questioning whether it is following the right route and whether it meets or exceeds customer expectations. The organisation's practice in setting measurement criteria and targets will affect the motivation of the design team and business executives to meet these targets (Holland & Lam, 2014).

Measures of innovation effectiveness

In Jacoby and Rodriguez's (2008) strategic innovation management framework, the organisation must evaluate the strategic innovation activities undertaken, in terms of three measures of innovation effectiveness: (1) *financial measures*, determining what is the net present value of the innovation initiatives – in other words, identifying whether the activities create or destroy value; (2) *brand measures*, measuring whether the activities are creating loyal fans in the marketplace by building emotional currency for the brand; and (3) *learning measures*, where the organisation in a reflexive manner must question what it has learned from the process and identify what the options are for the future.

Design strategies for innovation diffusion

In 1943, Ryan and Gross published a research paper in the *Rural Sociology* journal discussing the diffusion of hybrid seed corn in two Iowa communities in the United States. What they did not predict at the time is that their findings would provide the roots for the development of one of the most fundamental marketing concepts, Everett Rogers' seminal 'diffusion of innovation' theory. According to Rogers (1962), consumers adopt ideas, technologies, and products at varying speed, due to their differentiating psychological disposition to new ideas. To remind the reader, Rogers (1962) classified consumers in five categories: (1) the *innovators* (2.5% of the population) who are the first to adopt an innovation as they are risk-takers who have the desire and the resources to try new things, even if they fail; (2) the *early adopters* (13.5% of the population) who are more selective about which innovation they adopt and are considered the ones to 'check in with' for new information which can reduce the uncertainty associated with adopting the innovation; (3) the *early majority* (34% of the population) who take more time to adopt an innovation; they do so only when they understand how it fits into their lives; (4) the *late majority* (34% of the population) who adopt the innovation because of peer pressure, emerging social norms, or as a result of economic necessity, and before they adopt the innovation, any uncertainty must be resolved; and finally (5) the *laggards* (16% of the population) who are quite conservative, are economically constrained to take risks, and make decisions based on past experiences.

Drawing from Rogers' (1962) work, Canada et al. (2008) explored how the effective application of design strategy can ensure the successful adoption, diffusion, and management of new technologies. They identified six different design strategies, of which the first five correspond to the five categories in Rogers' (1962) typology (Figure 4.7). When introducing a new technology to the world, the organisation will need to appeal to innovators and early adopters. At this stage the firm needs to '*endorse*' the new technology by explaining its benefits and functions to the population and showcasing its viability. It is essential that the organisation shows that the new technology complies with regulations and is designed in a way that it leverages its strengths and minimises any potential problems (Canada et al., 2008).

Next, the organisation will need to '*curate*' the new technology as it starts to reach the early adopters. Here, companies need to emphasise aspects of the offering that demonstrate specific benefits and a particular use. Curating is often achieved through iconic and simple designs which are easily understood. Therefore, it makes sense that many unfamiliar technologies have adopted the formal clarity of Bauhaus Modernism and its intellectual successors. This stage "is a lot like being the curator of a museum. You need to select your pieces, have a clear point of view, and guide visitors through the experience" (Canada et al., 2008, p. 63). However, if the organisation wants to start reaching the mainstream market – the early majority – it has to '*integrate*' the offering into people's habits and routines. The technology has to be able to adapt, connect, and respond to other offerings the early majority already uses. The goal here is to make sure the new offering 'looks good in the living room' rather than it stands out. Such integrating design strategy will render the new offering with its mass appeal, transforming it from novel niche to household name. Flexible platforms will allow the organisation to customise the offering for a multiplicity of applications, customer segments, and distribution channels.

Further market penetration, i.e., reaching the late majority, can be achieved by cost-cutting and commoditising strategies. At this stage, the organisation will choose to '*economise*', in other words, create more economical solutions that reduce the barriers to adoption of the new offering, because the late majority are often convinced to try something new because of peer pressure or economic necessity. Such strategy is suitable to firms which operate in mature product sectors where the value of the technology is

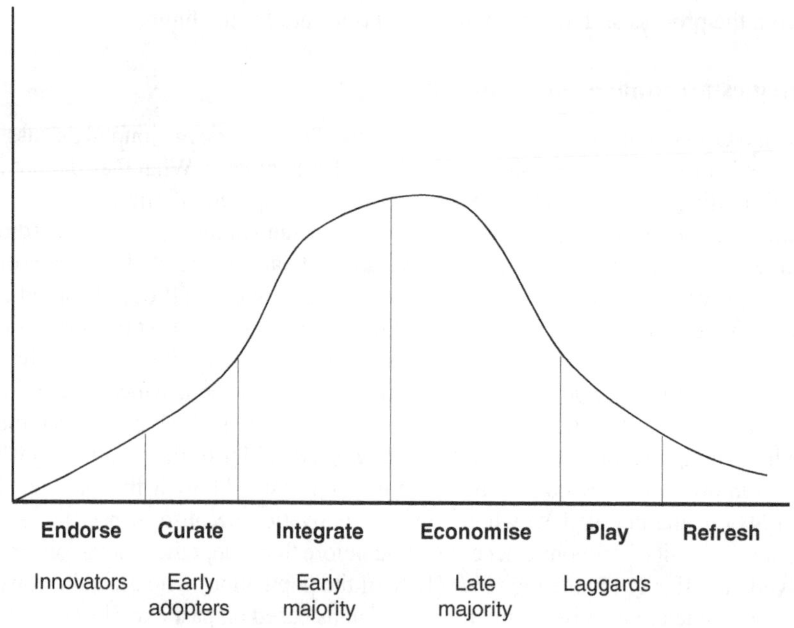

Figure 4.7 Design strategies for innovation diffusion.

generally accepted. Canada et al. argue that "the secret of designing to economise [is] not cutting corners arbitrarily, but analysing successful high-end solutions in a market and figuring out which corners could be cut to create a new low-cost alternative" (2008, p. 65). The journey of the new offering is not however finished. The organisation can try to appeal to laggards too. The challenge here is to uncover ways to create value which are not dependant on technical differentiation. Due to the wide adoption of the new offering, designers have the opportunity to '*play*' with something different by bringing innovative forms to established product categories, making the familiar unfamiliar. Consider, for instance, the launch of the *Swatch* brand in the early 1980s, where the omnipresence of wrist-watches meant consumers were ready for a play of artsy, cheeky, and unconventional watch designs, resurrecting the fortunes of Swiss market leader *SMH* (later the organisation changed its own corporate name to *Swatch*).

Going beyond the stage where the technology has reached universal adoption requires the organisation to find ways of reinventing the category by identifying ways to '*refresh*' the technology, which at this point might have become obsolete. Refreshing the technology might involve identifying novel ways of using it. Canada et al. (2008) raise the example of LP records and record-players still used by amateur and professional DJs in an era where all consumers use *iPods* and *iPhones* to listen to music. *Technics* has responded to DJs' needs by creating products that have refreshed the way an old technology is used, designing products that better handle reverse spins, audio fades, and variable speeds. In conclusion, by making connections between the diffusion of innovation theory and design strategy, design managers instead of giving up the introduction of "new technologies to the market or relying on random luck for success … [they] can craft strategies that play to their strengths, minimise risk, drive adoption, and ultimately fulfil their companies' larger growth objectives" (Canada et al., 2008, p. 66).

Chapter review questions

The following questions can help you reflect on the material we have covered in Chapter 4:

1 Discuss the overall contribution of design to corporate strategy, making references to marketing strategy and strategic management concepts.
2 Explain the concept of strategic renewal and illustrate the process by which design can contribute to strategic renewal of an organisation.
3 How does design contribute to the visual recognition of brands?
4 Provide strategic recommendations to organisations wishing to use design styling as a strategic tool.
5 Discuss the stages of developing a design strategy making connections with strategic marketing management and innovation management frameworks.
6 Recommend the appropriate design strategy for a new organisational offering in relation to Rogers' (1962) diffusion of innovation stages.

Recommended reading

1 Karjalainen, T. M., & Snelders, D. (2010). Designing visual recognition for the brand. *Journal of Product Innovation Management, 27*(1), 6–22.
2 Jacoby, R., & Rodriguez, D. (2008). Innovation, growth, and getting to where you want to go. In T. Lockwood, & T. Walton (Eds.), *Building design strategy: Using design to achieve key business objectives*. New York: Allworth Press.
3 Canada, A., Mortensen, P., & Patnaik, D. (2008). Design strategies for technology adoption. In T. Lockwood, & T. Walton (Eds.), *Building design strategy: Using design to achieve key business objectives*. New York: Allworth Press.

Reflective thoughts

Let's get emotional about design strategy

Dr. Mary Maclachlan
Senior Lecturer in Product Design
Glasgow Caledonian University, Glasgow, UK

This chapter outlines the differences and coherences between design strategy and strategic design and describes how strategic design can drive design philosophy to influence purchasing behaviour and brand loyalty. In today's competitive and crowded marketplace, organisations are challenged to differentiate themselves, stand out, and sustain and grow their customer base. The chapter discusses how design strategies can be used to do this by creating emotional connections with consumers. The strategies surrounding emotional aspects of design are becoming more embedded in common design practice and are more widely recognised in how organisations are defining their design philosophies. The most prevalent strategies can be categorised

(Continued)

(Continued)

into the following: pleasure, memories and product narrative, personality, self-expression and product personalisation, and novelty and sensory design.

Jordan (2000) advocates a *pleasure* approach to design, encouraging designers to address the emotional needs of their consumers. He compares Maslow's (1943) 'hierarchy of needs' to a hierarchy of consumer needs. He describes Maslow's theory in simple terms; when people get used to having something, they begin to look for something more. In relation to products, users expect, first and foremost, that a product performs the function for which it was intended. Once the user is satisfied that the product can perform the intended task, they will begin to expect it to be easy to use. Once usability is satisfied, they will begin to seek emotional benefits. Jordan (2000) argues that current human factor considerations within design ironically are de-humanising, as they consider humans as little more than cognitive and physical processors and ignore the emotional responses that users have from using and experiencing products. Furthermore, consumers have now come to expect usability in the products they use; they are no longer pleasantly surprised when a product is easy to use but are unpleasantly surprised if it is difficult to use, resulting in negative emotional connections. Using a pleasure approach as a design strategy, which seeks to satisfy the top tier of the hierarchy of consumer needs, could provide enhanced user experience and product attachment.

Product attachment presents an interesting and conflicting strategic direction for an organisation, as it implies that consumers will be so satisfied with their products that they will have no need to upgrade or trade in, which creates a marketing paradox. However, product attachment does have significant value in supporting a sustainable design philosophy and is therefore a very commendable and desirable strategic direction for some organisations. Csikszentmihalyi and Halton (1981) investigated consumers' attachments to material objects and found that *memories* play a significant role in establishing emotional and lasting relationships. They proposed that memories provide consumers with a reminder of who they are and where they have been. Chapman (2005) shares this view and proposes *product narrative* as a design strategy for responsible design, claiming that if users emotionally invest in their products they create a narrative that encourages them to cherish their products, therefore reducing the overconsumption of products.

Product personality is perhaps the most widely used and documented design strategy with leading researchers such as Jordan (2002) and Mugge, Govers, and Schoormans (2009) developing product personality scales to enable designers to profile the personalities of their products. Govers and Mugge (2004) advanced product personality as a design strategy to include Sirgy's (1982) 'self-congruity' theory. Self-congruity implies that consumers prefer products that reflect their own self-concept (e.g., Belk, 1988; Sirgy, 1982). Sirgy's (1982) self-congruity theory suggested that if a consumer makes a psychological comparison between their self-concept and a product, then their evaluation of that product would be positively influenced. Sirgy (1982) relates this to the human need to express and create a positive and consistent view of one self. This is something which the chapter relates to within the increasing role of culture in consumption. Based on Sirgy's (1982) self-congruity theory that consumers respond more positively to products that reflect their own self-concept, *product personalisation and self-expression* are also proposed as design strategies to enhance the emotional experience of the user (e.g. Franke & Piller, 2005; Kleine, Kleine, & Allen, 1995; Moreau & Herd, 2009). This is because product personalisation affords the user some control to express themselves through the personalisation of some aspect of the product.

The final strategy to reflect on is concerned with *sensory aspects* and the introduction of *novelty*. A study conducted by Schifferstein and Spence (2008) found that products that stimulated multiple senses created more pleasing user experiences. Ludden and Schifferstein (2009) further investigated multisensory experiences and suggested that in addition to engaging multi-senses to create coherent messages, creating incongruent messages could evoke an emotion of surprise. She also found that surprising products are perceived by consumers to be more interesting to interact with and can lead to increased product recognition. Introducing novelty and *surprise* within product design has always been of interest to designers due to the human nature to seek new and unfamiliar things (Hekkert, Snelders, & Van Wieringen, 2003). However, Whitfield's (1983) 'preference for prototypes' theory rejected novelty in favour of typicality, suggesting that people prefer the most typical examples within a product category. Conversely, Hekkert et al. (2003) argue that people prefer products with an optimal combination of both typicality and novelty. Introducing novelty as a design strategy should therefore be considerate to product heritage, and, as the chapter suggests, strike a balance with familiarity.

This chapter describes the intermediary goals of using design styling as a strategic tool to create symbolic meaning, draw attention, and establish recognition. Targeting the specific emotional design strategies presented in this reflection could provide focus to achieve these goals.

References

Belk, R. W. (1988). Possessions and the extended self. *Journal of Consumer Research, 15*(2), 139–168.

Chapman, J. (2005). *Emotionally durable design*. Trowbridge, UK: Cromwell Press.

Csikszentmihalyi, M., & Halton, E. (1981). *The meaning of things: Domestic symbols of the self.* Cambridge, UK: Cambridge University Press.

Franke, N., & Piller, F. T. (2005). Value creation by toolkits for user innovation and design: The case of the watch market. *Journal of Product Innovation Management, 21*(6), 401–415.

Govers, P. C. M., & Mugge, R. (2004). I love my jeep because its tough like me: The effect of product – personality congruence. In A. Kurtgözü (Ed.), *Proceedings of the Fourth International Conference on Design and Emotion*. Ankara, Turkey.

Hekkert, P., Snelders, D., & Van Wieringen, P. C. W. (2003). Most advanced, yet acceptable: Typicality and novelty as joint predictors of aesthetic preference in industrial design. *British Journal of Psychology, 94*(1), 111–124.

Jordan, P. W. (2000). *Designing pleasurable products: An introduction to the new human factors*. London: Taylor & Francis.

Kleine, S. S., Kleine, R. E., & Allen, C. T. (1995). How is a possession 'me' or 'not me'? Characterizing types and an antecedent of material possession attachment. *Journal of Consumer Research, 22*(3), 327–343.

Ludden, G. D. S., & Schifferstein, H. N. J. (2009). Should Mary smell like biscuit? Investigating scents in product design. *International Journal of Design, 3*(3), 1–12.

Maslow, A. (1943). Theory of human motivation. *Psychological Review, 50*(4), 370–396.

Moreau, C. P., & Herd, K. B. (2009). To each his own? How comparisons with others influence consumers' evaluations of their self-designed products. *Journal of Consumer Research, 36*(5), 806–819.

Mugge, R., Govers, P. C. M., & Schoormans, J. P. L. (2009). The development and testing of a product personality scale. *Design Studies, 30*(3), 287–302.

Schifferstein, H. N. J., & Spence, C. (2008). Multisensory product experience. In H. N. J. Schifferstein, & P. Hekkert (Eds.), *Product experience* (pp. 133–161). London: Elsevier.

Sirgy, M. J. (1982). Self-concept in consumer behaviour: A critical review. *Journal of Consumer Research, 9*(3), 287–300.

Whitfield, T. W. A. (1983). Predicting preference for familiar, everyday objects: An experimental confrontation between two theories of aesthetic behaviour. *Journal of Environmental Psychology, 3*(3), 221–237.

References

Ansoff, H. I. (1957). Strategies for diversification. *Harvard Business Review, 25*(5), 113–124.

Barney, J. (1991). Firm resources and sustained competitive advantage. *Journal of Management, 17*(1), 99–120.

Bloch, P. H. (1995). Seeking the ideal form: Product design and consumer response. *Journal of Marketing, 59*(3), 16–29.

Borja de Mozota, B. (2003). Design and competitive edge: A model for design management excellence in European SMEs. *Design Management Journal, 2*(1), 88–103.

Brown, S. L., & Eisenhardt, K. M. (1997). The art of continuous change: Linking complexity theory and time-paced evolution in relentlessly shifting organizations. *Administrative Science Quarterly, 42*(1), 1–34.

Brown, T. (2009). *Change by design: How design thinking transforms organisations and inspires innovation.* New York: HarperCollins.

Burgelman, R. A. (1991). Intraorganisational ecology of strategy making and organizational adaptation: Theory and field research. *Organization Science, 2*(3), 239–262.

Canada, A., Mortensen, P., & Patnaik, D. (2008). Design strategies for technology adoption. In T. Lockwood, & T. Walton (Eds.), *Building design strategy: Using design to achieve key business objectives.* New York: Allworth Press.

Cooper, R., & Press, M. (1995). *The design agenda: A guide to successful design management.* Chichester, UK: John Wiley & Sons.

de Bono, E. (1992). *Serious creativity: Using the power of lateral thinking to create new ideas.* New York: HarperCollins.

Dougherty, D. (1992). A practice-centered model of organizational renewal through product innovation. *Strategic Management Journal, 13*(1), 77–92.

Fuller, C. B., & Stopford, J. M. (1994). *Rejuvenating the mature business: The competitive challenge.* Cambridge, UK: Harvard Business Press.

Grant, R. M. (1996). Toward a knowledge-based theory of the firm. *Strategic Management Journal, 17*(S2), 109–122.

Holland, R., & Lam, B. (2014). *Managing strategic design.* London: Palgrave.

Jacoby, R., & Rodriguez, D. (2008). Innovation, growth, and getting to where you want to go. In T. Lockwood, & T. Walton (Eds.), *Building design strategy: Using design to achieve key business objectives.* New York: Allworth Press.

Jo Hatch, M., & Schultz, M. (1997). Relations between organizational culture, identity and image. *European Journal of Marketing, 31*(5/6), 356–365.

Jun, C. (2008). An evaluation of the positional forces affecting design strategy. *Design Management Journal, 3*(1), 23–29.

Karjalainen, T. M. (2004). *Semantic transformation in design: Communicating strategic brand identity through product design references.* Helsinki, Finland: University of Art and Design Helsinki.

Karjalainen, T. M., & Snelders, D. (2010). Designing visual recognition for the brand. *Journal of Product Innovation Management, 27*(1), 6–22.

Keinonen, T. (2008). Design in business: Views from the nucleus and the periphery. *Design Management Review, 19*(3), 30–36.

Keller, K. L., Apéria, T., & Georgson, M. (2012). *Strategic brand management: A European perspective* (2nd ed.). Harlow, UK: Pearson Education.

Kotler, P., & Alexander Rath, G. (1984). Design: A powerful but neglected strategic tool. *Journal of Business Strategy, 5*(2), 16–21.

Liedtka, J. (2015). Perspective: Linking design thinking with innovation outcomes through cognitive bias reduction. *Journal of Product Innovation Management, 32*(6), 925–938.

Loewenstein, G., & Angner, E. (2003). Predicting and indulging changing preferences. In G. Loewenstein, D. Read, & R. Baumeister (Eds.), *Time and decision: Economic and psychological perspectives on intertemporal choice* (pp. 351–391). New York: Russell Sage Foundation.

McCracken, G. (1986). Culture and consumption: A theoretical account of the structure and movement of the cultural meaning of consumer goods. *Journal of Consumer Research,* 71–84.

Manville, B., & Foote, N. (1996). Strategy as if knowledge mattered. *Fast Company, 2*(1), 66–67.

Mintzberg, H. (1994). *The rise and fall of strategic planning: Preconceiving roles for planning, plans, planners*. New York: Free Press.

Monö, R. (1997). *Design for product understanding: The aesthetics of design from a semiotic approach*. Stockholm, Sweden: Liber.

Olson, E. M., Cooper, R., & Slater, S. F. (1998). Design strategy and competitive advantage. *Business Horizons, 41*(2), 55–61.

Page, C., & Herr, P. M. (2002). An investigation of the processes by which product design and brand strength interact to determine initial affect and quality judgments. *Journal of Consumer Psychology, 12*(2), 133–147.

Pavlov, I. P. (1927). *Conditioned reflexes*. Oxford, UK: Oxford University Press.

Person, O., Snelders, D., Karjalainen, T. M., & Schoormans, J. (2007). Complementing intuition: Insights on styling as a strategic tool. *Journal of Marketing Management, 23*(9–10), 901–916.

Porter, M. E. (1979). How competitive forces shape strategy. *Harvard Business Review, 57*(2), 137–145.

Porter, M. E. (1980). *Competitive strategy: Techniques for analyzing industries and competitors*. New York: Free Press.

Porter, M. E. (1985). *Competitive advantage: Creating and sustaining superior performance*. New York: Free Press.

Quelch, J. A., & Kenny, D. (1994). Extend profits, not product lines. *Harvard Business Review, 72*(5), 153–160.

Ravasi, D., & Lojacono, G. (2005). Managing design and designers for strategic renewal. *Long Range Planning, 38*(1), 51–77.

Rogers, E. (1962). *Diffusion of innovations*. New York: Free Press.

Ryan, B., & Gross, N. C. (1943). The diffusion of hybrid seed corn in two Iowa communities. *Rural Sociology, 8*(1), 15.

Senge, P. (1990). *The fifth discipline: The art and science of the learning organization*. New York: Currency Doubleday.

Southgate, P. (1994). *Total branding by design: How to make your brand's packaging more effective*. London: Kogan Page.

Stabell, C. B., & Fjeldstad, Ø. D. (1998). Configuring value for competitive advantage: On chains, shops, and networks. *Strategic Management Journal, 19*(5), 413–437.

Stevens, J., & Moultrie, J. (2011). Aligning strategy and design perspectives: A framework of design's strategic contributions. *The Design Journal, 14*(4), 475–500.

Stopford, J. M., & Baden-Fuller, C. W. (1994). Creating corporate entrepreneurship. *Strategic Management Journal, 15*(7), 521–536.

Treacy, M., & Wiersema, F. (1993). Customer intimacy and other value disciplines. *Harvard Business Review, 71*(1), 84–93.

Warell, A. (2001). *Design syntactics: A functional approach to visual product form, theory, models, and methods*. Göteborg, Sweden: Chalmers University of Technology.

Wernerfelt, B. (1984). A resource-based view of the firm. *Strategic Management Journal, 5*(2), 171–180.

Wilson, R. M., & Gilligan, C. (1999). *Strategic marketing management*. London: Routledge.

5 Understanding individual and organisational creativity

Chapter aims and learning outcomes

This chapter aims to:

1 Define and understand the concept of creativity from a number of different perspectives.
2 Examine the different theoretical models of the creative process.
3 Discuss individual creativity as a function of a number of different elements.
4 Explore the concept of group creativity in the organisational context.
5 Discuss the determinants of organisational creativity.

Understanding design management cannot be achieved without a deep understanding of the concept of creativity and the different stages of the creative process. Creativity is the cornerstone of design and its process. A comprehension of creativity and how a creative act takes place can help us understand how designers and design teams work and how to improve the way we attempt to manage the design process. This chapter seeks to provide an understanding of the concept of creativity from different perspectives, as well as aims to discuss the different models of the creative process developed by social psychologists through a multiplicity of empirical studies. On the basis of such knowledge, we will also explore individual creativity, group creativity in the organisational setting, and identify the factors that affect organisational creativity. This will provide us with a deeper understanding of how we can ignite, facilitate, and enhance creativity among organisational members in a corporate setting.

Understanding creativity

There are three parameters by which creativity has been defined: (1) the creative process, (2) the creative person, and (3) the creative product (Warr & O'Neill, 2005). Our attempt to define and understand the concept of creativity will be structured in accordance with these parameters. We will also explore creativity from a macro- and a micro-perspective, referring to Simonton's (1975, 1980, 1999) work for the former and examining in depth Amabile's (1979, 1982, 1983a, 1983b) work for the latter.

The creative process perspective

Defining creativity in terms of the creative process involves understanding the internal human process through which ideas are generated. Gabora (2002) compares the human mind to a map of memory locations represented in neurons. Boden (1994) argues that the creative process is the individual's exploration and transformation of '*conceptual spaces*'. The exploration of conceptual spaces relates to the recall of memory locations, whereas the transformation of conceptual spaces relates to the formation of new associations between neurons to generate new ideas. Creativity, according to Koestler (1964), involves a 'bi-sociative process' whereby a person deliberately connects 'matrices of thought' which were previously unrelated, in order to produce a creative idea. A *matrix of thought* is an idea or concept in an individual's mind (Koestler, 1964). Adding to the current discourse on this perspective, Warr and O'Neill (2005) view creativity not only as an individual process but as a social or collaborative process, whereby the "matrices of thought that are to be combined in the generation of creative ideas are not necessarily in the mind of a single individual but may come from more than one person in the group" (Warr & O'Neill, 2005, p. 119). In addition, these matrices of thought are not only in the minds of the individuals but can exist as significant features in the environment that support cognition. Therefore, creativity is rather a 'multi-sociative' process of two or more related or unrelated matrices of thought in individuals' minds and the environment (Warr & O'Neill, 2005).

The creative person perspective

Defining creativity in terms of the creative person refers to earlier scholarly work of the 1950s to the 1970s. Scholars viewed creativity as a quality that few people possessed; these people were considered different in talent and personality, enough to be branded as 'geniuses' (Amabile & Pillemer, 2012). Creativity was seen as dependant on special qualities of unusual individuals, leading to the production of novel and appropriate ideas. The creative person has the personality traits that enhance the creative process because they allow the individual to explore and transform conceptual spaces more easily than other people who do not have these personality traits (Guildford, 1950). Although scholars in this stream of literature argue that it is the personality traits that lead to creativity, they seldom explain what these personality traits are. Gough (1979) attempted to determine these personality traits by developing the 'creativity personality scale' using an 'adjective check list', where some adjectives relate positively, and some other negatively, to creativity. Amabile (1983a, 1983b) questioned the appropriateness of such test scores, arguing that we should not label the score results as direct indication of creativity. The myth of the creative genius, i.e., the notion that creativity is only associated with geniuses who possess special qualities, has caused many problems in the creative industries, because it has separated creative from managerial work.

This means that there is often a lack of appropriate internal and external systems and processes to facilitate and enhance creativity within organisations. It is important to remember that creative and managerial work must not be separated. Especially in the case of the design sector, design is not art in its purest form; designers do not self-express; they have a design brief and a client to answer to. Design is 'commercial art'; it is all about the marriage of art and commerce, hence a synergy between the two is of absolute significance.

Amabile and Pillemer (2012) argue that there were five indications hinting that creativity was much more than what it was thought to be by scholars in this school of thought. First, if we study autobiographies and journals of well-known creative professionals, we would see that even these geniuses have good and bad days. "Their production of novel, appropriate work ebbed and flowed – often as a function, it seemed, of pressures, constraints, and other events impinging on them from their social environment" (Amabile & Pillemer, 2012, p. 4). Second, this fluctuating performance of these creative individuals was, as it appeared, the result of changing levels of motivation shifting from day to day and even from moment to moment. Third, there were other suggestions in early creativity literature that creativity was not a fixed quality of certain rare individuals, but a skill that can be learned, practiced, and improved over time. For instance, methods such as Osborn's (1957) brainstorming process promised to improve group problem-solving. Fourth, psychologist Crutchfield (1955, 1962) started publishing some provocative work on the situational forces that can affect conformity and its opposite which is creativity. Finally, Kruglanski, Friedman, and Zeevi (1971), using a randomised control experiment, showed that a manipulated socio-environmental factor, such as a desirable external reward for participation, can cause differences in creative behaviour. Interestingly, when participants were contracted to receive a reward, both the creative output and the participants' enjoyment of the task were lower.

The creative product perspective

Other scholars attempted to define creativity through understanding the 'creative product'. By creative product, we mean the creative result, not necessarily a physical product per se. The creative product is explained through two characteristics: novelty and appropriateness. Warr and O'Neill (2005) suggest that a novel idea is the combination of two or more matrices of thought, considered new or unusual. However, *novelty* is quite a subjective construct since what is considered novel by one person may seem conventional to another person. Boden (1994) likens novelty as belonging to one of two categories: (1) *psychological novelty* (*P-Novel*), which is an idea that is new to the mind in which it arose, although this does not mean that it might not have been thought by others before, and (2) *historical novelty* (*H-Novel*), which is an idea that is *P-Novel* and has never been thought of by anyone else before. Assessing whether the idea is *P-Novel* is much simpler than evaluating whether or not it is *H-Novel*. The former requires simply asking the individual to think retrospectively, whereas the latter requires crossing cultures and time to ensure that the idea had not occurred before. This means that assessing the *H-Novelty* of an idea is quite impossible. Bilton and Leary (2002) suggest that creativity which is related to *H-Novelty* demonstrates greater social significance and higher economic potential, but the principle in both cases is the same; it is all about novelty. The distinction might actually be a matter of good luck – having the right idea at the right time in the right place (Novitz, 1999).

Although novelty is important, it is not a sufficient characteristic of creativity. *Appropriateness* is the second characteristic that can moderate the creative (or no-creative) nature of the idea. An idea is considered appropriate when it conforms to the characteristics that have been set at the problem definition and preparation stage of the creative process. During the first stages of the creative process, individuals explore the problem determining a number of characteristics of the potential solutions. However, it is very likely that these characteristics vary from domain to domain, and from culture to culture. Hence, besides novelty, appropriateness too can be considered subjective. "The appropriateness of the [idea] should be assessed in relation to the setting for which the [idea] was intended" (Warr & O'Neill, 2005, p. 120).

Pulling together the research studies from these three different streams of literature, Warr and O'Neill (2005) provide a more comprehensive definition of creativity:

> Creativity is the generation of ideas, which are a combination of two or more matrices of thought, which are considered unusual or new to the mind in which the ideas arose and are appropriate to the characteristics of a desired solution defined during the problem definition and preparation stage of the creative process.
>
> (Warr and O'Neill, 2005, p. 122)

Micro- and macro-perspectives on creativity

Driven by the limitation of early definitions of creativity related to the creative person, many scholars sought to explore creativity in more depth and as a skill that can be taught and nurtured. Both Amabile

(1979, 1982, 1983a, 1983b) and Simonton (1975, 1980) embarked on exploring the social psychology of creativity, almost at the same time, albeit unbeknown to each other. They used different methods to explore the creativity phenomenon from different perspectives. Amabile (1979, 1982, 1983a, 1983b) concentrated on the immediate micro-level and sought to explore "how differences in the social environment surrounding task engagement might alter the creative behaviour of ordinary people" (Amabile & Pillemer, 2012, p. 5). In contrast, Simonton (1975, 1980) analysed archival data on great inventors and creators in history through historiometry, a sophisticated statistical method to understand how a number of social, cultural, and political factors affect creative success indicated by fame, eminence, originality, and productivity. Thus, he developed a social psychology of creativity from a macro-level perspective, exploring the wider social influences on well-respected creative persons in history. His work led to a 'Darwinian' theory of creativity (Simonton, 1999).

In this chapter we will concentrate on the micro-level perspective on creativity, and we will draw extensively from Amabile's (1979, 1982, 1983a, 1983b) work, which has been extremely influential in creativity research. Through her empirical work, Amabile (1982) developed a *consensual definition* of creativity, where she defined creativity as follows:

> A product or response is creative to the extent that appropriate observers [those familiar with the domain in question] independently agree it is creative … the quality of products or responses judged to be creative … and the process by which something so judged is produced.
>
> (Amabile, 1982, p. 997)

In addition, Amabile (1983b) provided a *conceptual definition*, which is comprised of two very important elements. She argues that "a product or response will be judged as creative to the extent that (a) it is both a novel and appropriate, useful, correct or valuable response to the task at hand, and (b) the task is heuristic rather than algorithmic" (Amabile, 1983b, p. 33). We can see a connection of this definition with the creative products' characteristics of novelty and appropriateness discussed above. However, there is also an extra element involved: the process.

Of course an important question here is what makes a task *algorithmic* or *heuristic*. Let us explore some examples. A chemist applying a well-known step-by-step synthesis chain process to produce a new hydrocarbon complex would not be considered a creative task even if the output was novel and appropriate. The same applies on the case of "an artist who followed the algorithm 'paint pictures of different sorts of children with large sad eyes, using dark-tinted backgrounds' would not be producing creative paintings, even if each painting were unique and technically perfect" (Amabile, 1983b, p. 33). One would, of course, wonder if this strips any design project with a well-defined design brief containing detailed instructions, off its creative nature. Such argument is certainly debatable. In general terms, there are many tasks that can be considered either algorithmic or heuristic, depending on the level of knowledge of the individual performer and on the goal at hand. If the goal is to produce an output with a predetermined process, the task is algorithmic, whereas if the goal is to produce the same output with a process that can be invented or thought out while the task is being pursued, then the task is certainly heuristic (Amabile, 1983b). With regard to the performer's knowledge about the task, if an algorithm for a certain task exists, but the performer is unware of it, then the task can be considered a heuristic task for this particular individual. In addition, for a task to be considered creative, judges must be able to determine whether the task is algorithmic or heuristic for this individual; in order to do so, they must rely on normative as well as ipsative criteria. The latter criteria involve information used to assess the nature of the task and the appropriate comparison group in a less subjective manner. Amabile (1983b) adds that creativity is also culturally and historically bound. The observers' judgements are certainly influenced by the cultural context and the historical time. This highlights the importance of 'reliable subjective judgement' that underpins creativity assessment (Amabile, 1983b).

Theoretical models on the creative process

Over the years, many empirical studies have attempted to map out the creative process. As a result, we have many models to explain the different stages that occur in the process of an individual being creative. Wallas (1926) was one of the first scholars to develop a model of the creative process. His model has four phases. First, *preparation* is the stage where the individual develops an understanding of the problem at hand in order to be able to develop a solution to this problem. This stage requires the individual to gather and review relevant data about the problem. Second, *incubation* requires the individual to step away from the task and refrain from consciously considering the problem. This is the stage where the individual might find himself/herself engaging in another activity. This, however, does not mean that the individual is wasting his/her time. In fact, "although conscious thought is suspended, the problem remains as an ambient thought awaiting some creative insight" (Warr & O'Neill, 2005, p. 120). Third, *illumination* is the stage where this creative insight occurs. This stage is often called the eureka or the 'aha!' moment. Nemiro suggests that this is when "there is a sudden change in perception, a new idea combination or a transformation that produces an acceptable solution to a problem at hand" (2004, p. 8). However, it is important that the individual verifies that the idea generated, indeed, provides the best solution to the problem. Hence, the individual must go through the final, *verification*, stage where he/she will evaluate the idea with respect to its novelty and appropriateness.

A later model of the creative process proposed by Osborn (1957) moved away from the notion of the unconscious stages of incubation and illumination, towards a more conscious process of intentionally coming up with ideas. He argued that the creative process is comprised of two main stages: (1) idea generation and (2) idea evaluation. *Idea generation* includes two sub-stages: *fact-finding* which is the process of defining the problem and preparing for the task, and *idea-finding* which is the process of generating novel ideas through the combination of old existing ideas. *Idea evaluation* is the stage where these novel ideas are evaluated for their appropriateness to the problem at hand.

Amabile's (1983a, 1983b) work led to a componential framework of the creative process which includes five stages. The first stage, *problem or task presentation*, involves the individual being presented with a problem or a task and what is involved. It is vital that the individual is highly motivated at this stage in order to have sufficient interest in pursuing the necessary activities that will lead to a solution. *Preparation*, as the second stage of the process, includes the individual accumulating knowledge about the problem or task and carrying out research about what might be the possible solution required. The third stage of the process is where the individual generates a response to the problem or task at hand; *response generation* is the illumination stage, otherwise known as the eureka moment we described above. *Validation* is the natural stage after, where the individual, based on his/her knowledge, needs to assess the validity of the idea generated, to ensure its novelty and appropriateness to the problem or task at hand. Finally, Amabile (1983a, 1983b) argues that there are three possible *outcomes* achieved at the last stage: (1) a complete attainment of the goal at which point the process ends, (2) no reasonable response possibilities generated, at which point the individual recognises that the process has failed and the process ends, and (3) there has been some progress towards the goal, at which point the individual understands that he/she must return to the first stage, i.e., the problem or task presentation, where the individual needs to reassess the problem or task at hand.

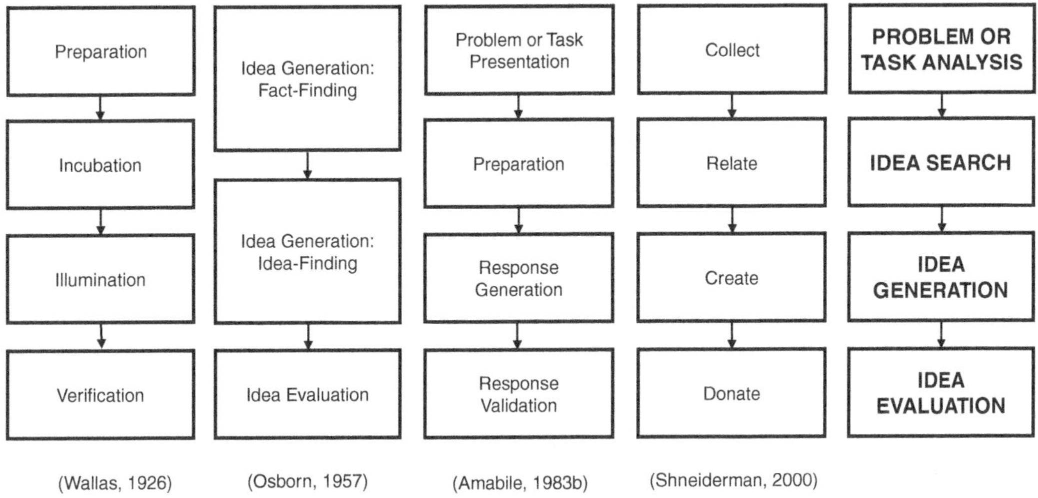

Figure 5.1 Theoretical models on the creative process.

More recently, Shneiderman (2000) described the creative process in terms of four stages. First, *collect* is about collecting information about the problem or task at hand, using a number of print and online resources. Second, *relate* is a very important stage which in fact is not actually a stage but an ongoing activity that needs to be performed throughout the process. Relate is about the individual consulting with peers and mentors; such consultation should be performed in an iterative manner, interweaved with the other stages. Third, *create* is the stage where the individual proposes, explores, and evaluates possible solutions. Fourth, *donate* is the stage where the results of the previous stages are disseminated. As Warr and O'Neill comment, "this stage may cause new needs to be identified or cause new ideas to be generated by the community who view the solutions, resulting in returning to previous stages in the model" (2005, p. 121).

If we were to compare the aforementioned models, we can see major similarities among them. The common themes we can identify is that all models suggest that there is an analytical stage, where the individual develops an understanding of the problem and prepares for the rest of the process. Once this has been achieved, the individual consciously or unconsciously searches for a solution to the problem or task at hand. This leads to idea generation and finally idea evaluation where the individual assesses the novelty and appropriateness of the solution proposed (Figure 5.1). It is important to clarify, at this point, that these models should not be viewed as linear processes; their stages are intertwined and iterative.

Individual creativity

With an interactionist model of creative behaviour at the individual level, Woodman and Schoenfeldt (1989, 1990) suggested that creativity is the complex outcome of a person's behaviour in a given situation. The situation is typified in terms of the contextual and social influences, which either allow or constrain creative accomplishment. This interactionist model combines the social psychology explanation of creativity (Amabile, 1983a, 1983b) with other explanations such as personality and cognition. Woodman and Schoenfeldt (1989, 1990) argue that individual creativity is a function of a number of different elements (Figure 5.2). Let us explore these in depth.

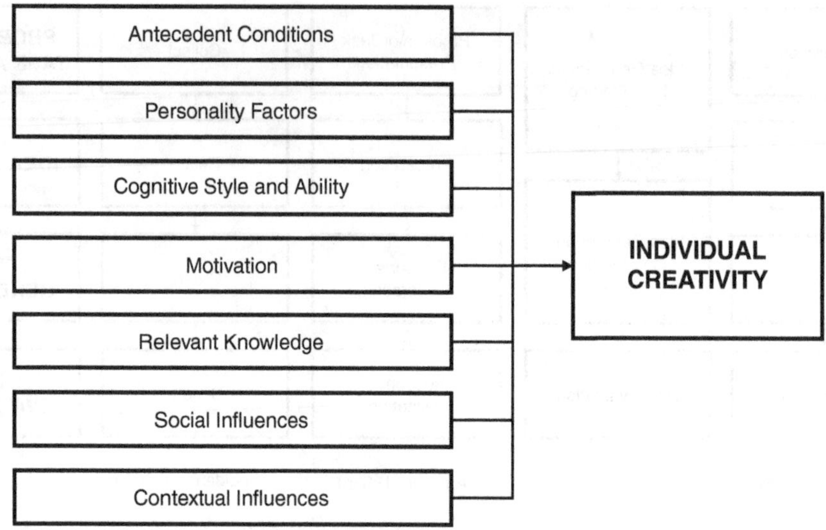

Figure 5.2 Determinants of individual creativity.

Antecedent conditions, personality, and cognitive factors

Antecedent conditions include biographical characteristics of the person in question and past reinforcement history. This element takes us back to the historiometric work of Simonton (1975, 1980). Results indicated specific sets of biographical variables that were differently associated with creative achievement, dependant on the area of achievement. Such conditions influence the personality and cognitive characteristics of the person, as well as the situation he/she is in (Woodman & Schoenfeldt, 1989, 1990). As far as *personality factors* are concerned, research has pointed towards a certain set of traits which include

> high valuation of aesthetic qualities in experience, broad interests, attraction to complexity, high energy, independence of judgement, autonomy, intuition, self-confidence, ability to resolve antinomies or to accommodate apparently opposite or conflicting traits in one's self concept, and a firm sense of self as creative.
>
> (Barron & Harrington, 1981, p. 453)

With respect to *cognitive factors*, Carrol (1985) determined eight factors that can influence idea generation, including associative fluency, fluency of expression, figural fluency, ideational fluency, speech fluency, word fluency, practical ideational fluency, and originality. In addition, individuals with high levels of field independence are capable of analysing situations without being distracted by irrelevant aspects. Guilford (1950) determined that individuals routinely engage in two different types of thinking, which constitute two different modes of operation: (1) *convergent thinking* which is all about concentrating, narrowing the mental focus until it converges on a solution, and (2) *divergent thinking* which is all about expanding, broadening the mental focus in many different directions to come up with new ideas. Guilford (1977, 1984) has identified that the cognitive processes of fluency, flexibility, originality, and elaboration are vital factors to divergent thinking, which is usually perceived as the cornerstone of creativity. However, we must emphasise that both types of thinking are important to

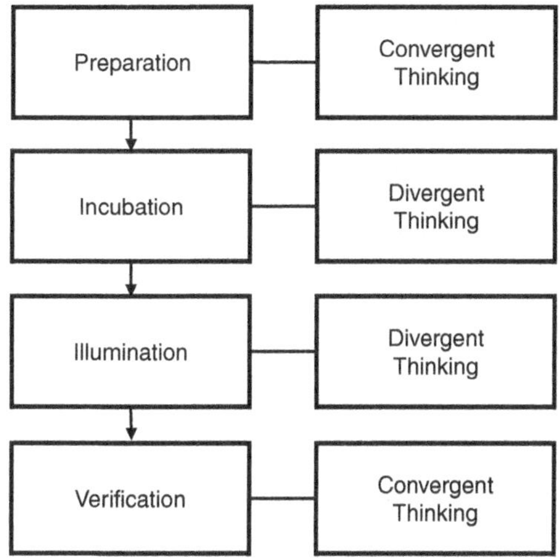

Figure 5.3 Types of thinking and the creative process.

creativity and the creative process, as we will explore further below, "for a creative person to produce socially useful products, his or her divergent thinking must come hand in hand with convergent thinking" (Woodman, Sawyer, & Griffin, 1993).

If we were to bring together the two types of thinking with the stages of the creative process previously discussed, we can argue that in the first stage of the process, the preparation stage, individuals engage in convergent thinking, where they need to narrow their mental focus in order to deeply understand the problem or task at hand. The next two stages of the creative process, the incubation and illumination stages, are all about divergent thinking because individuals need to expand their mental focus to explore different avenues and generate ideas. The final stage, the evaluation stage, requires individuals to engage in convergent thinking, because they need to refocus their mental effort to assess the novelty and appropriateness of the idea generated in the previous stage (Figure 5.3).

Motivation

Motivation is a fundamentally important element of individual creativity. The keystone for the micro-level social psychology of creativity is the intrinsic motivation hypothesis of creativity which proposed that intrinsic motivation is conducive to creativity, while extrinsic motivation is detrimental to creativity. Amabile explains that "when people are primarily motivated to do some creative activity by their own interest in, and enjoyment of, that activity, they may be more creative than they are when primarily motivated by some goal imposed on them by others" (1983b, p. 15). Following substantial empirical work by Amabile and other scholars, which ratified this hypothesis even further, Amabile (1996) revised the terminology to the *intrinsic motivation principle of creativity*, which indicates that intrinsic motivation is a central determinant of creativity across a multiplicity of contexts and populations. In comparison, motivational interventions such as evaluations and reward systems can negatively influence intrinsic motivation for the creative task because "they redirect attention away from the heuristic aspects of the creative task, and toward the technical or rule-bound aspects of task performance" (Woodman et al., 1993). We will explore evaluation and reward systems in more depth in the next section of this chapter.

The importance of intrinsic motivation to igniting creativity is undoubted. However, Grant and Barry (2011) examined variables, such as perspective taking, that could moderate the intrinsic motivation–creativity relationship. They determined that intrinsic motivation can focus the mind of the individual on the 'novel' aspects of creativity, which are especially important in activities like creating artwork, but may not relate as closely to the 'usefulness' aspect of creativity, which is vital in business. As already explored, creative ideas must be both novel and appropriate. Hence, Grant and Barry (2011) suggest that 'other-focused' psychological processes, such as prosocial motivation and perspective taking, can reinforce the link between intrinsic motivation and creativity.

Knowledge, social, and contextual elements

Another element that can influence individual creativity is the person's *relevant knowledge.* Amabile (1983b) suggested that there are two types of skills that may affect a person's creative behaviour: (1) *domain-relevant skills* which consist of the person's knowledge, technical skills, and innate talent in the relevant domains (Amabile, 1983b; Amabile & Pillemer, 2012), and (2) the *creativity-relevant skills* or processes, including flexible cognitive style, personality traits, e.g., openness to experience and ability to use creative thinking heuristics, and persistent work style (Amabile, 1983b; Amabile & Pillemer, 2012). The individual's creativity-relevant skills "determine the extent to which his product or response will surpass previous products or responses in the domain" (Amabile, 1983b, p. 72). There are also *social elements* that can influence an individual's creativity which include social facilitation and social rewards, as well as *contextual elements* including the physical environment and task and time constraints.

Organisational creativity

Understanding group and organisational creativity

Situating the concept of creativity in the organisational context is very important if we are to understand how creativity contributes to design management. Taylor, Berry, and Block (1958) suggest that the greater the number of ideas generated, the greater the possibility of achieving an effective solution. Therefore, the more creative we are during the design process, the greater the possibility of designing useful and usable offerings. Creativity contributes to design because it enables individuals to define and frame the design problem effectively and generate a successful solution to this problem. An in-depth comprehension of organisational creativity requires an understanding of the creative process, the creative product, the creative person, the creative situation, and the interaction of all these components with each other. Organisational creativity has been defined as

> [the] creation of a valuable, useful new product, service, idea, procedure, or process by individuals working together in a complex social system. It is therefore, the commonly accepted definition of creative behaviour, or the products of such behaviour.
>
> (Woodman et al., 1993, p. 293)

Woodman et al. (1993) extended Woodman and Schoenfeldt's (1989, 1990) interactionist model of creative behaviour, which explores creativity on the individual level, to explore creativity on the group level as well as the organisational level. Understanding group creativity is essential in design management because designers seldom work solely on their own. Designers tend to work in teams consisting of other designers or other professionals such as marketers, researchers, and/or engineers. It is undoubted that both individual and organisational creativity are very important to organisational life. Bharadwaj and Menon (2000) indicated that individual creativity is about the activities individual members pursue on their own to develop personal creativity, and organisational creativity is concerned with practices and formal procedures adopted by firms to promote creative behaviour. In their empirical study, they examined how each type impact innovation, and they identified the highest level of innovation, as reported by staff members, found in firms which had high levels of both individual and organisational creativity. However, regardless of this finding, they concluded that organisational creativity seems to have a stronger association with innovation performance (Bharadwaj & Menon, 2000).

Woodman and Schoenfeldt (1989, 1990) argue that *group creativity* is a result of (1) individual creative behaviour 'inputs', (2) the interaction of the people involved, i.e., the group composition, (3) the group characteristics, e.g., its norms, size, and level of cohesiveness, (4) the group processes, for example, the approaches taken to solve problems, and contextual influences, including organisational culture, reward systems, resource constraints, and the wider environment. In addition, they believe that *organisational creativity* is a result of the creative outputs of its component groups and the aforementioned contextual influences. As Woodman et al. (1993) articulately explain,

> the gestalt of creative output (new products, services, ideas, procedures, and processes) for the entire system stems from the complex mosaic of individual, group, and organisational characteristics and behaviours occurring within the salient situational influences (both creativity constraining and enhancing) existing at each level of social organisation.
>
> (Woodman et al., 1993, p. 296)

In their theory of organisational creativity, there are also a plethora of feedback loops. These include: (1) the effects of the consequences of behaviour on the successive individual and group behaviour,

Engaging in group creativity.

(2) the feedback provided to individuals and groups through social and contextual processes, and (3) the reciprocal influences on the social and contextual situation as the behaviour of individuals and groups unfolds over time (Woodman et al., 1993).

'Nominal' group vs. 'real' group creativity

Perhaps a question that we must address at this point is, which type of creativity, individual or group, is more productive in an organisational setting. On the one hand, we have individual creativity, which is often referred to as 'nominal' group creativity, where individuals would work on their own and then they collate their outputs to form a cumulative output and, on the other hand, we have 'real' group creativity, where there are face-to-face interacting groups which work together to generate ideas. Osborn (1957) argued that (real) groups which follow the brainstorming technique as a problem-solving process come up with more ideas (quantity) and better ideas (quality). However, Taylor et al. (1958) empirically tested Osborn's (1957) suggestion, and the results refuted his argument because 'nominal' groups produced almost twice as many non-replicated ideas as 'real' groups. These results are astonishing; naturally, we would expect that people working together have the potential to come up with more and better ideas (McGlynn, McGurk, Effland, Johll, & Harding, 2004). After all, idea exchange process in groups may be an important means for enhancing creativity and innovation (Paulus & Yang, 2000). Warr and O'Neill (2005) outline the theoretical potential of, what they call, social creativity, where individuals work together in groups to generate ideas. They theorised that

> each individual has a domain of knowledge and within this domain of knowledge has a collection of matrices of thought. An individual has only the matrices of thought available in her own domain of knowledge, but real groups can interact with each other, externalising their matrices of thought and making them available to others … Real groups have the potential to generate more creative ideas than nominal groups by taking advantage of these shared domains of knowledge. By externalising matrices of thought, more combinations of matrices of thought can be derived, producing more creative ideas.
>
> (Warr & O'Neill, 2005, p. 123)

However, in their paper, Warr and O'Neill (2005) do not present research results to empirically prove their theorem. In fact, as already mentioned, all empirical studies have indicated the contrary; 'nominal' group creativity is more productive than 'real' group creativity. Diehl and Stroebe (1987) and other scholars have tried to explain the substantial evidence that contradicts Osborn's (1957) claims. Warr and O'Neill (2005) indicate three explanations: (1) social influences of production blocking, (2) evaluation apprehension, and (3) the problem of free riding.

Production blocking occurs when ideas are verbally expressed within a 'real' group. This creates a situation of 'asynchronous interaction' where only one person can express their idea at one time. This means that while one person expresses his/her idea, the rest of the group members might subsequently forget their ideas or suppress them if they feel their ideas are not relevant or good as time passes. A second problem is that group members rehearse their ideas in their minds, while one person verbally expresses his/her ideas, preventing them from concentrating on what this person is saying. This renders ineffective the sharing of matrices of thought; such sharing is the main feature that could make 'real' groups more productive than 'nominal' groups (Warr & O'Neill, 2005). There is, however, one technique which might allow these matrices of thought to be shared effectively. In practice, it is extremely rare to have 'real' groups which depend exclusively on verbally expressing their ideas and then transcribing them at a later date. In fact, it is very common to see 'real' groups noting ideas down using notepads, flipcharts, post-its, or *iPads* as external shared media, dynamically incorporating such interpretations with verbal contributions (Warr & O'Neill, 2005).

Evaluation apprehension relates to the issue where 'real' group members fear criticism from other group members (especially when these members are seen as experts), which can lead to them avoiding externalising their matrices of thought and expressing their ideas. Thus, such evaluation apprehension can reduce the quantity of ideas, rendering the group less productive. To overcome this problem, Paulus and Yang (2000) have suggested that using anonymous means of expressing ideas can reduce evaluation apprehension, because individuals cannot be identified with an idea and hence can feel free to express their ideas without hesitation. This means that using externally shared media such as post-its and flipcharts, or, more recently, electronic brainstorming systems, allows ideas to be grouped together without identifying the originator. However, one could question whether the more you try to use such shared media, the more you progress from a 'real' group activity to a 'nominal' group activity. After all, in 'nominal' group activity, individuals generate ideas and then bring them together as a group.

Finally, the problem of *free riding*, also known as 'social loafing', stems from the situation where 'real' group members become lazy, rely on other members, and do not contribute much to the group. Surely, most of us have experienced this before, either as students on a university project or in a corporate setting. Free riding is particularly evident where there is pooled assessment in groups; many people who work in groups expect that their ideas will be presented altogether and judged as a group; therefore, some might choose to 'free-ride'. In contrast, when working alone, you are monitored as an individual; thus, it is almost impossible to avoid any poor performance being detected (Warr & O'Neill, 2005). Diehl and Stroebe (1987) identified that groups whose members knew they were going to be individually assessed produced more ideas than those groups whose members were going to be assessed collectively. They suggested that if you can make individuals identifiable with their ideas, you can avoid free riding. However, this would bring back evaluation apprehension, as discussed above. Therefore, we can say that there is a trade-off between evaluation apprehension and free riding. The question of whether the former or the latter is more detrimental to creativity remains empirically unanswered.

Determinants of organisational creativity

An important question springing to mind at this stage is what firms can do to enhance organisational creativity. This is an important question which directly relates to design management. The onus is on the design manager, along with other senior managers, to facilitate an environment where creativity can flourish. Rhodes (1987) has suggested that there are four variables that can influence creativity, which he calls the 4 Ps of creativity. First, the *person* variable includes the characteristics of the person which make him/her creative, such as intellect, temperament, traits, attitudes, self-concept, and values (some of these have been discussed above). This variable is similar to Amabile's (1983b) componential model of creativity in which she suggests that individual domain- and creativity-relevant skills work with intrinsic motivation to generate creative performance. Second, the *product* variable relates to the outcomes or artefacts that are generated as a result of creativity. According to Gilson, Lim, Lithfield, and Gilson (2015), although Rhodes (1987) "separated product into its own stream, the product perspective on creativity is considered to a certain degree in most organisational literature as the dependent variable or outcome" (Gilson et al., 2015, p. 180). Third, the *press* variable involves environmental and contextual factors that can influence creative endeavours. After all, creativity does not happen in a vacuum. This variable relates to issues of organisational culture, climate, leadership, structures and rewards, and the work context (Reiter-Palmon, Herman, & Yammarino, 2008), which will be explored further below. This variable connects well with

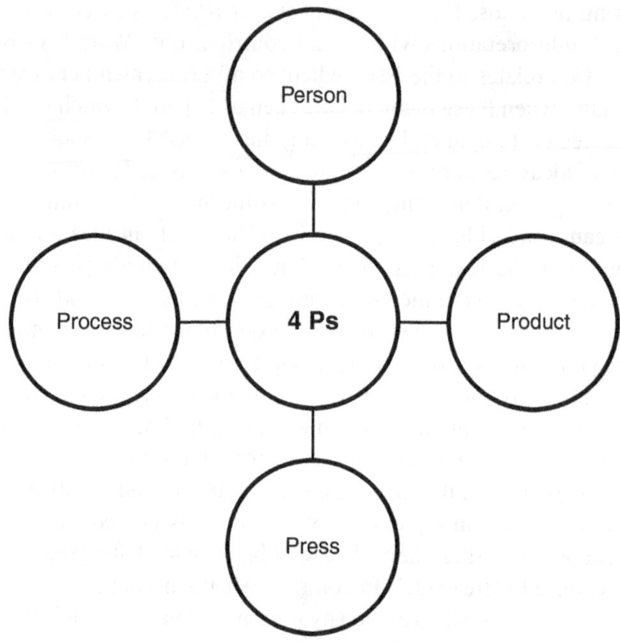

Figure 5.4 4 Ps of creativity.

Woodman et al.'s (1993) interactionist model of creative behaviour, which brings together individual, social, and contextual factors influencing group and organisational creativity. Finally, the *process* variable includes cognitive process and thinking techniques which can enhance the creative performance of the organisational teams. "Within team contexts, processes are what converts inputs into outcomes – the 'how' things get done" (Gilson et al., 2015, p. 180) (Figure 5.4).

A very thorough literature review conducted by Andriopoulos (2001) highlighted five major determinants of organisational creativity, i.e., organisational factors that enhance creativity in the work environment (Figure 5.5). It is important we discuss each of them in depth, drawing from the work of many scholars in organisational sciences.

Organisational climate and creativity

Organisational climate is different than organisational culture. It is concerned with the atmosphere or mood that exists in the work environment (Morgan, 1991). It has been an important concept in organisational sciences dating from Lewin's (1951) seminal work on motivation and was formalised through the human relations movement in the 1960s (Argyris, 1958). West and Sacramento argue that organisational climate is "primarily understood as the intervening variable between the context of an organisation and the responses and behaviour of its members" (2012, p. 362). It is all about the "perceptions of the events, practices, and procedures and the kinds of behaviour that are rewarded, supported, and expected in a setting" (Schneider, 1990, p. 384). Isaksen, Ekvall, Akkermans, Wilson, and Gaulin (2007) differentiated organisational climate from organisational culture by noting that climate is what staff members experience, whereas organisational culture is about what organisational members value. According to Ekvall (1983), organisational climate is all about the behaviours, feelings, and attitudes that characterise and distinguish life in an organisation.

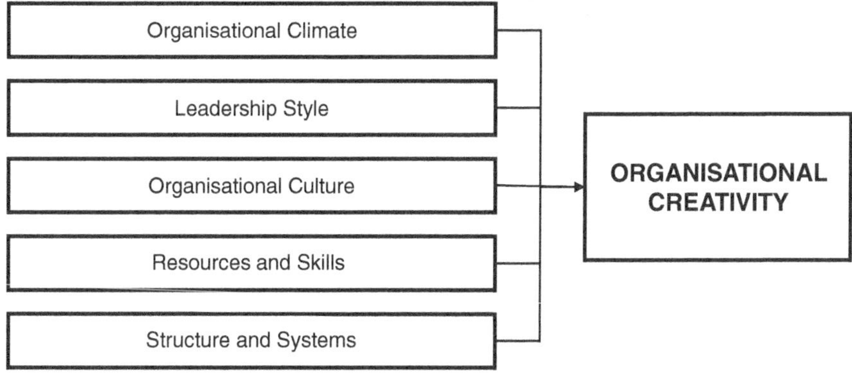

Figure 5.5 Determinants of organisational creativity.

Over the years, we have seen the development of many taxonomies of dimensions of organisational climate that is conducive to creativity (Amabile, Conti, Coon, Lazenby, & Herron, 1996; Isaksen, Lauer, Ekvall, & Britz, 2001; West & Anderson, 1996). In fact, Hunter, Bedell, and Mumford (2006) conducted a thorough review of 45 existing creative organisational climate taxonomies in order to generate an integrated version of a creative climate taxonomy which would encapsulate most of the dimensions in the previous conceptualisations. They identified 14 dimensions, as follows: positive peer group, positive supervisor relations, resources, challenge, mission clarity, autonomy, positive interpersonal exchange, intellectual stimulation, top management support, reward orientation, flexibility and risk taking, product emphasis, participation, and organisational integration. Some of these attributes have been explored in Chapters 2 and 3, where we discussed how we can create an environment where design research and design thinking can flourish. In a similar vein, Feurer, Chaharbaghi, and Wargin (1996) added that creativity can prosper in those organisations which can achieve: (1) interaction between individuals and teams with small barriers, (2) a large number of stimuli offered to individuals and teams, (3) individuals enjoying the freedom to experiment, and (4) processes which allow the possibility of building on earlier ideas. However, the importance of monitoring performance should not be underestimated; as Bower (1965) suggested, a 'working atmosphere' which enhances creativity and innovation not only demands participation and freedom of expression but also requires performance standards.

Leadership style and creativity

One of the most prominent variables in the organisational setting which can promote, facilitate, or hinder creativity is the leadership style and vision adopted by senior management (Locke & Kirkpatrick, 1995; Puccio & Cabra, 2010). The link between leadership behaviour and organisational creativity has been explored by many scholars over the years (e.g. Amabile, Schatzel, Moneta, & Kramer, 2004; Mumford, Scott, Gaddis, & Strange, 2002; Shalley & Gilson, 2004). Such research studies have led to the discovery of many leadership behaviours, abilities, and qualities, which facilitate and enhance creativity and consequently lead to innovation. Drawing from their work at the *Boston Consulting Group*, Andrew and Sirkin (2006) identified a specific set of qualities which leaders must have if they are to turn creative ideas to innovation. Leaders must have the ability to (1) be tolerant towards ambiguity, (2) assess and be comfortable with risk, (3) quickly and effectively assess an individual, (4) balance passion and objectivity, and (5) change. According to Puccio and Cabra (2010), there is one leadership theory which has received the greatest attention in relation to organisational creativity, which is the 'transformational leadership' model.

The theory suggests that transformational leaders assist their colleagues and staff to develop their full potential and motivate others to achieve more than what is expected.

> [Transformational] leadership … stimulates followers to be creative and innovative, and to challenge their own beliefs and values as well as those of the leader and the organisation. This type of leadership supports followers as they try new approaches and develop innovative ways of dealing with organisational issues.
>
> (Northouse, 2004, p. 177)

Organisational culture and creativity

Organisational culture has been defined as all the basic values, assumptions, and beliefs which organisational members share (Cook, 1998; Johnson & Scholes, 1984; Locke & Kirkpatrick, 1995; Morgan, 1991). These values, assumptions, and beliefs are usually manifested by the actions of organisational members, especially leaders and managers. Morgan (1991) uses the analogy of *mini-societies* to describe organisations, because they have their own patterns of culture and subculture. Similar to national cultures, organisations create and preserve values, traditions, and beliefs over time. Such beliefs are manifested in a multiplicity of ways like rites and routines within the organisation, the language used, the stories, legends and myths that are told and repeated within the organisation, as well as the symbols situated throughout the company (Irani, Sharp, & Kagioglou, 1997).

What distinguishes organisational from national culture is its reach, which means that within a national culture there might be many organisational cultures (Puccio & Cabra, 2010). Consider, for instance, the number of private and public holding companies that exist in the UK. This means that thousands of organisational cultures exist within the British culture. Morgan (1991) provides us with a clear description of organisational culture:

> One of the easiest ways of appreciating the nature of corporate culture and subculture is simply to observe the day-to-day functioning of a group or organisation to which one belongs, *as if one were an outsider*. Adopt the role of anthropologist. The characteristics of the culture being observed will gradually become evident as one becomes aware of the patterns of interaction between individuals, the language that is used, the images and themes explored in conversation, and the various rituals of daily routine. As one explores the rationale of these aspects of culture, one usually finds that there are sound historical explanations for the way things are done.
>
> (Morgan, 1991, pp. 129–130)

Martins and Terblance (2003) identified five factors which relate to organisational culture conducive to organisational creativity. First, an *innovation strategy* deriving from the organisation's vision, which concentrates on the development and implementation of new products and services. Second, the *organisational structure*, including variables such as flexibility, freedom, and cooperative teams. Third, *organisational support mechanisms*, for instance, reward and recognition programmes, along with the availability of resources such as time, information technology, and creative people. Fourth, *behaviour* which encourages innovation. Such behaviour includes the ability to respond to failure, generate ideas, take risks, support change, be competitive, manage conflict, and have a spirit of continuous learning. Fifth, the organisation needs to have *open communication*. Classic examples of organisations whose cultures support creativity are *Amazon* and *Google*. We can notice some similarities with the attributes included under the organisational climate construct, but as mentioned already, there are subtle, yet important, differences that we need to keep in mind.

In order to encourage creativity, organisations need to develop a divergent and learning culture, as well as a culture that is supportive, namely empowering and caring (Brand, 1998). As we have noticed, many scholars call for open flow of communication in order to encourage creativity in the organisational setting. Contrastingly, high conformity is considered to be anathema to creative behaviour (Amabile, 1988). In addition, the organisation's culture should encourage self-initiated activity, where individuals and team own problems and their solutions, which of course enhances intrinsic motivation (Robinson & Stern, 1997). Liu, Chen, and Yao (2011) increased our understanding of the role of intrinsic motivation through their concept of '*harmonious passion*'. They define harmonious passion as "the autonomous internalisation of an activity, making it part of one's identity and thus creating a sense of personal enjoyment and free choice about pursuing the activity" (Liu et al., 2011, p. 1). They determined that harmonious passion is a stronger motivation than simple intrinsic motivation because those people who experience harmonious passion internalise the activity (project) as part of their identity (Liu et al., 2011).

Finally, it is important that the organisational culture stimulates people's minds and maintains *participative safety* (Anderson et al., 1992). It is fundamental that staff members are not afraid of criticism and punishment, i.e., top management ought to be able to tolerate mistakes. This takes us back to what we have discussed in Chapters 2 and 3; teams must be given the time, space, and budget to make mistakes (Brown, 2009), by establishing a 'no-fear' climate (Andriopoulos & Gotsi, 2005), which encourages experimentalism, a significant precondition for design thinking and creativity to flourish.

Resources, skills, and creativity

The three most important organisational resources that affect creativity are *human resources*, *financial resources*, and *time*. Cook (1998) argues that any organisation which strives to facilitate and enhance creativity must attract, develop, and retain creative talent. Design projects need to be properly budgeted to ensure successful completion. Time is also a vital resource because teams must be given the time for proper experimentation. In addition, projects need to be appropriately scheduled so that designers are not asked for things at the last minute, or taken from one task to another without considering the fact that they need time to work on projects and generate ideas. Amabile (1988) has proposed the 'threshold of sufficiency'; creativity is not enhanced when resources are added above this threshold, whereas below this threshold a restriction of resources hinders creativity because organisational members concentrate on finding additional resources than carrying out what is expected of them.

Andriopoulos (2001) argues that the single most important factor for the creative mind to flourish within the organisation is the firm's attitude towards *accommodating personal idiosyncrasies*. Allowing some autonomy is important and should not be merely about the end result, but also about the processes within the organisation (Amabile, 1998). Nevertheless, autonomy does not mean complete independence; the latter can lead to anarchy within the organisation. This means that there should be some degree of pressure within the work environment because this can have a positive influence on creativity (Amabile, 1988; Amabile & Gryskiewicz, 1987). Such pressure, however, needs to be perceived to be arising from the urgent intellectually challenging nature of the creative problem at hand; otherwise, it might be perceived as tyranny.

Organisational members need to be matched to projects on the basis of their skills and interests. This will enhance the sense of positive challenge in the project and consequently can enhance organisational members' creative abilities (Amabile, 1998; Amabile & Gryskiewicz, 1987; Paolillo & Brown, 1978; Siegel & Kaemmerer, 1978). It is finally important to note that Amabile (1998) emphasises the importance of '*stretch*' within organisations. With this term she describes the organisations stretching their staff members beyond their comfort zone. This can enhance their creativity because it can challenge them. This means that organisational members should not be stretched too little because this will lead to boredom, or too much, because this will lead to them feeling overwhelmed and threatened by a sense of loss of control (Amabile, 1998).

Structure, systems, and creativity

Organisational structures are concerned with organisational hierarchy; therefore, they determine the relationships among organisational members, teams, and departments, as well as indicate lines of responsibility and authority within the organisational setting (Puccio & Cabra, 2010). Creativity can only be facilitated and enhanced when the entire organisation supports it. Thus, senior management must establish systems and procedures which highlight and communicate to everyone that creativity is top on the organisation's agenda (Amabile, 1998). Organisational structure and systems can include formal and informal processes and systems such as rewards, recognition, and career progression (Cook, 1998). Many organisations, such as design consultancies, often adopt a flat organisational structure which does not employ many levels of command. However, adopting such flat structure should not lead to an environment where everyone has an opinion on the strategic direction of the organisation, but no one has responsibility for it.

The use of *rewards* to enhance creativity has been the focus of many research studies in organisational creativity literature. As already discussed, extrinsic motivation can come from the promise of rewards and praise and despite appearances can be detrimental to creativity (Amabile, 1983a, 1983b). However, this does not mean that the firm should not give any rewards to its staff members. It is the nature of the rewards which needs to be carefully considered. The organisation should reward creativity, but such rewards should not be of financial nature in a way that they are perceived as the organisation 'bribing' staff to come up with innovative ideas (Amabile, 1998). In fact, many organisational scholars have argued that creativity can be enhanced by staff members expecting a reward perceived by them as a 'bonus', which is a confirmation of their competence and can take the form of a financial reward and/or verbal praise. So the difference lies on the fact that staff members should not be pursuing creativity only for the financial rewards they will receive; instead they should be trying to be creative because they find it interesting, enjoyable, satisfying, and positively challenging (Amabile & Pillemer, 2012). Therefore, Amabile suggests that "financial rewards *per se* do not necessarily make employees passionate about their work and hence may hinder creativity in the long run" (Andriopoulos, 2001, p. 838).

A topic closely linked with the use of rewards in organisational settings is the question of *evaluation* of organisational members' work. After all, staff members need to be appraised first, so that they can be rewarded with bonuses (beyond the remuneration they are anyway entitled to, under their employment contract). So the question that needs answering now is how expected evaluation affects creativity. The following explains Amabile's (1979) findings from her first experiments on the issue:

> In the first experiment to establish the negative effect of expected evaluation on creativity, Amabile (1979) had university students create a paper collage under one of several different expected-evaluation conditions; comparison groups did not expect evaluation. In general, compared to collages created by participants not expecting expert evaluation, judge-rated creativity was lower for those collages created by participants who expected evaluation by art experts – evaluations that would purportedly be shown to the participants. The only exception to this pattern was the group of participants who expected evaluation *on creativity* and were given *specific hints* on how to make a creative collage. Moreover, intrinsic interest in the collage activity was lowered by expected evaluation – even for participants in the specific-creativity-hints condition.
>
> (Amabile & Pillemer, 2011, p. 7)

Other studies added additional nuances to our understanding of the link between evaluation and creativity. Amabile, Goldfarb, and Brackfleld (1990) explored the issue of *surveillance* on creativity, i.e., the question of how creativity is affected when individuals feel they are being watched. The results indicated that surveillance has negative effects on creativity to the extent that individuals feel evaluated by those watching them. Shalley and Perry-Smith (2001) examined the difference between *informational evaluation* and *controlling evaluation*. The former is about evaluation that participants expect will provide them useful performance information, whereas the latter is about evaluation which individuals see as exclusively intended to monitor their behaviour. Their experiment indicated that both intrinsic motivation and creativity was substantially higher in the case of informational evaluation in comparison to controlling evaluation.

He, Yao, Wang, & Caughron (2016) explored the link between *failure feedback* and individual creativity and discovered a moderating role of goal orientation. Failure feedback is an antecedent to sense-making processes, and managers can use such feedback to influence how staff members make sense of their failures and ensure that attitudes, emotions, and behaviours, detrimental to the organisation, are redirected. Goal orientation governs intentions and expectations related to future achievement behaviours (Dweck & Leggett, 1988; Elliot & Church, 1997). There are two types of goal orientation. First, *avoidance goal orientation* which relates to individuals who are prevention-focused and risk-sensitive (Elliot & Church, 1997; Higgins, 1998; Simmons & Ren, 2009). These individuals, upon receiving failure feedback, pay attention to potential losses or shortfalls that they must avoid (Higgins, 1997). Second, *learning goal orientation*, which relates to individuals who, after receiving failure feedback, adopt growth and development goals to gain new knowledge and skills in order to counter failures or losses indicated by failure feedback (Brett & VandeWalle, 1999; Kozlowski et al., 2001). What He et al. (2016) found out was that learning goal orientation strengthens the positive link between failure feedback and creativity, whereas avoidance goal orientation weakens the positive relationship between the two.

Chapter review questions

The following questions can help you reflect on the material we have covered in Chapter 5:

1 Define creativity in relation to the creative product, the creative person, and the creative process, and from a micro- and a macro-perspective.
2 Outline the different models of the creative process and discuss their similarities.
3 Examine individual creativity and its determining elements, referring to the interactionist model of creative behaviour.
4 Define organisational creativity and compare 'nominal' and 'real' group creativity in an organisational setting. Which of these leads to greater and better production of ideas and why?
5 Discuss the various determinants of organisational creativity.

Recommended reading

1 Amabile, T. M., & Pillemer, J. (2012). Perspectives on the social psychology of creativity. *The Journal of Creative Behavior, 46*(1), 3–15.
2 Woodman, R. W., Sawyer, J. E., & Griffin, R. W. (1993). Toward a theory of organizational creativity. *Academy of Management Review, 18*(2), 293–321.

Reflective thoughts

Design, experiential learning, and team creativity

Professor Bruce M. Wood
Professor of Design Innovation
Director, Centre for Creative Industries
Glasgow Caledonian University, Glasgow, UK

This review of the theoretical considerations and thinking on the subject of creativity at the individual level and the organisational level provides an insight into a considerable amount of work already undertaken and published on the subject, from a business and a psychological perspective.

Design practitioners and design managers rarely consider this level of thought and background research that has occurred previously, or indeed is occurring in parallel with design practice.

Design education in general is based on problem-based learning, in that there is generally a wide range of subjects considered, then applied to a particular design brief or problem, and the results reviewed. It is generally accepted that designers are educated on a 'learn by doing' philosophy. This experiential learning develops individuals' ability to apply knowledge to a problem, provided in the form of a design brief and then assess the solutions proposed. The individual not only learns from the formal aspects of this process but also learns by experiencing the so-called 'transferrable skills', such as teamwork, time management, project management, communication skills, etc. Individuals improve their skills and confidence by this process. Design and design management are not pure subjects, and practitioners and students must have the ability to be agile, adaptive, and flexible in order to be able to direct their creative efforts in the pursuit of creative solutions.

It is generally accepted that teamwork is an essential set of skills for designers to operate, and there are several reasons for this. One obvious reason is the fact that products and services are now so complex that no single individual can possess all of the skills and knowhow to be able to deliver successful holistic solutions. Another important factor is that designers thrive in an environment where ideas are proposed, examined, expanded, and built on. This iterative process is clearly a journey, and it allows ideas to be developed into implementable solutions. Working in creative teams requires team members to propose and externalise their ideas; this means that team members need to develop their own creative confidence. There are a number of well-known techniques for this activity; 'brainstorming' and 'six-hat thinking' are two of the most common techniques.

In practice, design teams often work collectively, where and when appropriate, then retire to engage in different elements of the team task; this could be a more focused task element as a result of the collective team output. The outcomes of a more focused element of work are then fed back into the overall team task. These different modes of work reflect closely on the notion of divergent and convergent thinking, the former requiring generation of ideas, imagination, experimentation, and deferring judgement, whereas the latter requiring evaluation, organising, selection, focus, and refinement. Designers who operate in successful creative teams are used to this mode of working that could be seen as a 'pulsing' series of team-based divergent thinking activities, to be followed by focused convergent-based activities. Divergent thinking creates opportunities for solutions, and convergent thinking selects options. Both divergent and convergent thinking activities and skills are required in design and design management fields, and the two modes represent distinctly different methods and working practices.

Design firms and teams purposely and seriously consider the locations and working environments in order to get the best out of the teams' efforts. Some design companies establish team working locations, the so-called 'war rooms', where everything relating to the task or project is located; teams collectively meet there, all the facilitation resources are on hand. Once the project is concluded, the location is vacated or dismantled. Some design companies, on a planned basis, relocate all employees within the existing accommodation; this is believed to foster fresh thinking and stops individuals becoming territorial about 'their space'. Another reason that location and accommodation is considered carefully is that in some design/creative sectors, there can be a real business need to rapidly expand the team in order to deal with a project resources issue or task and then, once complete, contract back to the core team. This pattern can be often observed in the games design and visual effects sector. There are many variations on a theme of locations in design/creative companies; all of the companies do so on the basis of attempting to maximise their creative output for their client or customer, always bearing in mind the client/customer has engaged with the design company on the basis that they are genuinely creative and the resulting solutions will be creative and successful.

Design firms employ a wide range of techniques to both engender creativity and enhance the creative output. It is important to note that not every technique will be utilised on every project. Successful designers and design managers are aware and experienced in the use of most of the techniques, thus giving them an innate ability to select and match appropriate techniques to the appropriate project and client. This alone is not enough; successful designers and design managers are also skilled in adapting and refining any of the techniques to suit the situation that they are operating in.

While design practise, design management, and design thinking can be considered as processes, they are not only a simple series of mechanical steps and processes. Successful creative or design solutions are a result of a complex set of dynamically varying interconnected inputs and activities that are both proactive and reactive, depending on the situation, with people at the core of the system.

It is interesting to note that the empirical research undertaken into individual and organisational creativity, in psychology and management literature, is not normally taught on design curricula; yet, successful design organisations' strategic and operational activities align well with the empirical research findings discussed in this chapter.

It is also important to note that design professionals and firms are constantly developing their operations as the needs of society evolve. This allows their clients to react and respond to the rapidly changing demands of society. These changes in needs and demand are faster and more wide-ranging than anyone could have predicted.

It is the designers' role to bring new insights to the situation. As Marcel Proust (1871–1922) stated: "The real voyage of discovery consists not in seeking new lands but seeing with new eyes". This idea is even more relevant today for designers as it was then.

References

Amabile, T. M. (1979). Effects of external evaluation on artistic creativity. *Journal of Personality and Social Psychology, 37*(2), 221–233.

Amabile, T. M. (1982). Social psychology of creativity: A consensual assessment technique. *Journal of Personality and Social Psychology, 43*(5), 997–1013.

Amabile, T. M. (1983a). The social psychology of creativity: A componential conceptualization. *Journal of Personality and Social Psychology, 45*(2), 357–376.

Amabile, T. M. (1983b). *The social psychology of creativity*. New York: Springer-Verlag.

Amabile, T. M. (1988). A model of creativity and innovation in organizations. In B. M. Staw, & L. L. Cummings (Eds.), *Research in organizational behavior* (Vol. 10, pp. 123–167). Greenwich, CT: JAI Press.

Amabile, T. M. (1996). *Creativity in context*. Boulder, CO: Westview.

Amabile, T. M. (1998). How to kill creativity. *Harvard Business Review, 76*(5), 76–87.

Amabile, T. M., & Gryskiewicz, S. S. (1987). *Creativity in the R&D laboratory*. Technical Report No. 30, Center for Creative Leadership, Greensboro, NC.

Amabile, T. M., & Pillemer, J. (2012). Perspectives on the social psychology of creativity. *The Journal of Creative Behavior, 46*(1), 3–15.

Amabile, T. M., Conti, R., Coon, H., Lazenby, J., & Herron, M. (1996). Assessing the work environment for creativity. *Academy of Management Journal, 39*(5), 1154–1184.

Amabile, T. M., Goldfarb, P., & Brackfleld, S. C. (1990). Social influences on creativity: Evaluation, coaction, and surveillance. *Creativity Research Journal, 3*(1), 6–21.

Amabile, T. M., Schatzel, E. A., Moneta, G. B., & Kramer, S. J. (2004). Leader behaviors and the work environment for creativity: Perceived leader support. *The Leadership Quarterly, 15*(1), 5–32.

Anderson, N., Hardy, G., & West, M. (1992). Management team innovation. *Management Decision, 30*(2), 17–21.

Andrew, J. P., & Sirkin, H. L. (2006). *Payback: Reaping the rewards of innovation*. Boston: Harvard Business School Press.

Andriopoulos, C. (2001). Determinants of organisational creativity: A literature review. *Management Decision, 39*(10), 834–841.

Andriopoulos, C., & Gotsi, M. (2005). The virtues of 'blue sky' projects: How Lunar Design taps into the power of imagination. *Creativity and Innovation Management, 14*(3), 316–324.

Argyris, C. (1958). Some problems in conceptualizing organizational climate: A case study of a bank. *Administrative Science Quarterly, 2*(4), 501–520.

Barron, F., & Harrington, D. M. (1981). Creativity, intelligence, and personality. *Annual Review of Psychology, 32*(1), 439–476.

Bharadwaj, S., & Menon, A. (2000). Making innovation happen in organizations: Individual creativity mechanisms, organizational creativity mechanisms or both? *Journal of Product Innovation Management, 17*(6), 424–434.

Bilton, C., & Leary, R. (2002). What can managers do for creativity? Brokering creativity in the creative industries. *International Journal of Cultural Policy, 8*(1), 49–64.

Boden, M. A. (1994). *Dimensions of creativity*. Cambridge, MA: MIT Press.

Bower, M. (1965). Nurturing innovation in an organization. In G. A. Steiner (Ed.), *The creative organisation*. Chicago: Chicago University Press.

Brand, A. (1998). Knowledge management and innovation at 3M. *Journal of Knowledge Management, 2*(1), 17–22.

Brett, J. F., & VandeWalle, D. (1999). Goal orientation and goal content as predictors of performance in a training program. *Journal of Applied Psychology, 84*(6), 863–873.

Brown, T. (2009). *Change by design: How design thinking transforms organisations and inspires innovation*. New York: HarperCollins.

Carrol, J. B. (1985). *Domains of cognitive ability*. Paper presented at the Meeting of the American Association for the Advancement of Science, Los Angeles, CA.

Cook, P. (1998). The creativity advantage – is your organization the leader of the pack? *Industrial and Commercial Training, 30*(5), 179–184.

Crutchfield, R. S. (1955). Conformity and character. *American Psychologist, 10*(5), 191–198.

Crutchfield, R. S. (1962). Conformity and creative thinking. In H. Gruber, G. Terell, & M. Wertheimer (Eds.), *Contemporary approaches to creative thinking*. New York: Atherton Press.

Diehl, M., & Stroebe, W. (1987). Productivity loss in brainstorming groups: Toward the solution of a riddle. *Journal of Personality and Social Psychology, 53*(3), 497–509.

Dweck, C. S., & Leggett, E. L. (1988). A social-cognitive approach to motivation and personality. *Psychological Review, 95*(2), 256–273.

Ekvall, G. (1983). *Climate, structure and innovativeness of organizations: A theoretical framework and an experiment*. Stockholm, Sweden: Faradet.

Elliot, A. J., & Church, M. A. (1997). A hierarchical model of approach and avoidance achievement motivation. *Journal of Personality and Social Psychology, 72*(1), 218–232.

Feurer, R., Chaharbaghi, K., & Wargin, J. (1996). Developing creative teams for operational excellence. *International Journal of Operations & Production Management, 16*(1), 5–18.

Gabora, L. (2002). Cognitive mechanisms underlying the creative process. In *Proceedings of the 4th Conference on Creativity & Cognition* (pp. 126–133). New York: ACM.

Gilson, L. L., Lim, H. H., Lithfield, R. R., & Gilson, P. W. (2015). Creativity in teams: A key building block for innovation and entrepreneurship. In C. E. Shalley, M. A. Hitt, & J. Zhou (Eds.), *The Oxford handbook of creativity, innovation, and entrepreneurship*. Oxford, UK: Oxford University Press.

Gough, H. G. (1979). A creative personality scale for the adjective check list. *Journal of Personality and Social Psychology, 37*(8), 1398–1405.

Grant, A. M., & Barry, J. W. (2011). The necessity of others is the mother of invention: Intrinsic and prosocial motivations, perspective taking, and creativity. *Academy of Management Journal, 54*(1), 73–96.

Guilford, J. P. (1950). Creativity. *American Psychologist, 14*, 205–208.

Guilford, J. P. (1977). *Way beyond the IQ: Guide to improving intelligence and creativity*. Buffalo, NY: Creative Education Foundation.

Guilford, J. P. (1984). Varieties of divergent production. *The Journal of Creative Behavior, 18*, 1–10.

He, Y., Yao, X., Wang, S., & Caughron, J. (2016). Linking failure feedback to individual creativity: The moderation role of goal orientation. *Creativity Research Journal, 28*(1), 52–59.

Higgins, E. T. (1997). Beyond pleasure and pain. *American Psychologist, 52*(12), 1280–1300.

Higgins, E. T. (1998). Promotion and prevention: Regulatory focus as a motivational principle. In M. P. Zanna (Ed.), *Advances in experimental social psychology* (Vol. 30, pp. 1–46). San Diego, CA: Academic Press.

Hunter, S. T., Bedell, K. E., & Mumford, M. D. (2007). Dimension of creative climate: A general taxonomy. *Korean Journal of Thinking and Problem Solving, 15*, 97–116.

Irani, Z., Sharp, J. M., & Kagioglou, M. (1997). Improving business performance through developing a corporate culture. *The TQM Magazine, 9*(3), 206–216.

Isaksen, S. G., Ekvall, G., Akkermans, H., Wilson, G. V., & Gaulin, J. P. (2007). *Assessing the context for change: A technical manual for the situational outlook questionnaire, enhancing performance of organizations, leaders and teams for over 50 years* (2nd ed.). Orchard Park, NY: Creative Problem Solving Group.

Isaksen, S. G., Lauer, K. J., Ekvall, G., & Britz, A. (2001). Perceptions of the best and worst climates for creativity: Preliminary validation evidence for the situational outlook questionnaire. *Creativity Research Journal, 13*(2), 171–184.

Johnson, G., & Scholes, K. (1984). *Exploring corporate strategy*. Englewood Cliffs, NJ: Prentice-Hall.

Koestler, A. (1964). *The act of creation*. New York: Dell.

Kozlowski, S. W., Gully, S. M., Brown, K. G., Salas, E., Smith, E. M., & Nason, E. R. (2001). Effects of training goals and goal orientation traits on multidimensional training outcomes and performance adaptability. *Organizational Behavior and Human Decision Processes, 85*(1), 1–31.

Kruglanski, A. W., Friedman, I., & Zeevi, G. (1971). The effects of extrinsic incentive on some qualitative aspects of task performance. *Journal of Personality, 39*(4), 606–617.

Lewin, K. (1951). *Field theory in social science*. New York: Harper.

Liu, D., Chen, X. P., & Yao, X. (2011). From autonomy to creativity: A multilevel investigation of the mediating role of harmonious passion. *Journal of Applied Psychology, 96*(2), 294–309.

Lock, E. A., & Kirkpatrick, S. A. (1995). Promoting creativity in organizations. In C. M. Ford, & D. A. Gioia (Eds.), *Creative action in organizations: Ivory tower visions and real world voices.* London: Sage.

McGlynn, R. P., McGurk, D., Effland, V. S., Johll, N. L., & Harding, D. J. (2004). Brainstorming and task performance in groups constrained by evidence. *Organizational Behavior and Human Decision Processes, 93*(1), 75–87.

Martins, E. C., & Terblanche, F. (2003). Building organisational culture that stimulates creativity and innovation. *European Journal of Innovation Management, 6*(1), 64–74.

Morgan, G. (1991). *Images of organization.* Thousand Oaks, CA: Sage.

Mumford, M. D., Scott, G. M., Gaddis, B., & Strange, J. M. (2002). Leading creative people: Orchestrating expertise and relationships. *The Leadership Quarterly, 13*(6), 705–750.

Nemiro, J. (2004). *Creativity in virtual teams: Key components for success* (Vol. 6). Hoboken, NJ: John Wiley & Sons.

Northouse, P. G. (2004). *Leadership: Theory and practice.* Thousand Oaks, CA: Sage.

Novitz, D. (1999). Creativity and constraint. *Australasian Journal of Philosophy, 77*(1), 67–82.

Osborn, A. F. (1957). *Applied imagination: Principles and procedures of creative problem-solving.* New York: Scribner's.

Paolillo, J. G., & Brown, W. B. (1978). How organizational factors affect R&D innovation. *Research Management, 21*(2), 12–15.

Paulus, P. B., & Yang, H. C. (2000). Idea generation in groups: A basis for creativity in organizations. *Organizational Behavior and Human Decision Processes, 82*(1), 76–87.

Puccio, G. J., & Cabra, J. F. (2010). Organizational creativity. In J. C. Kaufman, & R. J. Sternberg (Eds.), *The Cambridge handbook of creativity* (pp. 145–173). Cambridge, UK: Cambridge University Press.

Reiter-Palmon, R., Herman, A. E., & Yammarino, F. J. (2008). Creativity and cognitive processes: Multi-level linkages between individual and team cognition. In M. D. Mumford, S. T. Hunter, & K. E. Bedell-Avers (Eds.), *Multi-level issues in creativity and innovation* (Vol. 7, pp. 203–267). Bingley, UK: Emerald.

Rhodes, M. (1987). An analysis of creativity. In I. G. Isaksen (Ed.), *Frontiers of creativity research: Beyond the basics* (pp. 216–222). Buffalo, NY: Bearly.

Robinson, A. G., & Stern, S. (1997). *Corporate creativity: How innovation and improvement actually happen.* San Francisco, CA: Berrett-Koehler.

Schneider, B. (1990). The climate for service: An application of the climate construct. In B. Schneider (Ed.), *Organizational climate and culture* (pp. 383–412). San Francisco, CA: Jossey-Bass.

Shalley, C. E., & Gilson, L. L. (2004). What leaders need to know: A review of social and contextual factors that can foster or hinder creativity. *The Leadership Quarterly, 15*(1), 33–53.

Shalley, C. E., & Perry-Smith, J. E. (2001). Effects of social-psychological factors on creative performance: The role of informational and controlling expected evaluation and modelling experience. *Organizational Behaviour and Human Decision Processes, 84*(1), 1–22.

Shneiderman, B. (2000). Creating creativity: User interfaces for supporting innovation. *ACM Transactions on Computer–Human Interaction (TOCHI), 7*(1), 114–138.

Siegel, S. M., & Kaemmerer, W. F. (1978). Measuring the perceived support for innovation in organizations. *Journal of Applied Psychology, 63*(5), 553–562.

Simmons, A. L., & Ren, R. (2009). The influence of goal orientation and risk on creativity. *Creativity Research Journal, 21*(4), 400–408.

Simonton, D. K. (1975). Sociocultural context of individual creativity: A transhistorical time-series analysis. *Journal of Personality and Social Psychology, 32*(6), 1119.

Simonton, D. K. (1980). Thematic fame and melodic originality in classical music: A multivariate computer-content analysis. *Journal of Personality, 48*(2), 206–219.

Simonton, D. K. (1999). *Origins of genius: Darwinian perspectives on creativity.* New York: Oxford University Press.

Taylor, D. W., Berry, P. C., & Block, C. H. (1958). Does group participation when using brainstorming facilitate or inhibit creative thinking? *Administrative Science Quarterly, 3*(1), 23–47.

Wallas, G. (1926). *The art of thought.* New York: Harcourt, Brace & World.

Warr, A., & O'Neill, E. (2005). Understanding design as a social creative process. In *Proceedings of the 5th Conference on Creativity & Cognition* (pp. 118–127). New York: ACM.

West, M. A., & Anderson, N. R. (1996). Innovation in top management teams. *Journal of Applied Psychology, 81*(6), 680–693.

Woodman, R. W., & Schoenfeldt, L. F. (1989). Individual differences in creativity: An interactionist perspective. In J. A. Glover, R. R. Ronning, & C. R. Reynolds (Eds.), *Handbook of creativity* (pp. 77–91). New York: Springer.

Woodman, R. W., & Schoenfeldt, L. F. (1990). An interactionist model of creative behavior. *The Journal of Creative Behavior, 24*(1), 279–290.

Woodman, R. W., Sawyer, J. E., & Griffin, R. W. (1993). Toward a theory of organizational creativity. *Academy of Management Review, 18*(2), 293–321.

6 Organising for design innovation
Organisational paradoxes and ambidexterity

Chapter aims and learning outcomes

This chapter aims to:

1 Provide a thorough understanding of paradoxes and their components.
2 Explore the different types of organisational paradoxes.
3 Discuss organisational paradoxes related to creativity and innovation.
4 Explore the concept of ambidexterity as a means to manage paradoxes of creativity and innovation.

As mentioned in the previous chapter, leaders wishing to facilitate and enhance creativity in their organisations must possess, among other qualities, the ability to balance the two elements of passion and objectivity (Andrew & Sirkin, 2006), which, from the outset, seem quite oxymoronic. This actually is not the only paradox leaders and managers are often faced within the organisational setting. In fact, organisational life is full of paradoxes, full of tensions between two opposite positions. For instance, the tensions between old and new, stable and dynamic, control and flexibility, the individual and the collective. In design firms in particular, tensions can arise between artistic and commercial identities, between evolutionary and revolutionary work, between profit and breakthrough projects. In his influential book, *The Age of Paradox*, Charles Handy explains the power and prominence of paradox in our contemporary, post-modern world with the following:

> Paradox I now see to be inevitable, endemic, and perpetual. The more turbulent the times, the more complex the world, the more paradoxes there are. We can, and should, reduce the starkness of some of the contradictions, minimise the inconsistencies, understand the puzzles in the paradoxes, but we cannot make them disappear, or solve them completely, or escape from them. Paradoxes are like the weather, something to be lived with, not solved, the worst aspects mitigated, the best enjoyed and used as clues to the way forward. Paradox has to be *accepted*, coped with, and made sense of, in life, in work, in the community, and among nations.
>
> (Handy, 1994, pp. 12–13)

Being faced with such paradoxes requires organisational members to have the ability to manage these tensions and a different way of thinking about the power and potential of tensions. Paradoxical thinking can enhance managers' ability to manage design effectively. Drawing from paradox literature, we will be able to address the important question of how firms can organise themselves in a way that design is effectively managed, leading to the highest levels of innovation. This chapter seeks to explore the paradox concept and provide an understanding of its role in organisational life. Over the years, research studies have identified a number of organisational paradoxes. In addition, contemporary empirical work on creativity has generated surprising findings that have led many scholars to identify a bundle of paradoxes related to creativity and innovation (Cropley & Cropley, 2012). Therefore, it is extremely important to understand these paradoxes and explore the ways organisations can cope with them. It is imperative to note, from the outset, that paradoxes cannot be managed, in the sense of resolving them. As Handy argues, a "paradox can only be 'managed' in the sense of coping with. Manage always did mean 'coping with', until we purloined the word to mean planning and control" (1994, p. 12). Thus, we will explore the different coping mechanisms pursued by organisations seeking to 'manage' these paradoxes. Such discussion will lead us to the concept of ambidexterity and its different types. Consequently, we will explore how ambidexterity can help firms organise themselves effectively in order to achieve design innovation.

Understanding the components of paradoxes

Lewis (2000) provides us with a very important definition of paradoxes; she determined that "a paradox denotes contradictory yet interrelated elements – elements that seem logical in isolation but absurd and irrational when appearing simultaneously" (Lewis, 2000, p. 760). From ancient Greek philosophy to existential philosophy, paradoxes have been very prominent and widely recognised. Philosophers have viewed the very human existence as paradoxical – grounded in tensions such as that of life and death, good and evil, or self and other. "A paradox is some 'thing' that is constructed by individuals when oppositional tendencies are brought into recognizable proximity through reflection or interaction" (Ford & Backoff, 1988, p. 89). This definition helps us to determine the *three characteristics of paradoxes*. First, paradoxes include a plethora of contradictory yet interwoven elements such as perspectives, feelings, messages, identities, demands, interests, or practices. Second, paradoxes are constructed through situations where organisational actors in their effort to understand the world simplify reality by polarising it in 'either/or' distinctions that conceal complex interrelationships. Third, paradoxes become obvious through self or social reflection or interaction that uncover the irrational coexistence of opposite entities (Ford & Backoff, 1988).

According to Lewis (2000), paradoxes have *three components*: (1) their fundamental tensions which act as the sources of the paradoxes, (2) their reinforcing cycles, and (3) their corresponding management tactics, the coping mechanisms, to 'manage' these paradoxes in an organisational setting (Figure 6.1). It is important to explore these three components in more detail.

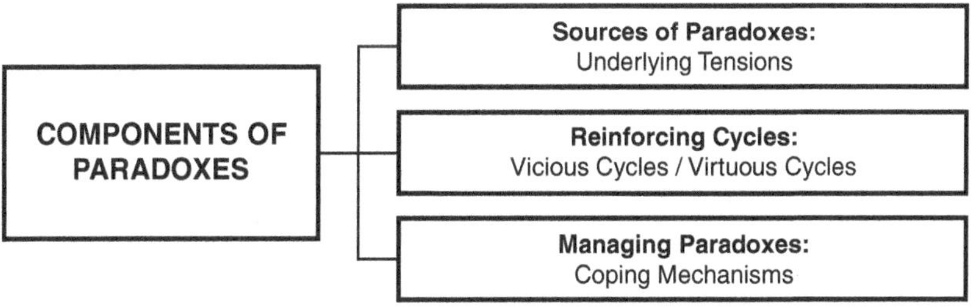

Figure 6.1 Components of paradoxes.

Sources of paradoxes: Underlying tensions

Tensions are the sources of paradoxes, but "unlike continua, dilemmas, or either/or choices, paradoxical tensions signify two sides of the same coin" (Lewis, 2000, p. 761). There are three interrelated types of tensions: (1) self-referential loops, (2) mixed messages, and (3) system contradictions. *Self-referential loops* are contradictions embedded within a cohesive concept, statement, or process, e.g., the liar's paradox: 'I am lying', which is a circular statement because if the person is lying then the statement is false, implying that he/she is telling the truth. *Mixed messages* derive from constructing ambiguous messages (Argyris, 1993), and they show inconsistencies between statements or between verbal and non-verbal responses that occur during social interactions. As time passes, these tensions could evolve to become *system contradictions*, present "within the goals, reward systems, resource demands, and division of labour of an organisation" (Putnam, 1986, p. 161). The emergence of system contradictions can be identified by contradictory messages and paradox cycles through the interactions of organisational members. Putnam adds that

> When contradictions appear within a reward system or an organisational ideology, they permeate the communication patterns that frame organisational events … By expanding alternatives, creating new insights, and reframing events, organisational members reconstruct the prevailing system to overcome its constraining effects.
>
> (Putnam, 1986, p. 164)

When faced with paradoxes, most individuals tend to follow Kelly's (1955) personal construct theory, where they increase the contradictions by interpreting their own or others' feelings, organisational practices, and cues from the environment in a way that they separate the opposites, instead of recognising that they are the two sides of the same coin, interrelated and reciprocally influenced. This deprives people the ability to understand complex realities and eventually makes them resistant to any change. Organisational members

> distinguish a phenomenon by placing brackets or boundaries around it, differentiating figure from ground to facilitate their understanding. But such distinctions become objectified over time, giving [organisational members] the impression that their perceptions are distinct and immutable entities.
>
> (Lewis, 2000, p. 762)

In order to avoid such simplistic distinctions, we need to follow notions from Eastern philosophies, such as Taoism. The Taoist symbol of Yin and Yang represents a natural wholeness composed of contradictions.

Morgan (1991) explains the meaning of the symbol:

> The diagram is a symmetrical arrangement of the dark *yin* and the bright *yang*, but the symmetry is not static. It is a rotational symmetry suggesting, very forcefully, a continuous cyclic movement: The *yang* returns cyclically to its beginning, the *yin* attains its maximum and gives place to the *yang*. The two dots in the diagram symbolise the idea that each time one of the two forces reaches its extreme, it contains in itself already the seed of its opposite.
>
> (Morgan, 1991, p. 284)

The Taoist philosophy indicates that many human situations can be balanced and improved by influencing the relationship between the opposing elements. Many of the Taoist principles were brought

The Taoist symbol of Yin and Yang: A natural wholeness composed of contradictions.

into Western philosophy through the work of the pre-Socratic Greek philosopher Heraclitus and evolved to what is now known as the dialectical view of reality by social theorists and scientists, influencing the work of philosophers such as Georg Hegel and social theorists such as Karl Marx (Morgan, 1991).

Reinforcing cycles: Vicious and virtuous cycles

The second component of paradoxes relates to the reinforcing cycles within which individuals become trapped as they attempt to resolve the aforementioned tensions. These reinforcing cycles perpetuate and aggravate the tensions. Smith and Lewis (2011) enhanced our understanding of the reinforcing cycles by arguing that paradoxical tensions once rendered salient, spur responses which can lead to negative or positive reinforcing cycles, which they call vicious or virtuous cycles, respectively.

Vicious cycles: Defensive reactions

Vicious cycles are a result of "cognitive and behavioural forces for consistency, emotional anxiety and defensiveness, and organisational forces for inertia" (Smith & Lewis, 2011, p. 391). Organisational members in their effort to resolve the paradoxical tensions become trapped within reinforcing cycles that preserve and aggravate the tension (Lewis, 2000). The first reactions from staff members are often defensive, holding to past understandings to avoid reorganising their cognitive and social shortcomings (Harris, 1996). There have been a number of defensive reactions to paradoxes identified (Smith & Berg, 1987; Vince & Broussine, 1996), such as: (1) *splitting*, which involves further polarising contradictions such as "forming subgroups, or artificial "we/they" distinctions that mask similarities" (Lewis, 2000, p. 763), (2) *projection*, which entails transferring

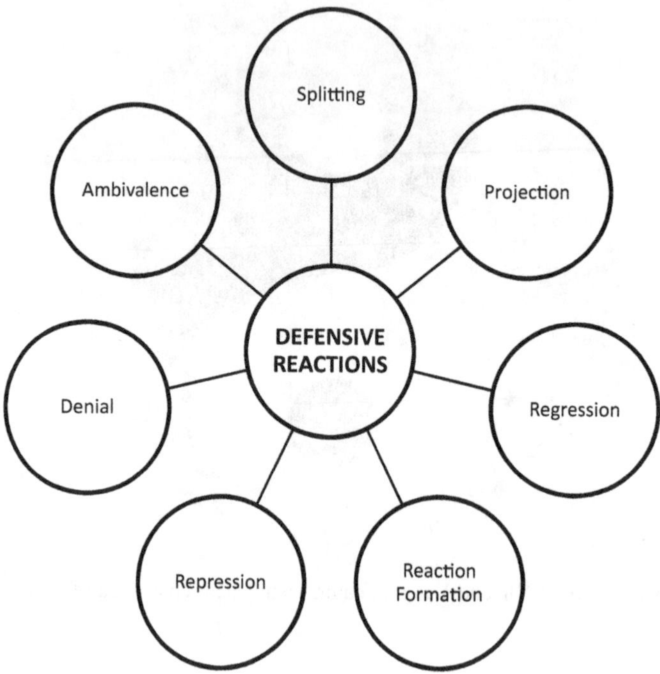

Figure 6.2 Defensive reactions to paradoxes.

conflicting attributes or feelings to others (a scapegoat), (3) *regression*, which signifies following actions which have offered some level of security in the past, (4) *reaction formation*, which involves "excessively manifesting the feeling opposite to the threatening one" (Vince & Broussine, 1996, p. 5), (5) *repression*, where staff members block unpleasant experiences from memory, (6) *denial* which includes employees' refusal to accept an unpleasant reality, and (7) *ambivalence*, which "signifies the compromise of conflicting emotions within 'lukewarm' reactions that lose the vitality of extremes" (Lewis, 2000, p. 763) (Figure 6.2). These defensive behaviours can be deceiving because they initially produce positive effects but ultimately lead to opposite unintended consequences that exacerbate the underlying tensions (Lewis, 2000).

Virtuous cycles: Embracing the paradoxes

On the other hand, *virtuous cycles* are a result of employees' acceptance and resolution strategies. Through their dynamic equilibrium model, Smith and Lewis (2011) proposed a more positive response to paradoxical tensions. They describe virtuous cycles where awareness of tensions triggers a management strategy that includes *acceptance* rather than defensiveness. This acceptance involves viewing tensions as an invitation for creativity and opportunity (Beech, Burns, de Caestecker, MacIntosh, & MacLean, 2004). Smith and Berg argued that "by immersing oneself in the opposing forces, it becomes possible to discover the link between them, the framework that gives meaning to the apparent contradictions in the experience" (1987, p. 391). This acceptance can be achieved through cognitive and behavioural complexity, and emotional equanimity at the individual level, and dynamic organisational capabilities at the organisational level (Smith & Lewis, 2011). *Cognitive complexity* involves an ability to recognise and accept the interrelatedness between underlying tensions. *Behavioural complexity* signifies the ability to adopt competing behaviours which enables acceptance of the paradoxical tensions (Denison, Hooijberg, & Quinn, 1995). *Emotional equanimity* involves emotional calm and evenness, which reduces anxiety and fear, caused by inconsistencies, and fosters paradoxical responses (Huy, 1999). Finally, with *organisational dynamic capabilities*, organisational leaders have the skills as well as the processes and routines that enable them to respond effectively to constantly shifting environments (Teece, Pisano, & Shuen, 1997).

Resolution strategies are a result of this acceptance achieved in an organisational setting, which provides employees a comfort with the underlying tensions (Smith & Lewis, 2011). Resolution strategies allow firms to respond to tensions through splitting and choosing between tensions or by identifying synergies that accommodate opposing poles. Splitting and synergies correspond to the concepts of differentiation and integration, respectively, which are explored in detail further below. Smith and Lewis' *dynamic equilibrium model* proposes that such strategies can be used together since "paradoxical resolution denotes purposeful iterations between alternatives in order to ensure simultaneous attention to them over time" (2011, p. 392).

Managing paradoxes: Coping mechanisms

The third component of paradoxes involves the mechanisms employed by organisational members to manage the paradoxical tensions. As previously emphasised, managing paradoxes does not mean resolving or eliminating them but taking advantage of their potential (Andriopoulos & Lewis, 2009). In many cases, when facing a paradox, organisational members tend to try to rationalise them and resolve them. However, successful managers are those who, instead, use the paradoxes they face, in a creative way, making sure both extreme opposite activities are captured (Eisenhardt, 2000). As opposed to trying to resolve or eliminate the paradoxes, managers ought to "recognise, become comfortable with, and even profit from tensions and the anxieties they provoke" (Lewis, 2000, p. 764). In fact, Eisenhardt and Westcott (1988) believe that paradoxes contribute enormously to management thinking by having the power to lead to creative insight and change.

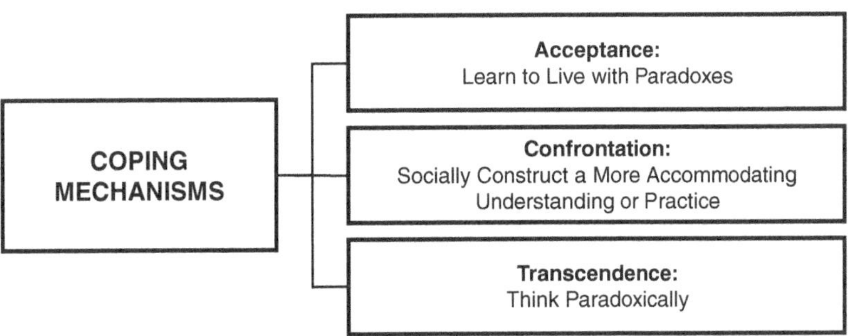

Figure 6.3 Managing paradoxes: Coping mechanisms.

Through a review of extant research studies, Lewis (2000) summarised three often interrelated approaches to managing paradoxes. The first involves *acceptance* where employees learn to live with the paradox which ultimately leads to a sense of freedom (e.g. Murnighan & Conlon, 1991; Schneider, 1990). The second approach to managing paradoxes involves *confrontation* where employees discuss the tensions to "socially construct a more accommodating understanding or practice" (Lewis, 2000, p. 764). Finally, another approach involves *transcendence* where employees have the capacity to think paradoxically (Figure 6.3). This is the most demanding approach because staff members have to go beyond 'first-order' thinking and employ 'second-order' thinking. First-order thinking would merely lead to a solution that is part of the problem and, therefore, aggravates it even further. Contrastingly, second-order thinking involves a higher level of thinking which goes beyond a basic analysis.

Lewis eloquently explains this level of thinking as one that involves

> critically examining entrenched assumptions to construct a more accommodating perception of opposites. Critical self- and social reflection might help actors reframe their assumptions, learn from existing tensions, and develop a more complicated repertoire of understandings and behaviours that better reflects organisational intricacies.
>
> (Lewis, 2000, p. 764)

This quote emphasises the maxim that managing paradoxes does not involve merely trying to resolve or eliminate them but in fact tap into their ability to bring change and drive innovation when embraced and celebrated within the firm.

Organisational paradoxes

Organisational paradoxes have been classified into four overarching categories: (1) paradoxes of learning which relate to knowledge, (2) paradoxes of organising which relate to organisational processes, (3) paradoxes of belonging, involving identity and interpersonal relationships, and (4) paradoxes of performing, related to organisational goals (Lewis, 2000; Smith & Lewis, 2011) (Figure 6.4). Let us explore these categories in more depth.

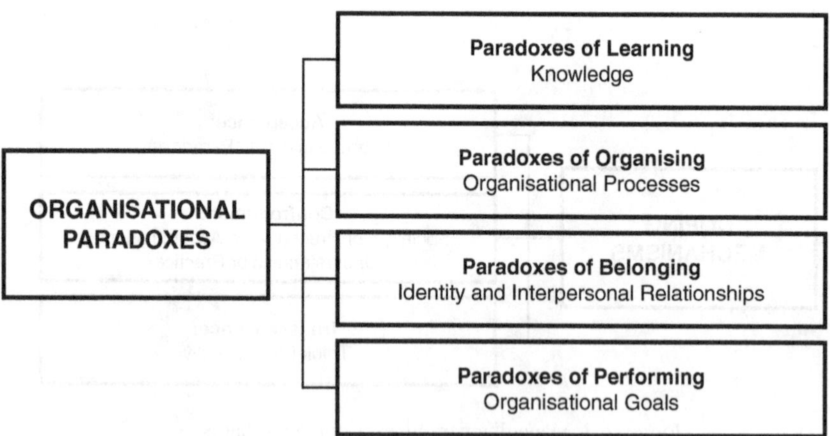

Figure 6.4 Overarching categories of organisational paradoxes.

Paradoxes of learning

Learning paradoxes emerge as dynamic systems change, renew, and innovate. These paradoxes relate to the efforts of employees to build upon, as well as destroy the past to create the future. As Cannon explains, "many paradoxes are caused by the hangover of one set of assumptions or beliefs into a new age or environment and proliferate when change is dramatic or rapid. Paradoxes emerge when beliefs or assumptions fail to keep up with external changes" (1996, p. 10). This describes the situations where employees fail to act when faced with inconsistencies between their own understanding and the information coming from the world around them, for instance, employees ignoring dramatic changes in the environment. Learning paradoxes stem primarily from the tension between the comfort of the past and the uncertainty of the future, a tension between old and new (Lewis, 2000). Paradoxes of learning are all about how the organisation engages with new ideas, including the tensions between radical and incremental innovation, as well as episodic or continuous change (Smith & Lewis, 2011).

After understanding the tensions which act as the sources of learning paradoxes, the question of course is how organisations manage such paradoxes. Lewis suggests that a combination of three elements, that allow social reframing, is required in order to cope with learning paradoxes. *Shock* is very important because it may impose employees to admit the limits of current understandings and practices; however, it cannot guarantee reframing. There is also a requirement for *open communication* and *experimentation* which can lead to social reflection (Westenholz, 1993). The leadership style within the organisation plays a very important role on how the firm copes with these paradoxes. There is need for a paradoxical leader who is able to think paradoxically, as well as guide social reflection, facilitating an environment where employees can examine the tensions instead of supressing them (Leonard-Barton, 1992; Westenholz, 1993).

Paradoxes of organising

Ford and Backoff (1988) argue that the organisation itself is a source of tension because "any action, any act of cognition, definition, or concept is based on, and establishes, distinctions. Thus, the very actions of organising involve the drawing of distinctions". Paradoxes of organising emerge from the tension between organisational attempts to operate efficiently and at the same time continuously adapt. Organising paradoxes relate to the conflicting aspects of organisational design (how organisations arrange their structure and their activities). Contingency theories which consider the differing impact of organic versus mechanistic structures, and distinguish organisations as stable or in flux, tend to downplay the complexities of organisational design and encourage an 'either/or' approach to such tensions. However, a paradox approach argues for the coexistence of opposing forces within organisations. Major tensions related to organising include that of control and flexibility, usually manifested in mixed messages (Argyris, 1993) and system contradictions (Putnam, 1986), as well as that of empowerment and formalisation.

There have also been more contextualised research studies on the paradoxes of creativity in the cultural industries. Two of the paradoxes identified can be incorporated under Lewis' (2000) organising paradoxes category: (1) the *difference* paradox which relates to the tension between crafting or standardising organisational policies, and (2) the *distance* paradox, which is concerned with the question of whether to couple or decouple creative and routine work (Cohendet & Simon, 2007; DeFillippi, Grabher, & Jones, 2007; Eikhof & Haunschild, 2007; Gander, Haberberg, & Rieple, 2007; Svejenova, Mazza, & Planellas, 2007; Thompson, Jones, & Warhurst, 2007).

In response to these organising paradoxes, many organisational members often resort to defensive strategies to comprehend the negative dynamics of these paradoxes. Such defensive strategies include repression and reaction formation. "Romanticising empowerment practices is a typical form of repression" (Lewis, 2000, p. 768), while employees overreacting to tensions of flexibility and control by focusing on one pole, can lead to a stronger pull from its opposite (Bouchikhi, 1998). Alternatively, organisational members often embrace the paradoxical tensions through the use of superordinate goals, humour, and behavioural complexity. The latter relates to the ability to have a wide range of actions to use when dealing with contradicting demands (Quinn, 1988). Again leadership plays a very important role in how the paradoxes of organising are managed. Organisational leaders must possess paradoxical behavioural repertoires that correspond to the contradicting elements of organisational life and are capable of achieving consistency, stability and control, *and* passion and courage within their firms (Lewis, 2000).

Paradoxes of belonging

The paradoxes of belonging are concerned with identity and interpersonal relationships (Lewis, 2000; Smith & Lewis, 2011). Social relationships are increasingly paradoxical because there is a blurring of hierarchical, occupational, and national distinctions in contemporary organisations. Paradoxes of belonging are about the issue of membership, and the tension between the identity of 'self' and the identity of 'other' (Smith & Berg, 1987). An underlying tension behind these paradoxes derives from employees' attempts to express themselves, demonstrate individuality, and at the same time achieve collective group affiliation. According to Smith and Berg (1987), the paradox of individuality is a self-referential cycle because

> the group exists, grows, and becomes strong, and resourceful only if the individuality of its members can be expressed. At the same time that a group requires connections, conformity, and similarity for its existence, it also requires discontinuities and differences. Both the differences that come as expressions of individuality and the similarities, expressed as connectedness, simultaneously jeopardise and strengthen the group. In like manner, the similarities and differences both support and threaten the individuality of group members.
>
> (Smith & Berg, 1987, p. 102)

Another paradoxical tension related to paradoxes of belonging arises in the construction of group boundaries. Group membership is often determined by differentiating one collective from another. However, things can get complicated because every employee is a member of different groups at the same time. Consider, for instance, the life of an academic in the university environment. He/she is a member of the organisation as a whole (the institution), a school (within this institution), a department (within this school), and often a team (discipline group or research stream within this department). He/she might also be a member of other groups outside the organisation. This can create different levels of membership and affiliation. Staff "are members of the organisation and of varied occupations and subcultures within and outside the organisation, provoking feelings of inclusion *and* exclusion simultaneously" (Lewis, 2000, p. 769).

This identity paradox was also identified by scholars investigating paradoxes in the specific context of the creative industries. The underlying tension relates to creating individual or collective identities, reputations, and careers (DeFillippi et al., 2007; Svejenova et al., 2007). Gotsi, Andriopoulos, Lewis, and Ingram (2010) explored the paradoxical identity of creative workers through a comparative case study of five new product development (NPD) firms. They recognised the tension between multiple identities that designers must take on. As they explain, one side of the same coin is 'creatives' trying to see themselves as unique in their artistry, passion, and self-expression, fostering an identity that invigorates their efforts for innovation. The flip side of the same coin is the fact that there are daily pressures to deliver projects within budgets, on deadlines, and in response to market demands. Such pressures require a more business-like identity that facilitates and enhances performance within the organisation. Gotsi et al.'s (2010) study explored the different ways these NPD firms manage the friction between these artistic and business identities.

On a more general level, beyond organisations, people also have multiple roles, and multiple identities. Handy (1994) discusses the paradox of belonging in relation to 'twin citizenship' and federalism. He explains that local citizenship is the easy part, as it is easy for each of us to identify with our neighbours and our local environment, especially if we are working with them. Yet people are also citizens of wider collectives. The following explains, in Handy's (1994) words, the benefits of a paradoxical approach to identity and the importance of twin citizenship and federalism to managing these paradoxes.

> Federalism is fraught with difficulty because it is trying to manage the paradox. Twin citizenship makes that possible. If there is a sense of belonging to something bigger as well as to something smaller, we can accept some restrictions on our local independence if it helps the larger whole ... In a business, it may be logical to combine functions, to group some regions together, to manage cash or purchasing centrally, but these actions steal power and decisions from independent units. Those units will be resentful, not understanding the paradox that in order to get the most value out of their independence it often pays to sacrifice some of that independence to a central function. That kind of compromise is only done willingly if there is confidence in the central function, a sense of belonging to a larger whole. We need that second citizenship.
>
> (Handy, 1994, p. 117)

He also added that "federalism, properly understood, can restore that sense of a local belonging and a broader, bigger citizenship, in both our organisations and in society" (Handy, 1994, p. 131).

Paradoxes of performing

Extending Lewis' (2000) work, Smith and Lewis (2011) identified paradoxes of performing as an additional overarching category of organisational paradoxes. Such paradoxes derive from the plurality of stakeholders and lead to the organisation having competing strategies and goals. In many organisations, there is a tension between the differing and frequently conflicting demands between internal stakeholders, such as employees, managers, and shareholders, and external stakeholders such as creditors, consumers, the government, and the local community (Donaldson & Preston, 1995).

Paradoxes of performing extend to an inter-organisational level through corporate partnerships between two or more organisations. Besides the aforementioned external stakeholders, competitors can also be considered an external stakeholder for an organisation. In fact, an organisation often enters into partnerships with other organisations, notwithstanding their rivalry in the same market sector. Such endeavours can lead to tensions between the need for cooperation between these partnering organisations and the need to continue to be competitive. Such 'coopetition' "is paradoxical in that the simultaneous cooperation and competition can give rise to important synergies as well as tensions" (Stadtler & Van Wassenhove, 2016, p. 655).

Smith and Lewis (2011) emphasise the interconnectedness among the aforementioned categories of organisational paradoxes. They claim that tensions do not only operate within these categories but also between these categories. They explain that learning and performing stimulate tensions between developing future capabilities while making sure success is possible in the present. "Tensions between learning and belonging reflect conflicts between the need for change and the desire to retain a developed sense of self and purpose. Organisational identities often become enablers and obstacles to development and change" (Smith & Lewis, 2011, p. 384). Organisational capabilities aiming for focus and efficiency while enabling change and agility can lead to organising and learning tensions. The need for dynamic capabilities creates tensions in looking to continuously change and renew stable routines within the organisation (Smith & Lewis, 2011).

Paradoxes of creativity and innovation

A specific stream within paradox literature has explored tensions related to creativity and innovation, pertinent especially in organisations whose aim is to deliver creative products and innovation, such as design consultancies. It is important to explore these paradoxes because this will demonstrate the tensions that design managers are called to manage in organisational life. Extant literature has identified a number of paradoxes related to innovation and creativity. It is now important to explore the typologies produced over the years, as these relate specifically to design firms and the discipline of design management.

Paradoxes of creativity: Connections with the 4 Ps typology

In the previous chapter, we discussed four important variables that can influence creativity: person, product, press, and process (4 Ps) (Rhodes, 1987). Cropley and Cropley (2012) make interesting

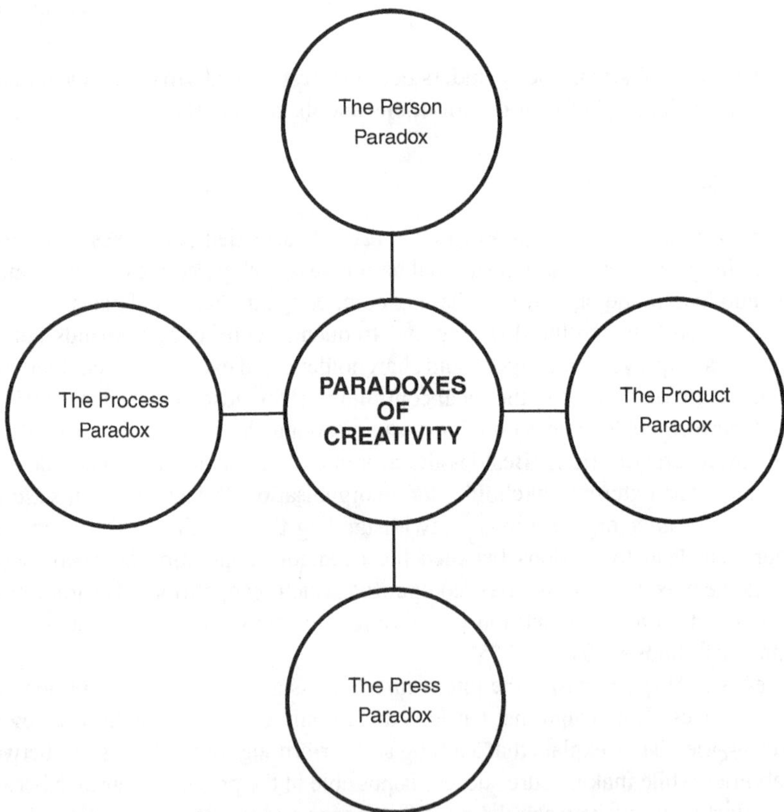

Figure 6.5 Paradoxes of creativity.

connections between this typology and the concept of paradox, by exploring the paradoxical nature of each of these elements. Our ensuing discussion demonstrates how in each element we can find two poles which, although antagonistic and of opposing nature, are both required in creativity and consequently in innovation. Understanding the paradoxical nature of each of these elements will highlight the tensions experienced in creativity and innovation (Figure 6.5).

The process paradox

As already explored, the 'process' element in Rhodes' (1987) typology includes cognitive process and thinking techniques which can foster and increase the creative performance of organisational teams. Early creativity research overemphasised the importance of divergent thinking in the creative process to the point that creativity came to be equated with divergent thinking immediately after Guilford's (1950) seminal work. However, more recent studies have identified that the individuals regarded as the most creative are those that can switch between convergent and divergent thinking (Ward & Kolomyts, 2010). Thus, both types of thinking are essential for creativity to flourish. More specifically, Ward and Kolomyts (2010) demonstrated that creative idea production requires the interaction of a plurality of cognitive factors, including not only the ability to combine concepts and images or associative thinking (related to divergent thinking) but also accurate representation, recall of information, evaluation of possible solutions, and selection of the best (related to convergent thinking). This indicates the process paradox, the tension between convergent and divergent thinking, their required contributions to creativity, and the need for designers and design managers to excel in both types of thinking.

The person paradox

The 'person' element includes the personal characteristics of the individual, including his/her personal traits, intellect, temperament, attitudes, self-concept, and values. As stated by Csikszentmihalyi (1996), creativity requires a complex, paradoxical personality that combines contradictions such as sensitivity with toughness, or high intelligence with naiveté. Both the adaptation of what exists and the development of something new can lead to useful novel products. Therefore, both adaptive *and* innovative personal characteristics are involved in creativity (Kirton, 1989). The former characteristics involve the preference to deal with the new by extending the already known, while the latter characteristics relate to the preference to deal with the new by generating something novel.

Extensive research studies have explored the relationship between mood and creativity. Kaufmann (2003) argues that mood is an antecedent to creativity, accompanies it, and results from it. Despite the widely accepted view that positive mood fosters creativity and negative mood opposes it, Baas, De Dreu, and Nijstad (2008) determined that some moods affect certain aspects of creativity but not other aspects, and some moods are more influential on creativity than others. Referring to Baas et al's. (2008) work, Cropley and Cropley explain that "positive moods do lead to more creativity when the task is framed as enjoyable and intrinsically rewarding, but to less when the task is framed as serious and extrinsically rewarding and performance standards are emphasized" (2012, p. 33).

Motivation has also been another important variable examined by many creativity scholars. As already explored in Chapter 5, a widely accepted stance is that intrinsic motivation is conducive to creativity, while extrinsic motivation is detrimental to creativity. Hence, higher levels of creativity are generated when the individual wishes to carry out the activity for the sake of the activity itself, regardless of any external reward (Amabile, 1983a, 1983b, 1996). However, more recently, Collins and Amabile (1999) have recognised that extrinsic motivation is not necessarily fatal to creativity. In fact, Eisenberger and Byron (2011) determined that both intrinsic and extrinsic motivation can foster creativity, depending on the product, i.e., the kind of task, "the way the task is presented and the kind of performance (e.g. generation of a novel product vs. generation of a large number of products) that is rewarded" (Cropley & Cropley, 2012, p. 33), which relates to the element of 'press' (in the 4Ps typology). In general terms, the opposing, yet interrelated nature of the aforementioned characteristics constitutes the paradoxical nature of the person element of creativity.

The product paradox

In Rhodes' (1987) typology, the 'product' element is concerned with the outcomes or artefacts that are generated as a result of creativity. As already mentioned, creative ideas must not only be novel but also appropriate (Warr & O'Neill, 2005). The requirement for both indicates the paradoxical nature of the product element of creativity because novelty and appropriateness can be deemed as antithetical, yet necessary poles. Novelty implies non-conformity, whereas appropriateness, the exact opposite, an idea is regarded as appropriate when it conforms to the characteristics predetermined during the problem identification and preparation stage of the creative process. Novelty that cannot be put into practice involves only quasi-creativity at best or pseudo-creativity at worst.

> In business, to be relevant and effective, novelty must not only work (do what is supposed to do), but it must also be understandable, usable, and acceptable to other people, not so much the experts in the field, but more frequently consumers … Thus, products need to be simultaneously novel, original, and even surprising, and yet routine (in the sense of reliable and effective).
>
> (Cropley & Cropley, 2012, pp. 33–34)

The press paradox

Finally, we have previously discussed how the 'press' element involves environmental and contextual factors that can influence creative performance including organisational culture, climate, leadership, structures and rewards, and the work context (Reiter-Palmon, Herman, & Yammarino, 2008). Amabile (1996) discusses the complex interaction between management pressure (press) and innovation. She determined that high levels of environmental demand facilitate performance in cases where the task involves carrying out predefined steps. In contrast, a low level of demand facilitates creativity, where the task involves exploring possibilities. Therefore, high managerial pressure is conducive to creativity, under certain circumstances, but an opponent to creativity under other circumstances (West, 2002). The paradoxical nature of the press element will become clearer in our discussion of the paradoxes of innovation typologies that follows below.

Paradoxes of innovation typologies

By engaging in a research study with a number of leading design firms, Andriopoulos (2003) identified six paradoxes in managing creativity. First, the need to *support employees' passions and achieve the organisation's financial goals* at the same time. This paradox means that the organisation has to, on the one hand, provide opportunities for staff members to work on exciting projects that reflect their employees' personal interests and enable creative thinking to prosper, *and*, on the other hand, ensure that financial goals are met. The latter, at times, means that the organisation will have to pursue projects which are deemed by organisational members monotonous and uninspiring, because such projects bring to the firm great financial returns. The onus is on design managers and project leaders to select the appropriate projects which are commercially promising or creatively interesting, and match employees to the right projects which utilise their skills and knowledge and at the same time challenge them at the right level. This relates to the notion of stretch (Amabile, 1998) which we discussed in Chapter 5. Therefore, such approach requires design managers to be aware of staff members' skills, needs, and aspirations, and facilitate challenging yet rewarding projects for them.

Second, Andriopoulos (2003) identified the importance of *challenging staff members and at the same time building their confidence.* This paradox, too, relates to the aforementioned concept of stretching because design managers should challenge their staff, but not in a way that it creates a climate of fear, but in a way that is rewarding. Creating a 'no-fear' climate and challenging employees are equally important (Andriopoulos & Gotsi, 2005). It is very often that employees who work on the same task for a long period of time become unproductive due to fatigue and boredom. "Involving employees in multiple projects or work stages is a means of nourishing their creativity" (Andriopoulos, 2003, p. 380).

Third, Andriopoulos (2003) identified the paradox of *personal initiative versus shared vision.* The underlying tension relates to the need to ensure that employees understand they are part of a collective (shared organisational vision), while encouraging personal initiative to allow an element of freedom to pursue their own interests. This means that employees need to be given the choice about what they do and how they do it, but at the same time they meet the objectives of the organisation and respect its norms and rules (Andriopoulos, 2003).

Fourth, at the project team level, there is also the need for *encouraging team diversity while assembling cohesive project teams* (Andriopoulos, 2003). Diversity within project teams is an important element for fostering higher levels of creativity. Staff members from different personal, disciplinal, and cultural backgrounds can challenge each other and demonstrate to each other an alternative way of thinking or doing things. Organisational culture should encourage diversity and non-conformism by valuing and celebrating members' individual skills, knowledge, expertise, and personality. As previously discussed, conformism is the opposite of creativity (Crutchfield, 1955, 1962), so much that it is considered to be anathema to creative behaviour (Amabile, 1988). However, too much diversity might be problematic as team members need to feel that they can associate with colleagues and talk the same language. Hence, it is important that design managers build cohesive work teams. Notwithstanding the need for cohesiveness, the need to talk the same language should not stand in the way of generating different viewpoints and challenging the ideas generated. It is all about the balance between diversity and cohesiveness.

From a learning perspective, the fifth paradox includes the need for firms to *learn from the past but at the same time seek new areas of knowledge.* This signifies the fact that past successes and failures can act as a pool of knowledge and experience for every staff member within the firm. Understanding the reasons for the success or failure of past projects allows the organisation to prevent mistakes reoccurring. Nevertheless, this does not mean that staff members should merely imitate previous work that has been successful. This would lead to unwanted stagnation. Besides, every project is unique and every client idiosyncratic. Firms must identify this fine line between learning from the past and creative conditioning. This certainly relates with the paradoxes of learning category discussed in the previous section (Lewis, 2000; Smith & Lewis, 2011). It is important that senior management encourages a knowledge-creating culture within the organisation.

Finally, in a paradox related to the strategic direction of an organisation, firms need to create a culture which promotes both *incremental risks* (repeat projects that maintain clients) *and breakthrough ideas* (which enhance the creative reputation of the firm). Hence, the organisation needs to encourage both types of thinking, incremental and radical, in order to balance conventional wisdom with 'blue-sky' ideas (Andriopoulos, 2003).

In a follow up paper, Andriopoulos and Lewis (2010) aimed at exploring how highly innovative companies manage tensions across top management, project, group, and individual creative worker levels.

On the individual creative worker's level, they identified the *passion–discipline* paradox which occurs because "passion fosters intrinsic motivation that builds commitment and excitement for the work, while discipline channels individual's efforts from ideas to fruition" (Andriopoulos & Lewis, 2010, p. 115). Passion leads to intrinsic motivation which is fundamental for enhancing creativity (Amabile, 1996) and discipline directs creativity and supports the execution of ideas. On a group level, they identified the group *diversity–cohesiveness* paradox (similar to Andriopoulos, 2003) while on the project level, they noticed the *possibilities–constraints* paradox where projects are driven by competing demands promoted by the design team or the client, regardless of the project goals, i.e., leading to radical or incremental innovation, respectively. Finally, on the senior management level, Andriopoulos and Lewis (2010) suggest that there has to be dual emphases on *experimentation* to address the needs of emerging clients through new approaches towards technologies and business processes *and* on *satisfying the needs of existing clients* through the application, improvement and extension of existing competencies, technologies and products.

In a different paper, Andriopoulos and Lewis (2009) identified three paradoxes of innovation as interwoven with each other. First, the *personal drivers* paradox includes an interdependence of discipline and passion (similar to Andriopoulos & Lewis, 2010). Second, the paradox of *customer orientation* includes an emphasis on both tight coupling and loose coupling. This paradox appears "during projects, grappling with the need to be tightly and loosely coupled to the client. Whereas clients stress competitive, market, and their own constraints ... [design] firms seek to explore emerging technologies and trends" (Andriopoulos & Lewis, 2009, p. 704) and relates to the possibilities–constraints paradox (Andriopoulos & Lewis, 2010). Third, the paradox of *strategic intent* involves an emphasis on both profit *and* breakthroughs, and relates to the strategic direction of the organisation as we have previously discussed (Andriopoulos, 2003). Organisations which are part of the creative industries must recognise the fact that they are 'creative businesses'. Design consultancies must be, by definition, creative, since this is the core of the professional services they provide to clients. "Creativity may indeed be the *a priori* currency of designers. However, the coordination of design labour – the management of design – is a necessary action to ensure its successful outcome" (Julier & Moor, 2009, p. 6). Thus, one must not forget that creative businesses are still 'businesses', and hence must be profitable too by maintaining effective client relationships and efficient management of creative accounts/projects (Lalaounis, Wood, & Harrison, 2012). The design work 'produced' is not developed for the sake of art (DeFillipi et al., 2007) but 'creatives' are required to innovate within certain boundaries since creative

Table 6.1 Paradoxes of innovation typologies.

Level	*Andriopoulos (2003)*	*Andriopoulos and Lewis (2010)*	*Andriopoulos and Lewis (2009)*
Organisational	Satisfy employees' passions *and* achieve the organisation's financial goals Learn from the past *and* seek new areas of knowledge Challenge staff members *and* build their confidence	'Long-term adaptability–short-term survival'	Strategic Intent
Project	Incremental risks (repeat projects) *and* breakthrough ideas	'Possibilities–Constraints'	Customer Orientation
Group	Encourage team diversity *and* assemble cohesive project teams	'Diversity–Cohesiveness'	
Individual	Personal initiative *and* shared vision	'Passion–Discipline'	Personal Drivers

production is embedded in an economic context, where art and commerce are interweaved (Eikhoff & Haunschild, 2007). Table 6.1 provides a classification of the paradoxes of innovation typologies on the basis of organisational, project, group, and individual levels.

Organisational ambidexterity

The next question we must address is of course how organisations and in particular design managers can manage the aforementioned paradoxes, especially those related to creativity and innovation. Organisational ambidexterity is considered the principle way of 'managing' the overarching tensions. The roots of the word ambidexterity include the Latin 'ambi' meaning both and 'dexter' meaning right or favourable (Maier, 2015). Ambidextrous organisations are defined by Tushman and O'Reilly as those organisations which have the "ability to simultaneously pursue both incremental and discontinuous (radical) innovation and change results from hosting multiple contradictory structures, processes, and cultures within the same firm" (1996, p. 23). Therefore, they are those with the ability to both exploit the present time and their current resources, products and knowhow, *and* explore the new, the radical, the unconventional, be it products, technologies, or markets. The concept of ambidexterity has been applied to different competing acts and broadly refers to the organisation being able to perform different and often opposing and competing strategic acts at the same time. Such competing acts have included the organisations' ability to achieve *both* search and stability, flexibility and efficiency, search scope and depth, exploitative and explorative learning, exploitative and explorative knowledge sharing, pro-profit and pro-growth strategies, alignment and adaptability, incremental and discontinuous (radical) innovation. The last two competing acts will be the focus of the rest of this chapter because they relate to innovation and creativity, and consequently with the work of the design manager, whose responsibility is to organise the firm to achieve the highest levels of design innovation.

Understanding ambidexterity

As mentioned above, ambidexterity provides the firm the ability to pursue incremental and radical innovation at the same time. Incremental innovation can be achieved through exploitation activities which refine and extend existing knowledge, improve current offerings, and seek greater efficiency for the organisation (Atuahene-Gima, 2005). In contrast, radical innovation relates to exploration activities which seek to develop new knowledge, experiment, and achieve a novel result. Many organisational scholars have argued that for an organisation to be innovative, it must excel at both types of innovation simultaneously or sequentially (Birkinshaw & Gibson, 2004; Gibson & Birkinshaw, 2004; Jansen, Volberda, & Van den Bosch, 2005; Raisch & Birkinshaw, 2008; Raisch, Birkinshaw, Probst, & Tushman, 2009; Tushman & O'Reilly, 1996). Yet attempting both can lead to tensions due to their different knowledge management processes (March, 1991). Ambidextrous organisations are those that can excel at both emphases, which makes them successful in product development (Sheremata, 2000) and leads to long-term performance (O'Reilly & Tushman, 2004; Tushman & O'Reilly, 1996). Nevertheless, achieving both requires a balance between these two approaches, not merely a split or a compromise between them.

There are two overarching dimensions which can help us understand the different approaches to achieving ambidexterity. First, the *spatial (or structural) dimension* refers to whether or not ambidexterity is realised within the same business unit or not. "When both exploitation and exploration are pursued by the same unit, the pursuit of ambidexterity is viewed as structurally independent. Conversely, when these pursuits involve two or more separate units, ambidexterity is viewed as structurally interdependent" (Simsek, Heavey, Veiga, & Souder, 2009, p. 868). Second, the *temporal (time) dimension* is concerned with whether or not exploitation and exploration are pursued simultaneously or sequentially over time.

With regard to spatial dimension, approaches can be classified under the overarching umbrellas of 'architectural ambidexterity' and 'contextual ambidexterity'. The former stands for differentiation, while the latter for integration.

> [Differentiation involves] recognizing and articulating distinctions [and] … helps overcome inertia both by reinforcing the needs of each product [incremental and radical] and being vigilant that the innovation is not crowded out by commitments to existing strategies and processes … [while integration includes] … shifting levels of analysis to identify potential linkages … [It] is associated with sustained attention to possible synergies between the exploitative and exploratory products. Attention to integration helps the team explicitly look for ways that the contradictory strategies can help each other.
>
> (Smith & Tushman, 2005, p. 527)

Therefore, with *architectural ambidexterity*, there are dual structures and strategies, allowing for efforts to be differentiated to focus either on exploitation or exploration (Gupta, Smith, & Shalley, 2006). This means that the organisation creates separate structures for different types of activities. For instance, core business units have the responsibility for aligning with existing products and markets, while the onus of preparing for new markets, developing new technologies and staying informed of emerging industry trends lies with the research and development (R&D) department and the business development group. Hence, structural separation is appropriate because these two sets of activities are seen as dramatically different which cannot co-exist. This notion is, however, questioned by Birkinshaw and Gibson (2004) who argue that this can lead to isolation where many R&D departments and business development groups fail to get their ideas accepted because they lack the necessary links with the core business units. Instead of architectural ambidexterity, they argue for what they call *contextual ambidexterity* which demonstrates the ways that exploitative and explorative innovation can be behaviourally and socially integrated. Contextual ambidexterity

> calls for individual employees to make choices between alignment-oriented and adaptation-oriented activities in the context of their day-to-day work. In business units that are either solely aligned or solely adaptive, employees have clear mandates and are rewarded accordingly. But in a business unit that is ambidextrous, the systems and structures are more flexible, allowing employees to use their own judgment as to how they divide their time between adaptation-oriented and alignment-oriented activities.
>
> (Birkinshaw & Gibson, 2004, p. 49)

The two approaches are two distinct cognitive processes associated with managing strategic contradictions, and are opposing, yet complimentary (Birkinshaw & Gibson, 2004). By addressing different aspects of paradoxical contexts, they reinforce one another. Organisations need to engage in both approaches to enable teams to carry out balanced decision making (Smith & Tushman, 2005). Many successful organisations such as *Hewlett-Packard*, *3M*, and *Intel* have used both architectural and contextual ambidexterity approaches to achieve both exploitative and exploratory innovation.

As far as the temporal (time) dimension is concerned, earlier studies suggested that in order for an organisation to be successful, it needs to pursue exploitation and exploration activities sequentially

(Burns & Stalker, 1961; Duncan, 1976; Thompson, 1967). Hence, *sequential ambidexterity* occurs as firms switch structures to initiate and then execute innovation. They begin the process with organic structures to achieve exploration, and then move to mechanistic structures to pursue exploitation. Such sequential approach to ambidexterity is suitable to certain scenarios, as our ensuing discussion will explain. However, there are also certain cases where an alternative conceptualisation is more appropriate: *simultaneous ambidexterity*. Due to the complexity of the market, and the pace of change, organisations might need to pursue both exploitation and exploration simultaneously (Tushman & O'Reilly, 1997; O'Reilly & Tushman, 2008).

The four types of organisational ambidexterity

The juxtaposition of these two dimensions leads to a two-by-two typology of four types of ambidexterity (Simsek et al., 2009). First, *harmonic ambidexterity*, which occurs when the organisation pursues exploitation and exploration simultaneously and within the same unit. Second, *cyclical ambidexterity* is concerned with the case where the same organisational unit pursues a long period of exploitation, with the associated stability, and sporadic episodes of exploration and the change this entails. The third type of ambidexterity, *partitional ambidexterity*, occurs when ambidexterity is pursued simultaneously across units, interdependently, where there is a dual structure, with different divisions, one to initiate and explore, and one to execute and exploit (as recommended by Duncan, 1976). Finally, *reciprocal ambidexterity* is the type which has received the least attention from organisational scholars. It occurs when the firm pursues exploitation and exploration across different, interdependent units, sequentially (Figure 6.6).

The following section will explore the antecedents of these four types of ambidexterity, which will allow us to comprehend how design managers can foster and maintain these types of ambidexterity within their organisations.

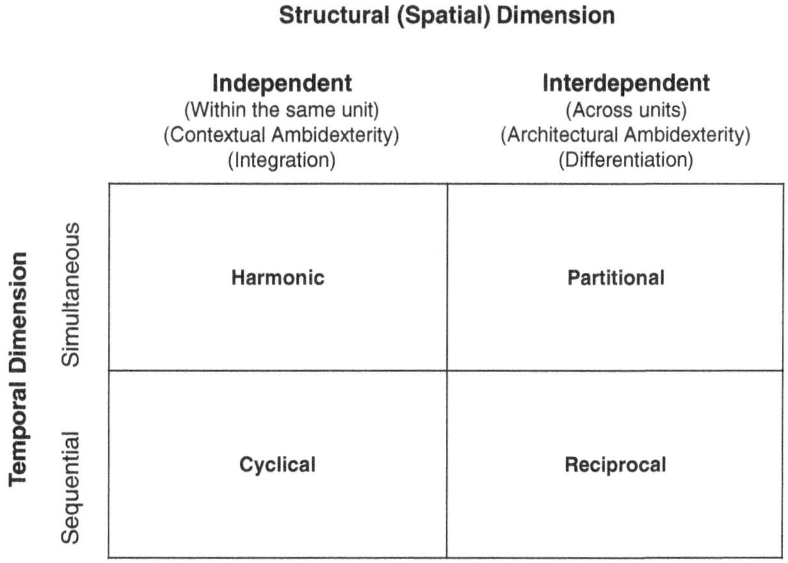

Structural (Spatial) Dimension

Temporal Dimension	**Independent** (Within the same unit) (Contextual Ambidexterity) (Integration)	**Interdependent** (Across units) (Architectural Ambidexterity) (Differentiation)
Simultaneous	**Harmonic**	**Partitional**
Sequential	**Cyclical**	**Reciprocal**

Figure 6.6 Types of organisational ambidexterity.

Building and maintaining organisational ambidexterity

Ambidexterity is extremely important for the performance of any organisation because it allows firms to achieve the combination of incremental and radical innovation, through exploitation and exploration. Achieving this can be very challenging because exploiting and exploring are contradictory to one another (Smith & Tushman, 2005). The epistemological belief of the 'unitary truth' (Ford & Backoff, 1988; Voorhees, 1986), where "contradictions and inconsistencies cannot coexist, leads to the notion that one of them must be right and the other wrong" (Smith & Tushman, 2005, p. 525). Hence, many organisations find achieving ambidexterity challenging or 'illogical' and they seldom manage to combine exploitation and exploration, putting an emphasis on either side, which creates vicious cycles (Smith & Lewis, 2011). In fact, many organisations tend to overemphasise exploitation because such activities bring out immediate returns and can maintain a healthy cash flow. Alas, such "tendencies to increase exploitation and reduce exploration make adaptive processes self-destructive" (March, 1991, p. 73). Other organisations emphasise exploration to the extent that they become too risky, ignore their current core competencies and work on imaginative projects at the expense of projects that can maintain a healthy cash flow (Birkinshaw & Gibson, 2004). Birkinshaw and Gibson (2004) raise the examples of *Lloyds TSB* bank and *Ericsson* as organisations where there has been an overemphasis on one pole of the equation, with serious detrimental effects on the organisations' performance. Building and maintaining ambidexterity is a challenging endeavour; therefore, it is very important to understand the steps design managers need to take in order to achieve and maintain an ambidextrous culture within their organisations.

The ambidextrous individual

First, managers need to employ organisational members who possess, or have the potential to develop, the personal characteristics required for ambidexterity to flourish. Employees need to be capable of recognising the times where adaptability or alignment is the appropriate course of action, in their daily work. For this reason, senior managers ought to employ those who: (1) take the initiative and are continuously aware of opportunities beyond the confines of their own jobs. This remind us of Brown and Wyatt's (2010) 'T-shaped people' who have depth of their own discipline and skills and the empathy for other disciplines; (2) are cooperative and look for opportunities to combine their efforts with others; (3) are 'brokers', and thus always seek to build internal links; and (4) are multi-taskers who are capable and comfortable of wearing more than one 'hat' (Birkinshaw and Gibson, 2004). The latter refers to the ability to develop and maintain multiple identities. For instance, Gotsi et al. (2010) demonstrated how creative workers have the ability to take on the different roles of the artist *and* the consultant at different times or simultaneously. As they explain

> segregating creatives' varied roles in time and space helped compartmentalise and leverage their distinct identities. To minimise identity conflict, however, socialisation efforts sought to cultivate an integrative meta-identity. Helping creative workers view themselves as 'practical artists' accentuated synergies between their identities, reducing the sense of tensions and resulting defensiveness that can fuel destructive extremes.
>
> (Gotsi et al., 2010, p. 782)

The aforementioned four characteristics of the ambidextrous individual have a number of commonalities. First, they call for the ability to act outside the narrow confines of the individual's job, as well as acting in the broader interest of the organisation. Second, ambidextrous individuals are those who are motivated and appropriately informed to act spontaneously without waiting for the permission or the support from their superiors. Third, these individuals can adapt to new opportunities *and* stay clearly aligned with the overall business strategy. "They illustrate how a dual capacity for alignment and adaptability can be woven into the fabric of an organisation on the individual level" (Birkinshaw & Gibson, 2004, p. 50). Let us now turn our attention on how we can build and maintain the four types of ambidexterity in different organisational contexts.

Developing harmonic ambidexterity

In order for organisations to develop harmonic ambidexterity where exploitation and exploration are pursued simultaneously and within the same unit, a context that promotes a behavioural orientation towards a combined capacity for both, needs to be developed. Senior managers can shape the organisational context through the systems and processes they establish and maintain within the firm, and through their daily actions. All these are then acted upon and reinforced through the attitudes, beliefs, and behaviours of all organisational members in the firm (Birkinshaw & Gibson, 2004). An organisation's context can be defined through the interaction of four set of attributes: (1) stretch, (2) discipline, (3) support, and (4) trust (Ghoshal & Bartlett, 1997). Birkinshaw and Gibson (2004) combine these four attributes to create two dimensions: (1) *performance management* (combining stretch and discipline) which is about motivating people to deliver high-quality results, as well as making them accountable for their actions, and (2) *social support* (combining support and trust) which is concerned with offering staff members the security and latitude they need to perform.

Performance management and social support are *both* vital for the organisation and are mutually reinforcing; strong presence of both can build harmonic ambidexterity, creating a 'high performance organisational context' (Birkinshaw & Gibson, 2004). An imbalance of these characteristics, or a lack of both, creates contexts which are less optimal, and less prone to ambidexterity. Organisations such as *Oracle* and *Renault* have been really successful in creating such context by striking the right balance of social support and performance management. In addition to an appropriate context, Adler, Goldoftas, and Levine (1999) suggested that organisational practices and routines such as job enrichment programmes and meta-routines can create harmonic ambidexterity because they can train staff members to pursue both exploitation and exploration, synchronise and integrate these activities, emphasising systematic reflection and conflict regulation.

Developing cyclical ambidexterity

Organisations which pursue cyclical ambidexterity, and hence sequential ambidexterity within the same unit, tend to be those with technological orientation because patterns of investment in technology-oriented companies follow an S-shaped curve. The start of the curve represents the early-stage effort and investment which is required until a dominant design is decided upon (exploration). Following this, in the next stage, this dominant design is exploited, and therefore, there is a dramatic increase in production results (Chen, 2005). Ultimately, at the top of the curve, the influence of exploitation decreases to marginal, and this cycle starts all over again. Research studies on product development alliances, such as between biotechnology firms or software development companies, have shown that organisations formed alliances to explore and develop new knowledge, and then formed other alliances to exploit that knowledge (Lavie & Rosenkopf, 2006; Rothaermel & Deeds, 2004). This demonstrates sequential ambidexterity where exploration, in terms of discovering, acquiring, and developing new products, services, or technologies, precedes exploitation which involves commercialisation, application, and leveraging of these new offerings (Simsek, 2009). In order to succeed in instigating and maintaining cyclical ambidexterity, organisations need to establish mechanisms to cope with any conflicts between managers resulting from the transition between episodes of exploitation and exploration. "Human resource practices that emphasize innovation, teamwork, and flexibility are apt to be the underpinnings of an adaptive organisational culture that enables these sequential shifts" (Simsek, 2009, p. 883).

Developing partitional ambidexterity

Partitional ambidexterity which involves interdependent units pursuing exploitation and exploration simultaneously requires the organisation to have a clear strategic intent which explains the importance of ambidexterity and an *overarching strategic vision* which can build a common identity across different units (O'Reilly & Tushman, 2008). As Jansen, George, Van den Bosch, and Volberda (2008) suggest, a strategic vision shared among senior managers can provide collective understanding of how tensions between exploitative and explorative units can be resolved, and how a collective response to various environmental demands can be developed. Structurally, partitional ambidexterity requires the development of separate units or divisions for exploitation and exploration, with their own strategic logics, cultures, and incentive systems, which need to be hosted within the same firm (Duncan, 1976; Tushman & O'Reilly, 1996). Achieving interdependence and loose coupling of the business units can be very challenging and requires, besides a shared vision, senior management team coordination, and systems for *knowledge integration*. The onus is on senior managers to emphasise that both exploitation and exploration are equally important to the organisational performance by institutionalising dual architectures and the processes to deal with costs and conflicts associated with ambidexterity. Senior managers (such as design managers) need to be able to embrace the paradoxes associated with pursuing both exploitation and exploration. Transformational leaders are well equipped to "force socially integrated teams to critically debate and openly discuss conflicting task issues" (Jansen et al., 2008, p. 22).

Developing reciprocal ambidexterity

In the case of reciprocal ambidexterity, where exploitation and exploration is pursued sequentially across different interdependent units, "the interplay between exploitation and exploration takes place both within and between organisations" (Holmqvist, 2004, p. 72). This means that this reciprocal relationship may involve an 'extension process' where a firm extends its experience to others, for instance, in the form of a strategic alliance, or an 'internalisation process' in which an organisation may internalise experiences as retrieved in inter-organisational rules (Holmqvist, 2004). In order to achieve reciprocal ambidexterity, senior managers need to be able to disseminate information across *and* within organisations, enabling the reciprocal information flows between exploitative and exploratory domains (Mom, Van den Bosch, & Volberda, 2007). Simsek et al. believe that "reciprocal ambidexterity is more likely to emerge in complex environments, where the depth (or requisite variety) of knowledge needed to both explore and exploit is more likely to reside in multiple units" (2009, p. 887).

Managing innovation paradoxes through ambidexterity

We previously stated that ambidexterity is the principle way of managing organisational tensions. With respect to design management, we are primarily concerned with managing those tensions which relate to creativity and innovation. Thus, it is important at this stage to refer back to Andriopoulos and Lewis' (2009) work, who identified the ways ambidexterity can be used to manage the 'strategic intent', 'customer orientation', and 'personal drivers' paradoxes, through their extensive research with successful international NPD firms. Although intertwined, let us explore the management of each of these paradoxes separately, referring to the coping mechanisms employed by these firms.

Managing the strategic intent paradox

Ambidexterity is the way of generating the necessary synergy between the profit and breakthrough emphases, which is the underlying tension in the strategic intent paradox. The NPD firms studied by Andriopoulos and Lewis (2009) demonstrated mixes of integration and differentiation in their management techniques, and hence a mix of contextual and architectural ambidexterity, respectively. These organisations demonstrated what Collins and Porras (1994) described as 'pragmatic idealism'; therefore, they had the vision to be highly profitable *and* highly idealistic. The firms worked on both unconventional design work which attracted attention and led to new clients, and incremental innovation work which funded the risky 'blue-sky' projects. "Supportive communications help avoid paradoxical visions being interpreted as oversimplified or unrealistic. Reiteration also may build trust and avoid mixed messages" (Andriopoulos & Lewis, 2009, p. 704) about what the organisation wants to achieve. The NPD firms studied, pursued exploitation projects that leverage and enhance their existing specialisation and knowledge, *and* exploration projects which sought to create new opportunities for them. Such opportunities could be through collaborating with clients or suppliers through joint ventures, and in general seizing entrepreneurial opportunities for revolutionary work (Andriopoulos & Lewis, 2009).

Managing the customer orientation paradox

When seeking to manage the customer orientation paradox, and the underlying tension between tightly or loosely coupling the design activities to the client, i.e., between sticking to existing markets or exploring emerging technologies and trends, the NPD firms pursued a combination of simultaneous and sequential ambidexterity. The former demonstrated the concept of purposeful improvisation which, according to Miner, Bassof, and Moorman (2001), refers to the ability to recombine existing elements in new ways. The projects the organisations worked on, involved both work which exploited existing routines, and work which explored within and pushed boundaries (Andriopoulos & Lewis, 2009). The latter took the form of temporal separation "splitting the tensions by iterating between project constraints and freedom" (Andriopoulos & Lewis, 2009, p. 705). The process described by the designers and managers involved in the research was as follows:

> The projects [start] by listening intently to the client, seeking to 'walk in their shoes' to fully grasp project goals. Teams then begin to pull away from initial constraints, most often using brainstorming to explore new domains. As projects progress, constraint–freedom iterations may increase in frequency.
>
> (Andriopoulos & Lewis, 2009, p. 705)

Managing the personal drivers paradox

An ambidextrous approach can also enable organisations to manage the paradox of personal drivers, and its underlying tension of the pursuit of discipline and passion on behalf of staff members. The mechanisms used by the NPD firms involved in Andriopoulos and Lewis' (2009) study pursued both integrative strategies which facilitated paradoxical thinking within their organisational environments, and differentiation strategies which compartmentalised opportunities for routine and radical work. Integrative strategies included nurturing paradoxical identities. This relates with Gotsi et al.'s (2010) findings on the meta-identity of 'practical artists', discussed in the previous section. Such identity was created through socialisation process including hiring and mentoring suitable staff members and conducting regular reviews to ensure this meta-identity was achieved and maintained (Andriopoulos & Lewis, 2009; Gotsi et al., 2010).

It is also very interesting that, with respect to differentiation strategies, Andriopoulos and Lewis (2009) identified a hybrid of temporal and spatial differentiation. The former was achieved by the NPD firms varying the nature of work at different times, for instance, during different projects and project phases, empowering staff members to leverage their discipline and passion. "As projects evolve, a team member's focus systematically shifts between exploitation and exploration" (Andriopoulos & Lewis, 2009, p. 707). In same vein, employees might work on a routine project during a certain period of time, and another time on a blue-sky unconventional ground-breaking product. Spatial differentiation was achieved through separating the roles between people and units; some people or units worked on execution and budgeting (discipline), while other individuals and units pursued experimentation and ideation (passion). Larger firms tended to use more division of labour, while employees in smaller firms wear multiple hats, relying more on paradoxical identities (Gotsi et al., 2010).

Outcomes of organisational ambidexterity

In this final section of the chapter, we must try to understand the outcomes that organisations, and in particular design firms can achieve through ambidexterity. We explained above that ambidexterity enables organisations to cope with the paradoxes of organisational life, and in particular for design firms, with the paradoxes associated with creativity and innovation. Now it is time to understand what the implications of ambidexterity, and of managing these paradoxes, are for these organisations. Let us refer back to the four types of ambidexterity, and explore the outcomes for each.

Harmonic ambidexterity outcomes

Achieving harmonic ambidexterity, where the same unit pursues exploitation and exploration simultaneously, provides a serious competitive advantage for the organisation because, such endeavours can be considered a valuable and hard-to-imitate resource (Simsek et al., 2009). The value of this resource stems from the interaction of exploitation and exploration and only exists in their relationship (Yang & Atuahene-Gima, 2007). Harmonic ambidexterity has also been connected with improved stakeholder satisfaction, in particular of senior managers and customers. The former tend to rate those units that achieve harmonic ambidexterity higher because their assessment is based on "creating breakthrough innovations, investing in disruptive technologies, developing strategic relationships with key external stakeholders, and providing funding for internal venturing activities" (Simsek et al., 2009). The latter relates to customer capital, determined by the existence of profitable customers, company reputation, and prestige.

Cyclical ambidexterity outcomes

Cyclical ambidexterity is the type of ambidexterity mostly associated with high levels of innovation, and in particular product innovation. Therefore, it may be the type that those involved with design management need to pay more attention to. The same unit (organisation) that sequentially pursues exploitation and exploration, has the ability to engage in long periods of exploration that can lead to new technologies that might prove ground-breaking and become the dominant design in their sector. Long periods of exploitation follow this, and the performance of these radical innovations can improve through process innovation. "Interestingly, by engaging in periods of exploitation interspersed by episodic bouts of exploration, business units avoid getting caught up in competency traps (over-exploiting) and failure traps (over-exploring)" (Simsek et al., 2009, pp. 883–884)

Partitional and reciprocal ambidexterity outcomes

Given the limited number of research studies which have explored partitional and reciprocal ambidexterity, the outcomes of these two types remain relatively unknown. With respect to partitional ambidexterity, where different interdependent units carry out exploitation and exploration simultaneously, emerging evidence suggests that it connects well with innovation and greater financial performance for the organisation (Simsek et al., 2009). As far as reciprocal ambidexterity is concerned, i.e. the case where different interdependent units pursue exploitation and exploration sequentially, there is one study which has suggested a connection with organisational performance. In a study of the logistics industry, Im and Rai (2008) indicated that exploitative and exploratory knowledge sharing in long-term inter-organisational relationships is positively related to relationship performance, which they define as "the extent to which partners consider their relationship to be worthwhile, equitable, productive, and satisfying" (Im & Rai, 2008, p. 1282).

Chapter review questions

The following questions can help you reflect on the material we have covered in this chapter:

1 What are the components of paradoxes, and how do these relate with each other?
2 Discuss the four categories of organisational paradoxes, making references to their components.
3 Making connections with the 4 Ps of creativity typology, discuss the four paradoxes of creativity.
4 Provide a critical discussion of the innovation paradoxes design firms are likely to encounter.
5 Explain the concept of ambidexterity and discuss its four types.
6 Recommend ways design managers can build and maintain organisational ambidexterity within their firms.
7 How can innovation paradoxes be managed through ambidexterity?
8 What are the outcomes of ambidexterity for corporate strategy and performance?

Recommended reading

1 Lewis, M. W. (2000). Exploring paradox: Toward a more comprehensive guide. *Academy of Management Review, 25*(4), 760–776.
2 Andriopoulos, C. (2003). Six paradoxes in managing creativity: An embracing act. *Long Range Planning, 36*(4), 375–388.
3 Andriopoulos, C., & Lewis, M. W. (2010). Managing innovation paradoxes: Ambidexterity lessons from leading product design companies. *Long Range Planning, 43*(1), 104–122.
4 Simsek, Z., Heavey, C., Veiga, J. F., & Souder, D. (2009). A typology for aligning organizational ambidexterity's conceptualizations, antecedents, and outcomes. *Journal of Management Studies, 46*(5), 864–894.

Reflective thoughts

Paradox theory and ambidexterity

Professor Constantine Andriopoulos
Professor of Innovation and Entrepreneurship
Vice-Dean for Entrepreneurship
Cass Business School
City, University of London, London, UK

This chapter sheds more light on a vital and timely question: how do organisational leaders and scholars bring paradox to awareness and manage competing demands simultaneously? As our world becomes more global, interconnected and fast paced, organisations more than ever before have to meet multiple, competing demands (Smith & Lewis, 2011). For instance, they face rising pressures to exploit existing opportunities, while simultaneously exploring new possibilities (Andriopoulos & Lewis, 2009; Smith, 2014; Smith & Tushman, 2005). Leaders, central to managing exploitation–exploration tensions, must improve existing capabilities and operations through a very disciplined resource allocation, while at the same time they must adapt to changing business environments. These two modes often require different attention and actions from organisations and, therefore, create competing tensions, which leaders and top management team members need to manage.

Interestingly, management history is replete with examples of companies whose leaders' inability to reach balance between the two activities has had drastic effects. Some leaders excessively focus on strategic planning that may enable improvements on existing capabilities. For instance, *Motorola* and *Kodak* faced dramatic technological changes in their respective industries. Even though both companies recognised the changing market requirements and took initial actions to adapt to them by creating new assets, they still failed to create coherence and support between exploitative and exploratory activities. Yet, this approach drove these organisations to a vicious success trap, where the developed solutions became obsolete. Others, seduced by the idea (as well as the financial and reputation benefits) of riding the next wave of innovation, take escalating risks, attempting to negate past innovation failures, while ignoring core competencies. Here, future opportunities are sought at the expense of today's operations. What those approaches have in common is that they aim to provide a stable solution by taking an 'either/or' approach. However, the inability to reach balance between the two activities can have severe effects. It can leave a firm exposed to either the risk of obsolescence or the risk of failure to appropriate.

Instead of having to choose one demand over another, organisations can strive to resolve the dilemma and pursue to become ambidextrous and balance both demands. Scholars have recently adopted a paradox lens to examine such competing demands (e.g. Andriopoulos & Lewis, 2009). Although this lens is relatively new to management, its early advocates have drawn from a rich history, grounded in the philosophies of Kierkegaard, Hampden-Turner, and Taoism, as well as the psychological insights of Freud, Bateson, and Watzlawick (e.g. Cameron & Quinn, 1988; Lewis, 2000; Smith & Berg, 1987). Scholars in management science attest that competing demands are inherent in organisational life (Ford & Backoff, 1988). The act of organising fosters contradictory, yet interrelated forces within organisations that persist over time, creating recurring cycles (i.e. Jarzabkowski, Lê, & Van de Ven, 2013; Smith, 2014). Such tensions may remain latent in organisations, becoming salient either through environmental conditions of complexity, scarcity and pluralism, or through individual cognition and sensemaking (Smith & Lewis, 2011). Scholars in this area approach tensions as ubiquitous and persistent forces that challenge and fuel long-term success. As such, the core premise is not problem solving through fit, but coexistence. Acceptance and engagement enable organisational members to live and thrive with tensions. Paradoxical thinking entails a 'both/and' mindset that is holistic and dynamic, exploring synergistic possibilities for coping with enduring tensions.

Paradox is a powerful word, evoking possibility and impossibility, energy and obstacles, intrigue and confusion. By definition, paradox refers to "persistent contradiction between interdependent elements" (Schad, Lewis, Raisch, & Smith, 2016, p. 6). Scholars have increasingly adopted a paradox lens to organisational ambidexterity to understand the source, challenges, and responses to competing exploitation–exploration demands. They have unpacked integrated approaches that leverage synergies between exploitation and exploration (e.g. Andriopoulos & Lewis, 2009; Raisch et al., 2009) and have investigated how paradox can fuel virtuous cycles as organisations learn to survive and/or thrive through innovation tensions (e.g. Smith and Tushman, 2005; Smith, 2014).

While much extant organisational ambidexterity research emphasises prescriptions that mainly rely on separation (structural differentiation or sequential attention), recently scholars have begun to embrace a paradox lens that has shifted the academic debate in this area towards more integrated approaches (Schad et al., 2016). For instance, studies have illustrated the value of a paradoxical perspective, focusing on the mutually reinforcing nature of exploration and exploitation (Andriopoulos & Lewis, 2009; Fourné, Jansen, & Mom, 2014; Heracleous & Wirtz, 2014) or the need for paradoxical recognition (Smith, 2014; Smith & Tushman, 2005) that enables senior managers to address strategic paradoxes when pursuing exploration and exploitation. Paradox "represents an ongoing challenge to our understanding of organisational processes and practices" (Jarzabkowski et al., 2013, p. 246).

In conclusion, I would like to highlight two areas in which I see the need for further development in this field. Firstly, scholars have tended to study paradox at either the organisational or the individual level. It is interesting for future research studies to focus on the interactions between levels. Secondly, while prior ambidexterity research has primarily examined static approaches to balance exploration and exploitation (O'Reilly & Tushman, 2013), a process perspective is deemed vital and could explicate how organisations shift this balance over time with changing requirements.

References

Andriopoulos, C., & Lewis, M. W. (2009). Exploitation–exploration tensions and organizational ambidexterity: Managing paradoxes of innovation. *Organization Science, 20*(4), 696–717.

Cameron, K. S., & Quinn, R. E. (1988). Organizational paradox and transformation. In R. E. Quinn, & K. S. Cameron (Eds.), *Paradox and transformation: Toward a theory of change in organization and management* (pp. 12–18). Cambridge, MA: Ballinger.

Ford, J. D., & Backoff, R. W. (1988). Organizational change in and out of dualities and paradox. In R. E. Quinn, & K. S. Cameron (Eds.), *Paradox and transformation: Toward a theory of change in organisation and management* (pp. 81–121). Cambridge, MA: Ballinger.

(Continued)

(Continued)

Fourné, S. P., Jansen, J. J., & Mom, T. J. (2014). Strategic agility in MNEs: Managing tensions to capture opportunities across emerging and established markets. *California Management Review, 56*(3), 13–38.
Heracleous, L., & Wirtz, J. (2014). Singapore airlines: Achieving sustainable advantage through mastering paradox. *The Journal of Applied Behavioral Science, 50*(2), 150–170.
Jarzabkowski, P., Lê, J. K., & Van de Ven, A. H. (2013). Responding to competing strategic demands: How organizing, belonging, and performing paradoxes co-evolve. *Strategic Organization, 11*(3), 245–280.
Lewis, M. W. (2000). Exploring paradox: Toward a more comprehensive guide. *Academy of Management Review, 25*(4), 760–776.
O'Reilly, C. A., & Tushman, M. L. (2013). Organizational ambidexterity: Past, present, and future. *The Academy of Management Perspectives, 27*(4), 324–338.
Quinn, R. E., & Cameron, K. S. (1988). Paradox and transformation: A framework for viewing organization and management. In R. Quinn, & K. Cameron (Eds.), *Paradox and transformation: Toward a theory of change in organisation and management* (pp. 289–308). Cambridge, MA: Ballinger.
Raisch, S., Birkinshaw, J., Probst, G., & Tushman, M. L. (2009). Organizational ambidexterity: Balancing exploitation and exploration for sustained performance. *Organization Science, 20*(4), 685–695.
Schad, J., Lewis, M. W., Raisch, S., & Smith, W. K. (2016). Paradox research in management science: Looking back to move forward. *Academy of Management Annals, 10*(1), 1–60.
Smith, K. K., & Berg, D. N. (1987). *Paradoxes of group life: Understanding of conflict, paralysis, and movement in group dynamics.* San Francisco, CA: Jossey-Bass.
Smith, W. K. (2014). Dynamic decision making: A model of senior leaders managing strategic paradoxes. *Academy of Management Journal, 57*(6), 1592–1623.
Smith, W. K., & Lewis, M. W. (2011). Toward a theory of paradox: A dynamic equilibrium model of organizing. *Academy of Management Review, 36*(2), 381–403.
Smith, W. K., & Tushman, M. L. (2005). Managing strategic contradictions: A top management model for managing innovation streams. *Organization Science, 16*(5), 522–536.

References

Adler, P. S., Goldoftas, B., & Levine, D. I. (1999). Flexibility versus efficiency. A case study of model changeovers in the Toyota production system. *Organization Science, 10*(1), 43–68.
Amabile, T. M. (1983a). The social psychology of creativity: A componential conceptualization. *Journal of Personality and Social Psychology, 45*(2), 357–376.
Amabile, T. M. (1983b). *The social psychology of creativity*. New York: Springer-Verlag.
Amabile, T. M. (1988). A model of creativity and innovation in organizations. In B. M. Staw, & L. L. Cummings (Eds.), *Research in organizational behavior* (Vol. 10, pp. 123–167). Greenwich, CT: JAI Press.
Amabile, T. M. (1996). *Creativity in context*. Boulder, CO: Westview.
Amabile, T. M. (1998, September–October). How to kill creativity. *Harvard Business Review, 76*(5), 77–87.
Andrew, J., & Sirkin, H. (2006). *Payback: Reaping the rewards of innovation*. Cambridge, MA: Harvard Business Press.
Andriopoulos, C. (2003). Six paradoxes in managing creativity: An embracing act. *Long Range Planning, 36*(4), 375–388.
Andriopoulos, C., & Gotsi, M. (2005). The virtues of 'blue sky' projects: How Lunar Design taps into the power of imagination. *Creativity and Innovation Management, 14*(3), 316–324.
Andriopoulos, C., & Lewis, M. W. (2009). Exploitation–exploration tensions and organisational ambidexterity: Managing paradoxes of innovation. *Organisation Science, 20*(4), 696–717.
Andriopoulos, C., & Lewis, M. W. (2010). Managing innovation paradoxes: Ambidexterity lessons from leading product design companies. *Long Range Planning, 43*(1), 104–122.

Argyris, C. (1993). *Knowledge for action: A guide to overcoming barriers to organizational change*. San Francisco, CA: Jossey-Bass.

Atuahene-Gima, K. (2005). Resolving the capability: Rigidity paradox in new product innovation. *Journal of Marketing, 69*(4), 61–83.

Baas, M., De Dreu, C. K., & Nijstad, B. A. (2008). A Meta-analysis of 25 years of mood-creativity research: Hedonic tone, activation, or regulatory focus? *Psychological Bulletin, 134*(6), 779–806.

Beech, N., Burns, H., de Caestecker, L., MacIntosh, R., & MacLean, D. (2004). Paradox as invitation to act in problematic change situations. *Human Relations, 57*(10), 1313–1332.

Birkinshaw, J., & Gibson, C. (2004). Building ambidexterity into an organization. *MIT Sloan Management Review, 45*(4), 47–55.

Bouchikhi, H. (1998). Living with and building on complexity: A constructivist perspective on organizations. *Organization, 5*(2), 217–232.

Brown, T., & Wyatt, J. (2010). *Design thinking for social innovation. Stanford social innovation review*. Palo Alto, CA: Stanford Graduate School of Business.

Burns, T., & Stalker, G. M. (1981). *The management of innovation*. London: Tavistock.

Cannon, T. B. (1996). *Welcome to the revolution: Managing paradox in the 21st century*. London: Pitman.

Chen, E. L. (2005). *Rival interpretations of balancing exploration and exploitation: Simultaneous or sequential*. Paper presented at the Annual Meeting of the Academy of Management, Honolulu, HI.

Cohendet, P., & Simon, L. (2007). Playing across the playground: Paradoxes of knowledge creation in the video game firm. *Journal of Organizational Behavior, 28*(5), 587–605.

Collins, J. C., & Porras, J. I. (1994). *Built to last: Successful habits of visionary companies*. New York: HarperCollins.

Collins, M. A., & Amabile, T. M. (1999). Motivation and creativity. In R. J. Sternberg (Ed.), *Handbook of creativity* (pp. 297–312). New York: Cambridge University Press.

Cropley, D., & Cropley, A. (2012). A psychological taxonomy of organizational innovation: Resolving the paradoxes. *Creativity Research Journal, 24*(1), 29–40.

Crutchfield, R. S. (1955). Conformity and character. *American Psychologist, 10*(5), 191–198.

Crutchfield, R. S. (1962). Conformity and creative thinking. In H. Gruber, G. Terell, & M. Wertheimer (Eds.), *Contemporary approaches to creative thinking*. New York: Atherton Press.

Csikszentmihalyi, M. (1996). *Creativity: Flow and the psychology of discovery and invention*. New York: HarperCollins.

DeFillippi, R., Grabher, G., & Jones, C. (2007). Introduction to paradoxes of creativity: Managerial and organizational challenges in the cultural economy. *Journal of Organizational Behavior, 28*(5), 511–521.

Denison, D. R., Hooijberg, R., & Quinn, R. E. (1995). Paradox and performance: Toward a theory of behavioral complexity in managerial leadership. *Organisation Science, 6*(5), 524–540.

Donaldson, T., & Preston, L. E. (1995). The stakeholder theory of the corporation: Concepts, evidence, and implications. *Academy of management Review, 20*(1), 65–91.

Duncan, R. B. (1976). The ambidextrous organization: Designing dual structures for innovation. In R. H. Killman, L. R. Pondy, & D. Sleven (Eds.), *The management of organization* (pp. 167–188). New York: North Holland.

Eikhof, D. R., & Haunschild, A. (2007). For art's sake! Artistic and economic logics in creative production. *Journal of Organizational Behavior, 28*(5), 523–538.

Eisenberger, R., & Byron, K. (2011). Rewards and creativity. In M. A. Runco, & S. R. Pritzker (Eds.), *Encyclopedia of creativity* (Vol. 2, pp. 313–318). San Diego, CA: Academic Press.

Eisenhardt, K. M. (2000). Paradox, spirals, ambivalence: The new language of change and pluralism. *Academy of Management Review, 25*(4), 703–705.

Eisenhardt, K. M., & Westcott, B. J. 1988. Paradoxical demands and the creation of excellence: The case of just-in-time manufacturing. In R. E. Quinn, & K. S. Cameron (Eds.), *Paradox and transformation: Toward a theory of change in organization and management* (pp. 169–194). Cambridge, MA: Ballinger.

Ford, J. D., & Backoff, R. W. (1988). Organisational change in and out of dualities and paradox. In R. Quinn, & K. Cameron (Eds.), *Paradox and transformation: Toward a theory of change in organisation and management*. Cambridge, MA: Ballinger.

Gander, J., Haberberg, A., & Rieple, A. (2007). A paradox of alliance management: Resource contamination in the recorded music industry. *Journal of Organizational Behavior, 28*(5), 607–624.

Ghoshal, S., & Bartlett, C. A. (1997). *The individualized corporation: A fundamentally new approach to management*. New York: Harper Business.

Gibson, C. B., & Birkinshaw, J. (2004). The antecedents, consequences, and mediating role of organizational ambidexterity. *Academy of Management Journal, 47*(2), 209–226.

Gotsi, M., Andriopoulos, C., Lewis, M. W., & Ingram, A. E. (2010). Managing creatives: Paradoxical approaches to identity regulation. *Human Relations, 63*(6), 781–805.

Guilford, J. P. (1950). Creativity. *American Psychologist, 14*, 205–208.

Gupta, A. K., Smith, K. G., & Shalley, C. E. (2006). The interplay between exploration and exploitation. *Academy of Management Journal, 49*(4), 693–706.

Handy, C. (1994). *The age of paradox*. Cambridge, MA: Harvard Business Press.

Harris, A. S. (1996). *Living with paradox: An introduction to Jungian psychology*. Belmont, CA: Wadsworth.

Holmqvist, M. (2004). Experiential learning processes of exploitation and exploration within and between organizations: An empirical study of product development. *Organization Science, 15*(1), 70–81.

Huy, Q. N. (1999). Emotional capability, emotional intelligence, and radical change. *Academy of Management Review, 24*(2), 325–345.

Im, G., & Rai, A. (2008). Knowledge sharing ambidexterity in long-term interorganizational relationships. *Management Science, 54*(7), 1281–1296.

Jansen, J. J., George, G., Van den Bosch, F. A., & Volberda, H. W. (2008). Senior team attributes and organizational ambidexterity: The moderating role of transformational leadership. *Journal of Management Studies, 45*(5), 982–1007.

Jansen, J. J., Volberda, H. W., & Van den Bosch, F. A. (2005). Exploratory innovation, exploitative innovation, and ambidexterity: The impact of environmental and organizational antecedents. *Schmalenbach Business Review, 57*, 351–363.

Julier, G., & Moor, L. (2009). Introduction: Design and creativity. In G. Julier, & L. Moor (Eds.), *Design and creativity: Policy, management and practice*. Oxford, UK: Berg.

Kaufmann, G. (2003). Expanding the mood-creativity equation. *Creativity Research Journal, 15*(2–3), 131–135.

Kelly, G. (1955). *The psychology of personal constructs*. New York: Norton.

Kirton, M. J. (Ed.). (1989). *Adaptors and innovators: Styles of creativity and problem solving*. London: Routledge.

Lalaounis, S. T., Wood, B. M., & Harrison, D. K. (2012). A framework for services evaluation in integrated design consultancies: A triangular approach. *The Design Journal, 15*(3), 265–298.

Lavie, D., & Rosenkopf, L. (2006). Balancing exploration and exploitation in alliance formation. *Academy of Management Journal, 49*(4), 797–818.

Leonard-Barton, D. (1992). Core capabilities and core rigidities: A paradox in managing new product development. *Strategic Management Journal, 13*, 111–125.

Lewis, M. W. (2000). Exploring paradox: Toward a more comprehensive guide. *Academy of Management Review, 25*(4), 760–776.

Maier, J. (2015). *The ambidextrous organization*. Basingstoke, UK: Palgrave Macmillan.

March, J. G. (1991). Exploration and exploitation in organizational learning. *Organization Science, 2*(1), 71–87.

Miner, A. S., Bassof, P., & Moorman, C. (2001). Organizational improvisation and learning: A field study. *Administrative Science Quarterly, 46*(2), 304–337.

Mom, T. J., Van den Bosch, F. A., & Volberda, H. W. (2007). Investigating managers' exploration and exploitation activities: The influence of top-down, bottom-up, and horizontal knowledge inflows. *Journal of Management Studies, 44*(6), 910–931.

Morgan, G. (1991). *Images of organization*. Thousand Oaks, CA: Sage.

Murnighan, J. K., & Conlon, D. E. (1991). The dynamics of intense work groups: A study of British string quartets. *Administrative Science Quarterly, 36*, 165–186.

O'Reilly, C. A., & Tushman, M. L. (2004). The ambidextrous organization. *Harvard Business Review, 82*(4), 74–83.

O'Reilly, C. A., & Tushman, M. L. (2008). Ambidexterity as a dynamic capability: Resolving the innovator's dilemma. *Research in Organizational Behavior, 28*, 185–206.

Putnam, L. L. (1986). Contradictions and paradoxes in organizations. In L. Thayer (Ed.), *Organization communications: Emerging perspectives* (pp. 151–167). Norwood, NJ: Ablex.

Quinn, R. E. (1988). *Beyond rational management: Mastering the paradoxes and competing demands of high performance*. San Francisco, CA: Jossey-Bass.

Raisch, S., & Birkinshaw, J. (2008). Organizational ambidexterity: Antecedents, outcomes, and moderators. *Journal of Management, 34*, 375–409.

Raisch, S., Birkinshaw, J., Probst, G., & Tushman, M. L. (2009). Organizational ambidexterity: Balancing exploitation and exploration for sustained performance. *Organization Science, 20*(4), 685–695.

Reiter-Palmon, R., Herman, A. E., & Yammarino, F. J. (2008). Creativity and cognitive processes: Multi-level linkages between individual and team cognition. In M. D. Mumford, S. T. Hunter, & K. E. Bedell-Avers (Eds.), *Multi-level issues in creativity and innovation, (7)*, pp. 203–267. Oxford: Elsevier.

Rhodes, M. (1987). An analysis of creativity. In I. G. Isaksen (Ed.), *Frontiers of creativity research: Beyond the basics* (pp. 216–222). Buffalo, NY: Bearly.

Rothaermel, F. T., & Deeds, D. L. (2004). Exploration and exploitation alliances in Biotechnology: A system of new product development. *Strategic Management Journal, 25*(3), 201–221.

Schneider, K. J. (1990). *The paradoxical self: Toward an understanding of our contradictory nature*. New York: Insight Books.

Sheremata, W. A. (2000). Centrifugal and centripetal forces in radical new product development under time pressure. *Academy of Management Review, 25*(2), 389–408.

Simsek, Z., Heavey, C., Veiga, J. F., & Souder, D. (2009). A typology for aligning organizational ambidexterity's conceptualizations, antecedents, and outcomes. *Journal of Management Studies, 46*(5), 864–894.

Smith, K. K., & Berg, D. N. (1987). *Paradoxes of group life: Understanding of conflict, paralysis, and movement in group dynamics.* San Francisco, CA: Jossey-Bass.

Smith, W. K., & Lewis, M. W. (2011). Toward a theory of paradox: A dynamic equilibrium model of organizing. *Academy of Management Review, 36*(2), 381–403.

Smith, W. K., & Tushman, M. L. (2005). Managing strategic contradictions: A top management model for managing innovation streams. *Organization Science, 16*(5), 522–536.

Stadtler, L., & Van Wassenhove, L. N. (2016). Coopetition as a paradox: Integrative approaches in a multi-company, cross-sector partnership. *Organization Studies, 37*(5), 655–685.

Svejenova, S., Mazza, C., & Planellas, M. (2007). Cooking up change in haute cuisine: Ferran Adrià as an institutional entrepreneur. *Journal of Organizational Behavior, 28*(5), 539–561.

Teece, D. J., Pisano, G., & Shuen, A. (1997). Dynamic capabilities and strategic management. *Strategic Management Journal, 18*(7), 509–533.

Thompson, J. D. (1967). *Organizations in action: Social science bases of administration.* New York: McGraw-Hill.

Thompson, P., Jones, M., & Warhurst, C. (2007). From conception to consumption: Creativity and the missing managerial link. *Journal of Organizational Behavior, 28*(5), 625–640.

Tushman, M. L., & O'Reilly III, C. A. (1996). Ambidextrous organisations: Managing evolutionary and revolutionary change. *California Management Review, 38*(4), 8–30.

Tushman, M. L., & O'Reilly III, C. A. (1997). *Winning through innovation: A practical guide to leading organisational change and renewal.* Cambridge, MA: Harvard Business Press.

Vince, R., & Broussine, M. (1996). Paradox, defense and attachment: Accessing and working with emotions and relations underlying organisational change. *Organisation Studies, 17*(1), 1–21.

Voorhees, B. (1986). Toward duality theory. *General Systems Bulletin, 16*(2), 58–61.

Ward, T. B., & Kolomyts, Y. (2010). Cognition and creativity. In J. C. Kaufman, & R. J. Sternberg (Eds.), *The Cambridge handbook of creativity* (pp. 93–112). Cambridge, UK: Cambridge University Press.

Warr, A., & O'Neill, E. (2005). *Understanding design as a social creative process.* In *Proceedings of the 5th Conference on Creativity & Cognition* (pp. 118–127). New York: ACM.

West, M.A. (2002). Sparkling fountains or stagnant ponds: An integrative model of creativity and innovation in work groups. *Applied Psychology: An International Review, 51*, 355–386.

Westenholz, A. (1993). Paradoxical thinking and change in the frames of reference. *Organization Studies, 14*(1), 37–58.

Yang, H., & Atuahene-Gima, K. (2007, August). *Ambidexterity in product innovation management: The direct and contingent effects on product development performance.* Paper presented at the Annual Meeting of the Academy of Management, Philadelphia, PA.

7 Human experiences and design management

Chapter aims and learning outcomes

This chapter aims to:

1. Provide an understanding of the relationships between humans and things through the concept of entanglement.
2. Define the concept of experiences and discuss the different ways of exploring the term using multiple perspectives in current academic discourse.
3. Explore the concept of experiences in marketing discourse and understand the nature of the experience economy and the experiential marketing process.
4. Discuss the different elements of experience design, with particular focus on aesthetics and emotions.
5. Provide a critique on the concepts of consumer experiences from a societal and a cultural perspective.
6. Provide an understanding of the role of designers as the 'cultural intermediaries' who understand users and create meaningful consumption forms for them.
7. Discuss how design management can contribute to the creation of holistic human experiences.

Our discussion in the last few chapters has made it very clear that design plays a fundamental role in society due to the fact that it directly contributes to the creation and development of objects and processes which make up an organisation's offering in the form of products and services. Such products and services (which themselves involve objects) are consumed by individuals; they are incorporated in people's daily lives and influence human relationships. However, with regard to objects in particular, their importance goes beyond an individual's mere ownership and consumption. According to Ian Hodder, a Stanford University archaeology professor,

> numerous different perspectives have converged on some version of the idea that subject and object, mind and matter, human and thing co-constitute each other. In these different approaches it is accepted that human existence and human social life depend on material things … We can say that we humans depend on things as technologies, that we depend on things as tools to feed us, to keep us warm, to forge social relations in exchange, to worship. Many would accept that as humans we have evolved with certain physical and cognitive capacities because of our dependence on things. It would also be widely acceptable to say that our perceptions and notions of desire, anger, love are always to some degree of or for something, including other persons.
>
> (Hodder, 2012, pp. 16–17)

Inspired by this statement, this chapter will start by exploring the concept of 'entanglement' which signifies Hodder's (2012) seminal thesis on the archaeology of the relationships between humans and things.

From a design management point of view, understanding this concept is imperative because it explores design beyond merely its relation with material culture, but also in relation to its contribution to human development. The focus of our discussion, therefore, will be on the consumer rather than on the organisation. Most importantly, we will go beyond the anthropocentric perspective and explore this entanglement from the perspective of things too, something that, according to Hodder (2012), has been neglected over the years. Following this discussion, we will then explore the concept of experiences, because "in our modern world our experiences are continuously shaped by and in the process of shaping many of the things around us" (Coxon, 2015). The creation of customer experiences constitutes the current economic offering in our contemporary post-modern society (Pine II & Gilmore, 1998, 1999, 2011); thus, it is essential we understand their nature and characteristics. Subsequently, our discussion will progress on understanding the nature of human experience and the potential of experience design, which will demonstrate clearly the role and influence of design in human life and societal development.

Entanglement: The relationships between humans and things

Defining things and objects

Hodder (2012) discussed the relationships between human and things in a way that highlights the importance of design in creating artefacts and shaping the world around us. Before we explore these relationships, we need to be clear about what we mean by 'things'. Things are entities that exist as contained and defined in a certain way, at least for the shortest of temporal moments. Things can be words, thoughts, institutions, events, and "create bundles of presence or duration in the continual flows of matter, energy and information. Just by having duration and presence we say they are things" (Hodder, 2012, p. 7). Therefore, things have a certain configuration. This is also the case for objects; thus, one

Jug: An object and a thing

could question whether or not the terms 'things' and 'objects' can be used in inter-exchangeable manner. Although both indicate configuration, objects tend to signify a more 'stable' configuration; therefore, not all things are objects. For instance, a cloud is a thing, but not an object, due to the fluidity of its configuration, although it can be an object of study. In comparison to objects, things are more evolving and transforming. Things are created through matter, energy, and information and are brought together for a period of time. Hence, things assemble, they are not isolated (this, however, does not make them less definable). "It is in their connections, and in their flows into other forms, that their thingness resides" (Hodder, 2012, p. 8).

However, objects can be considered things. Hodder (2012) refers to Heidegger's (1971) example of the jug as an object which is also a thing. A jug is created as a vessel to carry water, wine, or some other liquid. It stands up against us and can be described as an object as it is distant from us and set up against us. However, a jug's use is not merely to take in what it is poured into it; it also pours this liquid out. "The water and wine come from a rock spring or from rain or from the grape growing in the earth. The pouring out can quench thirst for humans or be a libation to the gods. So the jug connects humans, gods, earth and sky. It is this 'gathering' that makes the jug a thing" (Hodder, 2012, p. 8). We can, therefore, argue that things can bring humans and other things together in heterogeneous mixes.

In fact, Hodder (2012) argues that humans can also be considered things themselves. They are

> bundles of biochemical processes, flows of bloods and nerves and cells temporarily coalesced into an entity that is thoroughly dependent on and connected to air, water, food … a thing of particular kind, one that has developed a very large and complex nervous system, body and mind thoroughly dependent on other things to exist.
>
> (Hodder, 2012, p. 9)

As we will explore further, things can tie people together into relations of dominance and subordination. Things have been extremely important for human development; humans would never have evolved into the clever (and sometimes stubborn or plain stupid) species they have become without things. This human dependence on things has led to an entanglement between humans and things with implications for the ways we live our lives today (Hodder, 2012). It is this very premise that magnifies the importance of design and its management in society and human development. Designers can create objects, processes, and experiences, which enrich and determine the way we live; they are a particular class of things because they are made by humans.

Dependence and dependency

Humans depend on things (HT)

The notion of human dependence on things has two forms. The first form, and a more general focus, is *dependence* (plural: dependences) which views the human use of things as enabling. Using things, allows us to live, socialise, eat, think, move etc. Dependence also involves both reliance on things and contingency. People "depend on things, both in the sense of relying on things and in the sense of being contingent on the particular things relied upon" (Hodder, 2012, p. 17). The second form of human dependence on things, is what Hodder (2012) terms as *dependency* (plural: dependencies), which involves a form of constraint. He argues that people find themselves in different forms of dependencies which limit their abilities to develop and progress as societies and as individuals. "Such dependencies are not inherent in the things themselves but in the interactions between humans and things" (Hodder, 2012, p. 18) (Figure 7.1).

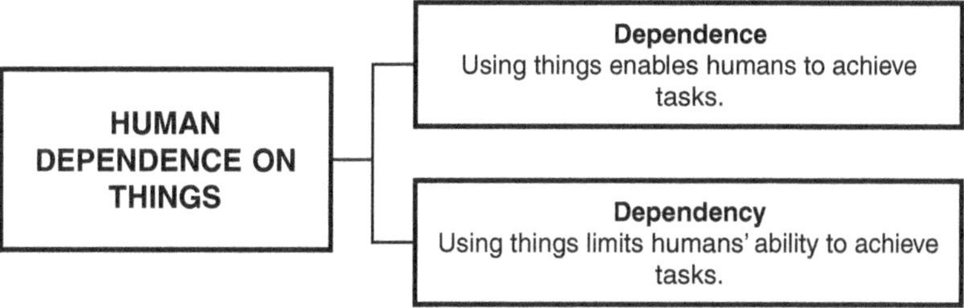

Figure 7.1 Forms of human dependence on things.

Various academic disciplines and schools of thought have discussed the human dependence on things, for instance, the phenomenology of the work by Heidegger (1973) and Merleau-Ponty (1963), material culture and material studies, and cognitive approaches. All these have concluded that humans are strongly dependent on things, so much that Webmoor and Witmore (2008) argue that humans cannot even exist without them. After all, "humans need sensory input in order to feel, touch, see, smell, hear, think. We would not have evolved as we are, with agile fingers and complex brains, were it not for the niches that made things provided for us" (Hodder, 2012, p. 38). The human need for this sensory input elevates the role of design in society and human development. The onus for creating the things which provide this input to sense, feel, think, act, and relate in this world, i.e., to experience, lies with designers. This directs our thinking to Schmitt's (1999a, 1999b) typology of the different types of experiences, which we will explore further below.

Things depend on things (TT)

Nevertheless, it is not only humans who depend on things, things also depend on things. To illustrate this, consider the example of a sail boat. The sail boat as a thing depends on many other things including its own components. Believe it or not, the main component of a sail boat is a small one-inch metal pin on the shackle which links the top of the mainsail to the halyard which pulls up and keeps up the mainsail.

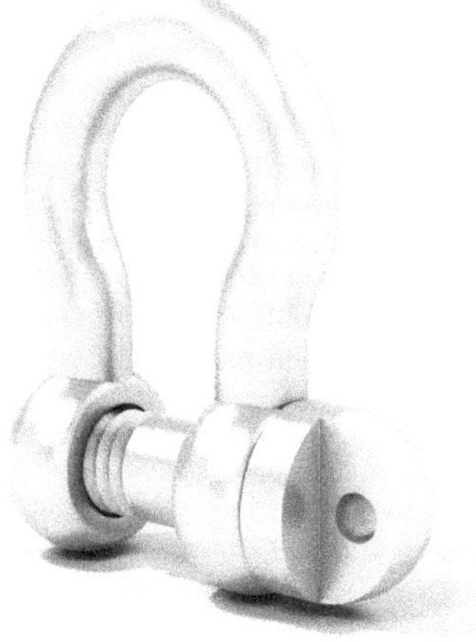

Metal pin: The main component of a sail boat.

Without this tiny component, the main function of the sail boat, sailing, cannot be performed, even when everything else is working fine. Certainly, many of us, if not all of us, have come across similar situations with things (think, for instance, technology products) that cannot function because of a small, yet vital, component malfunctioning (Hodder, 2012).

Things depend on humans (TH)

Similar to human dependence on things, things depend on humans too. Most things are entities made by humans (designers and manufacturers); therefore, they depend on humans who make them, use them, repair them, and discard them, all along the behavioural chains and throughout their use lives (Hodder, 2012). As already mentioned, things are evolving and transforming, and hence many things are not objects. However, although we assume that objects are more static than other things, they are not entirely static. Even objects change and morph as time passes. Think, for instance, our clothes, they wear off, their colours change after washes, or have a permanent scent, after spraying them with our perfume a number of times. Therefore, all things are "vibrant and have lives and interactions on human lives. As they grow, transform or fall apart, they have a direct impact on human lives" (Hodder, 2012, p. 68). Things' dependence on humans is evidenced by the fact that things fall apart. Things draw humans into their care because of this falling apart. Besides this, things also draw people in through the different stages of human use of materials, including procurement, manufacturing, exchange, use (and maintenance), and discard. Throughout their life-cycles, things draw people into labour, involvement, and a variety of responses to keep things as they are wanted. After all, if things are not maintained, they will fall apart sooner than later, and will stop functioning. A pot needs to be created first and then needs to be maintained so it does not break and leak. An *iPhone* needs to be protected so the screen does not break, and functions well. A computer needs to be switched on to work and upgraded when necessary. "The existence of these things in a specific form draws people into their care and into the lives of things" (Hodder, 2012, p. 70). Other disciplines like behavioural ecology and human behavioural ecology have also argued for this dependence of things on humans.

> Made things are not inert or isolated. Their connections with other things and their maintenance depend on humans … This dependence of things on humans draws humans deeper into the orbit of things. Looking after things as they get depleted or fall apart or as they grow and reproduce, traps humans into harder labour, greater social debts and duties, changed schedules and temporalities. This is true of all things that involve some form of human investment.
>
> (Hodder, 2012, p. 86)

Entanglement

The concept of entanglement is Hodder's (2012) attempt to bring all the above relationships together. As we have seen, humans depend on things (HT), as well as of course on other humans (HH), but also things depend on other things (TT) and on humans (TH). The addition of these four sets of dependences and dependencies, create what he calls entanglement.

Entanglement = (HT) + (HH) + (TT) + (TH)

Hodder (2012) articulately explains his concept of entanglement with the following:

> The defining aspect of entanglement with things is that humans get caught in a double bind, depending on things that depend on humans. Put another way, things as we want them have limited ability

> to reproduce themselves, so in our dependence on them we become entrapped in their dependence on us … Thing dependence on humans entraps humans into investment and care. But this is only because humans are so utterly dependent on things in the first place …, and it is amplified because things depend on other things. There is thus a dialectic relationship between dependence, often productive and enabling, and dependency, often constraining and limiting. Humans and things, humans and humans, things and things depend on each other, they rely on each other, produce each other. But that dependence is in continual tension with boundaries and constraints as things and humans reach various limits (of resources, of material and social possibility) that are overcome by, that demand, yet further dependence and investment. Entanglement can thus be defined as the dialectic of dependence and dependency.
>
> (Hodder, 2012, pp. 88–89)

The concept of entanglement aims to bridge the divide between materialism and social construction. "Real world issues entangle us in entrapments and necessities" (Hodder, 2012, p. 95). We engage in these necessities through our socially constructed world, and we are drawn into their webs of interconnections. The notion of entanglement allows "a materialism but embedded within the social, the historical and the contingent" (Hodder, 2012, p. 96). For instance, an old house that is considered a listed building of historic importance, requires extra attention and special care, not only because of the building itself and its age, but because of what it represents. Therefore, it is not just the building itself that entangles people, but also the ways people have come to value old buildings.

Hodder (2012) refrains from producing a classification of entanglements. The reason is that entanglements, i.e. the sets of interlinked dependences between humans and things, are not complete and holistic, quite the contrary, they are localised, partial, marginal, and open-ended. They are empirically identified as particular flows of matter, energy, and information, and continuously draw humans into them in order to carry out maintenance and fixing. However, some things require more investment from humans and more involvement from other things. Some could try to relate the degree of entanglement with the technological complexity of the object. "Thus very simple and widely available objects might be expected to have fewer material, practical, human entanglements than complex objects made with parts that are scarce" (Hodder, 2012, p. 106). For example, a *Mercedes-Benz* car involves fewer entanglements than an *Airbus A380*. Nevertheless, such generalisation is very hard to maintain beyond material entanglements, i.e., the social, religious, ideological, semiotic, phenomenological entanglements. An object might be simpler in material terms (thus lower material entanglement), but might enjoy higher level of emotional or spiritual importance and hence higher levels of emotional and spiritual entanglements. Consider, for instance, a gift given by a loved one; it has a lot of sentimental value regardless of its material value. As Hodder explains "because entanglement is both material and immaterial, involving debts, values, ownership and beliefs, it is not possible to generalise a priori about the overall entanglements of an object, although the material side certainly helps as a starting point in evaluating entanglement" (2012, p. 107).

The concept of experiences: Multiple perspectives

Understanding experiences

Drawing from our previous discussion of the relationships between humans and things, we can certainly argue that, in our contemporary world, things shape our behaviour and experiences, and are shaped by us. Our apartments, our workplaces, our cities, and our relationships with others influence our experiences, and are influenced by our behaviour. The relationship between environment and people is reciprocal. On the one hand, environments shape our behaviour. Consider, for instance, the beauty and order (or lack of) of the urban environment and how it can affect city residents' behaviour. Living in a leafy affluent area of a city can generate positive and orderly behaviour and increase people's wellbeing, in contrast with run-down areas which might lead to antisocial behaviour among their residents and visitors. On the other hand, people's behaviour influences the environment too. For example, urban populations can affect the environment: how much litter is thrown on the streets, how much (and the quality of) graffiti that can be found and where, or the levels of noise pollution. This indicates that the relationship between things and human experiences is mutually influential and could take the form of a vicious cycle (negative) or virtuous cycle (positive). Our human experiences are mediated by the things around us. It is, therefore, imperative at this stage to understand the concept of human experiences. This will enable our understanding of how we can design and manage design in a way that we positively contribute to the experience of individuals.

Philosophically speaking, we can argue that besides the definite beginning and end of a person's life (birth and death), most of our understanding of conscious life is created through our phenomenal way of being in, or of experiencing, the world around us as we live in it (Coxon, 2015). Coxon (2015) explains what we mean by the term 'phenomenal':

> The term phenomenal essentially means 'our' way of experiencing something based on all of our life experiences (of various phenomena) that have gone before, as interpreted through filters such as the social (family, friends, etc.) and cultural history (religion, ethnicity, etc.) that we bring to it. That is, all of the 'baggage' that helps us to see the world in the unique way that we do … Our experience of the world is coloured by our perception of it, and this is a product of the phenomenal (ontological) view that we have developed through our living of life in the way that we have done it, so far. This progressive absorption of life events adds to our 'cumulative experience' of the world and subsequent memory structures, which in turn contribute to and continually colour our ontological view – and so we go around again.
>
> (Coxon, 2015, p. 12)

Etymological perspectives on experiences

The question that begs an answer at this stage, is what exactly we mean by the term 'experience'. Etymologically, the word experience is dated from the 14th century but it can be loosely interpreted from the Latin word *experientia* or the French *esperience*, which mean 'to test' or 'to try out'. This therefore implies that an experience comes from a physical interaction with, or the exploration of, something, namely, to physically experience something. German philosophers such as Husserl, Heidegger, and Gadamer provided us with different variations of the meaning of experiences to determine different ways of looking at the term. Using the German terms, there are three ways of looking at experiences: (1) *erlenbis*, which refers to the *conscious experiences* an individual feels

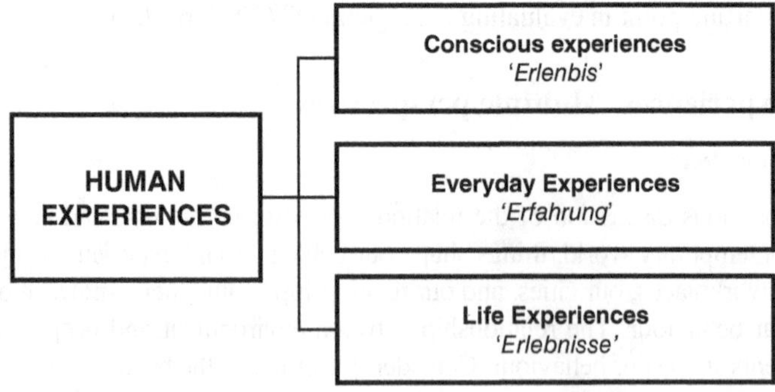

Figure 7.2 Types of human experiences.

deeply, and hence experiences which are 'lived' through or are personally felt, for example, reading this book; (2) *erfahrung*, involving *everyday experiences* that are undergone in a way that they are quite unremarkable or not extremely memorable, for example, walking or driving to work every day; and (3) *erlebnisse*, which is about the cumulative set of separate experiences that construct our *life experience* and our phenomenal view (Coxon, 2015) (Figure 7.2). "Experience is a complex word and refers not only to the here-and-now of experiencing an event, phenomenon, or design, but also to accumulated knowledge over time" (Schmitt, 2016, p. 197). In order to understand experience, we do not have to be always considering *erlenbis*, *erfahrung*, and *erlebnisse* all together. Modern phenomenologists tend to concentrate on the first way, *erlenbis*, because they tend to have a deep impact on the individual. However, from a design perspective, both the first two, *erlenbis* and *erfahrung*, are of importance because they are the ones that designers can directly influence through their practice. While it is possible to explore a person's *erlenbis* and *erfahrung* experiences for design purposes, we have to admit that it is impossible for us to understand the individual's cumulative experiences of life, his/her *erlebnisse*, in the design process (Coxon, 2015).

Unity and uniqueness of experiences

In our daily life, we go through a number of experiences. In order to understand these experiences and evaluate their nature, we have to be able to identify them as different units. This means that we need to define the beginning and the end of each experience. For instance, in order to understand the consumer's experience at *Waitrose* supermarkets, it would be appropriate to adopt the unity of the shopping experience and put a boundary around it, arguing that the experience starts when the consumer enters the parking lot to park his/her car, and it ends when the consumer exits the parking lot. As Dewey explains "an experience has a unity that gives its name … The existence of this unity is constituted by a single quality that pervades the entire experience in spite of the variation of its constituent parts" (1934, p. 38).

Coxon (2015) disagrees with Gadamer (1975) "who once suggested that real, original, or new experience only ever takes place once, and that all other experiences after that are repetitions of the original" (Coxon, 2015, p. 15), because although an experience might seem similar to a previous one in every way, it will never be the same, since the time and context will render it different to some degree. This means that we can never have the same experience twice. In similar vein, experiences are unique between people too; no two people can have the same experience. This means that two people cannot have a shared experience. Even though they might be present or participate in an experiential event (not an experience), having exactly the same experience is impossible due to the fact that an experience is always phenomenal. The experience is not the same, instead, what we are actually talking about is

> an episode of interaction or communication between two people about or in a similar event space … As an experience is always phenomenal, even if two people share the same event in close proximity, each of those people will always experience the event to some degree uniquely.
>
> (Coxon, 2015, p. 17)

In marketing literature, Pine II and Gilmore (1998, 1999, 2011) have argued the same: no two consumers can have the same experience of the brand. Each has a unique experience which is a result of the interaction between the brand and the individual's frame of mind, even when two consumers take part in the same experiential event. Naturally, based on this, one could question the ability for marketers and designers to plan and design a consistent customer experience of the brand. Despite the uniqueness of the experience with every consumer, it is likely that some general dimensions of the experiential event will be interpreted in the same way by the group of individuals who share similar characteristics and constitutes the brand's target audience.

A further way of looking at experiences, involves the intensity of the experience, in terms of how well we 'attend to' or are 'conscious of' the experience as it takes place (Coxon, 2015, p. 18). Heidegger (1962) used the terms '*authentic*' (*eigentlich*) and '*inauthentic*' (*uneigentlich*) to describe different levels of intensity and determine two facets of experience. As Moran explains,

> authentic moments are those in which we are most at home with ourselves ... we have a deep concrete experience of 'mineness', of 'togetherness'. However, in our more usual, normal, everyday moments, we do not treat things as affecting us deeply in our 'own-most' being. Heidegger thinks we live in an inauthentic way most of the time.
>
> (Moran, 1999, p. 240)

It is important to clarify at this stage that both facets always exist in the same experiential space simultaneously. We are in both modes at the same time, they are not separated facets; it is just the mix or balance which is different depending on the experiential context. Inauthentic experiences involve the "ordinary, everyday, often dream like way that we encounter every day" (Coxon, 2015, p. 18). This is the case when we are 'zoned out' or too 'lost' to notice our immediate surroundings, for instance, our daily routine of waking up, getting ready for work (or university) and walking to our office or class. In contrast, an authentic experience will be the case where we feel much more aware of our surroundings and ourselves, e.g., when entering an unfamiliar space, visiting a city for the first time, or the first day at a new job. Authentic experiences are those where we feel consciously aware of our self and who we are. Such experiences do not always have to be stressful or uncomfortable. Generally speaking, the importance of balance between authentic and inauthentic experiences should not be underestimated.

> If we were to live in a state of inauthentic experience all the time we would not be living very well – we would be in a quite robotic, dreamlike state. Conversely, if we were to try to be authentic all of the time we would be living in such an intense way that we would have no 'down-time' or periods where our brain activity and stress levels could slow down and relax – it sounds exhausting.
>
> (Coxon, 2015, p. 19)

Experience in marketing literature

The concept of experiences has been explored in marketing literature from different perspectives including consumer, product and service, offline and online, consumption, and brand experiences. Extant research has offered interesting frameworks and insights in these five areas using different research traditions as well as methodologies. This, according to Schmitt and Zarantonello (2013), has led to a lack of integration of findings among these five areas, resulting to experience issues been researched rather narrowly. Nevertheless, these research studies have provided an understanding of the experience process and interesting categorisations of experiences (Schmitt & Zarantonello, 2013). Current literature in the area of product and service experiences focuses on experiential targets, by exploring the interaction between the user and the product, either before or after purchase. Inspired by Kotler's (1973) seminal paper on the importance of store atmospherics, offline experiences have been studied for decades in retail literature, with regard to shoppers' experiences. Nowadays, thanks to the Internet and social media revolution, online platforms are equally significant in creating experiences before and after purchase. Studies on consumption experiences have concentrated on the emotional or hedonic aspects of consumption, introduced by Holbrook and Hirschman (1982) who argued that people's fantasies, feelings and urge for fun, can drive people's consumption behaviour. Finally, brand experiences have been defined as the "subjective, internal consumer responses (sensations, feelings, and cognitions) and behavioural responses evoked by brand-related stimuli that are part of a brand's design and identity, packaging, communications, and environments"

(Brakus, Schmitt, & Zarantonello 2009, p. 53). In marketing literature, two concepts stand out that need to be explored in more depth: the experience economy, and experiential marketing.

The experience economy

According to Pine II and Gilmore (1998, 1999, 2011), the world had moved from a services-based economy to the *experience economy*, where the new economic offering requires organisations to provide – in their language, 'to stage' – memorable personal experiences for their customers or 'guests'. These experiences are revealed 'over a duration' of time, and they are rich in sensations (Pine II & Gilmore, 1998, 1999, 2011). "An experience occurs when a company intentionally uses services as the stage, and goods as props, to engage individual customers in a way that creates a memorable event" (Pine II & Gilmore, 1998, p. 98). According to Svabo and Shanks (2015), Pine and Gilmore's view on experiences is performative, that "designing for experience is like staging, involving set, props, scripts – scenography and dramaturgy" (2015, p. 25), and is rooted in social and cultural theory.

Pine II and Gilmore's (1998, 1999, 2011) concept of the experience economy was a significantly revolutionary one, and as a consequence has attracted some criticism. In his monograph, Schmitt (2011) claims that the two authors fail to offer a clear picture of the numerical scale of the experience economy or empirical evidence for the very fundamental claim that economies are now entering a new stage of economic offerings. In addition, Raghunathan (2008) questioned whether experiential offerings are qualitatively different to those found in the previous two types of economies: the services and physical goods economies. Schmitt (2011) believes that Pine II and Gilmore's (1998, 1999, 2011) definition of experiences as 'events' or 'event-like' economic offerings (e.g. theme restaurants) means that the experience economy is only a small part of most economies. Similarly, Gupta and Vajic (2000) bemoaned the bandwagon of experience staging if this is executed in a superficial manner to add entertainment value that wears off once the novelty is gone, to reveal a hollow core. Schmitt suggests that

> rather than entering a new economic stage, it may be more appropriate to view business attention to experiences as a new way of marketing products and services, and even consumer commodities (such as salt, pepper, or produce). The experiential value would then not exist in the commodities, products or services per se, but in the marketing of these items.
>
> (Schmitt, 2011, p. 15)

The above quote highlights the fundamental difference between the concept of the experience economy and that of experiential marketing (Schmitt, 1999a, 1999b). While in the experience economy the organisation stages experiences as its offering, the experiential marketing paradigm explores the ways an organisation can 'experientially market' products and services; it is through the process of experientially marketing such offerings where the experiences emerge (Figure 7.3).

Experiential marketing

Schmitt's (1999a, 1999b) concept of experiential marketing ignited a paradigm shift in product and services marketing. He proposed a framework for experientially marketing products and services because customers "take functional features and benefits, product quality, and a positive brand image as a given" (Schmitt, 1999b, p. 22). Experiential marketing goes beyond product or service features and benefits, and focuses on experiences that provide sensory, emotional, cognitive, behavioural and relational values (Schmitt, 1999a, 1999b). It does not narrowly define product category and competition, but explores the possibilities of the consumption situation from a holistic perspective. It also acknowledges customers' rational and emotional motivations behind their consumption, and treats

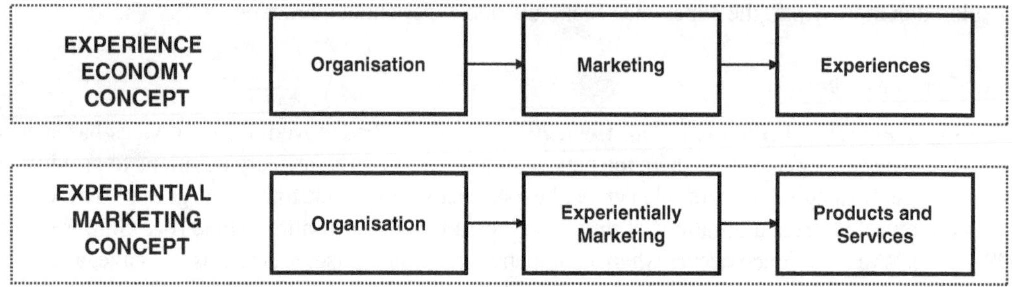

Figure 7.3 Differences between the experience economy and the experiential marketing concepts.

every consumption situation as an idiosyncratic event; therefore, the methods and tools used by the experiential marketer for gathering consumer intelligence are diverse and multifaceted. Consider marketing a shower gel for men for example; our focus should not be merely on the product function, i.e., body washing, but on how the product makes the user feel and the sensory delight he experiences. The product should be considered as part of a man's holistic grooming experience and should be placed in the mind of the consumer in a way that it is considered an integral part of a man's daily grooming experience. The designer should create the appropriate synergies with other products that can form part of that experience, such as a shaving razor and an aftershave lotion. Therefore, there are times competing products might become 'partners' in achieving the experiential result.

Schmitt (1999a, 1999b) suggested that it is the process of experientially marketing the organisation's offering which gives birth to the customer experience. The organisation can create five types of experiences which Schmitt (1999a, 1999b) calls the 'strategic experiential modules' (SEMs), and they form the objectives of an organisation's experiential marketing strategy. First, *sense experiences* which target the five senses in order to create sensory experiences through sight, sound, touch, taste and smell. Second, *feel experiences* which appeal to customer's inner feelings and emotions with the objective of creating affective experiences. Third, *think experiences* which aim at the customer's intellect in order to create cognitive, problem-solving experiences that engage him/her creatively and challenge his/her assumptions. Fourth, *act experiences* which seek to affect and enhance physical experiences, lifestyles, and interactions, as well as to demonstrate alternative ways of doing things. Finally, *relate experiences* which contain aspects of the above but expand beyond them in to order to relate the individual to his/her ideal self, to other people, or to cultures, and create brand communities (Muniz & O'Guinn, 2001).

Schmitt (1999a, 1999b) proposed that the five types of experiences can be created through the tactical implementation tools, in the hands of the experiential marketer, which he calls 'experience providers' (ExPros). These are: (1) communications activities, (2) visual and verbal identity, (3) product presence including product design, packaging and product display, and brand characters, (4) spatial environment including buildings, offices, factory spaces, retail and public spaces, and trade booths, (5) co-branding activities, such as events, sponsorship, and product placements, (6) people, including employees, managers, shareholders, and partners of the organisation, and finally (7) website and electronic media, including the organisation's Internet capabilities and of course nowadays, its social media activities (Figure 7.4).

In similar fashion, Gentile, Spiller, and Noci (2007) identified six experiential components: *sensorial, emotional, cognitive, lifestyle, relational,* and *pragmatic*. As we can see the first five components connect with Schmitt's (1999a, 1999b) sense, feel, think, act, and relate experiences, respectively. However, their sixth component, the pragmatic, is an extra dimension. It comes from the practical act of doing something, and includes the question of usability. Schmitt (2011) suggests this was due to design-oriented literature on user experience and interactions between human and object.

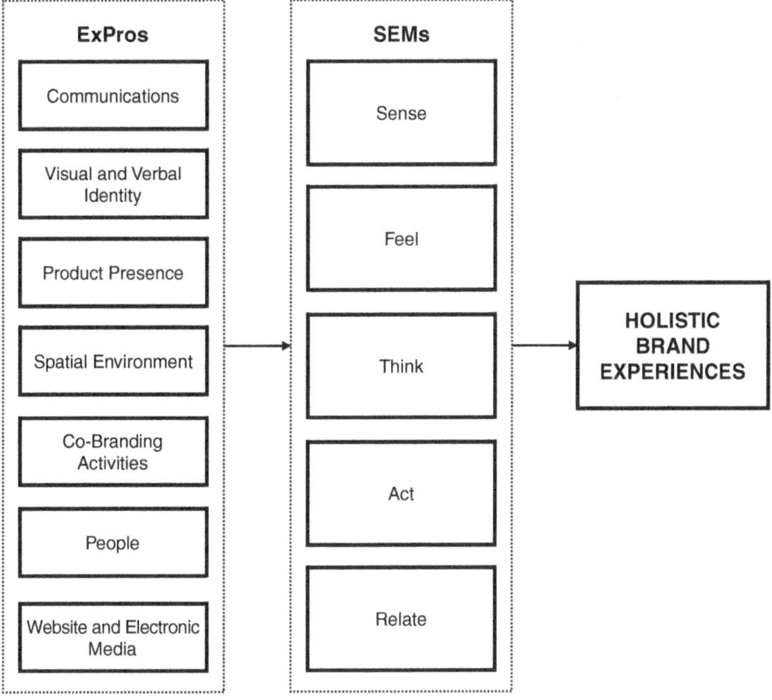

Figure 7.4 The experiential marketing framework.

An important question at this point is what the role of the designer is in this new economic setting, where "the entire system of production and consumption has undergone a profound shift" (Press & Cooper, 2003, p. 22). Advocates of Consumer Culture Theory view consumption as an activity that creates and transmits meaning, and ultimately results in cultural production. Culture – the creation and interpretation of meaning – is central in today's creative or cultural economy. Press and Cooper suggest that, consequently, designers have a new role to play as 'cultural intermediaries', "understanding users and creating meaningful forms of consumption for them" (2003, p. 22). The new forms are the experiences created by designers resulting in customer sensations, feelings, thoughts, actions, and relations with others and the wider society.

Experience design and design experiences

Experience design

Our post-modern, contemporary world is saturated with design. We live in environments designed by architects and interior designers, we are surrounded by objects created by product designers, we use software and digital platforms developed by software designers, and in many instances, our attention, capacity, and movement is negotiated by design. As material culture suggests, we live in artificial worlds; design is everywhere (Highmore, 2009). However, this design saturation leads to a certain challenge: "not only to design singular objects, services systems and environments, but also to understand imagine, connect, and choreograph all of these different designs" (Svabo & Shanks, 2015, p. 24). This goes in line with Brown's prediction that "as more of our basic needs are met, we increasingly expect sophisticated experiences that are emotionally satisfying and meaningful. These experiences will not be simple products. They will be complex combinations of products, services, spaces, and information" (Brown, 2008, p. 92). This challenge has led design scholars and practitioners to *human-centred design* whose main premise is that "design may be unified and improved by focusing upon the human component" (Svabo & Shanks, 2015, p. 24). Ultimately human-centred design aims to improve individuals' wellbeing, has an ethical orientation, and leads to innovation that positively impact people's lives. Such combinations of products, services, spaces, and information can be holistically created through *experience design*. Svabo and Shanks (2015) explain the power of experience design:

> An interesting potential of Experience Design lies in the ability to transcend singular design field … Experience Design may help draw forward the interrelations and complex combinations that emerge when people engage with multiple designs in complex physical environments and manifold social constellations. Experience Design analytically should make it possible to follow experience as a phenomenon that is enacted in relations between heterogeneous elements, for example, in human interactions with a place, modes of transportation, mobile mediation as well as the potential influence exerted by, say, a pair of high-heeled shoes. All of these singular designs contribute to and shape experience … this makes it a central challenge for design research and practice to be able to conceptualise and choreograph the on-going experience of combinations of designs.
>
> (Shanks, 2015, p. 26)

In order to achieve a human focus in experience design, we need to pay close attention to situations of use. Experience design is site-specific; therefore, it is imperative that designers understand the individuals and situations they design for. This takes us back to the concepts of design research, and in particular, design ethnography, explored in Chapter 2. The onus is on the multidisciplinary team to understand and imagine human needs and desires and fulfil them through the design of compelling experiences. In order to do so, design can aim at experience through three processes: (1) cognition, (2) sensory perception, and (3) emotion. Desmet, Hekkert, and Schifferstein (2011) highlight the fact that the distinctions between these three processes are helpful because they enable us to assess the experiential impact from multiple angles, but are also theoretical in nature because "in daily product experiences the layers are closely intertwined and they may influence each other" (Desmet et al., 2011, p. 5). Svabo and Shanks (2015) are not entirely keen on breaking down experience into these constituent components because such reductionist analytical acts might take our minds away from the need of understanding and designing experiences of complex combinations of objects, services, spaces, and information. They fear that breaking down experience into three constituent components

> may overlook the entanglements and shifting flows of movement and attention, which also constitute experience … [The alternative] to understanding experience is to unfold it as fluidity. Experience is well conceived as shifting entanglements and engagements, as vectors of movement. This honours that Experience Design … may be interesting for its ability to follow engagements and entanglements across different spatial, object, and digital relations, and over time.
>
> (Svabo & Shanks, 2015, p. 28)

The above statement takes us back to the concept of entanglement, and the relationships between humans and things, which we explored in the first section of this chapter. What follows in the next section is a discussion of aesthetics and emotional design, as two of the aforementioned constituent components. Despite Svabo and Shanks' (2015) disapproval, for the purpose of understanding extant literature on these topics, we shall explore them separately, while of course keeping in mind that they are intertwined with each other and with cognition.

Aesthetics and sensory perception

The term aesthetics was coined for the first time in the 18th century by Alexander Baumgarten, a German philosopher. The word derives from the Greek word *aesthetikos* (*αισθητικός*), which means perceptive, especially by feeling. Aesthetics is a special branch of philosophy, which aims to understand the impact of physical features on human experiences. Aesthetics "produce a science of sensuous knowledge, in contrast with logic whose goal is truth" (Schmitt & Simonson, 1997, p. 18). Aesthetics appeal to our five senses: sight, sound, touch, taste and smell, and create sensory experiences, which subsequently influence cognition and generate emotions. Sensory experiences can be generated through things (as defined by Hodder (2012)) and their aesthetics, in the form of objects, services, events, and/or environments. Consider, for instance, the plurality of times, certain scents have delighted your olfactory sense, brought back to your mind memories and maybe made you feel nostalgic. As Gobé elegantly puts it, "the nuance of an image, the delight of an unfamiliar taste, the memory of a familiar sound, the gentle caress of a soft fabric, the associations of an ancient smell – these are the cues which form indelible imprints on our emotional memories" (2009, p. 70). It is true that our whole perception and understanding of the world is experienced through our senses; they are a link to our memory and tap into our past and present emotions (Lindstrom, 2010).

Schmitt proposes that the overall purpose of sense experiences is to "provide aesthetic pleasure, excitement, beauty, and satisfaction through sensory stimulation" (1999b, p. 99). He highlights that senses should not only be stimulated but also delighted. Carefully crafting and planning a brand's aesthetic elements can result to customer preference and loyalty, making the brand stand out in overcrowded markets with fierce competition (Gobé, 2009). Schmitt and Simonson (1997) proposed a framework for creating and managing brand aesthetics. They indicated that brand expressions are projected through brand identity elements. Identity elements entail their own aesthetic elements which are created through primary elements, styles and themes. All these lead to customer impressions, the customer interpretations of these brand expressions. Let us explore this framework in a little more detail.

Schmitt and Simonson (1997) use an analogy to the concept of the 4 Ps of the marketing mix, and propose the 4 Ps of the identity elements mix, which consists of: (1) '*properties*', which include buildings, office interiors, retail spaces and company vehicles, (2) '*products*', including specific aspects or attributes of physical goods or services, (3) '*presentations*' referring to the surroundings of the physical product, including packaging, labelling, and tags, or the surroundings of the service such as shopping bags, interior graphics, employee uniforms, and finally (4) '*publications*' involving promotional materials, advertising, business cards, and stationery (Figure 7.5). Primary elements are vital in creating sensory experiences. Their importance lies on that fact that "primary elements are the building blocks of style" (Schmitt, 1999b, p. 103). Primary elements include shapes, colours, typefaces, sounds, materials and textures, and scents, corresponding to human senses. One shall not forget that consumption is a multisensory experience; hence, all primary elements need to be taken care of. Therefore, it is rather absurd how "99 percent of all brand communication today is focused on our two senses: what we hear and see. In sharp contrast, 75 percent of our emotions are generated by what we in fact smell" (Lindstrom, 2005, p. 85).

As mentioned before, primary elements and styles need to be explored together since "styles are composed of primary elements and can be analysed in terms of them" (Schmitt & Simonson, 1997, p. 85). At this stage it is essential we define the term '*style*'. One might instantly think the totality of someone's dress sense; although this is not entirely incorrect, the concept of style is much more encompassing. Shapiro suggests that style is "the constant form – and sometimes the constant elements and expression – in the art of an individual or a group" (1953, p. 287). Over the centuries, the concept of style has been used in a plethora of disciplines ranging from art history and literature, to architecture, fashion, and design. It is imperative that the design team associate the brand with a certain style through appropriate primary elements. The goal is to create an integration of the primary elements, to achieve 'synesthesia' – from the Greek *syn*

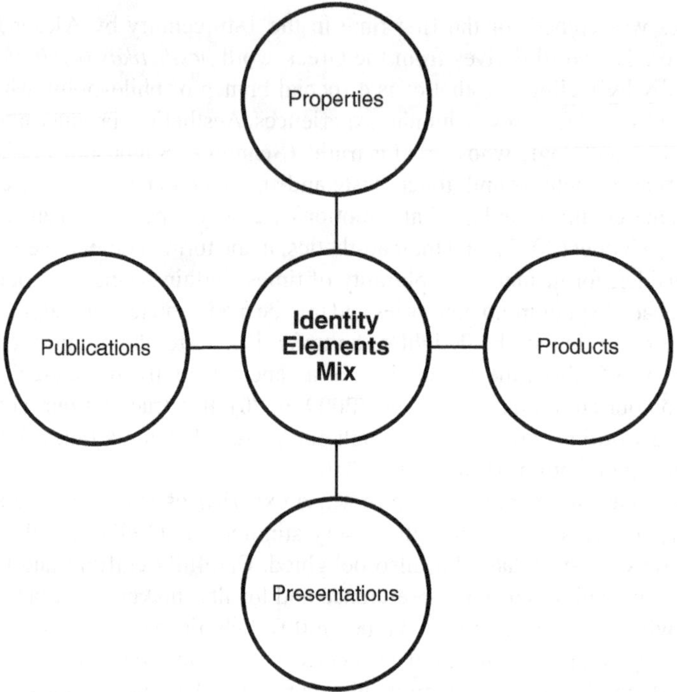

Figure 7.5 The 4 Ps of the identity elements mix.

(*σύν* – together) and *aisthanesthai* (*αισθάνεσθαι* – perceive) – that will ultimately express a brand style. The concept of store atmospherics (Kotler, 1973; Schmitt & Zarantonello, 2013) relates directly with the concept of style because store atmospherics combine different primary elements to create a certain style and bring this desired synesthesia to shoppers.

For style to work effectively, it must be combined with *themes*, which communicate the brand mantra more laconically and directly (Schmitt & Simonson, 1997). Schmitt (1999a, 1999b) argues that themes are messages communicating content and meaning about the brand. "Themes provide mental anchors, reference points, and memory cues, [and] appear in the form of corporate and brand names, visual symbols, verbal slogans, jingles, general concepts, or in a combination of these theme elements to evoke sensory imagery" (Schmitt, 1999b, p. 107). Essentially, designers and marketers create corporate and brand themes which act as signs and symbols to express brand characteristics. Themes should be used as "prototypical expressions of an organisation's and/or brand's core values or mission" (Schmitt & Simonson, 1997, p. 124). They should also be used on a repeat basis and, if needed, adapted over time. Designers and marketers should also ensure that they are developed into a system of interrelated ideas to ensure consistency and avoid confusion.

Affect and emotional design

Creating emotional experiences requires the organisation understanding how to attach affect to the organisational offering through Schmitt's (1999a, 1999b) aforementioned experience providers (ExPros). The design team needs to appreciate how to create positive emotions among the target audiences during their experience of the offering, be it a physical product, a service, an environment, or a piece of software.

Feelings are important because as human beings, we are pleasure-seekers; we want to feel good and avoid feeling bad. Feelings are important in branding because brands that create good feelings for their customers on a continuous basis can create strong and long-term brand loyalty (Schmitt, 1999a, 1999b). Organisations which establish unique, strong and favourable performance and imagery associations for their brands will evoke positive emotional reactions from consumers. This will ultimately lead to brand resonance, i.e., a long-term loyalty relationship between the brand and the consumer, leading to high levels of brand equity (brand resonance is the top layer in the Brand Equity Pyramid model – see Keller, Aperia, & Georgson, 2012).

Elements of emotional design

Candi and Saemundsson (2011) argue that once an organisation's offering meets the basic requirements of technological ability and functionality, its competitiveness can be improved by increasing emotional connections with the user. Such connections can be generated through the use of design which focuses also on the non-functional aspect of the offering which is often referred to as *emotional design* (Beltagui, Candi, & Riedel, 2012). According to Norman (2004), the concept of emotional design includes three elements: 'behavioural', 'visceral', and 'reflective' design. These elements resonate with what Bloch (2011) has described as the utilitarian, hedonic and semiotic benefits of the offering, or in other words, the offering's functional, the sensual, and the symbolic value, respectively. Norman's (2004) concept of emotional design builds upon and expands his previous work which concentrated on making sure the products developed by designers are usable (Norman, 1990). This early work, although very insightful from a usability perspective, was somehow incomplete because his prescriptions, if followed by designers, would result in usable but ugly products. Drawing from Tractinsky, Katz, and Ikar's (2000) work on the link between aesthetics and usability, "the emotional design concept explores the interplay between logical and emotional product aspects. Emotional design combines considerations of both usability and emotional appeal in the design of products [or services, environments etc.]" (Beltagui et al., 2012, p. 113).

Norman's (2004) first element of emotional design, *behavioural design* seeks to make the offering functional as well as understandable. The focus here is successful function; however, following this approach exclusively means that appearance and other non-functional attributes may be neglected. *Visceral design* appeals to the senses, through visual, audial, and tactile stimuli, and as already mentioned, sensual appeal can lead to emotions.

> Sensory stimuli are interpreted by the brain in a primitive and impulsive manner, rather than a logical one. Therefore, visceral design can produce emotional response quickly. This means irrational judgements of what is good or bad are made rapidly and tend to override the logical consideration of behavioural design attributes.
>
> (Beltagui et al., 2012, p. 114)

Finally, *reflective design* appeals to the highest layer of cognition. This element of emotional design targets abstract and non-verbal connections between people and things, and needs to resonate with the users' self-images and their group memberships. Reflective design is about the meaning of the offering for the individual and/or a group of people, including the memories and associations the offering creates for the user. Hence, reflective design is well connected with Hodder's (2012) concept of entanglement.

Emotional design's success lies in the combination of these three elements. "While focusing on behavioural design should result in intuitive and usable [offerings], emphasizing visceral and reflective design is likely to create the kind of emotional attachment that can potentially override usability problems" (Beltagui et al., 2012, p. 114). The physical form of the product should appropriately balance functionality, aesthetic appeal, and a deeper meaning, i.e., it should provide utilitarian, hedonic, and semiotic benefits (Bloch, 2011).

Moods and emotions

Affective experiences include experiences of different degrees of intensity, ranging from moods to intense emotions (Schmitt, 1999a, 1999b). Moods are very unspecific, and they can be positive, negative or neutral. We often find ourselves in a certain mood but we do not know the reason for this particular state. Specific stimuli, such as irritating music in a retail shop or an inattentive waiter at a restaurant, might trigger our mood states but we often remain unware of the reasons. In contrast to moods, emotions are much more intense, and we have the ability to recognise them and recognise the stimuli that elicited them. Schmitt (1999a, 1999b) suggests that there are two types of emotions: 'basic' and 'complex' emotions. He argues that basic emotions "constitute the basic components of our affective lives, similar to chemical elements" (Schmitt, 1999b, p. 124). Examples of basic emotions include positive emotions of joy and excitement, and negative emotions of anger, disgust and sadness, which of course are universal emotions across all races. The facial expressions made by people experiencing these emotions are also incredibly similar across cultures; this could endow them with a global appeal, ideal for global communications campaigns (Schmitt, 1999a, 1999b). Complex emotions are combinations of basic emotions. An example of a complex emotion is nostalgia, defined by Stern as "an emotional state in which an individual yearns for an idealised or sanitised version of an earlier time period" (1992, p. 11), which combines both positive and negative basic emotions. These positive and negative components yield a bittersweet quality which renders the emotion with its most distinguishing characteristic (Havlena & Holak, 1991).

Triggers of emotions

It is important to identify the causes of human emotions and how these can be utilised in experience design. Basic or complex emotions are triggered by three aspects or changes: (a) 'events', namely situations that occur, (b) 'agents', which include people and institutions, and (c) 'objects' (Schmitt, 1999a, 1999b). Indeed, Belk suggests that nostalgia, for example, "may be prompted by an object, a scene, a smell or a strain of music" (1990, p. 671). If we replace objects with products or brands, agents with companies, spokespeople or staff, and events with consumption situations, then this highlights how this concept can be applied in creating affective experiences in marketing (Schmitt, 1999a, 1999b).

In consumption situations, the most significant trigger for strong feelings is face-to-face interactions. In fact, feelings are the strongest when they occur during consumption and involve personal contact and interactions. Feelings created during consumption are much stronger than feelings created as a result of advertising. However, it is important to remember that not all consumption situations trigger positive feelings; badly designed processes, unhelpful staff, and irritating environments can create negative feelings. Any contact and interaction with staff should be carefully designed and facilitated.

A typology of consumption emotions

It is very important to understand the plethora of emotions that could occur during consumption. Inspired by the work of Richins (1997), who came up with sixteen emotions related to marketing situations, Schmitt (1999b) provides a useful perceptual map to place these emotions based on two dimensions: 'inward–outward' and 'positive–negative'. As shown in Figure 7.6, inward positive emotions include when the consumer feels warm-hearted, sentimental, and loving. Such emotions make the customers feel special and they will probably demonstrate loyalty to the brand albeit not publicly outward. Outward positive emotions include situations where customers feel pleased, excited, and enthusiastic – such emotions will make customers walk around and praise, spend money and make recommendations to others.

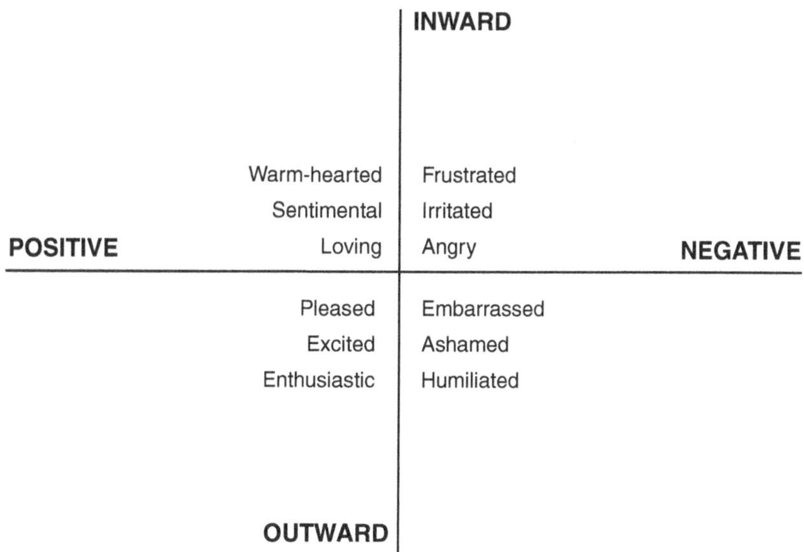

Figure 7.6 Typology of consumption emotions (based on Schmitt, 1999b).

On the other hand, inward negative emotions involve feeling frustrated, irritated, and angry. Such feelings are likely to make customers complain or, in the worst case, sabotage everything the organisation offers. Finally, outward negative emotions include situations that make customers feel embarrassed, humiliated and ashamed. Such feelings can possibly make customers never return to the brand, which of course would be a catastrophe for the brand and its equity. It is obvious that the organisation should do its outmost to avoid negative inward and outward emotions. Negative emotional reactions to the brand will not generate brand resonance with consumers, the ultimate layer in building successful brand equity, and will ultimately harm organisational performance in the long term (Keller et al., 2012).

Properties of objects and models of design experiences

Press and Cooper (2003) suggest that in order to understand the human experiences that design can create, we must explore the properties of objects, and the experiences that each of these properties can provide customers with. This leads us to the work of Tim Dant, a sociologist of material life, who proposed that there are six properties of objects, which result in six experiences. According to Dant (1999), the first property, '*function*', involves the ability of an object to extend or enhance human physical action. Press and Cooper (2003) use the example of a personal computer and the task of writing to explain this property. Consider the difference of using a computer to write a novel, compared with using a typewriter, or even a pen. A computer makes the task faster and more efficient because we can edit the text easier. The experience of writing, as a consequence, has changed because we now have the ability to play around with the text more easily, copy previous drafts onto a new document and manipulate the page design. Sometimes, it feels that we use computers for writing to such an extent, that in few years we will not be able to hold a pen to handwrite our names.

The second property, '*signification*', involves the product signifying membership of a social group (Dant, 1999). For instance, using *Beats by Dre* headphones to listen to music while on the go does not only solve functionality problems but makes a statement about oneself, creating a sense of belonging to a group of 'cool' and 'edgy' music lovers. Press and Cooper (2003) use the example of the *Apple iMac* to explain the signification property; they suggested that an *Apple iMac* user aimed to identify with creative people who adhere to the 'think-different' ethos that is associated with this product, signifying the users' membership to a more eclectic social group. Perhaps this example is rather outdated because one could argue that nowadays *Apple* has become too mainstream to signify such a 'sub-cult' ethos; in fact, quite the contrary, using an *iMac* nowadays might be seen by some as just a way to conform to the wider trend. We shall bear in mind that mass adoption of a brand can reduce its eclectic character and might eventually dilute or harm its brand personality.

'*Sexuality*', as an object property, includes the ability for a product to be sexually arousing in some certain way, or to signify sexual identity or activity (Dant, 1999). Of course, perfume, jewellery and clothing are items that can communicate this property (Press & Cooper, 2003). Think, for example, the homoerotic identity of *Jean Paul Gautier's Le Male* perfume, or the femininity of the *J'Adore* perfume by *Dior*. Besides sexuality, '*knowledge*' is another property that communicates messages to the user, and to some extent, the people around. Knowledge involves the product capability to impart knowledge or information to the user (Dant, 1999). Press and Cooper (2003) suggest that such knowledge products include maps, train timetables, books or computers since they transmit knowledge or allow the user to gather information. Essentially, the experience of learning has been transformed over the years; students have a plethora of sources of information beyond the traditional book and journal publications, which include the Internet and digital databases.

According to Dant (1999), '*aesthetics*' includes the emotional experiences resulting from the form or style of a product or a service. Similar to Gobé (2009) and Schmitt (1999a, 1999b), he connects aesthetic experience with the resulting emotional experience. Press and Cooper add that "we are moved by a work of art, a craft object, but also increasingly by the products of industrially based design. It is all part of the aestheticisation of our material culture" (2003, p. 73). Finally, '*mediation*', as an object property, includes the ability for a product to enable or enhance communication between people (Dant, 1999). Nowadays, certainly, our smartphones have evolved so much that we have multiple options of communicating with people; we can phone them, send them an SMS text, email them, message them on platforms such *WhatsApp* or *Viber*, or even video call them through *FaceTime* or *Skype*.

Press and Cooper (2003) claim that all designed objects are part of social life to some extent. However, the paradoxical nature of technology (Mick & Fournier, 1998) and of mobile phone technology in particular (Jarvenpaa & Lang, 2005), means that technology can disable mediation at the same time. Mick and Fournier (1998) call this the paradox of 'assimilation–isolation', where technology can bring people together while at the same time it can isolate them. The authors found that females are more attuned to this paradox because of their tendency to be concerned with human relations and communal issues. Consider, for instance, how many times your phone allows you to stay in touch with many people far away, but at the same isolates you from the people around you, much to their annoyance.

Cultural critique on experience concepts

The concepts and frameworks explored above, developed in the work of Pine II and Gilmore (1998, 1999, 2011), Schmitt and Simonson (1997), Schmitt (1999a, 1999b), and Press and Cooper (2003), provide very important guidelines for organisations aiming to create effective, personal and memorable experiences for their customers, and compete successfully in the experience economy arena. However, there have been some scholars who have criticised the failure of these concepts to consider the nature of human experiences from a societal and cultural perspective.

Carù and Cova (2012) emphasise the fact that we shall not forget that an experience is a subjective process. Therefore, they argue that organisations cannot offer experiences but experiential platforms or contexts. This goes in line with the notion of the phenomenal nature of experiences and the fact that two people can never have the same experience; merely, they might go through the same experiential event (Coxon, 2015). This means that although Pine II and Gilmore (1998, 1999, 2011) and Schmitt (1999a, 1999b) suggest that organisations can offer experiences, what they actually do offer are "devices and stimuli that consumers mobilise to realise their own experiences" (Carù & Cova, 2012, p. 165). In fact, according to Carù and Cova (2012), there are three qualities that establish the underlying foundations of the experiential context.

First, '*enclavisation*' includes the fact that the experience must be 'enclavised' within specific boundaries which allows customers to enter a separate world of entertainment, stepping outside their daily lives and escaping from their worries and hardships. This resonates with the concept of the experience as a unit, with a beginning and an end (Dewey, 1934). Consider, for instance, the *Abercrombie and Fitch* stores, which make their guests feel they are in a night-club-like environment. Second, '*security*' involves the fact that the experiential context needs to be secure and closely monitored in order to remove the customers' need to pay attention to themselves, their possessions, or even their concerns. Lastly, '*thematisation*' includes the fact that the context must be thematised. This thematisation "acts as a sort of symbolic packaging of the context, notably by ascribing meaning to the act of consumption. A theme can be an activity, era, region, population, or any combination of these elements and must be very distinctive" (Carù & Cova, 2012, p. 166).

This agrees with what Pine II and Gilmore (1998, 1999, 2011), Schmitt and Simonson (1997) and Schmitt (1999a, 1999b) have talked about with regard to the responsibility of the designer to theme the experience appropriately. Consider, for instance, how, in the past, *Abercrombie and Fitch* sought to communicate a US East Coast theme in their advertising (bizarrely different to the 'clubbing' theme which used to be created in their stores). Even when the organisation is mainly product-based, it is recommended that it creates its own retail premises which act as its own 'theatre of consumption'. This strategy was followed by *Nike* or *Apple*, which launched their own stores years ago. Since then, the *Nike Town* or *Apple* stores have become 'temples of worship' for the brands' followers.

Carù and Cova (2012) have identified four brand experience contexts. Firstly, '*brand stores*', such as the previous examples, which go in line with Pine II and Gilmore's (1998, 1999, 2011) suggestion of promoting shopping experiences that are fun, such as the experiences found at *Disney World*. Secondly, '*brand plants*' such as *Volkswagen's Autostadt* in Wolfsburg, the *Guinness Brewery* in Dublin, or the *Heineken Experience* in Amsterdam, which connect the concepts of tourist attraction and factory, where people are willing to pay a fee to visit production plants. Equally, theme parks have been combined with retail experiences such as the *Legoland* theme parks. Thirdly, '*brand fests*', which create a festival experience where customers can have a direct contact with the brand in an ephemeral and dynamic context, such as events organised by *Harley-Davidson* and *Ducatti*. Finally, '*brand websites*', designed to provide online experiences using 'immersion technologies' (often found in online games), such as the *Fiat 500* and *Nutella* websites.

A cultural approach to production of experiences indicates a '*continuum of experiences*' that customers go through, which of course can be associated with certain marketing activities. At one extreme of this continuum lie experiences constructed mainly by consumers, which can involve products and services provided by an organisation, like consuming food in our private homes (Carù & Cova, 2007). The organisation has the only option of following traditional product or service marketing and the customer has the ability to organise his/her experience. In the middle of this continuum reside experiences that have been co-developed by customers and organisations. In this case the organisation can provide the experiential platform based on which customers can develop their own experiences. Carù and Cova (2012) provide sport tourism, adventure packages, rock concerts, and cultural events, as examples of such experiences. Finally, at the other extreme lie experiences that have been developed by organisations, where consumers

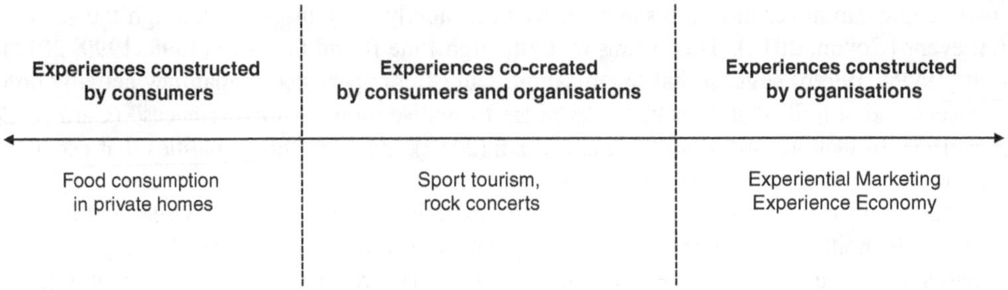

Figure 7.7 Continuum of experiences.

find themselves immersing in a hyper-real context. According to Carù and Cova (2012), this is the type of experiences that the experience economy concept (Pine II & Gilmore, 1998, 1999, 2011) and experiential marketing (Schmitt, 1999a, 1999b) have focused on (Figure 7.7).

However, based on our discussion of experiential marketing, one could counterargue that the organisation can also experientially market products and services which consumers use privately; thus, it can dictate (in the positive meaning of the word) the first type of experiences to a certain extent too. That being said, what we can distil from Carù and Cova's work (2012) is that using a consumer culture lens, we shall not forget the fact that customer experiences by definition are phenomenal (Coxon, 2015), as well as that experiences are sometimes found out with the control of the design team and the organisation in general.

Design management and experiences: A symbiosis

It is important now to examine the role of design management in the creation and management of human experiences. Throughout the previous sections, it became obvious that marketers and design managers can form brand experience teams in order to deliver the experiential objectives of the organisation and/or brand. Marketing and design share similar ambitions; they are both human-focused and aim to improve the quality of life of people around the world through offerings that enhance human experiences (Bruce, 2011). There is a symbiotic relationship between design and marketing; both focus on the individual and the wider society. In fact, we have used the terms 'consumers' and 'humans' interchangeably, to highlight that all humans are consumers since consumption is an inherent part of human life, and all consumers are humans, i.e., not only rational but also emotional and social species.

If we compare Schmitt's (1999a, 1999b) experiential marketing framework with Dant's (1999) models of design experience, we can find direct synergies between the two concepts. There can be connections drawn between all object properties (Dant, 1999) with the five types of experiences (SEMs) (Schmitt, 1999a, 1999b) (Table 7.1).

Another significant point that arises from the discussion above is that it is evident that design and subsequently design management, can deliver all three types of experiences in Carù and Cova's (2007) 'continuum of experiences'. Dant's (1999) work, and the different examples provided to explain his concept demonstrate that design can certainly influence the first type, i.e., those experiences mainly constructed by consumers, because although these experiences are organised by them, they incorporate products and services which are indeed designed by the design team. Design management can certainly influence the second type through the design of appropriate experiential platforms based on

Table 7.1 Properties of objects and strategic experiential modules.

Properties of objects	*SEMs*
Function	Act experiences
Signification	Relate experiences
Mediation	Relate experiences
Sexuality	Sense experiences Feel experiences
Knowledge	Think experiences
Aesthetics	Sense experiences Feel experiences

which customers can develop their own experiences. Finally, design management can determine and control the experiences developed by organisations, the 'hyper-real contexts', where consumers can immerse themselves.

Design management has a leading role in the creation of human experiences, regardless of what type of experience (in Carù & Cova's (2007) 'continuum of experiences') the organisation aims to influence or direct. In the case of experiential marketing, it becomes apparent from our discussion of Schmitt's (1999a, 1999b) framework, no matter what the experiential marketing objectives are, i.e., the intended SEMs, it is an investment in design that will deliver all the ExPros which lead to these types of experiences. Bruce highlights that "design is a tangible asset through the products and services generated and an intangible asset through the emotive value, meaning and experience embedded or associated, with the offerings, the X factor of design" (2011, p. 332).

Undoubtedly, design is related to all the aforementioned ExPros and design management plays a catalytic role in creating and managing these experience providers in a way that they create appropriate customer experiences. Press and Cooper (2003) use the example of a sushi bar (where the two authors met to discuss progress on their book *The Design Experience*), to illustrate the role of design in the creation of brand experiences. In their description of their experience of the sushi bar, they noted that the bar chefs – cooking and preparing every dish in front of the customers – provided a sense of theatre in the consumption situation, a form of performing art. They also described how everything from the interior décor to the menu, the tableware, staff uniform and attitude, had been meticulously orchestrated – designed – to provide the appropriate experience, one that is surprising, stimulating and pleasing. Design management, through the careful conception, planning and execution of design elements, enables the organisation to experientially market a product or service, and leads to a meaningful and personal experience for the customer (in this case, the two authors meeting over lunch).

If we attempt to match the seven ExPros with DCMS' (1998, 2001) typology of creative industries, we can argue that communications require graphic, and digital design, visual and verbal identity includes graphic, and digital design, as well as typography, product presence involves product design, and process design (for services offerings), and spatial environment requires architectural, interior design, and graphic design services (for interior graphics). With regard to the other ExPros, co-branding activities require exhibition design, and interior design, people's activities are influenced by fashion design (uniforms), and process design (the nature of the process followed to provide the service and the availability of resources), and finally website and social media require graphic design, digital design, and software design (Table 7.2).

The onus is on the organisation to organise project teams which include individuals from different backgrounds: marketers, designers, design managers, psychologists, and even engineers. Design is not

Table 7.2 Experience providers and design disciplines.

Experience providers	*Creative industries*
Communications (advertising, public relation campaigns, and external and internal company communications).	Graphic design and digital design.
Visual and verbal identity (name, logos, and signage).	Graphic design, typography and digital design.
Product presence (product design, packaging and product display, and brand characters).	Product design and process design.
Spatial environment (includes buildings, offices, factory spaces, retail and public spaces, and trade booths).	Architecture, interior design, and graphic design.
Co-branding activities (event marketing and sponsorship, and product placement).	Exhibition design and interior design.
People (salespeople, company representatives, service/ customer service providers, and partners).	Fashion design and process design.
Websites, electronic media, social media.	Graphic design, digital design and software design.

only vital for creating sensory experiences; its value and function goes beyond aesthetics. Montaña, Guzmán, and Moll argue that

> design is an unequivocal source of differentiation and has become a key element for branding; not only because aesthetically pleasing products and services better compete for consumer's short attention span, but also because design may serve as the cohesive factor for all elements that configure a brand experience.
>
> (Montaña et al., 2007, p. 829)

Brand building has evolved over the last twenty years beyond the notion of the brand as merely the identifying part of a product. Nowadays brands are acknowledged as "the full 'personality' of the company … the interface between a company and its audience" (Davis, 2009, p. 12), which go beyond the physical and into the psychological sphere, and hence they can be extremely powerful (Lewis, 1991). Montaña et al. (2007) argue that design (and design management) plays a leading role in creating and managing coherence within the portfolio of brand meanings. In fact, the relationship between design and experience is reciprocal. Not only brand experiences benefit from effective design, but also the other way round; the concept of experience is very important for design itself. Press and Cooper argue that "the concept of experience is essential as a unifying issue between the culture and economy of design, as a means of understanding the context of design today, and as a window through which to view the possibilities and challenges facing design in the future" (2003, p. 70).

Chapter review questions

The following questions can help you reflect on the material we have covered in this chapter:

1 What are the differences between a thing and an object according to Hodder (2012)?
2 Explain the concept of entanglement, making references to the different relationships this entails.
3 What are the different types of experiences? What makes experiences phenomenally different?
4 Provide critique on the concept of the experience economy and explain its difference with experiential marketing.
5 Discuss the power of experience design and its different elements.

6 How can organisations use aesthetics to create sensory experiences?
7 What are the triggers of emotions and what are the elements of emotional design?
8 Explain Dant's (1999) six properties of objects as models of design experiences.
9 Provide a critique on the experience concepts, from a cultural perspective.
10 Explain how design management can contribute to the creation of brand experiences.

Recommended reading

1 Coxon, I. (2015). Fundamental aspects of human experience: A phenomeno(logical) explanation. In P. Benz (Ed.), *Experience design: Concepts and case studies*. London: Bloomsbury.
2 Schmitt, B. H. (1999). Experiential marketing. *Journal of Marketing Management, 15*(1–3), 53–67.
3 Pine, B. J., & Gilmore, J. H. (1998). Welcome to the experience economy: As goods and services become commoditised the customer experiences that companies create will matter most. *Harvard Business Review, 76*, 97–105.
4 Carù, A., & Cova, B. (2012). Experience consumption: Appropriating and marketing experiences. In L. Peñaloza, N. Toulouse, & L. M. Viskonti (Eds.), *Marketing management: A cultural perspective*. London: Routledge.

Reflective thoughts

Design 'charrette': Dealing with time constraints in the design process

Tony Coffield
Lecturer in Interior Design
Glasgow School of Art, Glasgow, UK
Director, make., Glasgow, UK

This chapter looks at various ways in which our experiences as designers can be shaped by people, place and context, and time. The outcomes are often determined by how we allocate our time to each of the above, but if time itself becomes the driving factor then how do we cope with this impossible task?

While teaching Interior Design I noticed students approached design briefs in a familiar pattern and worked through the design process in a rhythm unique to them, in the knowledge they had the 'right' amount of time to complete the tasks. There is nothing wrong with this, in fact, most students demonstrate the ability to manage their time and ensure they make the necessary transition from start to finish. But what if conditions permit a change in the parameters which could occur when out with the controlled environment of learning? Surely something has to give? What if students only had three days to complete a three-week project?

While working on an individual project where time was a contributing factor (I had to condense a three-month project into three weeks), I realised that the outcome would be influenced by the use of time, and so I broke with my familiar pattern of working, and looked to borrow time by adopting the concept of a 'charrette'. With encouraging results, I decided to introduce this

(Continued)

(Continued)

method into the studio to see if students could adopt some of the strategies to help them complete the impossible task set.

Designers and architects know the concept of a "design charrette" all too well: long days and late nights in the studio, trying to complete a design project within a short, intense period of time. A charrette, in its simplest form, is a period of intense design and planning for solving a design challenge. Dating back to the glory days of the Ecole des Beaux Arts in Paris, the charrette became synonymous with students working feverishly to complete a project on a cart pulled by a friend on the way to a professor's home ('charrette' in French means cart).

The charrette has become one of the most powerful and effective tools for creative and collaborative problem solving. The soul of a charrette is found in bringing together designers with a broad and diverse range of ideas to address challenges collaboratively. The charrette is highly adaptive and responsive to change.

The charrette process is straightforward and simple. First, a team is assembled that has the expertise needed to address the issue at hand. Then, over the course of several days, a series of input sessions are held to gain an understanding of the issues from various perspectives (technical, emotion, practical etc.). All of these charrette sessions are open and fluid. Next, the charrette design team, or the individual, formulates responses to the issues based on what they have heard and their knowledge through research and endeavour. Finally, at the end of the charrette, the design team makes a presentation where they may offer solutions to the problems at hand or present different options for consideration.

Nevertheless, the concept of the charrette is not perfect, so what is the appeal? As a learning tool or experience, the charrette was effective as it highlighted the value of understanding that each outcome is arrived via a process of transitions. This was clearly understood as an important way of advancing design ideas. It became effective because it condenses traditional timescales and once a direction is established and momentum is gathered, it is the 'community' that drives and guides the answer.

Some of the values or benefits in condensing the design process can be observed as follows. First, input from staff promoted short and frequent design feedback loops, which promoted intensive conversation and generation of creative ideas. Implementing ideas through iterative making, drawing, discussing was encouraged with emphasis on unified thinking and agreeing on key 'issues'. Second, having contributed to the planning, participants are in a position both to understand and support a project's rationale, and all interested parties must be involved from the beginning which promotes mutual trust and dependence. Third, the charrette encouraged uninhibited decision making and reduced some of the negative practices which designers can dwell on, such as overthinking or exploring unfertile territory. Finally, during the charrette, design ideas are encouraged to be focused upon the delivery of a vision, and presented initially for review, critique, and refinement at a later stage.

Regular stakeholder input and reviews quickly build trust in the process and foster true understanding and support of the product. A feedback loop occurs when a design is proposed, reviewed, changed, and re-presented for further review within a short timescale. The use of design charrettes has been to create a disturbance or 'spike' in the curriculum in order to represent a set of conditions which are often out with our control, such as time. The intention is to empower students with the ability to distil the essence of the project and propel ideas forward without over thinking their actions in any negative sense. Through the introduction of the charrette way of working, our students distilled some of their thoughts and expressed them as a way of (1) learning through making various iterations and building from each stage, (2) being forced to distil or edit quickly and make decisions without fear of being wrong, and (3) having the confidence to stand by decisions which are derived from instinct rather prolonged planning.

During the project completion, one of the greatest challenges designers face is presenting ideas to clients in a way that feels authentic and desirable. Interior designers or architects build scale models, graphic designers create mock ups, but short of actualising the 'real' thing we often rely on a verbal narrative to fill in the gaps, provide assurances to clients' hesitations or to embellish what information they detect is missing.

In the Art School, we teach students how to visually and verbally present their ideas to clients. We also have to assess student presentations to determine their performance on the course. Reflecting on my experience, I still remember the presentation of one particular student. The student had found a way of introducing a low tech restaurant solution and had developed an exquisite model of a South East Asian-inspired food eatery. He was pitching his ideas to fellow classmates, and when his turn approached he seemed slightly nervous and stood silently before his model until the room went quiet. Quite casually he took out his phone, inserted into a concealed slot in the model, and pressed play. The sound from the phone was a recording of a Singapore hawkers food stall, complete with screaming chefs, bursts of flames, crashing tills, laughter, children crying and the scraping of plastic furniture on hard tiles surfaces. It is possibly the most authentic presentation I have witnessed because it encapsulated the essence of experiential design. His presentation went beyond the visual and introduced the audio element, which elevated his work to an experiential level. His presentation responded to the need of designing in a way that we create product, interior, building, or digital experiences which appeal to human senses and create an emotional connection with the user.

References

Belk, R. W. (1990). The role of possessions in constructing and maintaining a sense of past. *Advances in Consumer Research, 17*(1), 669–676.

Beltagui, A., Candi, M., & Riedel, J. C. K. H. (2012). Design in the experience economy: Using emotional design for service innovation. In K. S. Swan, & S. Zou (Eds.), *Interdisciplinary approaches to product design, innovation, & branding in international marketing. Advances in international marketing* (Vol. 23, pp. 111–135). Bingley, UK: Emerald.

Bloch, P. H. (2011). Product design and marketing: Reflections after fifteen years. *Journal of Product Innovation Management, 28*(3), 378–380.

Brakus, J. J., Schmitt, B. H., & Zarantonello, L. (2009). Brand experience: What is it? How is it measured? Does it affect loyalty? *Journal of Marketing, 73*(3), 52–68.

Brown, T. (2008). Design thinking. *Harvard Business Review, 86*(6), 84–92.

Bruce, M. (2011). Connecting marketing and design. In R. Cooper, S. Junginger, & T. Lockwood (Eds.), *The handbook of design management*. Oxford, UK: Berg.

Candi, M., & Saemundsson, R. J. (2011). Exploring the relationship between aesthetic design as an element of new service development and performance. *Journal of Product Innovation Management, 28*(4), 536–557.

Carù, A., & Cova, B. (Eds.). (2007). *Consuming experience*. London: Routledge.

Carù, A., & Cova, B. (2012). Experience consumption: Appropriating and marketing experiences. In L. Peñaloza, N. Toulouse, & L. M. Viskonti (Eds.), *Marketing management: A cultural perspective*. London: Routledge.

Coxon, I. (2015). Fundamental aspects of human experience: A phenomeno(logical) explanation. In P. Benz (Ed.), *Experience design: Concepts and case studies*. London: Bloomsbury.

Dant, T. (1999). *Material culture in the social world*. Maidenhead, UK: McGraw-Hill International.

Davis, M. (2009). *The fundamentals of branding*. Lausanne, Switzerland: AVA Publishing.

Department for Media, Culture and Sport. (1998). *Creative industries mapping document 1998*. Retrieved from www.gov.uk/government/publications/creative-industries-mapping-documents-1998

Department for Media, Culture and Sport. (2001). *Creative industries mapping document 2001*. Retrieved from www.gov.uk/government/publications/creative-industries-mapping-documents-2001

Desmet, P., Hekkert, P., & Schifferstein, H. (2011). Introduction. In P. Desmet, & H. Schifferstein (Eds.), *From floating wheelchairs to mobile car parks, selected work from TU delft: A collection of 35 experience-driven design projects*. The Hague, The Netherlands: Eleven International Publishing.

Dewey, J. (1934). *Art as experience*. New York: Minton, Balch, and Company.

Gadamer, H. G. (1975). *Truth and method* (G. Barden & J. Cumming, Trans.). London: Sheed & Ward and Continuum.

Gentile, C., Spiller, N., & Noci, G. (2007). How to sustain the customer experience: An overview of experience components that co-create value with the customer. *European Management Journal, 25*(5), 395–410.

Gobé, M. (2009). *Emotional branding: The new paradigm for connecting brands to people*. New York: Allworth Press.

Gupta, S., & Vajic, M. (2000). The contextual and dialectical nature of experiences. In J. A. Fitzsimmons, & M. J. Fitzsimmons (Eds.), *New service development: Creating memorable experiences* (pp. 33–51). London: Sage.

Havlena, W. J., & Holak, S. L. (1991). The good old days: Observations on nostalgia and its role in consumer behavior. *Advances in Consumer Research, 18*(1), 323–329.

Heidegger, M. (1962). *Being and time*. New York: Harper & Row.

Heidegger, M. (1971). *Poetry, language, thought* (A. Hofstadter, Trans.). London: Harper.

Heidegger, M. (1973). *Being and time*. Oxford, UK: Blackwell.

Highmore, B. (2009). A sideboard manifesto: Design culture in an artificial world. *The Design Culture Reader* (pp. 1–12). London: Routledge.

Hodder, I. (2012). *Entangled: An archaeology of the relationships between humans and things*. Chichester, UK: John Wiley & Sons.

Holbrook, M. B., & Hirschman, E. C. (1982). The experiential aspects of consumption: Consumer fantasies, feelings, and fun. *Journal of Consumer Research, 9*(2), 132–140.

Jarvenpaa, S. L., & Lang, K. R. (2005). Managing the paradoxes of mobile technology. *Information Systems Management, 22*(4), 7–23.

Keller, K. L., Aperia, T., & Georgson, M. (2012). *Strategic brand management: A European perspective* (2nd ed.). Harlow, UK: Financial Times/Prentice Hall.

Kotler, P. (1973). Atmospherics as a marketing tool. *Journal of Retailing, 49*(4), 48–64.

Lewis, M. (1991). Brand packaging. In D. Cowley (Ed.), *Understanding brands: 10 people who do*. London: Kogan Page.

Lindstrom, M. (2005). Broad sensory branding. *Journal of Product & Brand Management, 14*(2), 84–87.

Lindstrom, M. (2010). *Brand sense: Sensory secrets behind the stuff we buy* (2nd ed.). London: Kogan Page.

Merleau-Ponty, M. (1963). *The structure of behavior*. Boston: Beacon Press.

Mick, D. G., & Fournier, S. (1998). Paradoxes of technology: Consumer cognizance, emotions, and coping strategies. *Journal of Consumer Research, 25*(2), 123–143.

Montaña, J., Guzmán, F., & Moll, I. (2007). Branding and design management: A brand design management model. *Journal of Marketing Management, 23*(9–10), 829–840.

Moran, D. (1999). *Introduction to phenomenology*. New York: Routledge.

Muniz, A. M., Jr., & O'Guinn, T. C. (2001). Brand community. *Journal of Consumer Research, 27*(4), 412–432.

Norman, D. (1990). *The design of everyday things*. New York: Basic Books.

Norman, D. A. (2004). *Emotional design: Why we love (or hate) everyday things*. New York: Basic Books.

Pine II, B. J., & Gilmore, J. H. (1998). Welcome to the experience economy: As goods and services become commoditised, the customer experiences that companies create will matter most. *Harvard Business Review, 76*, 97–105.

Pine II, B. J., & Gilmore, J. H. (1999). *The experience economy: Work is theatre & every business a stage*. Boston: Harvard Business Press.

Pine II, B. J., & Gilmore, J. H. (2011). *The experience economy* (Rev. ed.). Cambridge, MA: Harvard Business Press.

Press, M., & Cooper, R. (2003). *The design experience: The role of design and designers in the twenty-first century*. Farnham, UK: Ashgate.

Raghunathan, R. (2008). Some issues concerning the concept of experiential marketing. In B. H. Schmitt, & D. L. Rogers (Eds.), *Handbook of brand and experience management*. Cheltenham, UK: Edward Elgar.

Richins, M. L. (1997). Measuring emotions in the consumption experience. *Journal of Consumer Research, 24*(2), 127–146.

Schmitt, B. H. (1999a). Experiential marketing. *Journal of Marketing Management, 15*(1–3), 53–67.

Schmitt, B. H. (1999b). *Experiential marketing: How to get customers to sense, feel, think, act, relate*. New York: The Free Press.

Schmitt, B. H. (2011). *Experience marketing: Concepts, frameworks and consumer insights* (Vol. 5, No. 2). Boston: Now Publishers.

Schmitt, B. H. (2016). The design of experience. In R. Batra, C. Seifert, & D. Brei (Eds.), *The psychology of design: Creating consumer appeal*. London: Routledge.

Schmitt, B. H., & Simonson, A. (1997). *Marketing aesthetics: The strategic management of brands, identity, and image*. New York: The Free Press.

Schmitt, B. H., & Zarantonello, L. (2013). Consumer experience and experiential marketing: A critical review. In N. K. Malhotra (Ed.), *Review of marketing research* (Vol. 10, pp. 25–61). Bingley, UK: Emerald.

Shapiro, M. (1953). Style. In A. L. Kroeber (Ed.), *Anthropology today*. Chicago: University of Chicago Press.

Stern, B. B. (1992). Historical and personal nostalgia in advertising text: The fin de siècle effect. *Journal of Advertising, 21*(4), 11–22.

Svabo, C., & Shanks, M. (2015). Experience as excursion: A note towards a metaphysics of design thinking. In P. Benz (Ed.), *Experience design: Concepts and case studies*. New York: Bloomsbury.

Tractinsky, N., Katz, A. S., & Ikar, D. (2000). What is beautiful is usable. *Interacting with Computers, 13*(2), 127–145.

Webmoor, T., & Witmore, C. L. (2008). Things are us! A commentary on human/things relations under the banner of a 'social' archaeology. *Norwegian Archaeological Review, 41*(1), 53–70.

8 Human-centred design

Co-creation and design management

Chapter aims and learning outcomes

This chapter aims to:

1 Present the history of co-creation activities in society and the marketplace.
2 Discuss the characteristics of co-creation activities.
3 Explore the role of human-centred design in social welfare and discuss the concept of the democratisation of design.
4 Provide an understanding of the relationship between human-centred design and prosumption.
5 Present the positive and negative aspects of prosumption and how the phenomenon is magnified through the advent of Web 2.0.
6 Discuss the notion of prosumption as a new form of capitalism facilitated through co-creation activities.
7 Explore the concept of anthropomorphism and its connections with co-creation activities, product design evaluations, and consumption goals.

In the previous chapter, we explored the concept of experiences and highlighted the phenomenal nature of experiences, i.e., the fact that no two humans can have the same experience and the fact that a person cannot have the same experience twice. The personality of the individuals and the context of the experiential event render every human experience unique and specific to that moment in time. We have also explored in Chapter 3 that one of the three important changes and additions which are regarded as critical elements of business design thinking is the question of *who* designs. We talked about how Buchanan (1992) envisaged a move from the general notion that it is design which has the *sole* responsibility to come up with socially acceptable results, to recognising the need for many opportunities where designers can work with different stakeholders including users, in order to reach appropriate design solutions, leading to the creation of a community of 'co-designers' (Garud, Jain, & Tuertscher, 2008), and the boundaries between organisations and individuals to be blurred (Brown, 2009).

Over the last few years, there have been significant changes in the market, especially with regard to the role of the consumer. With the advent of the Internet and social media, it has been recognised that "the role of the consumer in the industrial system has changed from isolated to connected, from unaware to informed, from passive to active" (Prahalad & Ramaswamy, 2004a, p. 4). This has led organisations to realise that co-creating adverts, products, services, and experiences with their consumers provides enormous potential. Nowadays, consumers aim to have an influence on every part of the business system, interact with organisations, and as a result, they co-create value with them. "The use of interaction as a basis for co-creation is at the crux of our emerging reality" (Prahalad & Ramaswamy, 2004a, p. 4). This co-creation is neither merely outsourcing activities to consumers, nor providing some degree of customisation of products and services, nor simply staging customer events around the organisation's offerings. What we are talking about is a deep and meaningful personalised interaction with each consumer, resulting in a co-creation experience, which acts as the basis for the unique value provided to the consumer. The nature of this experience, like any other experience, is phenomenal, and each person's idiosyncratic characteristics affect the co-creation process and the co-creation experience.

> Quality depends on the infrastructure for interaction between companies and consumers, oriented around the capacity to create a variety of experiences. The firm must efficiently innovate 'experience environments' that enable a diversity of co-creation experiences. It must build a flexible 'experience network' that allows individuals to co-construct and personalise their experiences. Eventually, the roles of the company and the consumer converge toward a unique co-creation experience, or an 'experience of one'.
>
> (Prahalad & Ramaswamy, 2004a, p. 5)

History of co-creation: From factory workers to social media users

The concept of co-creation has evolved dramatically over the years. The initial adoption of a co-creation approach involved practicing "user-centred design from an 'expert perspective' in which trained researchers observe and/or interview largely passive users, whose contribution is to perform instructed tasks and/or to give their opinions about product concepts that were generated by others" (Sanders & Stappers, 2008, p. 5). Since this somehow watered down approach to co-creation, there has been an increase on the influence, power, and room for initiative given to various stakeholders (e.g. users, managers, suppliers, distributors), leading to a plethora of cases where they provide expertise and take part in the informing, ideating, and conceptualising activities in the early stages of the design process. This means that their involvement nowadays is not merely to test or validate the creative concepts in the latter stages of the design process but to collaboratively come up with ideas with the designers, leading to those creative concepts.

The above drive towards greater participation from the different stakeholders influenced by design has led to the development of the area of 'participatory design' and the notions of 'co-creation' and 'co-design'. All these terms are often treated synonymously with one another. However, Sanders and Stappers (2008) draw a subtle distinction between co-creation and co-design. They believe that co-creation refers

> to any act of collective creativity, i.e. creativity that is shared by two or more people. Co-creation is a very broad term with applications ranging from the physical to the metaphysical and from the material to the spiritual ... By co-design we indicate collective creativity as it is applied across the whole span of a design process ... Thus, co-design is a specific instance of co-creation ... [It is] the creativity of designers and people not trained in design, working together in the design development process.
>
> (Sanders & Stappers, 2008, p. 6)

Historically speaking, the approach of collective creativity in design has been around for nearly 50 years under the more encompassing term of 'participatory design'(later replaced by the terms 'co-creation' and 'co-design'). However, quite surprisingly, this phenomenon was first observed a couple of centuries earlier by Adam Smith (1776) who pointed out the importance of invention of many machines which facilitate labour and allow one man to do the work of many and noted that

> a great part of the machines made use of in those manufactures in which labour is most subdivided, were originally the invention of common workmen, who, being each of them employed in some very simple operation, naturally turned their thoughts toward finding out easier and readier methods of performing it.
>
> (Smith, 1776, p. 6)

In more recent history, most of the activity in this area has been located in Europe, with research projects on user participation in systems development dating back to the 1970s. Engaging the workforce in developing new systems for the work environment was viewed as a successful way to increase the value of industrial production in countries such as Sweden, Norway, and Finland. Such activities led to the establishment of the so-called 'collective resource approach', which combined the expertise of systems designers and researchers with the expertise of those people whose work routines and life was to be influenced by the change (Bødker, 1996).

The Internet has revolutionised the potential of co-creation activities between organisations and consumers. Nowadays, organisations have the capability to create virtual environments for their brands and engage consumers in collaborative innovation in a multiplicity of ways. The traditional approach to customer engagement was very firm-centric where although consumers were engaged through focus groups and customer surveys at different stages of the design process, most information flowing was one-directional from the customer to the firm (Prahalad & Ramaswamy, 2004b). Such an approach viewed consumers as passive recipients of innovation and the organisation had a very limited understanding of consumer knowledge caused by the absence of iterative dialogue to refine and enhance ideas. In contrast, virtual environments (such as social media platforms) have increased the speed and persistence of customer engagement, and have enhanced interactivity, magnifying the organisation's capacity to understand the social dimension of consumer knowledge by facilitating the creation of virtual communities of consumption (Kozinets, 1999). This means that these platforms have provided three key benefits: (1) mutual direction of communication, which is now reciprocal, (2) higher intensity and richness of communication; such communication is no longer episodic but continuous and long-term, and (3) greater size and scope of the audience, which has expanded beyond comprehension (Sawhney, Verona, & Prandelli, 2005). For instance, think about the potential that *Facebook*, *Twitter*, *Instagram* and *Snapchat* provide organisations today – it is immense.

As far as academic literature is concerned, the most well-known advocates for co-design originate from business or marketing literature and not from the design practice (Sanders & Stappers, 2008). Despite this, in marketing or management literature the term co-creation is much more popular than the term co-design, perhaps because the former is a broader term than the latter, as already explained. In management terms, Perks, Gruber, and Edvardsson define co-creation as involving "the joint creation of value by the firm and its network of various entities (such as customers, suppliers, and distributors) … Innovations are thus the outcomes of behaviours and interactions between individuals and organisations" (2012, p. 935). In their book, *The Future of Competition: Co-creating Unique Value with Customers*, Prahalad and Ramaswamy (2004c, 2013) proposed that "the meaning of value and the process of value creation are rapidly shifting from a product- and firm-centric view to personalised consumer experiences. Informed, networked, empowered and active consumers are increasingly co-creating value with the firm" (Prahalad & Ramaswamy, 2004c, p. 5). Other scholars who explored the concept of co-creation of value include Tseng and Piller (2003) who explored the concept of mass customisation as a successful approach to increasing product sales, and Von Hippel (1986, 2005) who argued that organisations need to work with 'lead users' in co-creative activities, a concept which we explored in Chapter 2. Lead users are those people who are 'truly' creative (Seybold, 2006), and have explored innovative ways to get things done and want to share their expertise and approaches with others (Von Hippel, 2005).

Nevertheless, as already mentioned, co-creation of value should go beyond Tseng and Piller's (2003) mere mass customisation of parts of the organisation's offering. In addition, while the concept of lead users is very useful in design research, it is rather limiting from a co-creation perspective. The Von Hippel (1986, 2005) and Seybold (2006) approach to co-creation can be accused of limiting the participation in the design process to an elite and a very strictly selected group of people.

Ind and Coates emphasise that the idea of 'creation' in co-creation "is not simply about creation of things, it is also about interpretation and meaning making. Meaning is always co-created" (2013, p. 87). For instance, brand meanings are created by different stakeholders in a process of interaction. This means that firms might be able to influence the field of possible meanings because they write the brand narratives, however meaning itself is dialogic (Morris, 2003) therefore socially constructed. The development of brand communities can be seen as evidence of the move towards constructing brand meanings beyond the organisation (Fournier & Lee, 2009; Muñiz & O'Guinn, 2001; Schau, Muñiz, & Arnould, 2009). In addition, Grönroos (2011) argues that while the producer generates potential value, it is in the act of usage that real value is created. Ind and Coates (2013) explain Grönroos' (2011) argument by suggesting that: "the nature of value co-creation depends on perspective. Is it the firm that leads and invites the consumer to participate or is it consumers who are in charge of value creation? If co-creation is perceived to be concerned with value in use, then it is the user that creates value for the user" (Ind & Coates, 2013, p. 87).

A participatory approach to design should be applied throughout the creative process, from preparation to verification (Wallas, 1926), and at all stages of decision making. Sharma et al. (2008) argue that participatory design seeks to develop solutions with the close collaboration among different stakeholders through cycles of requirements gathering, prototype development, implementation, and evaluation. It is, therefore, essential that there is flow of information and feedback shared among designers, users, and other stakeholders, at every stage of the design and development process (Wilkinson, Walters, & Evans, 2016). The importance of individual input at all stages of the process resonates with Sanders' (2002) notion of participatory design

> as a belief that *all* people have something to offer *at every stage* of the design process and that when given the appropriate tools with which to express themselves, they can be articulate, creative, and inspirational, in terms of generating new ideas and in developing current thinking. This approach appreciates the diverse needs and requirements of users by involving them with a process that fosters ideation, and insights can then be used to develop products that are more immediately accessible and usable to a wider proportion of the population.
>
> (Wilkinson et al., 2016, p. 71)

Thus, participatory design as seen by the aforementioned scholars directly opposes Von Hippel's (1986, 2005) and Seybold's (2006) approach to co-creation which limits the participation in the design process to a strictly selected group of people, the lead users. There are, however, other scholars who have questioned whether it is indeed best for the organisation to seek to facilitate co-creation at all stages of the design process. Lehrer, Ordanini, DeFillippi, and Miozzo (2012) explored business-to-business services provision in the form of knowledge-intensive business services (KIBS) firms, and determined that "under certain circumstances, both KIBS providers and clients might desire to regulate the level of co-production, and that at certain project stages a reduced level might actually improve the quality of the final output" (Lehrer et al., 2012 p. 499). They note that a possible liability in co-creation activities can be the incompatible types of motivation, for instance, the more intrinsically motivated creative people of KIBS firms (see Chapter 5 about intrinsic motivation and creativity) may not entangle well with the more extrinsically motivated members of the client organisations.

However, they accept the fact that giving too much autonomy to KIBS firms during the design process might prove hurtful for the project because of "insufficient diversity in outlook and knowledge to produce novel ideas. An obvious advantage of co-production is precisely that it enhances such diversity by bringing together individuals of different backgrounds and differing cognitive orientations" (Lehrer et al., 2012, p. 500). Their research with KIBS firms identified a U-shaped pattern of KIBS firm–client co-production intensity over the lifetime of a project. They determined that during the initial and final stages of the project, a high level of co-creation is beneficial. This contrasts with the intermediate stage of the project delivery where in fact some degree of separation (instead of co-creation) is preferred by both KIBS firms and clients (Lehrer et al., 2012).

Understanding co-creation activities

Building blocks of co-creation activities

In management writings, Prahalad and Ramaswamy (2004a, 2004c, 2013) proposed the DART model of co-creation of value which includes four *building blocks* of co-creation activities. First, '*dialogue*' "means interactivity, engagement, and a propensity to act on both sides. Dialogue is more than listening to customers; it implies shared learning and communication between two equal problem solvers. Dialogue creates and maintains a loyal community" (Prahalad & Ramaswamy, 2004a, p. 6). Second, '*access*' is all about providing the tools and platforms to facilitate this co-creation of value. Third, '*risk assessment*' is all about evaluating the possibility of harm to the consumer. An important question that we need to address is whether or not consumers, as active co-creators, should shoulder responsibility for the risks associated with the design process too. As the cases of consumers co-creating products, services, and experiences with organisations increase, firms need to inform consumers "fully about risks, providing not just data but appropriate methodologies for assessing the personal and societal risk associated with products and services" (Prahalad & Ramaswamy, 2004a, p. 7). Finally, '*transparency*' questions the information asymmetry between the firm and the consumer which has traditionally existed in the marketplace. When the organisation and its consumers co-create value such asymmetry should disappear. It is crucial that there is transparency about products, technologies, and business systems; opaqueness of process, costs, and profit margins should be avoided (Prahalad & Ramaswamy, 2004a) (Figure 8.1).

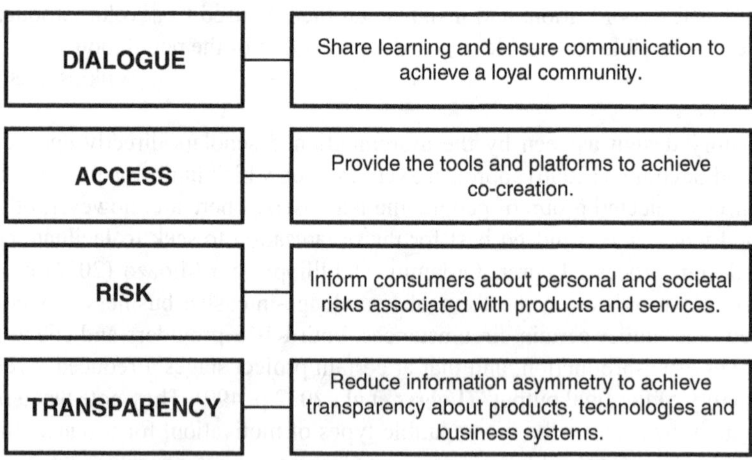

Figure 8.1 Building blocks of co-creation activities.

Characteristics of co-creation activities

Motives of co-creation activities

Before any organisation engages in co-creation activities, it is important that it understands the *motives* behind the drive to pursue such an endeavour. Drawing from an extensive literature review and their own workshops, interviews, and meetings, Frow, Nenonen, Payne, and Storbacka (2015) identified nine motives which drive organisations to engage in co-creation activities: (1) access to resources, in the form of access to networks, resource integration, or a kind of outsourcing activity, (2) increasing the differentiation of the organisation's offering through the creation of personalised experiences and customisation, (3) gaining commitment from the target users, (4) developing better self-service technologies that work intuitively with the consumers, (5) creating more competitive offerings, (6) reducing the costs of production, especially in co-production of the core product, (7) "speedier development and therefore a reduced time to create and launch new products" (Frow et al., 2015, pp. 471–472), because it allows the firm to further develop its capabilities, (8) opting "for non-predictive, evolving strategies, in which co-creation with other [stakeholders] occurs" (Frow et al., 2015) in cases where the organisation operates in uncertain environments, and (9) from a branding perspective, building brand awareness through co-promotion. Stronger brand awareness coupled with distinctive and favourable associations, as well as with positive emotional reactions can lead to brand resonance, i.e., a loyalty relationship between the brand and the consumer. Consequently, consumers become brand enthusiasts and start developing relationships with other consumers who share the same passion for the brand, ultimately facilitating the creation of brand communities (Muñiz & O'Guinn, 2001; Schau et al., 2009). In addition, strategic alliances between network partners can create 'hybrid marketing systems' which can also promote the brands. The notion of co-promotion, i.e., the consumer advertising the product on behalf of the organisation is not always seen positively in extant academic literature. Ritzer (2015) has questioned the benefits of such activities for the consumer; his ideas will be explored later in this chapter.

Forms of co-creation activities

Building on the work of Sheth and Uslay (2007) and Vargo and Lusch (2006), Frow and Payne (2013) identified a number of different forms of co-creation activities. These include: (1) 'co-conception of ideas' (e.g. crowd-sourced solution for an organisation), (2) 'co-design' (e.g. customisation of a consumer product such as *Dell* computers), (3) 'co-production', (4) 'co-promotion' (e.g. *Harley-Davidson* brand communities), (5) 'co-pricing' (e.g. pay-what-you-want restaurants), (6) 'co-distribution', (e.g. *Unilever* works with 'last mile' local women distributors in India), (7) 'co-consumption', (8) 'co-maintenance' (e.g. *Tesco*'s consumer engagement for the recovery of trolleys), (9) 'outsourcing' (e.g. *Apple*'s outsourcing strategy for apps), (10) 'co-disposal' (e.g. technology organisations' recovery initiatives), (11) 'co-experience' (e.g. adventure holidays), and (12) 'co-meaning creation' (e.g. online gamers share meanings within a virtual world). It seems from the above that Frow and Payne (2013) view co-design as one specific stage and not as an entire process contrary to Sanders and Stappers (2008) who view it as collective creativity spanning the whole design process. Frow and Payne (2013) believe co-design is merely related to customisation, although, as already mentioned, co-creation should go beyond simple customisation of the organisational offering.

Engaging actors

The term 'actors' in co-creation activities is used to identify the co-creating parties involved. Drawing from relationship marketing literature, Frow et al. (2015) identified five broad actor categories including

(1) customers (upstream actors), (2) suppliers (downstream actors), (3) partners, who are collaborators for any types of exchange, (4) competitors (actors with similar offerings), and (5) influencers, for instance, opinion formers, media, government, and regulatory bodies, who can be considered as indirect collaborators.

Platforms for co-creation activities

As previously discussed, it is important that the organisation provides all collaborating parties the necessary access to tools and platforms which facilitate co-creation activities (Prahalad & Ramaswamy, 2004a, 2004b, 2013). Such engagement platforms enable actors to "share their resources and adapt their processes to each other" (Frow et al., 2015, p. 472) and can become part of the organisation's offering itself, e.g., *NikeID* or *Adidas'* engagement platforms for co-designing athletic shoes. In addition, in current literature the term 'platform' also denotes systems that enable innovation or communications systems such as the *Apple's iOS* or *Android* systems. Frow et al. (2015) have identified five types of engagement platforms: (1) 'digital applications' such as websites which facilitate far-reaching and fast interactions with multiple and diverse parties (Sawhney et al., 2005), (2) 'tools or products' which are used on a recurring or continuous basis as a way to connect the different parties involved, such as when software companies provide software development toolkits, (3) 'physical resources', such as actual physical locations where the different parties will come together to collaborate, for instance, retail stores offering the space for such collaboration like in the *Apple* stores, (4) 'joint processes' which involve multiple parties (e.g. *P&G*'s '*Connect + Develop'* innovation programme), and (5) 'dedicated personnel teams', such as call centre teams.

Levels of engagement

The level of engagement an actor shows during a co-creation activity depends on the social, cultural and political context of the activity itself (Brodie, Hollebeek, Juric, & Ilic, 2011; Vibert & Shields, 2003). Patterson et al. (2006) describe the intensity of interaction as a continuum of cognitive, emotional, and/or behavioural engagement, which can vary from 'non-engaged' to 'highly-engaged' actors. Inspired by Macey and Schneider (2008), Frow et al. (2015) indicated three categories for level of engagement: (1) *cognitive engagement*, where the actor cognitively acknowledges the situation and provides the group with his/her resources, (2) *emotional engagement*, where the collaborating actors feel committed and are willing to put the effort to engage with the rest of the group, and (3) *behavioural engagement*, where the collaborating actors, given a specific frame of reference, change their behaviour because of the rest of the group (Figure 8.2).

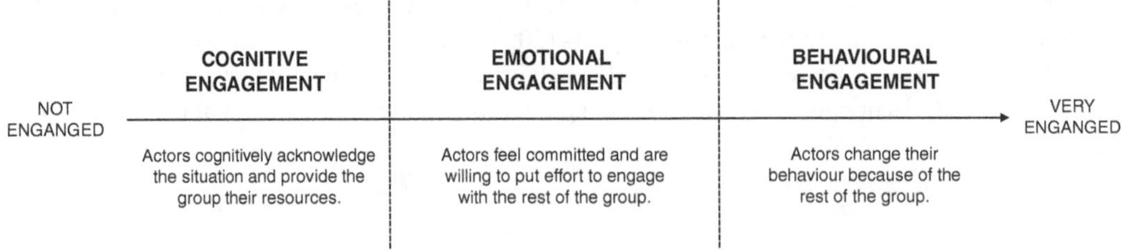

Figure 8.2 Continuum of engagement in co-creation activities.

Duration of engagement

Co-creation activities can differ in terms of the duration of both the interaction among the collaborating actors, and the collaborative relationship. Wasko and Faraj (2000) suggest that those actors who participate in co-creation over a long period of time will be more keen to maintain their relationship because there is more at stake in contrast with those situations where there is limited participation. Frow et al. (2015) have determined three categories of interactions: (1) one-off interactions, (2) recurring interactions, and (3) continuous interactions. They explain that

> selecting an appropriate category of duration for designing the co-creation initiative is important in terms of issues such as selection of an appropriate channel and the allocation of resources. One-off interactions may typically occur in a single channel, whereas continuous interactions may benefit from multiple channels that support continued interaction.
>
> (Frow et al., 2015, p. 473)

Human-centred design and society

Human-centred design and social welfare

Frediani (2016) explores the thought and practice of participatory design in the context of urban architecture and development, and in particular in relation to 'informal settlement upgrading'. The latter is concerned with issues associated with housing units which have been constructed on land that the occupants do not have legal claim to. He explains that in this context, participatory design has been associated with a multiplicity of agendas and purposes. It has been seen as a mechanism for "'inclusion' for a pre-defined vision and ideal of the city" (Frediani, 2016, p. 98), as well as a way to expand the "collective power to reshape the process of urbanization" (Harvey, 2008, p. 23). There has also been an extended debate about the connection between democracy and design though collaborative creativity. There have been times where design has been considered a way of improving or enabling structures of governance, or as a means of generating novel arguments and bringing a paradigm shift through social change (Frediani, 2016).

Through the case of urban development, Frediani (2016) identified a number of trends in the field of participatory design. One trend in particular stands out due to the fact that it connects participatory design with human dignity and welfare in general.

> [An] evolving trend in the field of participatory design refers to the *use* of design, and it is often associated with the process of participation in the design of artefacts, as well as information and communication technologies. Sometimes referred to as human-centred design, participation is practiced with the objective of improving communication in the process of design and generating not only responsive results, but also sustained results over time. Debate focuses on the relationship between the designer and the user, and the argument is that co-design has the potential to find solutions and possibilities that would not otherwise emerge if not for the exchange between the technical knowledge of the designer and the practical knowledge of the user. Ultimately, participation is justified as a means to enhance users' satisfaction with the product of design.
>
> (Frediani, 2016, p. 102)

The aim of ensuring usability, however, has been a matter of interesting contestation. In a short essay, inspired by a conference speech by the South African Minister of Education (1999–2004)

Dr. Kadir Asmal, Buchanan (2001) reflected on the issue of usability in human-centred design. He recognised that there has been significant transformation from the old design theme of 'form and function' into the design theme of 'form and content'. This does not mean that design thinking rejects function, but it recognises that "unless designers grasp the significant content of the products they create, their work will come to little consequence or may even lead to harm in our complex world" (Buchanan, 2001, p. 35). Nevertheless, he argues that participatory design and *human-centred design* often focus too much on usability, i.e., making sure that the offering created is useful to humans, while it overlooks the issues of human dignity and human rights. According to Buchanan (2001), we discuss too often, the principles of various methods that are employed in design thinking, such as the principles of form and composition, aesthetics, usability, market economics, business operations, or the mechanical and technological principles that underpin products, but we fail to discuss the *first* principle upon which design is (or should be) based and justified – human dignity. He calls for human-centred design that is approached as the continuous search for means to support and strengthen the dignity of human beings as they go on about their lives. The notion that design is grounded in human dignity and human rights has a number of implications for design and its management, which need to be explored. Buchanan (2001) eloquently explains these implications with the following:

> [It] helps us to understand aspects of design that are otherwise obscured in the flood of poor or mediocre products that we find everywhere in the world. We should consider what we mean by human dignity and how all of the products that we make either succeed or fail to support and advance human dignity. And we should think carefully about the nature of human rights – the spectrum of civil and political, economic and social, and cultural rights – and how these rights are directly affected by our work. The issues surrounding human dignity and human rights provide a new perspective for exploring the many moral and ethical problems that lie at the core of the design professions … The major tenet of new design thinking [is] the central place of human beings in our work. Unfortunately, we often forget the full force and meaning of the phrase – and the first principle which it expresses. This happens, for example, when we reduce our considerations of human-centred design to matters of sheer usability and when we speak merely of 'user-centred design'. It is true that usability plays an important role in human-centred design, but the principles that guide our work are not exhausted when we have finished our ergonomic, psychological, sociological and anthropological studies of what fits the human body and mind. Human-centred design is fundamentally an affirmation of human dignity. It is an ongoing search for what can be done to support and strengthen the dignity of human beings as they act out their lives in varied social, economic, political, and cultural circumstances.
>
> (Buchanan, 2001, p. 37)

The notion of co-creation contributing to social welfare is also recognised by Von Hippel (2005). However, he adopts the term 'user-centred' despite Buchanan's (2001) call for a human rather than a mere user focus. Manzini and Rizzo (2011) move Buchanan's (2001) argument even further, taking a more political view on participatory design and its role in society. They argue that the best thing designers can do to "promote citizens' participation in large-scale transformations is to use their creativity and their design knowledge and skills 'to make things happen' and, in this way, to promote and sustain the social conversation on possible futures" (Manzini & Rizzo, 2011, pp. 213–214). Nevertheless, there can be certain circumstances where participatory design seems like a double-edged sword. In his research on urban development, Frediani (2016) identified a number of tensions of participatory design in informal settlements upgrading (urban regeneration programmes). One tension in particular demonstrates clearly the *challenges of participatory design*. Frediani (2016) explains this tension:

> [Another] tension identified … has been the challenge for participatory design to engage with issues of social diversity and asymmetries of power. Although often motivated by concerns of recognition and empowerment, participatory design has faced challenges in recognising social diversity without homogenising needs and aspirations, while also proposing viable collective actions. Meanwhile, efforts focused on diversity have often been criticised for treating difference from an essentialist perspective, creating initiatives that target people from certain labelled 'vulnerable' identities, rather than challenging the relations that cause exploitation. As a result, such practices could end up fragmenting communities and weakening social mobilisations, rather than achieving the desired empowerment outcomes. Therefore, practitioners in participatory processes have often been short-sighted regarding issues of diversity of power because of the challenges imposed both by complex sets of social relations shaped by various asymmetries of power, and by donors' demand for measurable and product-driven outputs in short timeframes for activities.
>
> (Frediani, 2016, p. 104)

Readers familiar with the field of *social marketing*, would immediately see connections between the above challenges of participatory design with the challenges that social marketers face when planning intervention programmes. Social marketing is "the adaptation of commercial marketing technologies to programmes designed to influence the voluntary behaviour of target audiences to improve their personal welfare and that of society of which they are part" (Andreasen, 1994). This means that social marketing aims to develop and implement initiatives that contribute to social welfare, including programmes tackling health and social issues such as, domestic abuse, bulling, drug addiction, alcohol addiction, mental health stigmas, homophobia, and obesity. Like any other marketing programme, it is essential that the population is segmented on a number of variables (geodemographic, psychographic, and behavioural characteristics), segments are selected to be targeted based on a number of criteria, and a positioning programme is formulated to achieve the marketing objectives (the 'segmentation–targeting–positioning' process). Trying to follow such human-centred approach in social marketing is achieved by targeting specific well-defined segments of society who need most help and tend to cluster in certain locales, e.g., teenagers engaged in antisocial behaviour in deprived urban settings, and by tailoring the 'offering' to target those groups' needs and desires. However, following such strategy, there is the danger of social marketers being accused of discrimination, stigmatisation and isolation (Hastings, 2007). The groups not selected to be targeted may complain their needs are ignored, like assuming that there is no antisocial behaviour in affluent urban areas and hence intervention is not needed, while the groups selected to be targeted may complain they are stigmatised, creating the notion that all of city's problems are caused by people in these specific areas only. What this shows is that participatory design and social marketing programmes, if not carefully planned and implemented might manage to fix one problem while creating others due to lack of integration of different social groups. The bottom line is that, by merely concentrating on specific social groups, albeit helpful to face their problems, may in the long term create feelings of separation, distinctiveness and lead to less social mobility. There is a need for a very careful planning and a well-balanced approach. This renders social marketing and participatory design programmes very demanding from a resource planning perspective, yet very rewarding when successfully throughout and executed.

The democratisation of design

Earlier in this chapter, we discussed how the 'collective resource approach' in Scandinavian countries in the 1970s spurred the development of the notion of co-creation and participatory design. The Scandinavian approach was based on the idea that if you want to create usable products, services, and spaces, it is imperative to involve those people who will use them.

Ind and Coates (2013) explain that there is a powerful democratising element in co-creation because it can involve citizens and influential groups in co-creating social innovation in governmental affairs, public services, and healthcare and education. The development of design thinking and the open source movement have been significantly influenced by the democratising principle of participatory design. Offerings such as *Linux*, and *Wikipedia*, have been the descendants of the democratisation of design facilitated by participatory design. For instance, *Wikipedia* has challenged the traditional notion of encyclopedia and has become the most prominent form of disseminating knowledge. Consider, for example, how many times when you need instant information on something, the first thing you do is visit the *Wikipedia* portal. Drawing from the work of Raymond (1999), Ind and Coates (2013) explain the power of the open source movement:

> Indeed *Wikipedia* and other participative processes have undermined what has been called Royal science – knowledge determined by elites – and replaced it with minor (or nomad) science – knowledge agreed among a community. The underpinning of open source (and indeed most forms of co-creation) is that it is based on a gift. Individuals are often willing to help others for the intellectual, social, and hedonic benefits of sharing. While there is still structure and often very detailed guidelines that enable participation in participative processes, there is a far greater opportunity for individuals to influence content by bringing their cognitive diversity to help elaborate problems and share solutions … The resulting, bottom up, structure [is] more like a bazaar (or souk) and less like top-down structures, such as a cathedral. Cathedrals are highly planned, highly controlled and beautiful, but less organic. The souk has its own order, its own logic, its own patterns, but it does allow people to lose themselves.
>
> (Ind & Coates, 2013, p. 89)

Co-creation and prosumption

The notion of democratisation has also been explored in marketing literature. Smith and Zook (2011) have argued that social media have enabled collaborative co-creation of value leading to the marketing practice becoming more democratised. "Customers not companies are controlling the flow of marketing information as they shut out interruption marketing and use, instead, social media to find products, ratings and reviews" (Smith & Zook, 2011, p. 9). Brands and consumers form strong loyalty relationships but in the form of equal partnerships. Consumers become the co-producers of adverts, products and brands, which they eventually consume; they become *prosumers*. This term is generally attributed to Alvin Toffler (1980) who, in his book *The Third Wave*, argued that 'prosumerism' was prominent in pre-industrial societies (which he called the 'first wave'). What followed this was a 'second wave' of marketisation that led to a "wedge into society, that separated these two functions, thereby giving birth to what we now call producers and consumers" (Toffler, 1980, p. 266). Contemporary society is now moving away from such separation of production and consumption. What we are experiencing nowadays is a move towards a 'third wave' which drives the reintegration of production and consumption and the rise of the prosumer. Ritzer (2009) claims that even during the Industrial Revolution, production and consumption were never truly distinct since producers needed to consume materials to develop their products, and consumers produced their own meals.

Positive and negative aspects of prosumption

The concept of 'prosumption' has been the subject of increased debate. On the one hand, some scholars discuss the positive aspects of prosumption. For instance, Zwick, Bonsu, and Darmody (2008) have related prosumption to theories developed by Foucault and neo-Marxist theorists by claiming that prosumption means companies are offering new freedoms to consumers. They believe that "the ideological recruitment of consumers into productive co-creation relationships hinges on accommodating consumer needs for recognition, freedom, and agency" (Zwick et al., 2008, p. 185). This is particularly true in the case of the Internet and social media, which will be explored further below. On the other hand, other scholars have questioned the concept and have been troubled by it, in terms of its impact on society. As previously discussed, organisations seek to involve consumers in participatory design activities for a multiplicity of reasons including access to resources, enhanced differentiation, increased customer loyalty, increased competitiveness, production cost reduction, speedier product development, reduction of uncertainty, and co-promotion. One could argue that all these motives are marketing-driven, and that co-creation activities in fact exploit consumers. Indeed, many scholars have raised questions about customer involvement in product development (Cova & Dalli, 2009; Ind, Fuller, & Trevail, 2012; Zwick et al., 2008).

Ritzer (2015) has explored prosumption as part of his *McDonaldisation* thesis, which suggests that the principles of fast-food restaurants, i.e., efficiency, predictability, calculability, and control, dominate social systems rendering them as rational systems where humans feel trapped, a notion similar to Weber's (1978) 'iron cage'. In their rationality these systems have many irrationalities manifested in higher degrees of inefficiency, loss of control, and ultimately the dehumanisation of society. He argues that organisations' co-creation activities are merely a way of putting customers to work, expecting them to do unpaid labour. He discusses such activities in the context of the fast-food restaurant (used as the prime metaphor in his thesis) where customers are expected to perform self-service work, such as taking their food to their table, and disposing their leftovers upon departure from the restaurant. In such cases, customers co-create the fast-food service with the organisation, which in Ritzer's (2015) eyes, means that they perform work which was once performed by paid workers. He argues that prosumers are not only working consumers, but also consuming workers, since "all workers consume all sorts of things as they work such as the raw materials they use and their own labour time and capacities" (Ritzer, 2015, p. 102). Ind and Coates suggest that in order "to counter charges that co-creation exploits consumers and other stakeholders who gift their time and intellect for the benefit of organisations, it needs to move beyond the co-opting lens and engage stakeholders in a reciprocally useful way" (2013, p. 86). It is absolutely critical that co-creation activities should aim to contribute to social welfare besides organisational profit.

Prosumption and Web 2.0

Prosumption is not confined only in the retail services sector, but has expanded in, and thanks to, social media and Web 2.0. Web 2.0 is the "platform whereby content and applications are no longer created and published by individuals, but instead are continuously modified by all users in a participatory and collaborative fashion" (Kaplan & Haenlein, 2009, p. 61). Based on the fact that Web 2.0 has been highly involved in, as well as a popular location of, prosumption, we can argue that Web 2.0 is both the most important facilitator as a means of prosumption, and the most prominent platform upon which this prosumption takes place (Ritzer & Jurgenson, 2010). Ritzer suggests that "the implosion of the consumer and the producer on Web 2.0 has led to the pre-eminence of the prosumer" (2015, p. 205). However, he argues that

> Web 2.0 has a huge advantage over web 1.0. In one sense, Web 2.0 has reduced or eliminated the irrationalities of rationality associated with Web 1.0. In another sense, it could be argued that it has greatly heightened the rationality of these systems by figuring out how to get the most out of the people who use the sites without allowing them to compromise the basic functioning of the system. In this way, while Web 2.0 can be viewed as a rational next step, often pushed by profit-based motives, it exists partially outside the principles outlined by the McDonaldisation thesis, and thus Web 2.0 can be seen as having, to some degree, a tendency toward *de*-McDonaldisation.
>
> (Ritzer, 2015, pp. 206–207)

The outcome of such prosumption activities on the Internet is what scholars often call '*user-generated content*'. Social media are "the group of Internet-based applications that build on the ideological and technological foundations of Web 2.0 and that allow the creation and exchange of user generated content" (Kaplan & Haenlein, 2009, p. 61). Consumers are now able, through social media and based on the technical capabilities of Web 2.0, to develop their own content.

Human-centred design, prosumption, and capitalism

Ritzer and Jurgenson (2010) explore the relation of the world of prosumption, especially as it occurs on the Internet, with the capitalist system of society. Their main thesis is that (online) prosumption is "capitalist, but it has enough unique characteristics to allow us to begin to think of it as possibly a new form of capitalism" (Ritzer & Jurgenson, 2010, p. 22). Let us explore their argument in more detail.

The original conceptualisation of capitalism (especially by Marx and early Marxist theorists) concentrated on the relationship between producers (workers, the proletariat) and capitalists. Although workers needed to consume raw materials in order to produce, and consumers had to buy and use what came out of those capitalist factories, consumption in early capitalism was always subordinate to production (Ritzer & Jurgenson, 2010). However, over the years, in the developed world in particular, the power of the consumer and consumption has increased and that of production has declined. Some societies evolved to the point where they are defined more by consumption than production. Yet, this is still a form of consumer capitalism and as Ritzer and Jurgenson note "capitalists clearly 'overcharged' consumers and this served to enhance their profits in a way similar to the way that subsistence wages paid to workers ('underpaying' them) were key to the high profits reaped by early capitalists" (2010, p. 20). The important question we must answer then is whether the idea of capitalism as we have known it, can be extended to the prosumer, as well as whether we can claim that we are entering the age of 'prosumer capitalism'.

Ritzer and Jurgenson (2010) argue that in order to answer these questions, we need to understand the difference between traditional prosumers and the contemporary prosumers. The *traditional prosumers* are those who clean up after them in fast-food restaurants (as already described). Therefore, as far as this type of prosumers is concerned, it is impossible to suggest that we have entered a new stage of capitalism. Instead, one could argue that capitalists have found another group of people to exploit beyond workers. On the other hand, *contemporary* prosumers are those associated with Web 2.0, who develop and collaboratively modify user-generated content. In this case, there can be two ways of interpreting this phenomenon. The first way is that we can argue that these prosumers take part in an extended form of traditional capitalism since they simply encompass the dual role of producer and consumer under the control of the capitalist. The second way is what Ritzer and Jurgenson (2010) suggest with the following:

> There are also unique characteristics involved in the relationship between capitalism and prosumption on the Internet that make it possible to argue that capitalism has indeed entered a new and very different phase. There are indications that capitalism is having a difficult time gaining control over at least some of the prosumers than it has with producers, consumers, or more traditional prosumers (e.g., in fast food restaurant). More extremely, it may well be that capitalism itself will be transformed, perhaps, radically in the prosumer age.
>
> (Ritzer and Jurgenson, 2010, p. 21)

Drawing the conclusion that capitalism is being transformed due to Internet prosumption can be explained by four factors. First, Internet prosumption makes capitalists *unable to control contemporary prosumers* in the same way and to the same degree that they have been able to control producers, consumers, and traditional prosumers. "There is greater resistance to the incursions of capitalism (e.g. efforts to gain greater control and greater profits) by at least some contemporary prosumers than by any of the others" (Ritzer & Jurgenson, 2010, p. 21). Second, it would be difficult to argue that prosumers are being exploited in the same way as producers and consumers. Any notion of exploitation of prosumers is contradicted by the fact that *prosumers choose to co-create* with the organisation, they enjoy or even love the process and are willing to devote long hours engaged in such activities for no pay (Ritzer & Jurgenson, 2010). Third, it is certainly possible to claim that there is an emerging whole new economic form, especially on the Internet. The typical form of capitalism involves the exchange of money for goods and services, resulting in a profit out of this exchange. However, there is *no exchange of money* between website users and owners, for example, *Twitter* and *Facebook* users do not have to pay for the services. Organisations are certainly unwilling to pay for the work done by prosumers, but also prosumers prefer and are able to pay little or nothing for what they consume on the Internet in the form of news, blogs, and social networking sites (Anderson, 2009). This leads Ritzer and Jurgenson to wonder, "if capitalism is ultimately based on (unequal) exchanges based on a money economy, in such a 'free' economy can it be said to have capitalism in its traditional sense, or are we beginning to see the emergence of the outlines of a new form of capitalism?" (2010, p. 22). Rothery (2008) suggests that exchanges online do not focus on monetary value but on what it takes for consumers to give their attention, engagement and permission to the organisation.

Finally, traditional producer or consumer capitalism is based on scarcity, but online prosumer capitalism offers a *high degree of abundance*. According to Weber (1968[1921]), a system where

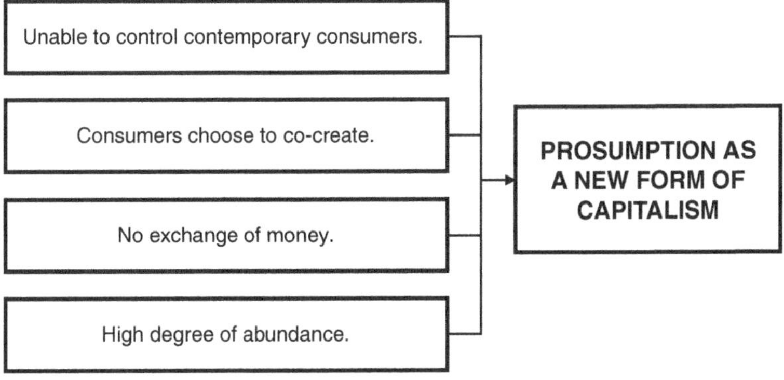

Figure 8.3 Prosumption as a new form of capitalism: The reasons.

there is scarcity, is based on rationality, and in particular, efficiency. In comparison, prosumer capitalism does not pay too much attention on maximising efficiency, but instead it seeks to increase effectiveness (Jurgenson & Ritzer, 2009). This means that the "concern is with the *quality* of what is produced irrespective of what it takes to produce products or services" (Ritzer & Jurgenson, 2010, p. 30). One could wonder if this drive from quantity to quality is another sign of *de*McDonaldisation of society due to the decreasing levels of calculability which is a dimension associated with cases where quantity surrogates for quality as one of the primary aims of social systems (Ritzer, 2015) (Figure 8.3).

Naturally, following this discussion it is important to reflect on the connections of design management with this new form of capitalism. In Chapter 3 we mentioned that design thinking is an antecedent to human-centred design. As we explained design thinking challenges the status quo and articulates to organisations an alternative way of thinking, managing, and doing business. Therefore, we could argue that a recognition of design as a human activity and an increasing attention to design thinking, has empowered design management to drive fundamental changes in traditional economic systems, and as a result, human-centred design, through co-creation and prosumption, has led to a new form of capitalism which has been gradually embraced by society.

Co-creation and anthropomorphism

Understanding anthropomorphism

As we discussed earlier, co-creation can also involve interpretation and meaning making (Ind & Coates, 2013), for example, in the form of brand meanings which are co-created by a multiplicity of stakeholders through a process of interaction. Aggarwal and McGill (2012) argue that consumers can engage themselves in a 'give and take' relationship with a brand and enjoy a feeling of reciprocity, when the brand is humanised, rendering its consumption (purchase and use) a social act. Brand anthropomorphism is a very interesting phenomenon, well connected with the notion of co-creation of value. "From a consumer's perspective, the verb to anthropomorphise describes the psychological process

Automobile design: A typical example of product anthropomorphism.

of attributing human form (e.g. visual features such as face, hands and eyes) or human mental states (e.g. intention, emotions) to a non-human agent such as a consumer product" (Miesler, 2012, p. 374). Seeing the human in non-human forms and events, is not something strange, quite the contrary, it pervades human judgement (Guthrie, 1993). People tend to see the human in nature (faces on clouds or the moon) and in artefacts too.

Explaining anthropomorphising tendencies

Guthrie (1993) provided us with three explanations for the tendency of all of us to anthropomorphise products and nature. First is that by attributing human characteristics, goals, beliefs, and emotions to objects and nature, we feel *comfort* because by doing so we create a relationship or companionship with them. Perhaps this connects with the popular belief that people who wish to have more relationships in their day-to-day lives, use products to fill this void. In fact, Epley, Waytz, and Cacioppo (2007) have argued that people feel the need to anthropomorphise because they have a desire to establish social connections with other humans. This need is satisfied through anthropomorphising because it enables the perception and creation of a human-like connection with non-human agents (Epley et al., 2007). In a journal paper which discusses the craft and handicraft profession in India as a way to spur innovative and creative thinking in sustainable design, Botnick and Raja have explained that due to the fact that "people in India are traditionally quite connected socially … even a temporary disconnect from the social context may result in the manifestation of anthropomorphism" (2011, p. 46).

The second explanation is that people anthropomorphise artefacts and nature, to make *better sense of the world* around them. "People use what they are familiar with – their knowledge of themselves – and ascribe human-like characteristics to events or entities to better account for outcomes and things that they know less about" (Aggarwal & McGill, 2007, p. 469). Again, drawing upon the work of Epley et al. (2007), the common drive for people to anthropomorphise enables them to interact more effectively with their environment. This allows them to make sense of the actions of non-human agents, artefacts and nature, reducing any uncertainty associated with the environment, and even enables them to predict how it might behave in the future. Therefore, it could be argued that anthropomorphism could be linked with the fear of uncertainty (Botnick & Raja, 2011; Epley et al., 2007). Finally, the third explanation involves the notion that anthropomorphising is a *cognitive and perceptual strategy* similar to making a bet that the world is human-like with a more upside than downside risk (Figure 8.4).

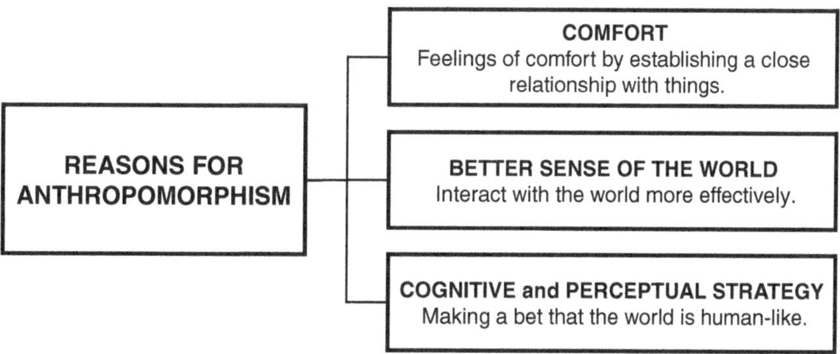

Figure 8.4 Reasons for anthropomorphising tendencies.

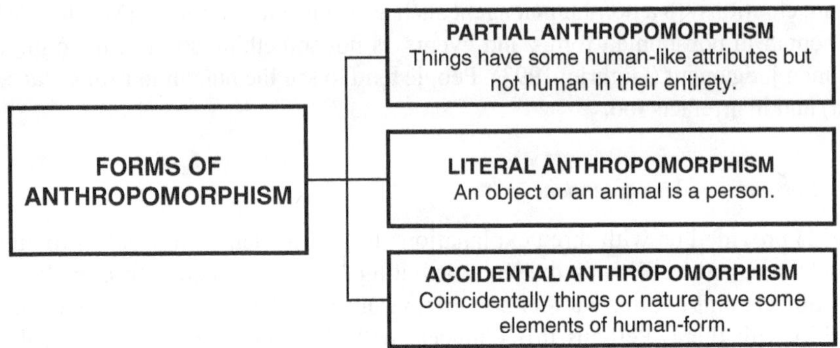

Figure 8.5 Forms of anthropomorphism.

Forms of anthropomorphism

Consequently, the above explanations led Guthrie (1993) to suggest that there are three forms of anthropomorphism. First, *partial anthropomorphising* "occurs when people see objects and events as having some important human traits but do not consider the entity as a whole to be human" (Aggarwal & McGill, 2007, p. 469). This form of anthropomorphism is relevant in product design where consumers might assign their possessions with some human traits and interpret them using schema for people, but they do not go as far as to see these possessions as fully, literally, human. Drawing from DiSalvo and Gemperie (2003), Miesler (2012) argues that products might have anthropomorphic qualities because they can be easily anthropomorphised due to their visual appearance imitating human features. Apart from the visual appearance of the product, designers can endow the product with human-like features and thus foster anthropomorphising in consumers by making the product mimic human gesture, human movement or human sound (Miesler, 2012). The second form of anthropomorphism is *literal anthropomorphising*, when individuals believe that an object or animal is a person. *Accidental anthropomorphising* is the third form, and this occurs when people coincidentally see some elements of human form in artefacts or nature, for instance, seeing a person's face in a rock or cloud. The focus of our discussion will be on the first form of anthropomorphism, partial anthropomorphising because there are clear connections between this form and product design and design management (Figure 8.5).

Anthropomorphism and product design evaluations

Aggarwal and McGill (2007) have presented three empirical studies which focused on partial anthropomorphising. Their overarching research aim was to explore whether presenting products in human terms affects the evaluation of the product and if so, how. Marketers often advise the design team to use presentational elements that humanise the products because there is a general belief that by doing so, the organisation can achieve more salient and more appealing presentations for their products. Notwithstanding such popular expectation, Aggarwal and McGill found that "the effect of presentational devices that humanise the product does not always lead to more positive evaluations and may even lead to less positive evaluations" (2007, p. 468).

Analytically their research studies aimed to investigate whether consumers' liking of a product is dependent on the perceived fit between product features and an activated human schema.

Fiske and Linville (1980) define schema as a stored framework of cognitive knowledge representing information on a particular stimulus (including its attributes and the relation among the attributes), a topic, or a concept. Previously scholars such as Fiske (1982) and Meyers-Levy and Tybout (1989) have suggested that new product evaluations could depend on congruity levels between the features of the product and the category schema in which it is presented. Congruity levels express the degree to which product features match those of the category schema (Fiske, 1982; Meyers-Levy & Tybout, 1989). The results of Aggarwal and McGill's (2007) studies support the schema-congruity hypothesis as the basis for explaining consumers' evaluation of anthropomorphised products. The schema-congruity model was first proposed in the 1980s to explain the match between products and their categories (Fiske, 1982; Mandler, 1982). Thus, the complex phenomenon of anthropomorphism offers a new application of this model in a new context (Aggarwal & McGill, 2007). Consistent with the model, Aggarwal and McGill's (2007) work provides evidence for the following thesis: how easy products can be anthropomorphised by consumers is dependant on the schemata in which products are presented and whether product features that are human-like are present or absent. Consequently, the consumers' ability to see the products as human, affects the evaluation of that product. "Products that are presented as human but which lack human features are evaluated less positively than products that are presented as human and which have human-like features" (Aggarwal & McGill, 2007, p. 477).

Aggarwal and McGill (2007) empirical research has provided an extra nuance to our current understanding of anthropomorphism. Consistent with the previous work by Fiske (1982), Aggarwal and McGill determined that "the overall evaluation of the product may be influenced both by the degree of satisfaction from seeing the fit between the product feature and the activated human schema as well by the 'affective tag' associated with that schema" (2007, p. 477). This means that the extent of congruity with an evoked schema is not the only source of evaluative information used by consumers to assess products. Prior research studies have identified that schemata are stored in human memory with an associated emotion; hence, when a product is perceived by consumers as having a good fit with an evoked schema, consumers may also evaluate this product according to the emotion associated with the particular schema (Fiske, 1982; Fiske & Pavelchak, 1986). Simply put, this means that there are conditions where anthropomorphising the product does not lead to higher product evaluations. If the product is anthropomorphised in a way that connects with a schema that evokes negative feelings from memory, the product will not be evaluated as favourably as it would if it was connected with a schema that evokes positive feelings from people's memory. Therefore, this point acts as caution to marketers and designers interested in anthropomorphising product offerings. Aggarwal and McGill suggest that "anthropomorphising a product may lead to more positive evaluations only when the type of person brought to mind is associated with positive feelings" (2007, p. 477).

Anthropomorphic design and consumption goals

Aggarwal and McGill's (2007) work, as well as other consumer and design research studies (e.g. Windhager, Hutzler, Carbon, Oberzaucher, Schaefer, Thorstensen, Leder, & Grammer, 2010; Windhager, Slice, Schaefer, Oberzaucher, Thorstensen, & Grammer, 2008) have explored what happens psychologically when people anthropomorphise products. As already discussed, there is a great human tendency to anthropomorphise; in fact, the presence of other humans is the most significant cue to human survival in our natural environment (Guthrie, 1993). Therefore, we could argue that we have the natural disposition to detect human forms quickly and without much thinking, and we are naturally attracted to human-like forms such as faces. This means that it is very tempting for designers to create a human look to products to increase the products' potential to trigger attention and attract consumers (DiSalvo & Gemperle, 2003). Miesler (2012) argued that most research studies on the topic were not embedded in a realistic product choice context, where most real-life situations require more reflection from consumers. For instance, when consumers need to purchase a product, they have to take into consideration the product features, situational factors such as price, and their own consumption goals. This means that whether individuals prefer and choose anthropomorphically designed products could depend on the consumption and purchase context. Marketers and designers "need to know such contextual factors which enhance or hinder overt preferences for anthropomorphic forms" (Miesler, 2012, p. 376).

In a choice situation, visible product design features such as how elements are arranged, and the shapes and materials used, might enable consumers to infer the value of a product, be it emotional or functional. From a functional value perspective, the relationship between product form and inferred product value can be explained through ergonomics, i.e., if a product has clearly arranged buttons and simple form, it will be easy to use; therefore, it will be functional. However, from an emotional value perspective, things might not be as clear. Miesler (2012) postulates thus that

> with regard to anthropomorphic designs ... even the emotional value of a product could be assessed by consumers based on its visual appearance before they interact with the product. Hereby, the process of anticipation becomes important, a concept, which has been neglected in design appreciation research so far – consumers need to *anticipate* the consumption (e.g. the interaction with a product) and possible consequence of this consumption (e.g. they anticipate that they will be proud of using a product due to its unique design).
>
> (Miesler, 2012, p. 377)

Consequently, Miesler (2012) proposed that anthropomorphic forms enhance the perceived emotional value of a product as a result of the associations evoked by the design features. Based on these associations, anthropomorphic designs make individuals build, or anticipate the potential of building, stronger emotional relationships with human-like products, for instance, in terms of commitment and loyalty, than the case where products are merely seen as objects only. Miesler hypothesised that "when consumers expect future interactions with a product to fulfil emotional goals, consumers prefer anthropomorphic designs over less anthropomorphic designs at the moment of purchase. When they expect to fulfil functional goals, less anthropomorphic designs should be preferred" (2012, p. 378). The results of her empirical study confirmed this hypothesis. Research participants who were stimulated to imagine emotional consumption goals preferred anthropomorphic designs, in contrast with participants asked to imagine functional goals, who preferred less-human-like designs. This means that Miesler (2012) identified situations within which the positive human bias to prefer human-like forms to non-human-like forms is not present.

Miesler's (2012) empirical study tested a second hypothesis which had two parts. First, individuals who prefer anthropomorphically designed products, have more positive emotions towards the product, and anticipate a stronger emotional relationship with that product (this anticipation might not be the same as the feelings experienced during actual product interactions but they can certainly influence product choice), than those individuals who prefer neutral designs. Empirical results demonstrated a positive relationship between a person's preference for anthromorphic designs and general emotional constructs such as liking the product and perceiving it as pleasant. However, there was not a positive relationship with more complex emotional constructs; for example, individuals did not anticipate they would develop a strong bond, a strong relationship with the product. The second part of the hypothesis involved the argument that perceiving a product as human-like magnifies the emotional responses to it, independent of the product's actual design. To answer this, it was essential to understand an individual's ability to perceive design features as human-like in the first place. This offered "additional evidence for the point that anthropomorphic forms (or product form in general) are not always directly linked to consumer responses. Designers should understand such characteristics which explain variation between individuals in emotional responses to design" (Miesler, 2012, p. 388). These characteristics can be differences in sensitivity to perceive certain forms (some people are more observant than others), gender, or hormonal influences (Durante, Griskevicius, Hill, Perilloux, & Li, 2011). Drawing from her research, Miesler (2012) advises designers by offering the following implications for anthropomorphic design:

> Overall, … [the research study] found that responses to anthropomorphic forms are complex, and cannot be explained by innate responses to product-inherent features only. Rather, when consumers make overt product choices, many different factors are involved, as in our case, the interplay of product appearance, consumption goals and personal characteristics. It is important for designers to understand such interplays to create product designs which match with consumers' needs, goals and perceptions.
>
> (Miesler, 2012, p. 388)

Chapter review questions

The following questions can help you reflect on the material we have covered in this chapter:

1 Explain the development of co-creation activities, comparing previous with current practice.
2 Discuss the characteristics of co-creation activities.
3 How can human-centred design contribute to social welfare?
4 Explain the concept of prosumption and its relationship with co-creation activities.
5 What are the positive and negative aspects of prosumption? What are the changes that Web 2.0 have brought to co-creation and the prosumption phenomenon?
6 Discuss the notion of prosumption as a new form of capitalism facilitated through co-creation activities.
7 Why do people tend to anthropomorphise objects? How does anthropomorphic design influence product design evaluations?
8 How do consumption goals influence people's preference for anthropomorphic design?

Recommended reading

1 Sanders, E. B. N. (2002). From user-centred to participatory design approaches. In J. Frascara (Ed.), *Design and the social sciences: Making connections* (pp. 1–8). London: Taylor & Francis.
2 Ritzer, G., & Jurgenson, N. (2010). Production, consumption, prosumption: The nature of capitalism in the age of the digital 'prosumer'. *Journal of Consumer Culture, 10*(1), 13–36.
3 Aggarwal, P., & McGill, A. L. (2007). Is that car smiling at me? Schema congruity as a basis for evaluating anthropomorphized products. *Journal of Consumer Research, 34*(4), 468–479.
4 Miesler, L. (2012). Product choice and anthropomorphic designs: Do consumption goals shape innate preferences for human-like forms? *The Design Journal, 15*(3), 373–392.

Reflective thoughts

Anthropomorphism and marketing challenges

Dr. Katerina Karanika
Senior Lecturer in Marketing
University of Exeter Business School, Exeter, UK

The attribution of human-like characteristics to products and brands is an important and widespread phenomenon in contemporary consumer culture (Belk, 1988; Fournier, 1998; Kniazeva & Belk, 2010; Landwehr, McGill, & Herrmann, 2011; Puzakova, Kwak, & Rocereto, 2009; Rauschnabel & Ahuvia, 2014). As this chapter rightly points out, anthropomorphised products and brands provide functional and emotional values. Basic reasons why people anthropomorphise non-human agents is that anthropomorphism helps to counteract the negative emotions associated with a sense of lack of control over one's environment or with a sense of lack of social connection, by enabling a sense of efficacy or a sense of connection, respectively. Therefore, a key point readers should consider is that anthropomorphism can enhance subjective well-being (Burgoon, Bonito, Bengtsson, Cederberg, Lundeberg, & Allspach, 2000; Epley, Waytz, Akalis, & Cacioppo, 2008; Tam, Lee, & Chao, 2013; Waytz, Cacioppo, & Epley, 2010). This in turn poses the challenge of how anthropomorphic designs can be used in order to positively impact on consumers' well-being.

As this chapter highlights, consumers do not always prefer human-like forms to non-human-like forms, when it comes to products and brands. Indeed, consumer research has discussed not only positive but also negative consequences of anthropomorphism for the evaluation of products and brands (Aggarwal & McGill, 2007; Delbaere, McQuarrie, & Phillips, 2011; Kim & McGill, 2011; Landwehr et al., 2011; Puzakova, Kwak, & Rocereto, 2013; Rauschnabel & Ahuvia, 2014; Veer, 2013; Waytz et al., 2010). In other words, consumer research has focused on consumers' positive and negative relationships with anthropomorphised products and brands, and has suggested that the challenge for marketers is how to ensure the design of anthropomorphised brands that guarantees positive consumer–brand relationships and promises the avoidance of negative consumer–brand relationships. Ambivalence or mixed emotions (the existence of multiple, both positive and negative feelings in one consumption episode) is central to consumer experience (e.g. Karanika & Hogg, 2016; O'Donohoe, 2001; Otnes, Lowrey, & Shrum, 1997; Stevens, Maclaran, & Brown, 2003; VOICE group, 2010) when shopping, consuming and watching advertisements, raising the question on whether marketers should try to anthropomorphise ambivalent products and brands (which are consumer goods experienced with mixed, both positive and negative feelings). Therefore, Hur, Koo, and Hofmann (2015) recently explored the impact of anthropomorphising ambivalent and tempting products on consumer behaviour. For example, they examined the impact on consumer behaviour when anthropomorphising entertaining but time-consuming products that can also isolate the consumer such as TVs, as well as the impact on consumer behaviour when anthropomorphising tasty but unhealthy products, e.g., cookies which can be desirable in the short run but harmful in the long run. In their experiments Hur et al. (2015) found that anthropomorphising an ambivalent product reduced self-control and increased indulgence during consumption. This in turn raises ethical concerns regarding the consequences of anthropomorphism that readers should consider.

Another critical point for discussion regards the multiplicity of meanings in brand anthropomorphism. Fournier's seminal (1998) paper identified that different consumers can attribute different social roles to the same brand. Similarly, more recently Kniazeva and Belk (2010) suggested that multiple brand personalities exist in the same brand as consumers anthropomorphise the brand. This raises important questions for marketers on how to use anthropomorphism when designing products, brands and advertising campaigns in order to try to navigate this multiplicity of meanings in brand anthropomorphism. These challenges also connect to the important discussion on co-creation and co-promotion earlier in this chapter. More specifically, marketers are presented with the challenge of how to invite and include consumers in the process of brand anthropomorphism after taking into consideration consumers' multiple perceptions of, and experiences with, the brand. How marketers dealing with anthropomorphic marketing can co-design, co-create, and co-promote brand meaning with consumers. A final point readers should consider is that managers dealing with anthropomorphic marketing should be concerned not only about co-creation that stems from a positive deep and meaningful interaction with the consumer but also about how to take on board the negative views that are expressed, for example, in communities against particular brands, and even how to engage into a dialogue with such communities.

Questions for discussion

1 Think of a brand that you really like. If this brand was a person what kind of person would he or she be? What would his/her lifestyle, values, physical and mental characteristics be? Then, consider a brand you like less or a brand you do not like at all. If this brand was a person what kind of person would he or she be? What would his/her characteristics be? Now consider if, how and to what extent your brand anthropomorphisms have been influenced by marketers and/or by your own experiences and interactions with the brand.
2 Choose a brand and take interviews from consumers asking them to think of the brand as a person. Repeat the above questions: If this brand was a person what kind of person would he or she be? What would his/her lifestyle, values, physical and mental characteristics be? Ask also about your interviewees' experiences with the brand and their recollection of advertisements and promotional activities of the brand. Based on your findings, what would be the recommendations you would give to marketers in terms of using or not anthropomorphism for designing products, packaging and advertising campaigns for this brand?

References

Aggarwal, P., & McGill, A. L. (2007). Is that car smiling at me? Schema congruity as a basis for evaluating anthropomorphized products. *Journal of Consumer Research, 34*(4), 468–479.

Belk, R. W. (1988). Possessions and the extended self. *Journal of Consumer Research, 15*(2), 139–168.

Burgoon, J. K., Bonito, J. A., Bengtsson, B., Cederberg, C., Lundeberg, M., & Allspach, L. (2000). Interactivity in human–computer interaction: A study of credibility, understanding, and influence. *Computers in Human Behavior, 16*(6), 553–574.

Delbaere, M., McQuarrie, E. F., & Phillips, B. J. (2011). Personification in advertising. *Journal of Advertising, 40*(1), 121–130.

(Continued)

(Continued)

Epley, N., Waytz, A., Akalis, S., & Cacioppo, J. T. (2008). When we need a human: Motivational determinants of anthropomorphism. *Social Cognition, 26*(2), 143–155.

Fournier, S. (1998). Consumers and their brands: Developing relationship theory in consumer research. *Journal of Consumer Research, 24*(4), 343–373.

Hur, J. D., Koo, M., & Hofmann, W. (2015). When temptations come alive: How anthropomorphism undermines self-control. *Journal of Consumer Research, 42*(2), 340–358.

Karanika, K., & Hogg, M. K. (2016). Consumption through the ambivalent prism of intergenerational support. *European Journal of Marketing, 50*(3/4), 575–601.

Kim, S., & McGill, A. L. (2011). Gaming with Mr. Slot or gaming the slot machine? Power, anthropomorphism, and risk perception. *Journal of Consumer Research, 38*(1), 94–107.

Kniazeva, M., & Belk, R. W. (2010). If this brand were a person, or anthropomorphism of brands through packaging stories. *Journal of Global Academy of Marketing, 20*(3), 231–238.

Landwehr, J. R., McGill, A. L., & Herrmann, A. (2011). It's got the look: The effect of friendly and aggressive 'facial' expressions on product liking and sales. *Journal of Marketing, 75*(3), 132–146.

O'Donohoe, S. (2001). Living with ambivalence attitudes to advertising in postmodern times. *Marketing Theory, 1*(1), 91–108.

Otnes, C., Lowrey, T. M., & Shrum, L. J. (1997). Toward an understanding of consumer ambivalence. *Journal of Consumer Research, 24*(1), 80–93.

Puzakova, M., Kwak, H., & Rocereto, J. F. (2009). Pushing the envelope of brand and personality: Antecedents and moderators of anthropomorphized brands. *Advances in Consumer Research, 36*, 413–420.

Puzakova, M., Kwak, H., & Rocereto, J. F. (2013). When humanizing brands goes wrong: The detrimental effect of brand anthropomorphization amid product wrongdoings. *Journal of Marketing, 77*(3), 81–100.

Rauschnabel, P. A., & Ahuvia, A. C. (2014). You're so lovable: Anthropomorphism and brand love. *Journal of Brand Management, 21*(5), 372–395.

Stevens, L., Maclaran, P., & Brown, S. (2003). 'Red time is me time' advertising, ambivalence, and women's magazines. *Journal of Advertising, 32*(1), 35–45.

Tam, K. P., Lee, S. L., & Chao, M. M. (2013). Saving Mr. Nature: Anthropomorphism enhances connectedness to and protectiveness toward nature. *Journal of Experimental Social Psychology, 49*(3), 514–521.

Veer, E. (2013). Made with real crocodiles: The use of anthropomorphism to promote product kinship in our youngest consumers. *Journal of Marketing Management, 29*(1–2), 195–206.

VOICE Group. (2010). Buying into motherhood? Problematic consumption and ambivalence in transitional phases. *Consumption, Markets and Culture, 13*(4), 373–397.

Waytz, A., Cacioppo, J., & Epley, N. (2010). Who sees human? The stability and importance of individual differences in anthropomorphism. *Perspectives on Psychological Science, 5*(3), 219–232.

References

Aggarwal, P., & McGill, A. L. (2007). Is that car smiling at me? Schema congruity as a basis for evaluating anthropomorphized products. *Journal of Consumer Research, 34*(4), 468–479.

Aggarwal, P., & McGill, A. L. (2012). When brands seem human, do humans act like brands? Automatic behavioral priming effects of brand anthropomorphism. *Journal of Consumer Research, 39*(2), 307–323.

Anderson, C. (2009). *Free: The future of a radical price*. New York: Hyperion.

Andreasen, A. R. (1994). Social marketing: Its definition and domain. *Journal of Public Policy & Marketing, 13*(1)108–114.

Bødker, S. (1996). Creating conditions for participation: Conflicts and resources in systems design. *Human–Computer Interaction, 11*(3), 215–236.

Botnick, K., & Raja, I. (2011). Subtle technology: The design innovation of Indian artisanship. *Design Issues, 27*(4), 43–55.

Brodie, R. J., Hollebeek, L. D., Juric, B., & Ilic, A. (2011). Customer engagement: Conceptual domain, fundamental propositions, and implications for research. *Journal of Service Research, 14*(3), 252–271.

Brown, T. (2009). *Change by design: How design thinking transforms organisations and inspires innovation.* New York: HarperCollins.

Buchanan, R. (1992). Wicked problems in design thinking. *Design Issues, 8*(2), 5–21.

Buchanan, R. (2001). Human dignity and human rights: Thoughts on the principles of human-centered design. *Design Issues, 17*(3), 35–39.

Cova, B., & Dalli, D. (2009). Working consumers: The next step in marketing theory? *Marketing Theory, 9*(3), 315–339.

DiSalvo, C., & Gemperle, F. (2003). From seduction to fulfilment: The use of anthropomorphic form in design. In *Proceedings of the 2003 International Conference on Designing Pleasurable Products and Interfaces* (pp. 67–72). Pittsburgh, PA: ACM Press.

Durante, K. M., Griskevicius, V., Hill, S. E., Perilloux, C., & Li, N. P. (2011). Ovulation, female competition, and product choice: Hormonal influences on consumer behaviour. *Journal of Consumer Research, 37*(6), 921–934.

Epley, N., Waytz, A., & Cacioppo, J. T. (2007). On seeing human: A three-factor theory of anthropomorphism. *Psychological Review, 114*(4), 864–886.

Fiske, S. T. (1982). Schema-triggered affect: Applications to social perception. In M. S. Clark, & S. T. Fiske (Eds.), *Affect and cognition: 17th annual Carnegie Mellon symposium on cognition* (pp. 55–78). Hillsdale, MI: Lawrence Erlbaum.

Fiske, S. T., & Linville, P. W. (1980). What does the schema concept buy us? *Personality and Social Psychology Bulletin, 6*(4), 543–557.

Fiske, S. T., & Pavelchak, M. A. (1986). Category-based versus piecemeal-based affective responses: Developments in schema-triggered affect. In R. M. Sorrentino, & E. T. Higgins (Eds.), *Handbook of motivation and cognition: Foundations of social behavior* (pp. 167–203). New York: Guilford Press.

Fournier, S., & Lee, L. (2009). Getting brand communities right. *Harvard Business Review, 87*(4), 105–111.

Frediani, A. A. (2016). Re-imagining participatory design: Reflecting on the ASF-UK change by design methodology. *Design Issues, 32*(3), 98–111.

Frow, P., & Payne, A. (2013). *Co-creation: A typology and framework.* Working Paper, Discipline of Marketing, University of Sydney, Australia.

Frow, P., Nenonen, S., Payne, A., & Storbacka, K. (2015). Managing co-creation design: A strategic approach to innovation. *British Journal of Management, 26*(3), 463–483.

Garud, R., Jain, S., & Tuertscher, P. (2008). Incomplete by design and designing for incompleteness. *Organization Studies, 29*(3), 351–371.

Grönroos, C. (2011). Value co-creation in service logic: A critical analysis. *Marketing theory, 11*(3), 279–301.

Guthrie, S. E. (1993). *Faces in the clouds: A new theory of religion.* Oxford, UK: Oxford University Press.

Harvey, D. (2008). The right to the city. *New Left Review, 6*, 23–40.

Hastings, G. (2007). *Social marketing: Why should the devil have all the best tunes?* Oxford: Butterworth-Heinemann.

Ind, N., & Coates, N. (2013). The meanings of co-creation. *European Business Review, 25*(1), 86–95.

Ind, N., Fuller, C., & Trevail, C. (2012). *Brand together: How co-creation generates innovation and re-energizes brands.* London: Kogan Page.

Jurgenson, N., & Ritzer, G. (2009). Efficiency, effectiveness, and web 2.0. In S. Kleinman (Ed.), *The culture of efficiency* (pp. 51–67). New York: Peter Lang.

Kaplan, A. M., & Haenlein, M. (2009). Users of the world, unite! The challenges and opportunities of social media. *Business Horizons, 53*, 59–68.

Kozinets, R. V. (1999). E-tribalized marketing? The strategic implications of virtual communities of consumption. *European Management Journal, 17*(3), 252–264.

Lehrer, M., Ordanini, A., DeFillippi, R., & Miozzo, M. (2012). Challenging the orthodoxy of value co-creation theory: A contingent view of co-production in design-intensive business services. *European Management Journal, 30*(6), 499–509.

Macey, W. H., & Schneider, B. (2008). The meaning of employee engagement. *Industrial and Organizational Psychology, 1*(1), 3–30.

Mandler, G. (1982). The structure of value: Accounting for taste. In M. S. Clark, & S. T. Fiske (Eds.), *17th annual Carnegie Mellon symposium on cognition* (pp. 3–36). Hillsdale, MI: Lawrence Erlbaum.

Manzini, E., & Rizzo, F. (2011). Small projects/large changes: Participatory design as an open participated process. *CoDesign, 7*(3–4), 199–215.

Meyers-Levy, J., & Tybout, A. M. (1989). Schema congruity as a basis for product evaluation. *Journal of Consumer Research, 16*(1), 39–54.

Miesler, L. (2012). Product choice and anthropomorphic designs: Do consumption goals shape innate preferences for human-like forms? *The Design Journal, 15*(3), 373–392.

Morris, P. (2003). *The Bakhtin reader: Selected writings of Bakhtin, Medvedev, Voloshinov*. London: Arnold.

Muñiz, A. M., Jr., & O'Guinn, T. C. (2001). Brand community. *Journal of Consumer Research, 27*(4), 412–432.

Patterson, P. G., Yu, T., & de Ruyter, K. (2006). Understanding customer engagement in services. Advancing theory, maintaining relevance, *Proceedings of ANZMAC 2006 Conference*, Brisbane, December.

Perks, H., Gruber, T., & Edvardsson, B. (2012). Co-creation in radical service innovation: A systematic analysis of microlevel processes. *Journal of Product Innovation Management, 29*(6), 935–951.

Prahalad, C. K., & Ramaswamy, V. (2004a). Co-creating unique value with customers. *Strategy & Leadership, 32*(3), 4–9.

Prahalad, C. K., & Ramaswamy, V. (2004b). Co-creation experiences: The next practice in value creation. *Journal of Interactive Marketing, 18*(3), 5–14.

Prahalad, C. K., & Ramaswamy, V. (2004c). *The future of competition: Co-creating unique value with customers*. Cambridge, MA: Harvard Business Press.

Prahalad, C. K., & Ramaswamy, V. (2013). *The future of competition: Co-creating unique value with customers*. Cambridge, MA: Harvard Business Press.

Raymond, E. (1999). *The cathedral and the bazaar: Musings on Linux and open source by an accidental revolutionary*. Sebastopol, CA: O'Reilly.

Ritzer, G. (2009, March). *Correcting an historical error*. Keynote Address at the Conference on Prosumption, Frankfurt, Germany.

Ritzer, G. (2015). *The McDonaldization of society* (8th ed.). London: Sage.

Ritzer, G., & Jurgenson, N. (2010). Production, consumption, prosumption: The nature of capitalism in the age of the digital 'prosumer'. *Journal of Consumer Culture, 10*(1), 13–36.

Rothery, G., (2008). The matchmaker. *Marketing Age,* November/December.

Sanders, E. B. N. (2002). From user-centred to participatory design approaches. In J. Frascara (Ed.), *Design and the social sciences: Making connections* (pp. 1–8), London: Taylor & Francis.

Sanders, E. B. N., & Stappers, P. J. (2008). Co-creation and the new landscapes of design. *CoDesign, 4*(1), 5–18.

Sawhney, M., Verona, G., & Prandelli, E. (2005). Collaborating to create: The internet as a platform for customer engagement in product innovation. *Journal of Interactive Marketing, 19*(4), 4–17.

Schau, H. J., Muñiz, A. M., Jr., & Arnould, E. J. (2009). How brand community practices create value. *Journal of Marketing, 73*(5), 30–51.

Seybold, P. B. (2006). *Outside innovation: How your customers will co-design your company's future*. New York: Collins.

Sharma, V., Simpson, R. C., LoPresti, E. F., Mostowy, C., Olson, J., Puhlman, J., . . . Cooper, R. (2008). Participatory design in the development of the wheelchair convoy system. *Journal of NeuroEngineering and Rehabilitation, 5*(1), 1.

Sheth, J. N., & Uslay, C. (2007). Implications of the revised definition of marketing: From exchange to value creation. *Journal of Public Policy & Marketing, 26*(2), 302–307.

Smith, A. (1776). *The wealth of nations. An inquiry into the nature and causes of the wealth of nations*. New York: The Modern Library.

Smith, P. R., & Zook, Z. (2011). *Marketing communications: Integrating offline and online with social media*. London: Kogan Page.

Toffler, A. (1980). *The third wave*. New York: William Morrow.

Tseng, M. M., & Piller, F. T. (2003). *The customer centric enterprise: Advances in mass customization and personalization*. Berlin, Germany: Springer.

Vargo, S. L., & Lusch, R. F. (2006). Service-dominant logic: What it is, what it is not, what it might be. In R. F. Lusch, & S. L. Vargo (Eds.), *The service-dominant logic of marketing: Dialog, debate, and directions* (pp. 43–56). Armonk, NY: M.E. Sharpe.

Vibert, A. B., & Shields, C. (2003). Approaches to student engagement: Does ideology matter? *McGill Journal of Education, 38*(2), 221–240.

Von Hippel, E. (1986). Lead users: A source of novel product concepts. *Management Science, 32*(7), 791–805.

Von Hippel, E. (2005). Democratizing innovation: The evolving phenomenon of user innovation. *International Journal of Innovation Science, 1*(1), 29–40.

Wallas, G. (1926). *The art of thought*. New York: Harcourt, Brace & World.

Wasko, M. M., & Faraj, S. (2000). 'It is what one does': Why people participate and help others in electronic communities of practice. *The Journal of Strategic Information Systems, 9*(2), 155–173.

Weber, M. (1968 [1921]). *Economy and society* (Vols. 3). Totowa, NJ: Bedminster Press.

Weber, M. (1978). *Economy and society: An outline of interpretive sociology* (E. Fischoff, Trans.). G. Roth & C. Wittich (Eds.). Berkeley, CA: University of California Press.

Wilkinson, C. R., Walters, A., & Evans, J. (2016). Creating and testing a model-driven framework for accessible user-centric design. *The Design Journal, 19*(1), 69–91.

Windhager, S., Hutzler, F., Carbon, C. C., Oberzaucher, E., Schaefer, K., Thorstensen, T., Leder, H., & Grammer, K. (2010). Laying eyes on headlights: Eye movements suggest facial features in cars. *Collegium Antropologicum, 34*(3), 1075–1080.

Windhager, S., Slice, D. E., Schaefer, K., Oberzaucher, E., Thorstensen, T., & Grammer, K. (2008). Face to face: The perception of automotive designs. *Human Nature, 19*, 331–346.

Zwick, D., Bonsu, S. K., & Darmody, A. (2008). Putting consumers to work: Co-creation and new marketing governmentality. *Journal of Consumer Culture, 8*(2), 163–196.

9 Design consultancies as professional service firms

Chapter aims and learning outcomes

This chapter aims to:

1 Define professions and professional service firms (PSFs).
2 Explore design consultancies from a PSF perspective and in particular investigate the characteristics of client relationships.
3 Discuss the effects of client relationships on design consultancies as PSFs.
4 Provide an understanding of different stages of the client relationships lifecycle pattern and how these can be successfully managed.
5 Discuss the nature of social, economic, intellectual, and symbolic capital produced and processed by design consultancies, drawing from the work of Pierre Bourdieu.
6 Discuss the lessons which design consultancies can offer for management practice, through the concept of 'managing as designing'.

The main theme explored in the previous chapter was the notion of co-creation in creativity and design, in the form of participatory design. Co-creation, and in particular co-production of services, is one of the defining features of professional service firms (PSFs). "The output of PSFs is co-produced through coordinated efforts of the PSF and the client firm, [therefore] close contact and ongoing communication between the two firms is necessary for the delivery of services to occur" (Broschak, 2015, p. 306). It has been argued that in such relationships both parties have valuable knowledge to offer in order to develop solutions to the client's problems; thus, it is essential that a shared meaning and understanding is developed between the two parties (Nikolova, Reihlen, & Schlapfner, 2009). Design consultancies can be considered professional services firms, a term which has been used to describe law firms, accounting firms, management consultancies, advertising agencies, engineering consultancies, investment banking, and public relations firms, on which significant empirical research has been carried out. It is important at this stage to explore design consultancies through the lens of PSFs because this will provide us with a greater understanding of their special nature, identifying their similarities to other PSFs, as well as highlighting their idiosyncrasies. It is imperative we understand the characteristics of the PSFs and in particular of the relationships PSFs develop with the client organisations (COs) which hire their services. This will provide us with a better insight on the organisational nature of design consultancies.

In addition, this chapter explores the different phases of the client–design consultancy relationship lifecycle. Understanding these phases can highlight how client relationships can be managed successfully. Furthermore, design consultancies, being a vibrant and dynamic part of the wider creative and cultural industries, produce and process different forms of capital, including significant social, economic, intellectual, and symbolic capital. It is important to understand these forms of capital, which are a result of the design work produced and the client relationships developed. Finally, there are many lessons that any organisation, regardless of its size and the industry it operates in, can learn from design consultancies. In fact, the latter can not only contribute to design innovation but also drive significant organisational change for the COs. This chapter discusses the role of design consultancies as agents of organisational change, through the concept of 'managing as designing'.

Understanding PSFs

Defining professions and PSFs

Before we attempt to understand the characteristics of PSFs, it is important to determine what we mean by the terms 'profession' and 'PSFs'. The term 'profession' implies a "method of gaining a living while serving as an agent of formal knowledge and implies as well the fact that bodies of formal knowledge, or disciplines, are differentiated into specialised occupations" (Freidson, 1988 ,p. 20). However, professions can be considered more than occupations because of the prestige attached to them, due to their formal knowledge. They can also be considered as occupations enjoying special form of protection from competition (Freidson, 1988). In fact, Wilensky (1964) attempted to separate professions from occupations claiming that not all occupations are professions. He determined a process which occupations must follow in their pursuit for professional status. This *professionalisation process* includes the following stages: (1) the emergence of the occupation, (2) the establishment of a training school, (3) the founding of professional associations, (4) a political agitation for legally protecting the job territory and its code of ethics, and, finally, (5) the formal adoption of such code of ethics (Wilensky, 1964) (Figure 9.1). In an examination of the professional status of design management, Lalaounis, Wood, and

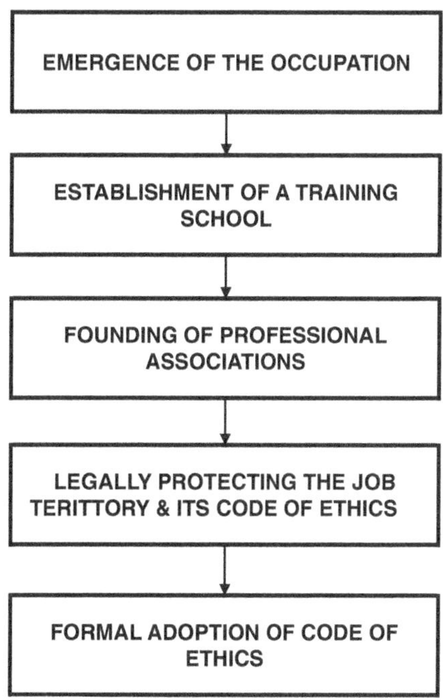

Figure 9.1 Process of professionalisation of occupations.

Evans (2011) view these stages more as criteria which can be achieved in different sequence and determined that design management can actually be characterised as a 'semi-profession' due to the fact that two of Wilensky's (1964) five stages have yet to be achieved: first, public recognition and legal support and, second, a code of ethics governing the professional conduct of design managers (Figure 9.1).

Contrastingly, Abbott (1988) suggests that the main distinguishing characteristic between professions and occupations is the fact that professions are based on abstract bodies of knowledge. Therefore, his argument emphasises, like Freidson (1988), the need for a body of knowledge, instead of the need for legal protection or code of ethics. He claims that "any occupation can obtain licensure (e.g. beauticians) or develop an ethics code (e.g. real estate). But only a knowledge system governed by abstraction can redefine its problems and tasks..." (Abbott, 1988, p. 9). How abstract a body of knowledge needs to be in order to be professional depends on time and place. What is important is that abstraction "is effective enough to compete in a particular historical and social context, not abstraction relative to some supposed absolute standard" (Abbott, 1988, p. 9). Consequently, in line with Freidson's (1988) thesis, Abbott provides a looser definition of professions as "exclusive occupations applying somewhat abstract knowledge to particular cases" (1988, p. 8). This means that contrary to previous research studies which attributed the prestige of profession to more traditional occupations such as law and medicine, Abbott (1988) broadened the definition to include other occupations such as accounting, architecture, and design (Sharma, 1997).

Following our discussion of the meaning of the term professions, it is now important to understand what we mean by the term 'professional service firms'. Drawing from various scholars (Bowen & Jones, 1986; Larsson & Bowen, 1989; Løwendahl, 2005; Sharma, 1997), Broschak defines PSFs as follows:

> [PSFs are] knowledge-intensive organisations, composed of individuals with prolonged and specialised training in an abstract body of knowledge, who customise their efforts for clients, exhibit a high degree of discretionary effort and exercise personal judgement in the delivery of their service, and who operate under the constraints of professional norms.
>
> (Broschak, 2015, p. 304)

The characteristics of PSFs

Von Nordenflycht (2010) identified three distinctive characteristics of PSFs. First, *knowledge intensity* is the most fundamental among the three and "indicates that production of a firm's output relies on a substantial body of complex knowledge" (Von Nordenflycht, 2010, p. 159). This goes in line with Abbott's (1988) aforementioned notion of abstract knowledge. Second, *low capital intensity* relates to the fact that "a firm's production does not involve significant amounts of non-human assets, such as inventory, factories and equipment, and even intangible non-human assets like patents and copyrights" (Von Nordenflycht, 2010, p. 162). It is important to emphasise that low capital intensity is not an implication of knowledge intensity. There are cases where production needs *both* an intellectually skilled team (knowledge) *and* significant non-human assets. For instance, hospitals' services operations require both staff who have a medical degree *and* specialised buildings with medical equipment. The third characteristic is *professionalised workforce* which involves professions that have (1) a particular knowledge base, (2) regulation and control of this knowledge base and its application, and (3) an ideology, i.e., a set of professional code of ethics (Von Nordenflycht, 2010) (Figure 9.2). The latter two characteristics go in line with two of the stages of Wilensky's (1964) professionalisation process.

Based on the above, Von Nordenflycht (2010) developed a taxonomy of PSFs including four categories, each with a specific combination of these three characteristics. The first category is the '*classic PSFs*' which meet all three characteristics, such as law, accounting, and architecture firms. They are

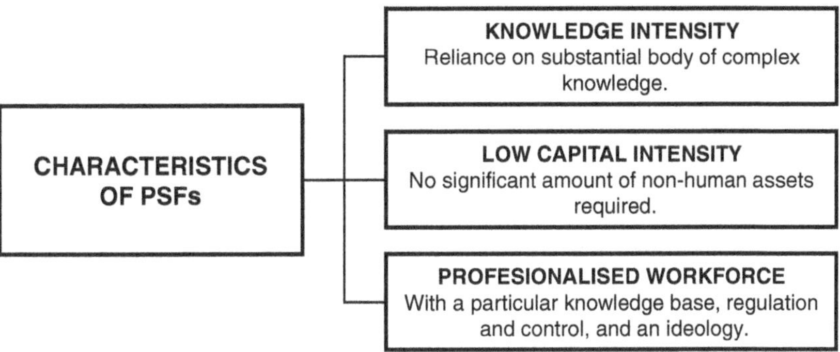

Figure 9.2 Characteristics of professional service firms.

the organisations with the highest degree of professional service intensity, and as a classic or archetypal category of professions, they have high levels of ideology and self-regulation. In the UK, creative firms which deliver architectural services must employ architecturally trained staff, who have passed examinations by the Royal Institute of British Architects (RIBA-3) (regulation) and adhere to a code of ethics set by RIBA (ideology).

The second category is the '*professional campuses*' which involve knowledge intensity, a professionalised workforce, but these firms are more capital-intensive, because they require specialised equipment and facilities. Hospitals are a prime example in this category as already explained. '*Neo-PSFs*' is the third category in Von Nordenflycht's (2010) taxonomy, and they differ from the classic PSFs on the basis of having non-professionalised (or weakly professionalised) workforces. Management consultancies and advertising agencies are examples in this category. Although these organisations employ a workforce with specific knowledge, these professions have lower levels of regulation and ideology. However, at least in the case of advertising agencies, over the last few years, the Institute of Practitioners in Advertising has sought to regulate the industry more and establish a code of ethics in advertising services provision.

Finally, the fourth category is the '*technology developers*', which displays the lowest degree of professional service intensity as it includes knowledge intensity but neither low capital intensity nor a professionalised workforce. These are organisations "whose workforces are composed of engineers and scientists and that also require significant investments in equipment or significant up-front capital to fund development of new products" (Von Nordenflycht, 2010, p. 165). This example can be slightly problematic because one could argue that engineering and natural sciences tend to be regulated, and with their own code of ethics; thus, their workforces can be considered professionalised (Figure 9.3).

Maister (2003) argues that all PSFs must achieve the triple mission of (1) delivering outstanding client service, (2) fostering and facilitating careers which provide professional satisfaction to all organisational members, and (3) achieving financial success to reward themselves and grow. There needs to be a balance between these endeavours to ensure quality, satisfaction, and success simultaneously. PSFs produce output which is intangible and cannot be held in inventory (Mills & Marguiles, 1980; Sharma, 1997). To some extent, this is true in the case of design consultancies since such firms provide an intangible service by generating ideas and giving these ideas form and substance. However, one could argue that design consultancies also deliver a tangible output in the form of sketches, prototypes, blueprints, artwork, and artefacts, depending on the design service provided.

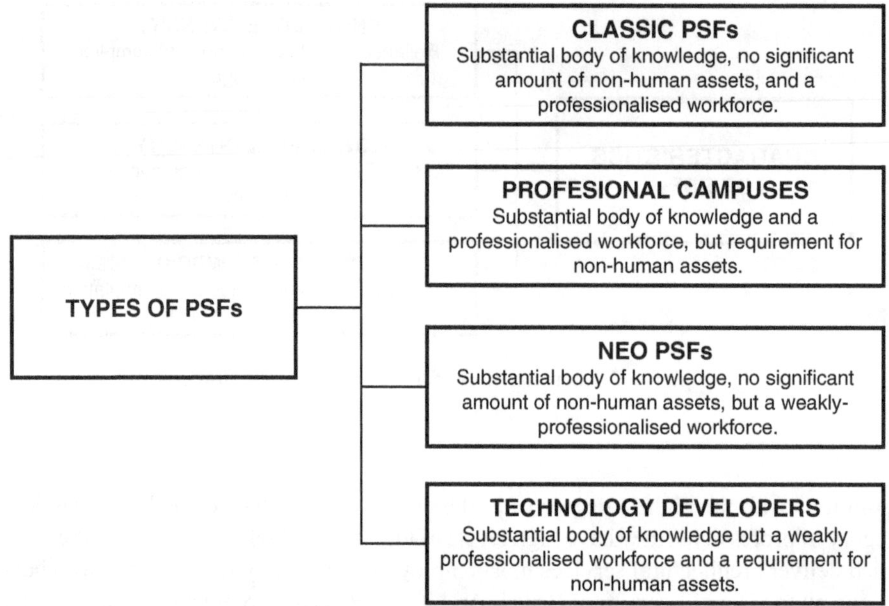

Figure 9.3 Types of professional service firms.

Although, PSFs produce this output collaboratively with COs, it is still the PSFs' expertise that makes all the difference; otherwise, COs could and would pursue these activities on their own, and there will not be a need for design services provided by design consultancies. This implies that "professionals have expertise that is outside the technical knowledge of their clients, while the work-related behaviours of professionals are difficult for clients to observe and assess" (Broschak, 2015, p. 306). As a result, the relationships between PSFs and COs are characterised by *information asymmetry* and *uncertainty*. Referring to the work of Mills and Moshavi (1999) and Bagdoniene and Jackstaite (2009), Broschak explains information asymmetry:

> information asymmetry in client relationships refers to how informed parties are about each other in a contractual relationship, to the differing amount of information clients and service providers have that must be shared for the professional service to be performed, and to the fact that clients and service providers may have different understandings of the information that needs to be shared.
>
> (Broschak, 2015, p. 306)

Professionals as agents

Sharma (1997) explored professionals through the lens of agency theory, in which information asymmetry is one of the main concepts. This theory explores the exchanges in which one party (principal) delegates work to another party (agent). In the case of design consultancy work, the principal is the CO and the agent is the design consultancy. "The agency theory endeavours to surface contractual problems arising from the assumption that the agents will behave opportunistically if their interests conflict with those of the principals" (Sharma, 1997, p. 760). Resolving these problems can be difficult due to the information asymmetry which favours agents, as well as the different attitudes to risk held by the two contracting parties (Sharma, 1997). Comparing professionals with other types of agents, Sharma (1997) identified not only similarities such as self-interest and bounded rationality but also distinctive characteristics such as co-production of an intangible service product, which we have already touched upon, and an oversight by the community of peers. The latter is concerned with the fact that the cost of monitoring the agent's actions and of measuring the agent's contribution is higher than other agency exchanges.

However, the main attribute which makes the principal–professional agency exchange different to those typically explored in agency theory research studies, is the *power asymmetry* favouring professional agents (Sharma, 1997). In other types of agency exchanges there is the assumption that the principal is the dominant party because he/she has the power to formulate and enforce contractual agreements, as well as the ability to reduce information asymmetry by establishing suitable information systems. In contrast, Sharma (1997) argues that in principal–professional agent exchanges, the agent might be considered the dominant party because in such exchanges

> professionals have power over lay principals by virtue of their expertise, functional indispensability, and intrinsic ambiguity associated with the services they provide. Such agency exchanges involve information asymmetry that is particularly severe, since principals do not possess the technical knowledge to evaluate the effort invested or the outcome accomplished by professional agents.
>
> (Sharma, 1997, p. 768)

Evidently, Sharma (1997) makes a distinction between *knowledge asymmetry* and information asymmetry. Not knowing *how* the professional agent does a job (knowledge asymmetry) is different from, and multiplies, the problem of not knowing *what* the professional agent does (information asymmetry). There is, therefore, a distinction between 'knowing-what' and 'knowing-how' which is a primary characteristic of PSFs. In the case of design consultancies, we can certainly argue that there is such knowledge asymmetry as clients do not know *how* to solve problems through design. This means that design consultancies as agents might have more power than COs. Yet, we have to be cautious here. COs (principals) still have the power to form and dissolve client–design consultancy relationships. In addition, one could suggest that instilling design thinking in COs (explored in Chapter 3) might reduce this knowledge asymmetry to some extent, because design thinking demonstrates to managers *how* designers think, frame and solve problems, and enables managers to follow such process. This does not, however, mean that managers will be able to replace designers in the future because there is always going to be a lack of abstract knowledge and experience, which designers acquire through their formal institutionalised training and work.

Smith and McKinlay (2009) argue that

> agents in the creative industries are not simply labour and capital; governments play a role because some of the goods produced in the sector are treated as a public goods, for example those with educational value; others have national or cultural value [such as architectural projects of national importance], both for internal purposes of social or ideological control, and also for inter-country competition and prestige. Finally, state intervention might also be about supporting nascent industries which have innovative or strategic commercial power – as in the 1997 [UK] Labour Government championing of creative industries in the UK.
>
> (Smith and McKinlay, 2009, p. 8)

Client–consultancy relationships

Relational vs. transactional client relationships

Scholars exploring the characteristics of PSFs have identified two categories of client relationships developed by these organisations: (1) relational and (2) transactional (Figure 9.4). Broschak explains the difference between these categories:

> whereas *relational client relationships* are long-lasting and involve considerable interaction between firms, *transactional client relationships* resemble the competitive markets of neo-classical economics where client firms are indifferent between suppliers. Transactional client relationships are short-lived and episodic, with clients keeping PSFs at arm's length, dispersing business among many competitors, limiting the amount of and type of information that is shared, and letting price and profit, rather than commitment, drive relationships.
>
> (Broschak, 2015, p. 305)

COs maintain a portfolio of relationships in their operations, the characteristics of which can determine their orientation, relational or transactional, towards markets for professional services. This means that the proportion of relational and transactional relationships COs have can indicate whether or not these COs prefer long-term, stable relationships or short-term transactions with PSFs (Baker, 1990). This logic can of course extend to PSFs; the characteristics of the portfolio of client relationships PSFs maintain reflects the approach PSFs take, relational or transactional, in their work.

An important question we must address at this stage is about how we can determine whether a client relationship is relational or transactional. Therefore, it is essential we understand where the dichotomy lies. The *duration of the relationship* is the main indicator of the category the client relationship belongs to (Broschak, 2015). This is because, scholars believe that relationships become stronger as time passes due to the relationship-specific investments all parties make over time (Levinthal & Finchman, 1988). Such investments can take the form of routines, software, hardware, facilities, and extra staff members, from the firms' perspective, and investments in relationship-specific skills, in-depth knowledge of the exchange partner's business, and the development of personal relationships with exchange partner counterparts, from an individuals' perspective (Broschak, 2004; Uzzi, 1996). In the case of design consultancies, it is very often that recruitment of extra staff occurs as the relationship with important clients grows. Such recruits are assigned to these 'big' accounts to ensure the quality and the breadth of service required by clients. However, there is a negative side to this, as "clients have a plethora of design consultancies to

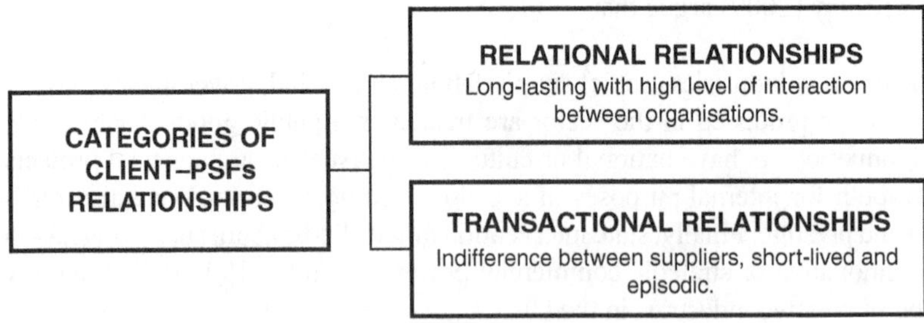

Figure 9.4 Categories of client–PSFs relationships.

choose from, … if they decide to offer their work to another studio, which could be smaller, equally creative, but more cost-effective, an account's withdrawal could be disastrous for a consultancy's existence" (Lalaounis, Wood, & Harrison, 2012, p. 268).

In general terms, the duration of the client relationship can be considered as the determinant criterion for categorising it as either relational or transactional, on the assumption that investments in these relationships increase over time, and the client relationships become more embedded in social relationships (Granovetter, 1985). If we were to provide a specific number for relationship durations, Uzzi and Lancaster (2003, 2004) have identified that "as short as two years have been used to mark the threshold for the transactional-relational transition" (Broschak, 2015). However, the categorisation of client relationships as relational or transactional is very dichotomous and perhaps not representative of the nuances in the nature of client–consultancy relationships. Instead, Laing and Lian (2005) determined a number of criteria that can be used to understand the nature of client relationships in more depth. Such criteria include the degree of trust in the relationship, the degree of relational closeness, and type of organisational policy. Consequently, based on these criteria, they identified five different 'ideal' types: (1) elementary relationships which are similar to transactional relationships, (2) interactive, (3) embedded, (4) partnering, and (5) integration relationships. Laing and Lian's (2005) key argument is that client relationships do not necessarily become relational as time passes, rather the category the client relationship belongs to is a strategic choice made by clients or jointly by PSFs and clients.

Effects of client relationships on PSFs

Through the service co-production process occurring during client–PSF relationships, PSFs are exposed and are receptive to influences from COs. Such influences often shape the structures and internal processes PSFs adopt and operate with. Broschak (2015) identified four main effects of client relationships on PSFs. First, PSFs tend *to match the expansion efforts of COs* to provide better quality of service, gain higher reputation and more referrals from existing clients, which can contribute to attracting new business. Second, PSFs tend to *adapt organisational structure and control systems* to disperse their own structure geographically by decentralising decision making powers to the local offices they open because they can respond better to local legal requirements, can maintain face-to-face interaction with clients, and can indicate a PSF's commitment to a long-term client relationship because it is a relationship-specific investment in physical assets (Broschak, 2015).

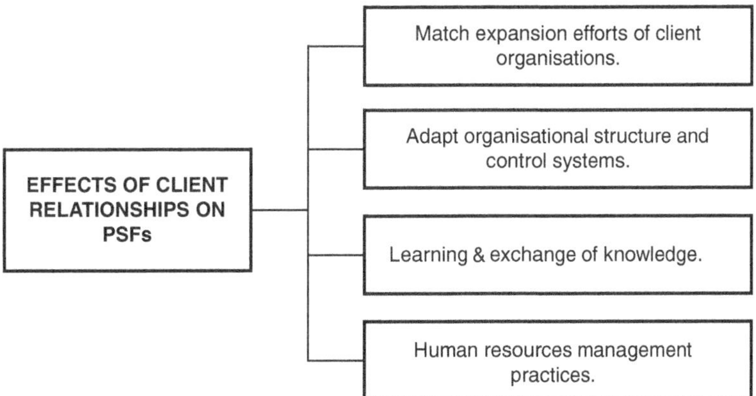

Figure 9.5 Effects of client relationships on PSFs.

Third, client relationships can influence PSFs through *learning and the exchange of knowledge*. Client relationships can be considered an important source of knowledge development for PSFs. For instance, as a result of working with a specific client, e.g., a pharmaceutical firm, the PSF can develop specialist knowledge about the pharmaceutics industry. Such knowledge can be integrated into the PSF's own knowledge and become part of its intellectual capital. Finally, scholars have identified that clients can influence *human resources management practices*, and in particular employee recruitment practices, skill development, promotion patterns (such as gender equality), and job security within PSFs in order for their needs to be better served (Beckman & Phillips, 2005; Grimshaw & Miozzo, 2006) (Figure 9.5).

Client relationships life cycle pattern

A very important question which requires a discussion at this point is concerned with the *life cycle pattern* that client relationships typically exhibit. Such life cycle pattern includes three stages and applies in the case of design consultancies too (Figure 9.6). Let us explore each stage in depth.

Client relationship formation

The first stage of the life cycle pattern is the *client relationship formation* stage. As previously said, the markets of PSFs are very idiosyncratic due to the asymmetry of power which characterises them. Although client relationships are more consequential for PSFs, and clients do have more power and incentive than the PSFs to form relationships, there is a lack of objective data that could be used to assess and compare the output or processes of PSFs. After all, every project, every account, and every client is different; hence, the outcome and procedures used by PSFs cannot be objectively benchmarked because they are very context-specific. This means that forming client relationships is rendered with uncertainty and selecting an exchange partner can be quite difficult (Broschak, 2015). Due to the lack of such objective criteria, COs need to rely on the reputation of the PSFs as a social signal of potential quality and attractiveness of PSFs as prospective partners. This means that reputation actually acts as a surrogate for quality and positive reputation will increase PSF's attractiveness.

Other criteria that client firms use to make decisions to form exchange relationships with a specific PSF include demographic characteristics such as size and scope of the PSF. A client firm might opt to form a relationship with a PSF which has the same geographical span of operations or has similar size and market orientation (transactional or relational) to a previous PSF the client firm had used, which reduces any uncertainty about the selection (Broschak & Niehans, 2006). In addition, *homophily*, i.e., dealing with firms that resemble one's organisation, can play a role in the formation of client–PSF relationships. Scholars such as Broschak and Niehans (2006) and Somaya, Williamson, and Lorinkova (2008) have also identified that managers in COs "prefer forming relationships with PSFs with whom they have had prior dealings or who employ professionals with whom they have personal relationships or know through other social settings" (Broschak, 2015, p. 312). However, this is also contingent on the task at hand; Richter and Niewiem (2009) identified that this is the case when client-specific or proprietary knowledge

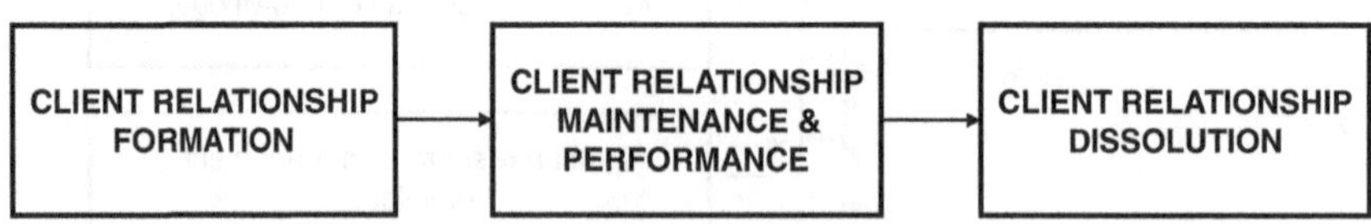

Figure 9.6 Client relationships life cycle pattern.

is involved, but not when projects required functional, industry-specific, or methodological knowledge. This means that a PSF developing in-depth client relationships might not bring additional work for the PSF because it might no longer be perceived as functional or industry specialist. Finally, it is important that PSFs "understand how potential clients see themselves relative to the profession's domain, and utilise this knowledge in presenting themselves to clients, [in order] to be more effective at signalling legitimacy and at securing new client relationships" (Broschak, 2015, p. 313).

Client relationship maintenance and performance

Once client relationships are formed, they need to be *maintained and reinforced* on a continuous basis. Such continuity of the relationships formed is a primary goal for all PSFs, including design consultancies, no matter whether they have a relational or transactional market orientation. There are several reasons that this is the case. Relationship continuity, (1) increases the level of trust between the exchange parties, (2) reduces the information asymmetries, (3) promotes the sharing of private information, (4) reduces uncertainty over the behaviour of both parties, (5) reduces the cost for monitoring the relationship, and (6) enables PSFs with relational client relationships to offer clients lower prices (Lancaster & Uzzi, 2012; Uzzi, 1999; Uzzi & Lancaster, 2003, 2004). Nevertheless, there is also a downside to PSFs, such as design consultancies, maintaining close relationships with clients. Managers in COs which have a long-term relationship with a PSF are more inclined to challenge or criticise the PSF's work, feel more confident to negotiate for lower prices, and pressure for politically correct recommendations from the (design) consultants (Ram, 1999). This adds stress on the client relationships, and clients end up behaving like 'partial employees' of the PSF in the co-production process (Mills & Morris, 1986), or consultants feel 'captured' by the clients (Broschak, 2015).

The above highlights the need for the development of *trust* between the exchange parties. Despite the fact that the power to make and break a relationship lies with the client firm, scholars often assign the responsibility for maintaining client relationships to PSFs, and trust is the recipe for doing so successfully. Trust allows PSFs to minimise conflict with client firms, fulfil client performance quality expectations, and increase client commitment to the relationship (Glückler, 2005; Labahn & Kohli, 1997). Maister (2003) highlights the need to market to existing clients as it is more likely to generate more business than marketing to new clients. "This is so because the ability to win the client's trust and confidence is a dominant influence in the sales process of professional services" (Maister, 2003, pp. 97–98).

Trust is also vital in design consultancy–client relationships because it allows clients to have creative input into the design work (co-production) not in an instructional but in an advisory manner. Unlike law and accounting services, which tend to adhere to rigid legal and accounting practices, design is more open to interpretation and subjectivity. This often makes clients more inclined to give their opinion about what the design solution should be like, or even instruct what the solution should be. Trust helps to mitigate this phenomenon because it helps clients recognise that design consultants are professionals who possess disciplinal knowledge which they lack. This can make them understand that they need to trust that design consultants will be able to advise on the best design solution for the problem in hand. In other words, similar to a manager in a client firm refraining from instructing a lawyer how to represent the CO, or from instructing an accountant how to keep the CO's management accounts, trust enables managers in client firms to let design professionals do their job, without dictating the solution, but rather co-constructing it with them.

A number of activities which help PSFs to minimise conflict with client firms and promote smooth working relationships have been proposed by many scholars. Bourland (1993) argued for a consistent communication flow between the exchange parties to ensure they know each other's business, while Bettencourt, Ostrom, Brown, & Roundtree (2002) proposed specifying roles during the service provision to decrease ambiguity, enhance clarity and cooperation. Other activities include making client-specific investments in infrastructure and training and building interdependence between the exchange partners (Manning, Lewin, & Schuerch, 2011), as well as PSFs using reassuring rhetoric that communicates high quality of service, expertise, and technical knowledge to client firms (Fincham, 1999; Sturdy, 1997).

Mills and Moshavi (1999) identified the *professional concern paradox* in client relationships; the need for PSFs to get close to client firms, yet remain detached from them. They argued that client role accountability is an important dimension of professional concern. However, Alvesson, Kärreman, Sturdy, and Handley (2009) emphasised that clients and their roles in exchange relationships are not monolithic. Broschak explains the idiosyncrasy of client relationships:

> Clients are diverse and roles are socially constructed, varying across firms, industries, and time, in part due to changing interactions with PSFs. Therefore, client roles are best viewed as negotiated in an ongoing manner over the course of a relationship rather than as a fixed structure common to all client relationships.
>
> (Broschak, 2015, p. 314)

Integrated design consultancy services evaluation framework

It is absolutely imperative that design consultancies assess the services they provide to their existing clients in order to monitor their performance, address any problems, and successfully maintain existing client relationships. In particular, design consultancies must carry out

> an assessment of the way [they] manage their design accounts, produce design work (and of what quality) and market their services to existing and potential clients, as part of their overall business development strategy, in order to maintain their existing clientele and develop their client base even further.
>
> (Lalaounis et al., 2012, pp. 268–269)

This responds to Cooper , Evans, and Williams' (2009) view that measuring and improving business performance is an issue which has still not been addressed by design consultancies. Many design consultancies are still ignoring questions about business development. Lalaounis et al. (2012) provided a conceptual framework for *services evaluation in integrated design consultancies* (those which provide a number of design services as a 'one-stop-shop' for clients), drawing from a single case study research. The framework is composed of three entities: (1) the *integrated design consultancy* (hereafter abbreviated to IDC), (2) the *CO*, and (3) the *design account* (hereafter abbreviated to DA). The latter is a notional entity, in its own right, which involves a team from the IDC and a team from the CO; hence "it is highly influenced by the activities of these two entities and requires their synergy" (Lalaounis et al., 2012, p. 271). It is important to note that adopting this framework to carry out the evaluation requires the participation of organisational members of both the IDC and CO, certainly those involved in the particular DA. Each of these entities is judged on its own set of criteria (see Figure 9.7), and each criterion includes its own factors outlined in Tables 9.1, 9.2, and 9.3.

In addition, there are two criteria which interconnect these entities and contribute to the success of the DA: (1) the *IDC–CO relationship* and (2) the *DA's future forecasts* (Table 9.4). The IDC–CO relationship has a profound effect on the DA. One could say this relationship *is* the account. The DA's future forecasts criterion relates to the forecasts on the CO's future business with the IDC. This is where both account managers from the IDC and staff from the CO forecast on the future

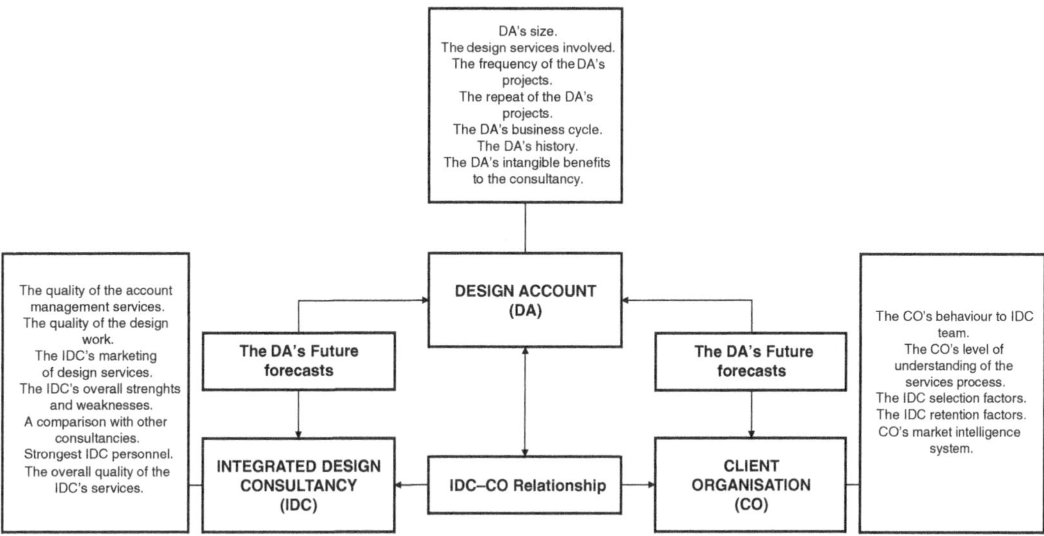

Figure 9.7 Integrated design consultancy services evaluation framework.

Table 9.1 The integrated design consultancy (IDC) criteria and factors.

Criteria	*Factors*
The quality of the account management services	Reliability
	Proactivity
	Easiness to work with the account manager
	The quality of response to CO's briefs
	Knowledge of the CO's markets and trends
	Strategic input to CO's campaigns
	Ability on concept development
	Quality of time planning and management.
	Attention to detail
	Flexibility
	Understanding of CO's organisation and procedures
	Problem-solving abilities
	Aptitude on handling budgets and production efficiently
	Overall professionalism
The quality of the design work	Originality
	Appropriateness to the CO's brand
	Meeting the brief's objectives
	Attention to detail
	Value for money
	Effectiveness
	Whether or not it can be considered risky and challenging
The IDC's marketing of its design services	The effectiveness of the IDC's own marketing efforts
The IDC's overall strengths and weaknesses	Overall strengths
	Overall weaknesses
	Clients' words to describe the IDC

(Continued)

Table 9.1 (Continued)

Criteria	*Factors*
A comparison with other design consultancies	Account management Strategic thinking Creativity and innovation Price and value for money
Strongest IDC personnel	Account management team Design team
The overall quality of the IDC's services	General assessment of the IDC and its services

Table 9.2 The client organisation (CO) criteria and factors.

Criteria	*Factors*
The CO's behaviour to IDC team	Responds to invoices according to contractual agreements Provides clear briefs Reliable and responsible Expects from the account management team to respond to briefs in realistic time Expects from the IDC to deliver pertinent level of innovation in realistic time Collaborative in an efficient and timely way Adventurous Understands and accepts the risks associated with innovation
The CO's level of understanding of the services process	The client's level of understanding of the process the IDC follows when providing its services Whether or not the IDC meets and/or exceeds client's expectations
The IDC selection factors	The initial pitch The IDC's knowledge and expertise The personal relationship (if pre-existing) between IDC staff and the CO contacts The IDC's creativity The possibility of integration of services The IDC's reputation The cost of the IDC's services
The IDC retention factors	The IDC's presentation abilities The IDC's knowledge and expertise The continuous personal relationship between IDC and the CO contacts The IDC's creativity The possibility of integration of services The effectiveness of the work provided The IDC's reputation The cost for the IDC's services
CO's market intelligence system	The way the CO stays informed on market trends Whether or not the CO wants the IDC to keep them up to date on market trends Whether or not the CO welcomes new ideas from the IDC

Table 9.3 The design account (DA) criteria and factors.

Criteria	*Factors*
The DA size	DA's revenue per year Revenue of individual projects per month Number of individual projects per month Duration of individual projects DA's cost to the IDC per month DA's profit per month
The design services (type of design work) involved	Type of design work involved in the DA The DA management process
The frequency of the DA's projects	Frequency of new briefs/new projects Whether or not IDC simultaneously works on multiple projects in the DA
The repeat of the DA's projects	Level of repetition of projects The way innovation is encouraged and ensured despite repetition of projects
The DA's business cycle (volume of work/month)	Fluctuation of the volume of work for the DA during the year
The DA's history	How the relationship started The way the IDC has managed to retain or increase the business with the CO over the time Type of design services before and at the time Past changes in the IDC team involved Changes on the size of the DA over time Effect of these changes on the IDC–CO relationship How the IDC has managed these changes, their effects, any other issues
The DA's intangible benefits to the IDC	Publicity of the DA Creative recognition (such as in creative media) Awards Networking opportunities IDC's intellectual property

Table 9.4 Connecting the entities.

Criteria	*Factors*
The IDC–CO relationship	Duration Values and characteristics Third parties involved in the DA (e.g. suppliers) Problems occurred in the past and how they were resolved
The DA's future forecasts	Number of projects (more or fewer projects) Size of future budgets Extra type of design services involved in the DA Potential changes on IDC, CO, and market levels

developments on the DA in question. This criterion makes connections between the IDC and the DA and between the DA and the CO and plays the dual role of re-enhancing the worthiness of the DA (Lalaounis et al., 2012). It is important to reiterate that the application of this services evaluation framework requires the participation of organisational members from both the IDC (agency) and the CO (principal) to pursue a mix of qualitative and quantitative research to provide an understanding of the current status of the DA and the effectiveness of the relational client relationship (we assume that the relationship is relational and not transactional because it is long-term and requires a high degree of information sharing to reduce any asymmetries).

Client relationship dissolution

Many research studies have started addressing the question about the reasons that client relationships end. It is important to note that the *end of a client relationship* does not necessarily imply that the relationship has failed. "The decision to terminate a client relationship may occur for reasons independent of the quality of PSF performance or any relationship dysfunction" (Broschak, 2015, p. 315). One reason for the dissolution of a client relationship is time. Levinthal and Fichman (1988) determined that the likelihood of client relationships dissolving initially rises with time because the preliminary honeymoon period at the start of the relationship (where goodwill, financial resources, and a sense of commitment which buffer the relationship from ending), gives way to normality, where resources are drawn down. Dissolution is more likely during this period until trust is developed and relationship-specific expertise is formed. Trust and expertise then act as powerful inertial forces (Levinthal & Fichman, 1988) which maintain the relationship and the status quo. Dissolution of the relationship might also occur when there is a misfit between the PSF's capabilities and the client's needs due to the latter's change of needs and the PSF's inability to serve these needs (Seabright, Levinthal, & Fichman, 1992).

Another reason for the dissolution of client relationships is the amount and frequency of attention PSFs give to their clients. Naturally the less attention clients receive the more likely the relationship will be dissolved. Such lack of attention to client's needs could be due to PSF's poor quality of service, but also might be attributed to the number of clients the PSF has in its portfolio as well as its size (Baker, Faulkner, & Fisher, 1998; Broschak, 2004; Heinz, Nelson, & Laumann, 2001). The small size of a PSF might have a knock-on effect on its ability to attend to a client's need. However, a growing size does not guarantee more attention, in fact it might too lead to less attention to client's needs because of the growing portfolio of clients that this might bring, as well as the fact that client relationships might become impersonal (Broschak, 2015). Mergers between PSFs is also a reason for the dissolution of client relationships because they might lead to an overlap between their pre-merger and post-merger clients' business. Interestingly, the most relational client relationships are the most vulnerable to dissolution due to mergers between PSFs (Rogan, 2014a).

The mobility of people in, and between, PSFs and client firms is another reason that client relationships might end. When managers at the client firm or members of the PSF (such as designers or project managers in the case of design consultancies) get promoted or exit their respective organisation, they take with them the relationship-specific tacit knowledge and expertise, as well as the personal relationship developed over time, reducing the level of relationship-specific investment, thus making dissolution of the client relationship more likely (Biong & Ulvnes, 2011; Broschak, 2004; Broschak & Block, 2014; Broschak & Niehans, 2006; Rogan, 2014b; Seabright et al., 1992). This means that PSFs need to ensure that such client-specific knowledge and expertise is disseminated within the organisation as possible, integrating it into the intellectual capital of the PSF. This is supported by Broschak (2015) who has suggested that "client relationships seem to be more resilient to the loss of executives and ... managers [from either or both sides] when there are multiple points of contact between the client and PSF" (Broschak, 2015, p. 317). The multiplexity of ties can take the form of multiple individuals assigned to the client relationship, multiple units of the PSF each maintaining connections with the client firm, knowledge sharing or client-specific routines which facilitate the dissemination of client relationship-specific knowledge, and expertise across both the PSF and the client firm (Broschak, 2015). In a study of advertising agencies, Broschak and Block (2014) determined that the exit of client firm executives has a greater effect on the dissolution of client relationships than the exit of staff members in the PSF. Broschak (2015) explains this:

> This is somewhat unexpected since it is a reasonable assumption to expect that the loss of key personnel from PSFs would be detrimental to their capabilities to serve client firms. However, the effect of the exit of PSF executives on client relationships is most pronounced in new relationships when fewer relationship-specific investments have been made and client relationships are sustained by the existence of trust and goodwill of the PSF's executives. As client relationships age, the loss of executives has little effect on the likelihood of client relationship dissolution.
>
> (Broschak, 2015, p. 317)

Design consultancies and forms of capital in the creative industries

In the previous section, we emphasised the importance of intellectual capital developed during the service provision, which forms part of the client-specific expertise and knowledge. It is important at this stage to explore the different forms of capital in the field of the creative industries, drawing from the work of French philosopher, Pierre Bourdieu. It is important because "an examination of the interrelationship between capital's various guises offers a means of transcending the culture/commerce dichotomy within which this sector [such as the design sector] is usually discussed" (Townley, 2015, p. 187). After all, as already argued, design is all about the nexus of art and commerce, in order to frame problems and provide the necessary solutions to them, and design management aims to organise and manage for this to be achieved.

Pierre Bourdieu (1930–2002), French sociologist, anthropologist, and philosopher.

Forms of capital

According to Bourdieu (1998), the social world is a 'space' whose dimensions are structured by 'principles of differentiation or distribution'. "Within this space, agents occupy structured positions according to how much capital they hold: social space is structured by the unequal distribution of capital in both its objective and symbolic forms" (Townley, 2015, p. 187). Bourdieu views capital as a social relation; however, he finds mere economic capital insufficient for his analysis. He argues that in order to understand power and domination in society, we need to go beyond a simple understanding of possession of material resources through the means of production. In his words, "it is impossible to account for the structure and functioning of the social world unless one introduces capital in all of its forms and not solely on the one form recognised by economic theory" (Bourdieu, 1986, p. 242). Therefore, social relations and relations of cultural production are as important as economic relations.

Bourdieu (1986) argues that there are three guises of capital: (1) economic, (2) social, and (3) cultural. *Economic capital* includes assets and property rights and can be immediately converted into money. *Social capital* is concerned with the possession of durable networks of relationships with different people, which is characterised by mutual acquaintance and recognition (Bourdieu, 1986). Social capital includes social obligations which derive from these relationships and is dependent "on the size of the network connections [a person can effectively mobilise] and on the volume of capital (economic, cultural, or symbolic) possessed in his own right by each of those to whom he is connected" (Bourdieu, 1986, p. 49). *Cultural capital* can exist in three states. First, the 'embodied state' takes the form of behaviour and forms of being (dispositions), developed through socialisation of family and peers, as well as the form of 'self-improvement' achieved through mastery of knowledge and cultivating habits and tastes of cultural appreciation and understanding. Second, the 'objectified state' involves the possession of valued cultural objects (such as a collection of paintings); and third, the 'institutionalised state' includes acquiring education, knowledge, and qualifications, such as academic degrees (Townley, 2015). *Time* is an important dimension in Bourdieu's understanding and use of capital. He argues that capital is transferred through time in a material, objectified form, or in an embodied form. The latter is achieved through a person immersing himself/herself in a field. Embodied capital is acquired through time and energy which allow individuals to profit from their investment. Immersing in a field and investing time and energy grant the individual *legitimacy* (Townley, 2015).

Distinct and discrete fields such as scientific, political, or literary fields have their own specific forms of capital – their own *symbolic capital*. Economic, cultural, and social capital can also act as symbolic capital depending on the field (Bourdieu, 2000). Symbolic capital acts as a field's currency, it is "capital with cognitive base" (Bourdieu, 1998, p. 85); it is all about what counts and what is at stake in a specific field. Symbolic capital is like a form of energy, driving the development of a field over time. According to Townley, "the valorisation of symbolic capital depends on the structure of the field – that is, its composition, the relations within it, and its relative position vis-à-vis other fields" (2015, p. 190) (Figure 9.8).

According to Bourdieu (1984), fields are defined by three fundamental dimensions of capital: (1) its volume or amount, (2) its structure or composition, and (3) the change which occurs in the first two dimensions over time. The *volume or amount* of capital includes the set of usable resources and powers, while the *structure or composition* is about the relative weight of capital. Fields represent the environment within which the conversation and transformation of different forms of capital occurs. "The efficacy of capital … depends on the field in which it operates … [and] struggles take place over the relationship among the various forms of capital distinctive to the field" (Townley, 2015, p. 191). As Bourdieu explains "the relative value of the different species of capital … is continually being brought into question, reassessed, through struggles aimed at inflating or deflating the value of one or the other type of capital" (1987, p. 10).

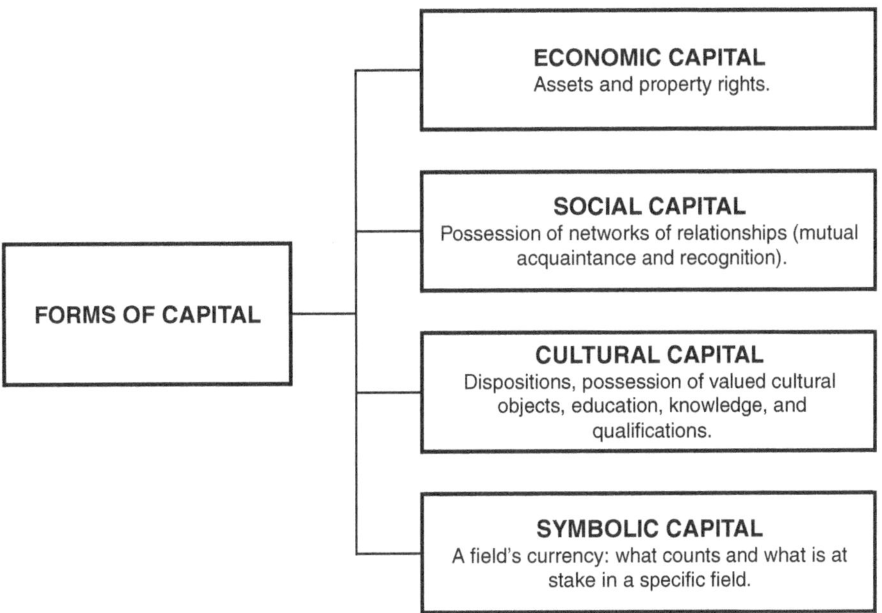

Figure 9.8 Forms of capital.

Nevertheless, generally speaking, fields tend to be organised along two poles, economic and cultural capital, leading to distinctions such as 'hard' and 'soft' sciences in academia, and 'elitist' and 'populist' culture (Townley, 2015).

Forms of capital in the creative industries

The aforementioned dichotomy between economic and cultural capital has been the basis for extensive debate regarding the appropriateness of the term 'cultural and creative industries' (CCI). There has been some criticism about the alignment of 'cultural' with 'industry', "the two supposed antithetical provinces of creativity and commerce representing the coupling of the sacred with the profane" (Townley, 2015, p. 196). Critics have questioned the emphasis on the 'economic role' and 'impact' of the CCI, as well as the wider role of the creative economy (as discussed in Chapter 1). However, regardless of the differences of the cultural market to the free market, there is still an economic logic. "Cultural appreciation is far from disinterested. Taste conforms to a market system with its own logic and own specific form of capital" (Beasley-Murray, 2000, p. 106). Bourdieu (1980) argues that symbolic, cultural capital can act as a form of economic or political capital in the market of symbolic goods, it is a sort of credit which can bring economic profit under certain conditions. The CCI are not different to any other industry in the sense that they are similarly implicated in structured inequalities of power (Bourdieu, 1984). The CCI "produce and regulate different forms of symbolic capital and police its distribution" (Townley, 2015, p. 197).

The CCI can be characterised as the amalgamation of four different but interrelated forms of capital: (1) intellectual, (2) cultural, (3) social, and (4) economic. Bourdieu's (1988) *Homo Academicus* makes a distinction between academic capital, the position within formal university hierarchies, and *intellectual capital* which explores "the creation and generation of ideas, their recognition, understanding, protection and dissemination" (Townley, 2015, p. 198). Management literature tends to use the term 'intellectual capital' as an intangible value or human capital. In the case of CCI, the term represents the idea that is behind the 'journey' from capital to intellectual property (Townley, 2015). Intellectual capital becomes transformed into intellectual property by its integration within a production process. A client relationship's (an account's) contribution to intellectual capital is recognised as an important criterion in the aforementioned design consultancy services evaluation framework (Lalaounis et al., 2012). Design consultancies must recognise and protect the value of their work, discussing intellectual property rights ownership with their clients.

As already explained, *social capital* involves the possession of networks of relationships. In the case of the CCI in particular, it includes "access to networks that transmit ideas, employment, project opportunities and sustain activity" (Townley, 2015, p. 198). Social networks are extremely important for organisations in the CCI because they facilitate recruitment and sustain their project work. The Internet and social media allow the creation of digital social networks which have been useful for crowdsourcing ideas, crowdfunding projects, and developing digital word of mouth. The physical and digital infrastructure that enable a wider engagement of people with the CCI is an important element of building social networks and social capital (Townley, 2015).

Cultural capital, as previously explored, relates to the knowledge of a cultural arena and an understanding and recognition of its codes. The acquisition of cultural capital and the participation in cultural forms is influenced by socio-demographics and income. Drawing from the *BBC's 2011 Great British Class Survey*, the largest survey of social class ever conducted in the UK, Savage, Devine, Cunningham, Taylor, Li, Hjellbrekke, Le Roux, Friedman, and Miles (2013) used questions on social, cultural, and economic capital to determine a person's social class, leading to a new seven-class model which can replace its predecessor, the 'Nuffield class schema', developed in the 1970s, which was codified in the UK's National Statistics Socio-Economic Classification (NS-SEC). The questions determining one's cultural capital aimed to understand the person's interests and hobbies. This new model highlights the connections between cultural, social, and economic capital. As Townley (2015) explains:

> Cultural capital underpins distinctions between social groups according to taste and consumption patterns and 'high-brow' and 'low-brow' art forms, and is seen being played out in attempts to widen a canon or introduce works that might be more widely seen or read. Also important is the role of the cultural intermediary [such as designers] in translating ideas and influencing their perception, as seen, for example in how museums function in their selection and presentation of material for exhibition, the role and range of digital sites that support cultural intermediation, and in how authority positions and the nature of evaluative discourse become established. The valorisation of this capital is reflected in the consecration practices of awards and prizes and the conferring of symbolic capital.
>
> (Townley, 2015, p. 200)

Such distinctions between 'high-brow' and 'low-brow' art forms refer back to the dichotomy between 'elitist' and 'populist' culture. Such distinctions are not only evident in CCI, but can be found in other professional services firms too. For example, by studying small accounting firms, Stringfellow, Shaw, and Maclean (2013) identified a distinction between two forms of individual business owners, (1) the 'traditional', who adheres to established norms of the professional field, and (2) the 'apostate', who renounces these established norms. The former is associated with 'elitist' accounting practices which adhere to higher professional values, whereas the latter with commercially led accounting practices which wish to break such norms. Back to the case of the CCI, Anheier, Gerhards, and Romo (1995) who studied the field of literature, discussed the distinction between the field of 'restricted cultural production' and the field of 'large-scale cultural production'. In the former, writers are seen as artists, in the latter, they are seen as commercial producers. They explained the differences between the two segments:

> Both fields differ to the extent to which economic and non-economic capital forms become dominant. The field of restricted production is relatively autonomous from market considerations. Economic success is secondary to symbolic value, and writers compete for cultural capital in the form of recognition, reputation, and legitimacy rather than for monetary rewards. In contrast, the field of large-scale cultural production is characterised by the predominance of economic considerations and market success. In the large-scale case, writers compete as producers in a market to seek financial returns first and foremost.
>
> (Anheier et al., 1995, p. 863)

The question that certainly arises after reading the above quote, is how such distinctions can be transferred in the case of the design profession. As already emphasised in Chapter 6, designers are 'practical artists' (Gotsi, Andriopoulos, Lewis, & Ingram, 2010) or 'commercial artists', a meta-identity which combines artistic ability with commercial acumen. Thus, designers might be considered as an intermediate form between the restricted and large-scale cultural production segments. Indeed, Bourdieu (1985) acknowledges that "cultural fields may contain a variety of intermediate forms between art as a commercial commodity and as a symbolic and cultural good" (Anheier et al., 1995, pp. 864–865). In Chapter 5, we discussed how an idea is considered creative when it is novel *and* appropriate; hence, a solution brought forward by a designer needs to be both artistically original *and* commercially viable. Therefore, design can be considered an intermediate form that combines the two aforementioned segments. However, Anheier et al. (1995) make it clear that

> for these intermediate positions, commercial success and critical acclaim do not necessarily coincide. Social capital, for example, may be a more important means of status competition in high-culture genres than in mass culture; moreover, some writers may regard membership in professional organisations and circles as inopportune, perhaps even contrary to their self-understanding as artists, while others see it as an important ingredient for the accumulation of the economic, cultural, and social capital needed for status competitions.
>
> (Anheier et al., 1995, p. 865)

One could argue that even in the intermediate form of the design profession, there could be subtle distinctions between design consultancies which focus on commercial success and those which concentrate on critical acclaim, or perhaps between design consultancies which adhere to professional norms and those which renounce them, similar to Stringfellow et al.'s (2013) work on accounting firms, although the design profession is less formally organised in terms of professional codes. However, such emphasis on either side can prove problematic. For a design consultancy to be truly successful, it must achieve both. This takes us back to our discussion in Chapter 6, and in particular the 'strategic intent' paradox (Andriopoulos & Lewis, 2009), where organisations must ensure they work on projects which generate profit *and* on breakthrough projects which enhance the organisation's creative reputation. In general terms, we have argued that the creative output must be paradoxical (novel *and* appropriate). As we previously explored, ambidexterity is the way to embrace this paradox by pursuing both exploitation *and* exploration, and hence commercial success and critical acclaim, simultaneously. Perhaps, viewing design consultancies as intermediate forms between these two segments goes in line with the need for ambidexterity.

Generally speaking, each form of capital in the CCI requires strategies and policies which enable its creation, reproduction, and accumulation. Admittedly, many people involved in the CCI emphasise their symbolic capital, i.e., the recognition and prestige deriving "from their symbolic cultural capital, their relative standing, and the relative standing of the symbolic cultural capital they profess" (Townley, 2015, p. 200). Symbolic capital in the CCI is created through the functioning, and interrelationship, of intellectual, social, cultural, and economic capital. Therefore, organisations in the CCI, such as design consultancies, trade their capitals, and in particular their symbolic capital, for other forms of capital, on a continuous basis, in order to survive and flourish as businesses (Townley, 2015).

Managing as designing: Design consultancies and management practice

Previously in the chapter, we explored how client relationships influence PSFs such as design consultancies, in terms of their growth and development, structure and control systems, learning and exchange of knowledge practices (contribution to intellectual capital), and human resources management policies. It is important at this stage to explore how such influence is, in fact, reciprocal. This means that COs are also influenced by client relationships and the PSFs they engage with. In the case of design consultancies in particular, the structures and processes of design consultancies can influence COs. As we explored in Chapter 1, a side of design management which is currently evolving, relates to the interconnectedness among the activities of designing, managing, and organising, which can lead to the transferability of design practices and methods to managerial problems (Cooper & Junginger, 2011). In the same chapter, we also talked about the concept of 'knowledge spillovers', which refers to the cases where ideas and technologies developed by firms in the creative industries, such as open models of collaboration, spread to COs which engage with them (Chapain, Cooke, De Propris, MacNeill, & Mateos-Garcia, 2010).

Guggenheim Museum in Bilbao, Spain, designed by Frank O. Gehry Architects.

The Peter B. Lewis Building of the Weatherhead School of Management, at Case Western Reserve University, Cleveland, USA, designed by Frank O. Gehry Architects.

There are indeed many lessons organisations of any kind can learn from designers and design consultancies. Boland, Collopy, Lyytinen, and Yoo (2008), drawing from their personal encounters with the architect Frank O. Gehry, who has designed the *Guggenheim Museum* building in Bilbao, Spain, and the *Peter B. Lewis Building* of the *Weatherhead School of Management*, at *Case Western Reserve University*, Cleveland, USA, explored "the importance of design as a mode of cognition and as an organisational practice" (Boland et al., 2008, p. 10). Exploring the way Gehry and his firm work can provide us with important lessons for design management, and management in general.

Boland et al. (2008) explained their drive to pursue this research study:

> Animating our interest in bringing together design and management is dissatisfaction with the way that design, as a *noun*, seems to overshadow design as a *verb* in the popular press, as well as in the practice of modern management. This results in an emphasis on design as a completed and whole *thing*, instead of design as a becoming and unfolding process. In the popular press, it means that design is treated as referring to style or fashion. In management discourse, it means that design is treated as referring to a finished product, or an established way of doing things in an organisation. Either way, the power of design as a verb – as a way of defining problems and projects, and of acting responsibly to seek betterment in the world – is lost.
>
> (Boland et al., 2008, p. 11)

Boland et al. (2008) argue that design is central to the process of managing. Managers need to capitalise on the value of design by engaging actively in the design and redesign of products, services, and experiences as a means to organisational survival and success. Nobel Laureate Herbert Simon emphasised the central role of designing in management and wrote about what is now called a 'design attitude' for managers. He argues for management education based on the understanding of manager's role as designer. According to Simon (1996), management is as a profession "whose training should be like that in the applied sciences … because the manager's professional responsibility is not to discover laws of the universe, but to act responsibly in the world to transform existing situations into more preferred ones"

(Boland et al., 2008, pp. 11–12). Similar to engineers and architects, and unlike natural scientists, the manager gives form and shapes organisations (which are social structures within society) and economic processes to create value (Boland et al., 2008). As he explains, "engineering, medicine, business, architecture, and painting are concerned not with the necessary but with the contingent – not how things are but how they might be – in short, with design" (Simon, 1996, p. xii).

Simon (1960) also argued that management is all about decision making which involves three essential intertwined aspects: (1) intelligence (research), (2) design, and (3) choice (models); all need to be attended to by managers. Interestingly, institutionalised study of management decision making reduced these three aspects to one, that of choice. Nowadays, management decision making is seen as making a choice from a number of alternatives which are presented to managers. This is extremely different to Simon's (1960) view that management decision is

> a robust and recursive process of collecting and interpreting evidence, designing possible courses of action, and testing multiple ideas … In keeping with the overly non-based uses of design, organisation leaders today are mere responders to situations presented to them, as opposed to active makers of a future worthy of us as human beings.
>
> (Boland et al., 2008, p. 12)

This means that design in its verbal form has been neglected by management scholars and education, despite the fact that it is a critical managerial skill. Management practice and education needs to nurture a *design attitude* which is vital for innovation. The term signifies the "expectation that each project is a new opportunity to create something remarkable, and to do it in way that has never been done before" (Boland et al., 2008, p. 13). Managers with a design attitude respect the conditions of a new project situation, including the beliefs, expectations, practices, and policies, but they foresee that these conditions could be other than they are and seek to change them for the better (Boland et al., 2008). This means that the organisation needs to employ members and work with partners, who share the design urge to question and search for new methods and ways of organising. Such an attitude helps the organisation refrain from typical organisational goals, e.g., growth by a certain percentage point per year, because these lead to stereotypical behaviours and stifle innovation and creative problem solving.

Besides the notion of design attitude, another important characteristic of Gehry's way of working is his awareness of his own vocabulary. '*Design vocabulary*' is about one's own language and how this affects design. It is fundamental that managers are aware of their own vocabulary including their own practices, routines, images, and non-verbal elements (Boland et al., 2008). This allows a level of reflexivity we rarely see in management practice. An awareness of their own vocabulary can make managers understand how this might or might not fit a situation at hand. A misfit might urge them to develop new vocabularies, providing new possibilities for making meaning and for making lives meaningful (Boland et al., 2008). Such reflexive practices might create opportunities for self-criticism, a characteristic seldom found in managers, and for a more thorough understanding of their motivations and consequences of their actions (Boland et al., 2008).

Part of management vocabulary is the word '*functional*' which means that something can be used; it works. This interpretation of the word, however, does not make connections with the emotional, or whether this functional artefact is human-centred. According to Gehry, "functional … has broader meaning … It means achieving a building that does all the things we want from our buildings" (Gehry, 2004, p. 34). A lack of functionality in organisations today contributes to many of the problems in the corporate world.

> Functionality begins with the desire to achieve efficiency and effectiveness in a traditional sense, and expands to include an enlarging circle of concern for emotions, customer experiences, ethical behaviour, environment, cultural norms, and aesthetic appeal … Functionality … [is] taken as a betterment of the human condition.
>
> (Boland et al., 2008, p. 23)

Another interesting element of the work process of Gehry's firm is its extensive use of multiple models in the design process, including *sketches and physical raw models*, acting as tools of thought and creating an emotional involvement for everyone participating in the process. This, of course, takes us back to the tools and principles of design thinking, explored in Chapter 3, including visualisation and prototyping to achieve empathy and using sketching and modelling as a means of 'thinking with your hands' (Brown, 2009; Collopy, 2004). Design thinking goes against institutionalised management theory which teaches managers to follow 'best practices' and refrain from trying to 're-invent the wheel'. This has made managers settling for solutions that are merely good enough, albeit not truly 'functional', depriving the corporate world from opportunities to invent new solutions to problems of the contemporary society (Boland et al., 2008). This does not mean that managers need to abandon their world of concepts and abstractions and replace them with sketches and physical models. In fact, they should engage in both worlds, combine concepts and abstractions, with sketches and physical models. This goes in line with Kant's argument that when the two worlds of concepts and images merge, we can achieve visualised thought, by having access to the real basis of nature (Boland et al., 2008).

Another characteristic of Gehry and his design practice is the need to *refrain from falling in love with an idea*. When we come up with an idea that we think is a good idea, we tend to become committed to it, and try to perfect it. This brings us back to the notion of cognitive biases in decision making, and in particular the 'hypothesis-confirmation' bias, where we look for data that confirms our idea, while we avoid or ignore data that disconfirms it. Gehry and his associates avoid falling in love with an

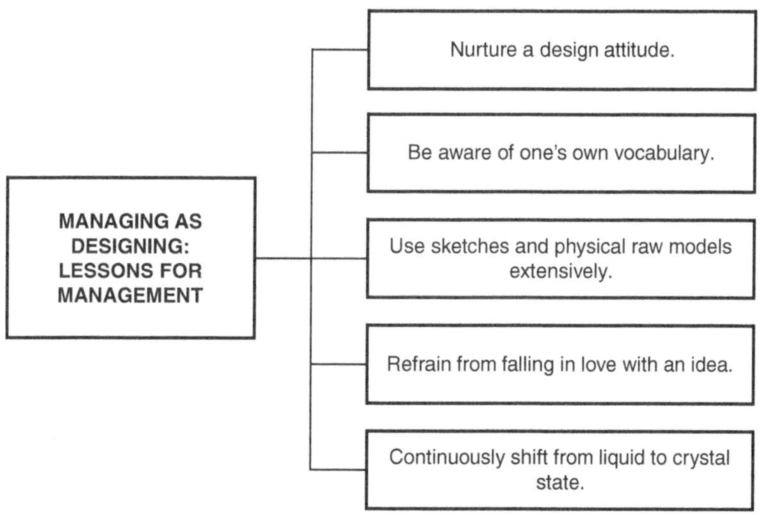

Figure 9.9 Managing as designing: Lessons for management.

idea; instead, they treat every idea as a step and not as the final destination. This way, they remember they need to keep searching for other approaches (Boland et al., 2008). "This paradoxical response to appealing ideas (avoiding an attachment to them) is mirrored by Gehry's response to the unappealing reality of constraints (embracing them)" (Boland et al., 2008, p. 21). Unlike typical management education and practice which view constraints as limiting, we should view constraints as opportunities. Constraints make a problem unique and worthy of our best effort. By embracing constraints, we are able to resist the temptation to fall in love with an idea too quickly, because only a truly great idea can 'solve' a strong set of constraints (Boland et al., 2008).

Finally, Boland et al.'s (2008) study demonstrates that organisational design is never complete. In fact, it is a human enactment that *shifts between liquid and crystal state* by applying doubt, asking questions and engaging in action continuously (Figure 9.9). They explain their thoughts on organisational design

> Like software design, organisational design is recursive in nature. Recursive design emphasises the criticality of meta-design (i.e. sustained flexibility in the functionality achieved by the design) as a good design practice. Meta-design helps to keep the design continuous and open, moving between liquid and crystal states … All organisational designs should be able to continue to be redesigned, and to change their form over time. That is, the elements and configurations set in place by managerial design should keep the organisation in dynamic motion … If meta-design is not achieved, an organisation is dead and lacks the capability to inspire and move us.
>
> (Boland et al., 2008, p. 24)

Chapter review questions

The following questions can help you reflect on the material we have covered in this chapter:

1 Provide definitions of professions and PSFs and explore the differences between professions and occupations.
2 Discuss the characteristics of information asymmetry, uncertainty, and power and knowledge asymmetry found in PSFs.
3 Explore the effects of client relationships on PSFs.
4 Critically explain the stages of the client relationships lifecycle pattern and how these can be successfully managed.
5 Discuss the nature of intellectual, cultural, social, and economic capital produced and processed by organisations in the CCI, drawing from the work of Pierre Bourdieu.
6 What are the lessons, managers can learn from design firms?

Recommended reading

1 Townley, B. (2015). Exploring different forms of capitals: Researching capitals in the field of cultural and creative industries. In A. Tatli, M. Ozbilgin, & M. Karatas-Ozkan (Eds.), *Pierre Bourdieu, organization, and management* (Vol. 34). London: Routledge.
2 Broschak, J. P. (2015). Client relationships in professional service firms. In L. Empson, R. Hinings, D. Muzio, & J. Broschak (Eds.), *The Oxford handbook of professional service firms*. Oxford, UK: Oxford University Press.

Reflective thoughts

Conceptualising design consultancies as PSFs: A nuanced approach

Dr. Lindsay Stringfellow
Senior Lecturer in Marketing and Organisation Studies
University of Exeter Business School, Exeter, UK

PSFs perform vital functions within modern society, and as a result of ongoing processes such as globalisation, the demand for the services of PSFs is higher than ever. It is commonly said that PSFs are 'different' from other types of organisations, and yet it is relatively rare that the core characteristics of such firms are studied and appreciated. This may be, in part, due to the fact that arriving at a theory of the PSF is problematic. PSFs differ hugely in terms of the services they deliver, they adopt different organisational structures, and they exhibit varied cultural and managerial styles. The organisation and regulation of PSFs will differ both across industries, and within industries where, for example, a small practice will have little in common with the activities performed by a large firm. And yet, as this chapter has outlined, we can tease out some core defining features that enable us to better understand the category and, furthermore, to conceptualise the specific nature of PSFs within the context of design consultancies.

Thinking firstly about knowledge, within professions such as accounting, law, and medicine, there exists a codified, fairly uniform set of rules and procedures to which professionals must adhere. Accounting firms, for instance, must follow International Financial Reporting Standards to ensure that globally, accountants produce a standardised, consistent, and comparable presentation of the financial performance of an entity. Cultural capital, you might say, is highly institutionalised, with professional bodies engaging in various types of institutional work to secure legitimacy for the profession, including setting examinations, controlling entry into the profession, and subsequently monitoring members and ensuring they engage in continuing professional development.

Design consultancies, by contrast, we might see as fitting into the 'Neo-PSF' category, characterised by lower levels of regulation, ideology, and professionalisation of the workforce. Cultural capital is, of course, institutionalised through formal qualifications, but design educators may have quite different notions of design culture, as a result of their particular trajectory in the field. Educators play an important role in socialising designers of the future in rituals, stylistic preferences, and language codes that influence the disposition, or habitus, of design graduates. Educational institutions are but one element of the field of production of design, which is comprised of relations between many different actors supporting the symbolic production of the work, in other words, the 'value' of the work. Internal to the field, agents engage in power struggles to determine design 'taste', and quality, therefore, is a relative term determined by where a designer or design consultancy fits within a complex and dynamic network of interests that makes up the field. As this chapter has noted, in fields orientated by cultural production, commercial success is often at odds with achieving critical acclaim, industry awards, and the admiration of your peers.

(Continued)

(Continued)

This insight has further implications for understanding professionals and the nature of client relationships within the design field, when we think about key concepts such as information and knowledge asymmetry and uncertainty. Clients of design consultancies, as with other professions, may lack the technical knowledge to evaluate the effort and outcomes accomplished by professional agents (Sharma, 1997). Yet clients, naturally, have their own habitus, orientating their own aesthetic sensibilities as a result of their upbringing, education, and position in the class structure that may help, or hinder, their own appreciation of the designer's efforts and output. This may make the social capital notion of homophily, the principle that 'birds of a feather flock together' even more important within the client–professional relationship in design consultancies. While the client might not comprehend the technical aspects of the design process, some kind of shared habitus may help in the consultation process and the co-creation of the desired outcome. It may also emphasise the need for design professionals to form stronger ties with their clients by sharing more content, for instance, social and friendship elements, which is often avoided for ethical reasons in traditional professions such as accounting, law, and medicine.

Elements of a shared disposition between the professional and client, and the involvement of the client in the design process should help the client to appreciate the outcome's aesthetic worth. There are a few further aspects to note about the outcome: it is tangible, an artefact whose value (culturally, symbolically, and economically) may change over time as a result of the design field being in constant flux; or more subjectively, its value may change as the clients themselves reflect on the practical consequences of living with the design; the outcome is ultimately, from a Bourdieusian perspective, the transfer of economic capital in exchange for objectified cultural capital, the value of which is, ultimately, symbolic and socially determined. These aspects are somewhat unique to the cultural-aesthetic professions such as architecture and design, as opposed to professions such as accounting and law.

The general characteristics of PSFs, professionals, and their relationships with their clients, and the idiosyncrasies of design consultancies outlined in this chapter, form an important insight into the practice and performance of professional entities. It may be, as Bucher and Strauss (1961) proposed, that professions are better understood from a process perspective, as 'segments in movement' rather as a single entity with a shared identity, values, and interests. In this perspective, all professions are fluid assemblages of professional identity, loosely amalgamated into a profession but in reality stratified and segmented on many dimensions such as occupational domain, autonomy, income, prestige, networks, and practices. This alternative view of the professions certainly suggests that we should interrogate and question the applicability of PSF criteria to different organisations and professional domains, and remain mindful of the tensions, struggles, and intra-industry variations that might exist.

References

Bucher, R., & Strauss, A. (1961). Professions in process. *American Journal of Sociology, 66*(4), 325–334.

Sharma, A. (1997). Professional as agent: Knowledge asymmetry in agency exchange. *Academy of Management Review, 22*(3), 758–798.

References

Abbott, A. (1988). *The system of professions: An essay on the division of expert labour*. Chicago: University of Chicago Press.

Alvesson, M., Kärreman, D., Sturdy, A., & Handley, K. (2009). Unpacking the client(s): Constructions, positions and client–consultant dynamics. *Scandinavian Journal of Management, 25*(3), 253–263.

Andriopoulos, C., & Lewis, M. W. (2009). Exploitation–exploration tensions and organisational ambidexterity: Managing paradoxes of innovation. *Organisation Science, 20*(4), 696–717.

Anheier, H. K., Gerhards, J., & Romo, F. P. (1995). Forms of capital and social structure in cultural fields: Examining Bourdieu's social topography. *American Journal of Sociology, 100*(4), 859–903.

Bagdoniene, L., & Jakstaite, R. (2009). Trust as basis for development of relationships between professional service providers and their clients. *Economics and Management, 14*, 360–366.

Baker, W. E. (1990). Market networks and corporate behaviour. *American Journal of Sociology, 96*(3), 589–625.

Baker, W. E., Faulkner, R. R., & Fisher, G. A. (1998). Hazards of the market: The continuity and dissolution of inter-organizational market relationships. *American Sociological Review, 63*(2) 147–177.

Beasley-Murray, J. (2000). Value and capital in Bourdieu and Marx. In N. Brown, & I. Szeman (Eds.), *Pierre Bourdieu: Fieldwork in culture* (pp. 100–122). Lanham, MD: Rowman & Littlefield.

Beckman, C. M., & Phillips, D. J. (2005). Interorganizational determinants of promotion: Client leadership and the attainment of women attorneys. *American Sociological Review, 70*(4), 678–701.

Bettencourt, L. A., Ostrom, A. L., Brown, S. W., & Roundtree, R. I. (2002). Client co-production in knowledge-intensive business services. *California Management Review, 44*(4), 100–128.

Biong, H., & Ulvnes, A. M. (2011). If the supplier's human capital walks away, where would the customer go? *Journal of Business-to-Business Marketing, 18*(3), 223–252.

Boland, R. J., Jr., Collopy, F., Lyytinen, K., & Yoo, Y. (2008). Managing as designing: Lessons for organization leaders from the design practice of Frank O. Gehry. *Design Issues, 24*(1), 10–25.

Bourdieu, P. (1980). The production of belief: Contribution to an economy of symbolic goods. *Media, Culture & Society, 2*(3), 261–293.

Bourdieu, P. (1984). *Distinction*. London: Routledge and Kegan Paul.

Bourdieu, P. (1985). The social space and the genesis of groups. *Theory and Society, 14*(6), 723–744.

Bourdieu, P. (1986). The forms of capital. In J. Richardson (Ed.), *Handbook of theory and research for the sociology of education* (pp. 241–258). New York: Greenwood Press.

Bourdieu, P. (1987). What makes a social class? On the theoretical and practical existence of groups. *Berkeley Journal of Sociology, 32*, 1–17.

Bourdieu, P. (1988). *Homo academicus*. Cambridge, UK: Polity Press.

Bourdieu, P. (1998). *Practical person*. Cambridge, UK: Polity Press.

Bourdieu, P. (2000). *Pascalian meditations*. Cambridge, UK: Polity Press.

Bourland, P. G. (1993). The nature of conflict in firm–client relations: A content analysis of public relations journal 1980–89. *Public Relations Review, 19*(4), 385–398.

Bowen, D. E., & Jones, G. R. (1986). Transaction cost analysis of service organization–customer exchange. *Academy of Management Review, 11*(2), 428–441.

Broschak, J. (2004). Will they miss you when you're gone? The effect of managers' career mobility on the dissolution of market ties. *Administrative Science Quarterly, 49*, 608–640.

Broschak, J. P. (2015). Client relationships in professional service firms. In L. Empson, R. Hinings, D. Muzio, & J. Broschak (Eds.), *The Oxford handbook of professional service firms*. Oxford, UK: Oxford University Press.

Broschak, J. P., & Block, E. S. (2014). With or without you: When does managerial exit matter for the dissolution of dyadic market ties? *Academy of Management Journal, 57*(3), 743–765.

Broschak, J. P., & Niehans, K. M. (2006). Social structure, employee mobility, and the circulation of client ties. *Research in the Sociology of Organizations, 24*, 369–401.

Brown, T. (2009). *Change by design: How design thinking transforms organisations and inspires innovation*. New York: HarperCollins.

Chapain, C., Cooke, P., De Propris, L., MacNeill, S., & Mateos-Garcia, J. (2010). *Creative clusters and innovation: Putting creativity on the map*. London: NESTA.

Collopy, F. (2004). 'I think with my hands': On balancing the analytical and intuitive in designing. In R. Boland, & F. Collopy (Eds.), *Managing as designing* (pp. 19–35). Palo Alto, CA: Stanford University Press.

Cooper, R., & Junginger, S. (2011). General introduction: Design management – A reflection. In R. Cooper, S. Junginger, & T. Lockwood (Eds.), *The handbook of design management*. Oxford, UK: Berg.

Cooper, R., Evans, M., & Williams, A. J. (2009). *Design 2020: Design industry futures* (pp. 1–48). Lancaster, UK: Lancaster University and University of Salford.

Fincham, R. (1999). The consultant–client relationship: Critical perspectives on the management of organizational change. *Journal of Management Studies, 36*(3), 335–351.

Freidson, E. (1988). *Professional powers: A study of the institutionalization of formal knowledge*. Chicago: University of Chicago Press.

Gehry, F. O. (2004). Reflections on designing and architectural practice. In R. Boland, & F. Collopy (Ed.), *Managing as designing* (pp. 19–35). Palo Alto, CA: Stanford University Press.

Glückler, J. (2005). Making embeddedness work: Social practice institutions in foreign consulting markets. *Environment and Planning A, 37*(10), 1727–1750.

Gotsi, M., Andriopoulos, C., Lewis, M. W., & Ingram, A. E. (2010). Managing creatives: Paradoxical approaches to identity regulation. *Human Relations, 63*(6), 781–805.

Granovetter, M. (1985). Economic action and social structure: The problem of embeddedness. *American Journal of Sociology, 91*(3) 481–510.

Grimshaw, D., & Miozzo, M. (2006). Institutional effects on the IT outsourcing market: Analysing clients, suppliers and staff transfer in Germany and the UK. *Organization Studies, 27*(9), 1229–1259.

Heinz, J. P., Nelson, R. L., & Laumann, E. (2001). The scale of justice: Observations on the transformation of urban law practice. *Annual Review of Sociology, 27*, 9–20.

LaBahn, D. W., & Kohli, C. (1997). Maintaining client commitment in advertising agency: Client relationships. *Industrial Marketing Management, 26*(6), 497–508.

Laing, A. W., & Lian, P. C. (2005). Inter-organisational relationships in professional services: Towards a typology of service relationships. *Journal of Services Marketing, 19*(2), 114–128.

Lalaounis, S. T., Wood, B. M., & Evans, D. (2011). Design management: A comparative analysis of the professional status of the occupation in the UK. *Design Principles & Practice: An International Journal, 5*(6), 639–665.

Lalaounis, S. T., Wood, B. M., & Harrison, D. K. (2012). A framework for services evaluation in integrated design consultancies: A triangular approach. *The Design Journal, 15*(3), 265–298.

Lancaster, R., & Uzzi, B. (2012). Legally charged: Embeddedness and profit in large law firm legal billings. *Sociological Focus, 45*(1), 1–22.

Larsson, R., & Bowen, D. E. (1989). Organization and customer: Managing design and coordination of services. *Academy of Management Review, 14*(2), 213–233.

Levinthal, D. A., & Fichman, M. (1988). Dynamics of interorganizational attachments: Auditor–client relationships. *Administrative Science Quarterly, 33*(3), 345–369.

Løwendahl, B. (2005). *Strategic management of professional service firms*. Copenhagen, Denmark: Copenhagen Business School Press.

Maister, D. (2003). *Managing the professional service firm*. London: Simon & Schuster.

Manning, S., Lewin, A. Y., & Schuerch, M. (2011). The stability of offshore outsourcing relationships. *Management International Review, 51*(3), 381–406.

Mills, P. K., & Margulies, N. (1980). Toward a core typology of service organizations. *Academy of Management Review, 5*(2), 255–265.

Mills, P. K., & Morris, J. H. (1986). Clients as 'partial' employees of service organizations: Role development in client participation. *Academy of Management Review, 11*(4), 726–735.

Mills, P. K., & Moshavi, D. S. (1999). Professional concern: Managing knowledge-based service relationships. *International Journal of Service Industry Management, 10*(1), 48–67.

Nikolova, N., Reihlen, M., & Schlapfner, J. F. (2009). Client–consultant interaction: Capturing social practices of professional service production. *Scandinavian Journal of Management, 25*(3), 289–298.

Ram, M. (1999). Managing consultants in a small firm: A case study. *Journal of Management Studies, 36*(6), 853–873.

Richter, A., & Niewiem, S. (2009). Knowledge transfer across permeable boundaries: An empirical study of clients' decisions to involve management consultants. *Scandinavian Journal of Management, 25*(3), 275–288.

Rogan, M. (2014a). Too close for comfort? The effect of embeddedness and competitive overlap on client relationship retention following an acquisition. *Organization Science, 25*(1), 185–203.

Rogan, M. (2014b). Executive departures without client losses: The role of multiplex ties in exchange partner retention. *Academy of Management Journal, 57*(2), 563–584.

Savage, M., Devine, F., Cunningham, N., Taylor, M., Li, Y., Hjellbrekke, J., Le Roux, B., Friedman, S., & Miles, A. (2013). A new model of social class? Findings from the BBC's Great British class survey experiment. *Sociology, 47*(2), 219–250.

Seabright, M. A., Levinthal, D. A., & Fichman, M. (1992). Role of individual attachments in the dissolution of inter-organizational relationships. *Academy of Management Journal, 35*(1), 122–160.

Sharma, A. (1997). Professional as agent: Knowledge asymmetry in agency exchange. *Academy of Management Review, 22*(3), 758–798.

Simon, H. A. (1960). *The new science of management decision.* New York: Harper & Brothers.

Simon, H. A. (1996). *The sciences of the artificial.* Cambridge, MA: MIT Press.

Smith, C., & McKinlay, A. (2009). Creative industries and labour process analysis. In A. McKinlay, & C. Smith (Eds.), *Creative labour: Working in the creative industries* (pp. 3–28). Basingstoke, UK: Palgrave Macmillan.

Somaya, D., Williamson, I. O., & Lorinkova, N. (2008). Gone but not lost: The different performance impacts of employee mobility between cooperators versus competitors. *Academy of Management Journal, 51*(5), 936–953.

Stringfellow, L., Shaw, E., & Maclean, M. (2013). Apostasy versus legitimacy: Relational dynamics and routes to resource acquisition in entrepreneurial ventures. *International Small Business Journal, 32*(5), 571–592.

Sturdy, A. (1997). The consultancy process: An insecure business. *Journal of Management Studies, 34*(3), 389–413.

Townley, B. (2015). Exploring different forms of capitals: Researching capitals in the field of cultural and creative industries. In A. Tatli, M. Ozbilgin, & M. Karatas-Ozkan (Eds.), *Pierre Bourdieu, organization, and management, Series 34.* London: Routledge.

Uzzi, B. (1996). The sources and consequences of embeddedness for the economic performance of organizations: The network effect. *American Sociological Review, 61*(4) 674–698.

Uzzi, B. (1999). Embeddedness in the making of financial capital. *American Sociological Review, 64*(4), 481–505.

Uzzi, B., & Lancaster, R. (2003). Relational embeddedness and learning: The case of bank loan managers and their clients. *Management Science, 49*(4), 383–399.

Uzzi, B., & Lancaster, R. (2004). Embeddedness and price formation in the corporate law market. *American Sociological Review, 69*(3), 319–344.

Von Nordenflycht, A. (2010). What is a professional service firm? Toward a theory and taxonomy of knowledge-intensive firms. *Academy of Management Review, 35*(1), 155–174.

Wilensky, H. L. (1964). The professionalization of everyone? *American Journal of Sociology, 70*(2), 137–158.

10 Conclusion

Leading through design

As we conclude our exploration of design management from organisational and marketing perspectives, it is important to discuss how the future is shaping for the discipline. This book has demonstrated how over the last few decades there have been significant developments in the area of design management, but there is still a lot to be done if design is to play an even stronger role in leading organisational and societal development. Undoubtedly, nowadays, private and public organisations recognise the power of design as a means of delivering solutions to social problems, contributing to human progress, while achieving organisational objectives. Based on the progress made in the academy and practice of design management as discussed in the previous chapters, many scholars have now started exploring the concept of *design leadership* (Joziasse, 2011), as the next level of design, which needs to be congruent with organisational strategies (Chiva & Alegre, 2009). According to Cooper (2012), design leadership is in a vortex of change. She explains that:

> The Internet, the digital world, and our ability to connect with each other through the medium; the technology that enables one-off and personalised production; the consideration of sustainability, of democracy, of social and ethical values; and lately a fixation on a growth agenda – all of these mean we really are seeing change happening from all directions and at all levels. There are exciting opportunities and extreme challenges. We see the roles and capabilities of design and designers changing; we see the type and nature of organisations and consumers changing. The question is, what do we know from the past that is omnipresent and constant, and what do we need to know in order to ensure design management moves with the times?
>
> (Cooper, 2012, p. 3)

Design leadership is a fairly new concept which was initially distinguished from design management. Turner and Topalian (2002) argued that design leadership involves a number of key responsibilities: (1) envisioning the future, (2) demonstrating strategic intent, (3) directing design investment, (4) managing corporate reputation, (5) fostering and maintaining an environment of innovation, and (6) training for design leadership. Turner and Topalian (2002) also argued that design leadership is essentially proactive, in contrast with design management which is rather reactive. Design leadership is more concerned with vision, whereas design management is more concerned with implementation.

Nevertheless, based on a closer examination of these responsibilities, one could argue the aforementioned responsibilities are similar to what we have described as 'strategic design management' (see Chapter 4), which concentrates on translating the vision into strategy (Joziasse, 2011). This means that design management and design leadership are not distinguished activities; on the contrary, they substantially depend on each other.

> Design management needs design leadership in order to know where to go and design leadership needs design management to know how to get there. This … means that (design) leaders and (design) managers have to cooperate and continuously assess the level of agreement about what to do and how to do it to be effective and efficient.
>
> (Joziasse, 2011, p. 399)

Hands (2009) is also sceptical of such separation of design leadership and design management and prefers to use the term 'strategic design management' to describe both. He explains his scepticism as follows:

> Who is the best person to lead and manage is more complex issue; more shades of grey than black or white. It could be argued that design management is inherently a proactive force similar to design leadership, but it applies its value and persuasive effects in very much a 'silent' or subtle manner. Rather than have two definitions competing for attention and utmost importance within the organisation, why not have one holistic term that embraces the values of both perspectives: strategic design management?
>
> (Hands, 2009, p. 101)

According to McCullagh (2008), a design leader must have three characteristics. First, he/she should be able to *envision the future* and identify changes and opportunities which flow from these changes. Second, a design leader should be capable of *thinking strategically*, questioning existing competencies, and identifying which competencies need to be built in the future in order to set the organisation apart from competition. Third, he/she should be able to *lead others* while developing, inspiring, and maintaining successful teams. Whitney (2014) suggests that in order for an organisation to adopt design methods successfully, there has to be "a leader who is willing to go down a path, even when they're not certain what the outcome will be" (Whitney, 2014, p. 14). This is opposite to the traditional business and management approach where research allows the organisation to select a target segment and then optimise towards it, following a very well-established path. Instead, *leading through design* means that "the senior executive needs to know the general direction they're going, needs to know what characterizes that direction, but crucially, needs to be open to proceeding without knowing where exactly they're going to end up" (Whitney, 2014, p. 14).

Similarly, other scholars have talked about the concept of a leader with a 'designerly' approach, who offers strategic and tactical advantages for the organisation, in contrast with traditional leaders trained through traditional management and business curricula (Brown 2009; Liedtka & Mintzberg, 2006; Liedtka & Ogilvie, 2011; Martin, 2009). According to Cross (2006, 2011), a designerly approach "privileges a discourse around and through making, aesthetic sensitivity, and human-centred perspectives" (Yuille, Varadarajan, Vaughan, & Brennan, 2015, p. 113). Yuille et al. (2015) argue that leaders with a designerly approach lead projects that support human experiences which are constructed through the lived perception of the people who engage with these projects. "*Designerly leadership* begins with a grounding principle: that framing what we do in terms of the experiences it supports is as applicable to the design of products and services as it is to the design of projects, organisations, and workplaces. In other words, leadership" (Yuille et al., 2015, p. 114).

The same authors suggest that designerly leadership includes two complementary qualities: (1) affinity and (2) ambiguity. There are three ways that *affinity* is modulated in designerly leadership. First, through 'spotting affinity' which is situated in the analysis stage of a design project, acting as the bridge between researching and changing the situation. Second, 'seeking affinity' which includes activities that assist building the set of elements used for spotting affinity. Third, "at some stage designerly leaders need to put something back into [the] world, to make changes. This process of creating things that solve problems can be framed as *making* affinity with a perceived *gap* that exists in the design situation" (Yuille et al., 2015, p. 118). The concept of affinity very much relates with the concept of empathy, a significant element of design thinking, as discussed in Chapter 3. The second quality of *ambiguity* can be achieved through three approaches: (1) pragmatic, (2) critical, and (3) enterprising. Yuille et al. (2015) explain these three approaches with the following:

> A pragmatic approach to designerly leadership seeks to *reduce* and *excise* ambiguity … [Design leaders] who use this approach aim to minimise the effects of cognitive load and reduce conceptual friction or dissonance in order to design things that are intuitive and usable … Conversely, a critical use of ambiguity seeks to *use* or *exercise* ambiguity in a project, often to draw attention to the relationship between an artefact and its context. This approach reframes design as an agent of critical reflection, where artefacts are intentionally designed to be ambiguous, in order to encourage people to interpret the artefact and situation themselves. . . . A third approach uses the second to achieve the first. An enterprising approach to ambiguity employs the ambiguous to scaffold mutual engagement in shared goal. It uses ambiguity as an invitation to negotiate and construct *meaning* between different stakeholders in a design project.
>
> (Yuille et al., 2015, pp. 118–119)

A number of scholars have argued that design leadership faces a number of issues and challenges which may limit its potential and ability to lead the development from design of artefacts and services into organisational transformation design, social transformational design, and business design (Joziasse, 2011). Topalian (2011) identified ten critical factors which underline the challenges facing design leadership. First, organisations need to focus on creating and managing experiences for consumers, an organisational reality explored in Chapter 7. Second, tangible products "are [nowadays] complemented by services and services incorporate tangible components that can be patented and branded" (Topalian, 2011, p. 381); thus, organisational offerings must work as integrated systems (Elliot & Deasley, 2007). Third, products need to be understood by users; hence, design needs to distil the essence of what is being offered through 'core platforms' which lead to resonance among users through effective use of the offering. Fourth, consumers 'personalise' organisational offerings through their use and amendment of these, as well as through their own impressions and emotions (Topalian, 2003). As a fifth factor, Topalian (2011) argues that design work tends to get compartmentalised, fragmented, and pigeonholed into predetermined silos, leading to a lack of a meaningful overview or formal responsibility for it and a reduction of the influence of design professionals on key decisions. Sixth, there is a strong drive towards co-creation of design solutions through collaboration between designers and other stakeholders, a phenomenon which we explored in Chapter 8. In addition, the fact that many ineffective products make it to the market but they represent "a waste … resulting from a poor understanding of product capabilities or a lack of confidence to demand more of them" (Topalian, 2011, p. 383) is a seventh factor which underlines the challenges facing design leadership today. Another factor is the legislative demands which limit organisations in (overregulated) advanced markets, while legislations in other, less regulated emerging economies fail to protect intellectual property. The latter is a factor in its own right too; the intellectual property of the organisation does not get the appropriate protection. Finally, a tenth factor is the fact that, sometimes, design is not taken seriously and is left to inexperienced people without any authority within the organisation.

On the basis of the aforementioned critical factors, Topalian (2011) has identified a number of challenges which design leadership currently faces. First, there is a need to achieve a '*prospect beyond the horizon*'. In order to achieve this, design leaders should explore new territories by encouraging organisational members "to be different, change mindsets, expand networks, update their ways of working, and challenge top executives, even in adverse circumstances" (Topalian, 2011, p. 385). This will allow organisations to envision needs, customers, and markets that do not yet exist (Topalian, 2000). For instance, *Apple* has been leading the way through the design and launch of the first *iPad* in 2010, which was a revolutionary product that kick-started an entire new consumer electronics product category (tablets). In addition, design leaders should continuously come up with new proposals about how to take their organisations forward and transform ideas into outputs which achieve a harmonious balance between the three important criteria: desirability, feasibility, and viability (Brown, 2009), as discussed in Chapter 3. This reinforces design's strategic contribution to organisational performance.

Furthermore, design leaders can "provide 'roadmaps to track trends in behaviour and identify emerging needs. These will help to make sense of the 'fuzzy front-end' when exploring new opportunities and solving problems generally" (Topalian, 2011, p. 386). In Chapter 2, we discussed how corporate managers often describe the early stages of the design process, which include design research, as the 'fuzzy front end'. This is because the research phase is often perceived by the corporate world as ill-defined, random, and mysterious (Rhea, 2003). The onus is on the design leader to make this front end as less fuzzy as possible. Appropriately planned and implemented design research can contribute to making things clear for all the stakeholders involved in the design process. Finally, design leaders need to be able to manage any change and transition as a result of the design solutions generated. They must ensure that responsibility for transitions is formally assigned to the right people. This would typically involve "explaining project configurations, justifying strategies pursued, protecting the integrities of journeys, [and] then championing the solutions generated" (Topalian, 2011, p. 386).

A second challenge is the importance of '*upgrading to business design*'; it is essential that design leaders establish design as the key unifying discipline at the heart of the organisation. A poor understanding of design management within organisations leads to problems in recognising the great potential of design and the outstanding contributions it can make to organisational success. The onus is on the design leader to communicate the value of design and its management by

> raising awareness of the design process and contributions across business, dismantling organisational silos that constrain and undermine design work, and integrating the administration of design so that it is handled as a powerful strategic resource that measurably enhances performance and warrants long-term investment.
>
> (Topalian, 2011, p. 387)

The design leader also needs to cultivate a distinctive voice and expertise. The aforementioned designerly approach to leadership "provides the holistic perspective and motivation to tackle complete problems and create total solutions, co-ordinating the contributions of different disciplines to serve shared visions of desired outcomes" (Topalian, 2011, p. 387). In addition, the design leader needs to develop deeper practical knowledge of users. Design research and design ethnography, discussed in Chapter 2, can lead to the development of such knowledge. Finally, the design leader needs to have a thorough insight into competitors' outputs through creative analyses of their outputs (Topalian, 2011).

A third challenge is the need to '*manifest corporate conscience through design*'. Design leaders need to 'do the right things right' and should be accountable for their actions, ensuring that they measure and document the impact of operations and outputs on the environment and the society in a transparent way (Topalian, 2011). It is also very important that design leaders ensure that design expertise is exercised with a consideration to professional and ethical values because while design is about creating desirable offerings, such seduction carries responsibilities. Design leaders need to embrace diversity and promote inclusion and sustainability which are important factors in the discharge of corporate social responsibility. Design solutions and design strategies pursued by organisations should not disadvantage any stakeholder (Topalian, 2011). In addition, it is vital that design leaders seek to achieve a better work/leisure balance for all organisational members and a work environment which fosters creativity and enhances human well-being. Finally, design leaders should build on achievement through 'virtuous cycles of development'; this means that there has to be a culture and infrastructure which nurtures continuous innovation (Topalian, 2011).

As a fourth challenge, Topalian (2011) suggests that it is vital we '*nurture future generations of leaders*'; therefore, it is important that centres of excellence in design are sustained. These centres are both academic (e.g., design schools) and commercial, i.e., design consultancies. Design leaders as well as the government should ensure that the reputation of these centres of excellence is continuously enhanced (Topalian, 2011). This highlights the need to revamp training to lead through design. Design schools need to ensure they train and nurture the best talent of designers and design leaders. Design leaders can have a central role in bringing academics and practitioners together. They can provide "clear briefs, plus guidance, for the refreshment of courses offered by design, engineering and business schools so they remain relevant to the future needs of client organisations and design practices – especially relating to continuous professional development" (Topalian, 2011, p. 391). They should also value their staff by championing their creativity. Design leaders are responsible in leading the introduction of design consultancy practices in client organisations' operations, as we explored in Chapter 9. They should also target and nurture new skills for development, as well as infiltrate 'non-design' jobs to widen perceptions of design and its value. It is important they improve professional practice by adopting a discipline of evaluating project progress and outcomes and documenting experiences in ways that they can be shared within and outside their organisations. Last but not least, they need to ensure continuity of successful design management by mentoring future generations of design leaders (Topalian, 2011).

Finally, design leadership faces the challenge of seeking to '*join the top table*'. Design leaders should step up to lead in business. This means that they should not only be leaders of design in business but also they should lead business through design, i.e., they should become leaders in designing business. "This ... requires design – whose essence is to devise effective means to achieve desired ends – to be acknowledged as the core discipline in business" (Topalian, 2011, p. 393). They should not feel afraid to borrow best practices from other fields (even out with design) that can be adopted as normal practice. It is vital they acknowledge diversity in design leadership. "'Friends of design' and potential leaders need to be identified across organisations (within and outside the professions), entrusted with design responsibilities, then supported to discharge those responsibilities effectively, with confidence" (Topalian, 2011, p. 394).

Looking into the future, there are indeed many opportunities for design leadership. Over the last few years, there are developments which indicate the fact that design leadership is making inroads in organisations. These developments take place in private organisations, but are also supported by national governments. Design management makes a number of contributions in organisations which elevate the status of design leadership too. These include, first, the presence of designers in organisations' boardrooms, which has been growing over the years. Second, the establishment of benchmarks to evaluate design management. Examples include the establishment of the Design Management Europe Award (as part of European Union's ADMIRE project) in 2007, as well as the Design Business Association's (DBA) Design Effectiveness Awards. Such initiatives demonstrate the value of design within organisations. The DBA's methodologies "are intended to determine the effectiveness and measurement of design efforts ... They show that design is taking leadership and no longer waits for others in the organisation to assign it its position" (Joziasse, 2011, p. 408). Third, there have also been developments in design management education in the form of undergraduate and postgraduate programmes. While most of them are situated in design schools, there have been some business schools that have been integrating design into their business programmes, such as schools at Lancaster University (UK), University of Toronto (Canada), University of Pennsylvania (USA), Massachusetts Institute of Technology (USA), and Aalto University (Finland). Additional opportunities include design management and leadership contributing to the development of value networks for small- and medium-sized enterprises, as well as understanding the role of design leadership in creating a sustainable world (Joziasse, 2011).

As we explored in Chapter 1, our society (especially in the developed world) can be characterised as post-materialistic, where after satisfying lower order material needs, people are looking to satisfy higher, less material needs like love and self-actualisation (Inglehart, 1981, 2008). In such *post-materialistic society*, there is a greater demand for sustainability, and design ought to play its significant role in achieving this. Design for sustainability must be human-centred, exploring and providing solutions to both environmental and social issues. Understanding and taking into account the social impact of design renders design for sustainability with a more holistically human-centred ethos. After all, in Buchanan's (2001) articulate words,

> Design is not merely an adornment of cultural life but one of the practical disciplines of responsible action for bringing the high values of a country or a culture into concrete reality, allowing us to transform abstract ideas into specific manageable form. This is evident if we consider the scope of design as it affects our lives. As an instrument of cultural life, design is the way we create all of the artefacts and communications that serve human beings, striving to meet their needs and desires and facilitating the exchange of information and ideas that is essential for civil and political life. Furthermore, design is the way we plan and create actions, services, and all of the other humanly shaped processes of public and private life. There are the interactions and transactions that constitute the social and economic fabric of a country. Finally, design is the way we plan and create the complex wholes that provide a framework for human culture – the human systems and sub-systems that work either in congress or in conflict with nature to support human fulfilment ... Design offers a way of thinking about the world that is significant for addressing many of the problems that human beings face in the contemporary culture. We believe that conscious attention to the way designers work in specialised areas of application such as communication or industrial design is relevant for work in other areas. And we believe that general access to the ways of design thinking can provide people with new tools for engaging with their cultural and natural environment. As we work toward improving design thinking in each of our special areas of application, we also contribute to a more general understanding of design that others may use in the future in ways that we cannot now anticipate.
>
> (Buchanan, 2001, pp. 38–39)

The main purpose of this book has been to explore design management from organisation and marketing perspectives. In our extensive discussion of the subject, we explored a number of areas. We began our journey with understanding the role of design management in today's creative economy, as well as the importance of design research in identifying design opportunities. Then, we discussed the process and tools of design thinking and how we can develop successful design strategies. We reflected on theories of individual, team, and organisational creativity, and we explored ways of organising for design innovation through paradoxical thinking and ambidexterity. Following this, we sought to understand human experiences and the role of design in creating experiential platforms, and we discussed the concept of co-creation, anthropomorphism, and human-centred design. We also explored design consultancies as professional service firms which produce and deliver different forms of capital. Finally, we brought our discussion together by exploring the future of design management through the concept of design leadership. As we explained earlier, by looking into the future, we can identify many opportunities and challenges for design management and leadership. It is essential to believe that if design is pursued and managed in a way that it contributes to society and human dignity (Buchanan, 2001) as we have previously highlighted, the future of design management although challenging, is also very promising in addressing social problems and improving human well-being.

References

Brown, T. (2009). *Change by design: How design thinking transforms organisations and inspires innovation.* New York: HarperCollins.

Buchanan, R. (2001). Human dignity and human rights: Thoughts on the principles of human-centered design. *Design Issues, 17*(3), 35–39.

Chiva, R., & Alegre, J. (2009). Investment in design and firm performance: The mediating role of design management. *Journal of Product Innovation Management, 26*(4), 424–440.

Cooper, R. D. (2012). Design leadership in a vortex of change. *Design Management Journal, 7*(1), 3–5.

Cross, N. (2006). *Designerly ways of knowing.* London: Springer.

Cross, N. (2011). *Design thinking: Understanding how designers think and work.* Oxford, UK: Berg.

Elliott, C., & Deasley, P. (2007). *Creating systems that work: Principles of engineering systems for the 21st century.* London: Royal Academy of Engineering.

Hands, D. (2009). *Vision and values in design management.* Lausanne, Switzerland: AVA Publishing.

Inglehart, R. (1981, December). Post-materialism in an environment of insecurity. *American Political Science Review, 75*, 880–900.

Inglehart, R. (2008). Changing values among Western publics from 1970 to 2006. *West European Politics, 31*(1–2), 130–146.

Joziasse, F. (2011). Design leadership: Current limits and future opportunities. In R. Cooper, S. Junginger, & T. Lockwood (Eds.), *The handbook of design management.* Oxford, UK: Berg.

Liedtka, J., & Mintzberg, H. (2006). Time for design. *Design Management Review, 17*(2), 10–18.

Liedtka, J., & Ogilvie, T. (2011). *Designing for growth.* New York: Columbia University Press.

McCullagh, K. (2008). *The many faces of design leadership.* Retrieved December 05, 2016 from www.core77.com/posts/9962/the-many-faces-of-design-leadership-by-kevin-mccullagh-9962

Martin, R. L. (2009). *The design of business: Why design thinking is the next competitive advantage.* Cambridge, MA: Harvard Business Press.

Rhea, D. (2003). Bringing clarity to the 'fuzzy front end': A predictable process for innovation. In B. Laurel (Ed.), *Design research: Methods and perspectives.* Cambridge, MA: MIT Press.

Topalian, A. (2000). The role of innovation leaders in developing long-term products. *International Journal of Innovation Management, 4*(2), 149–171.

Topalian, A. (2003). Experienced reality: The development of corporate identity in the digital era. *European Journal of Marketing, 37*(7/8), 1119–1132.

Topalian, A. (2011). Major challenges for design leaders over the next decade. In R. Cooper, S. Junginger, & T. Lockwood (Eds.), *The handbook of design management.* Oxford, UK: Berg.

Turner, R., & Topalian, A. (2002). *Core responsibilities of design leaders in commercially demanding environments.* London: Design Leadership Forum.

Whitney, P. (2014, July–September). Leading growth through design: An interview with Patrick Whitney. *Research-Technology Management*, 14–18.

Yuille, J., Varadarajan, S., Vaughan, L., & Brennan, L. (2015). Leading through design: Developing skills for affinity and ambiguity. *Design Management Journal, 9*(1), 113–123.

Index

Note: page numbers in **bold** refer to figures, images, or tables.